PAPAL GENEALOGY

To the memory of Pompeo Litta and the illustrious
Italian families that constitute the essence of this work

PAPAL GENEALOGY

The Families and Descendants of the Popes

by GEORGE L. WILLIAMS

McFarland & Company, Inc., Publishers
Jefferson, North Carolina, and London

Acknowledgments: The author is indebted to the early nineteenth-century Milanese historian Pompeo Litta, whose monumental work *Famiglie celebri italiane* served as an inspiration for this study on papal families, and this book is dedicated to him. The classic studies on the history of the popes by Ranke and Pastor were among those sources which have assisted the author. Ranke tends to place his emphasis on the nepotistic practices of pontiffs, presenting an abundance of evidence to document the fortunes that the families of the popes obtained from their pontifical relatives. On the other hand, Pastor's pen is broader in scope, and, while he deals with papal nepotism and simony, he looks at the strengths and weaknesses of those who wore the tiara and is quick to praise their accomplishments. To emulate the high standards of scholarship of Litta, Ranke and Pastor was always a goal to which this writer aspired.

The author wishes to thank those who have assisted him in his research, especially Dr. Aldo Coletto of the Brera Library (Biblioteca Nazionale Braidense) in Milan. Dr. Coletto helped to obtain difficult-to-find archival materials. And the author also thanks the members of the staff of that library, especially Dr. Giovanna Calati. They were of enormous help throughout the project, as was the staff at the Vatican Library and the National Library in Rome.

Additional materials were obtained from the main branch of the New York Public Library in Manhattan and from the Hofstra, Adelphi and C. W. Post university libraries and the Port Washington Public Library on Long Island, New York.

The author is grateful to his wife Adelia Musa Williams for her critical and insightful suggestions, for her patience and endurance, and especially for accompanying him to the Vatican Library and the National Library in Rome and for assisting him with the translations and the references so that the research could be completed while in the Eternal City. She has been a constant source of help during the entire project.

The present work is a reprint of the library bound edition of Papal Genealogy: The Families and Descendants of the Popes, *first published in 1998 by McFarland.*

LIBRARY OF CONGRESS CATALOGUING-IN-PUBLICATION DATA

Williams, George L.
   Papal genealogy : the families and descendants of the popes / by
George L. Williams.
     p.   cm.
   Includes bibliographical references and index.

   ISBN 0-7864-2071-5 (softcover : 50# alkaline paper)

   1. Popes — Genealogy.   2. Aristocracy (Social class) — Europe —
Genealogy.   I. Title.
CS39.P64   2004
929.7'088'22 — dc21   97-36093

British Library cataloguing data are available

Cover photograph: View of a colonnade arm of St. Peter's
Basilica in Rome (*Corbis Images*)

Manufactured in the United States of America

McFarland & Company, Inc., Publishers
  Box 611, Jefferson, North Carolina 28640
  www.mcfarlandpub.com

Table of Contents

So much time has gone by
and how far off everything seems
and so different.
It is so painful for me
to end my days in a city
which is no longer mine.
My Rome was not like this one.
We all knew each other.
Bishops, Cardinals, the Pope.
We were all friends.
We were all related to each other.
But now those close ties with the church are gone.

— Lament by Princess Domitilla, recalling her life as an aristocrat in Rome, longing for a bygone era when Roman nobility had power (from Fellini's Roma*)*

List of Tables

TABLES IN APPENDIX A

Author's Note

The translations were made by the author with the assistance of Dr. Adelia Musa, a linguist specializing in Italian-to-English translations. The Anglicized version of the names of the popes are used throughout the text. Many of these names are taken directly from the Latin. Since this is a study of Italian families, the author has decided to provide the given names of the members of Italian families in Italian. Most other names are in English. For example, since Bertha and Berengar (Berta and Berengario in Italian) are not Italian names, the author has decided to use the English names. Often the English version of a name is given in parentheses right after the Italian version, e.g., "Teofilatto (Theophylactus or Theophylact)."

Juan Borgia, the Spanish duke of Gandia, one of the sons of Pope Alexander XI, presented another problem. In Italian, Alexander's children would be called Geoffredo and Lucrezia, but Juan (Giovanni in Italian) was used through the book because the pope had another son Giovanni, "l'Infante Romano." Juan is called by his Spanish name to avoid confusion with this other son. Having used Italian, English, Latin, French, Spanish and German sources, the author often made decisions regarding the use of given names and surnames which he felt would assist the reader and which were consistent throughout the text and tables.

Preface

During the first half of the nineteenth century, Pompeo Litta began his prodigious research on the history of prominent Italian families. When he died in 1852, he had written about 113 of these families, presenting the history of Italy by examining the lives of the men and women within them. Using thousands of sources, Litta prepared a genealogical table for each family, and for each person within that family he wrote a biography, some very brief but others quite extensive, depending upon the material gathered for each individual entry. And so he wrote thousands of biographies, many of which were minor masterpieces, especially his accounts of Popes Paul III (Alessandro Farnese), Julius II (Giuliano della Rovere), Leo X (Giovanni de' Medici) and Clement VII (Giulio de' Medici). His study of noble Italian families, called *Famiglie celebri italiane*, was published in a series of tomes during his lifetime, and after Litta's death in 1852 other historians continued his work writing about these renowned Italian families. The last of the tomes was published in the early part of the twentieth century.

Pompeo Litta had a keen eye for detail, as when he noted how marriages were arranged. Queen Joanna (Giovanna) II of Naples (1371–1435), a friend of Pope Martin V (Oddo Colonna), was instrumental in planning to have the very young heiress of the marchese of Cotrone marry the pope's nephew. And that same pope's niece, Caterina Colonna, was promised to the duke of Milan so that Martin V could conclude an alliance with that dukedom. Later Julius II, pope from 1503 to 1513, married his niece to a Colonna and his own daughter Felice to an Orsini, the duke of Bracciano, to harmonize relations between these two rival Roman families. The aristocratic Bracciano, in turn, continually belittled his wife for her humble origins, being the bastard daughter of a Roman clergyman. A grandniece of Pope Paul IV (Giampietro Carafa), named Agnese Carafa, was destined to become the wife of the duke of Ferrara. When the pope died and his nephews were tried and found guilty of assorted crimes in 1561, the power of the Carafa family disintegrated. The family was disgraced, and Litta notes that Agnese became a nun instead of the wife of a duke. These papal familial decisions were constantly motivated by political, social and economic objectives. Litta did not write about every family that produced a pope, but he knew how pivotal these families were to understanding the history of Italy, if not of western Europe, over an extensive period of time.

The author of the current study wishes to bring to light the work of Litta, and he relies heavily on *Famiglie celebri italiane*. Unfortunately several families — the Conti, Caetani, Borgia, Cibo, Barberini, Pamfili and Borghese — crucial to a full comprehension of the papacy, were not investigated by Litta. But inspired by the observations of that historian, this writer has delved into other studies about the families of the popes, and even though the remarkable works of Pastor and Ranke revealed the nepotism of many of them, this study enters a new realm in dealing with the history of the papacy.

It is a study that centers on the families of the Supreme Pontiff and their influence on history and even on their descendants — in some cases up to the present time. *Genealogies* presents an interpretation of papal history based on the families of the pontiffs. These were families, related to ruling European dynasties, who constituted a royalty of their own. They were Italian families that united with the rich and powerful throughout Europe. They tended to intermarry in order to hold on to riches bestowed by popes related to their families. And once a pope was elected, his family moved into a frenzy of activities for the express purpose of acquiring wealth for themselves. These were families, mainly Italian, intent on acquiring more church wealth through the largess of the pope than had been given to the families of the previous popes. One of the main avenues of papal activities was to maintain, sustain and enrich the Italian aristocracy. During much of the Middle Ages and Renaissance, battles were fought among these families for territory and power.

Pope Alexander VI (Rodrigo Borgia) financed his son Caesar in wars against the Orsini, della Rovere and numerous other families to conquer territories that, once secured at others' expense, were readily distributed among the members of the Borgia family. A master manipulator, this pope had forced his daughter Lucrezia into a series of marriages for political reasons, allying the papacy with particular noble families — the Sforza, the Aragona, and the d'Este. When the marital alliance was no longer advantageous for the pope, as in the case of Lucrezia's second husband, her husband was brutally murdered. In later periods there were yet other battles, ones that involved these families into arranging new, strategic marital alliances. Much of the history of the popes is a history of terror.

This study places a new emphasis on the role of women in the history of the papacy. The power-hungry Marozia, who died around 940, placed her own son on the pontifical throne and murdered those who stood in her way. Olimpia Pamfili, the sister-in-law of Pope Innocent X (Gian Battista Pamfili), ruled the papal domain in the 1640s and '50s. Little could be done in the Vatican without her permission. Olimpia had the distinction of ransacking the papal palace for treasure while her dead brother-in-law, the pope, was placed in a corner for three days. Another influential woman, the sister of Pope Leo X, followed a similar course of action as her brother lay dying. Even in the twentieth century, vast power was held by a nun over Pope Pius XII.

But most women of these families were not placed in positions of power and authority. Many of them, like Lucrezia Borgia, became pawns in the hands of pontifical families. The heiresses of these families were desirable wives because of the enormous dowries, properties and titles that they brought with them. These, of course, were moneys and lands that had been obtained by the papal relative. Olimpia Aldobrandini was the fabulously wealthy heiress of the Aldobrandinis, the family of Clement VIII (who reigned as pope from 1592 to 1605). She was first married to Paolo Borghese, scion of the Borghese family. Pope Paul V (Camilio Borghese) had carved a position of imperial status for that family. When Paolo Borghese died, Olimpia was quickly married to Camilio Pamfili, the nephew and heir of Pope Innocent X. The wealth of these pontifical families — the Aldobrandini, Borghese and Pamfili — was distributed to the children of both marriage.

The demand for these heiresses increased as some of the papal families had reversals of fortune and were in need of cash. The consequences were to the detriment of the heiresses. Anna Borromeo, niece of Pope Pius IV (Giovanni Angelo de' Medici of Marignano), was only eleven years of age when she married Fabrizio Colonna. This marriage had been arranged to cement better relations with this Medici pope because the previous pope, Paul IV (Gian Pietro Carafa), had in 1555 seized Colonna land. The Colonna realized that it was absolutely essential to form an alliance with this new pontiff to regain lost possessions, and this little girl played into their hands. The very wealthy heiress of the Barberini family, Cornelia, was not even twelve years of age when she was made the wife of Giulio Cesare Colonna. She brought with her the lordship of Palestrina, which the Colonna had been forced to sell to the Barberini many years before. Desperation often was the motivating force, and when Federico Sforza, count of S. Fiora, whose family had been forced to sell many of its fiefdoms, wished to increase the coffers of his family, he proceeded to the convent where Livia, the oldest daughter of Giuliano Cesarini and his wife Margherita Savelli, was preparing to become a nun. Federico seized Livia, removed her from the convent, married her and inherited the Cesarini fortune. The lands and wealth of the Cesarini were legendary. In the process he changed his name to Sforza-Cesarini.

Another avenue has been explored in this study. Not only were these papal families intricately related over and over again, but there was an obvious attempt by them to establish an hereditary papacy. This began with the Conti of Tusculum in the ninth century, later continued with their descendants the Conti of Segni, and was subsequently followed by the Colonna. Fourteen members of these families obtained the tiara. Further, they married into other papal dynasties — the Orsini, Savelli, Caetani — to enhance their positions in Rome and within the church. Descendants from these alliances were the Medici popes, Leo X and Leo XI, and the Farnese pope, Paul III.

The machinations of the Conti and the Orsini, along with such other Roman families as the Frangipane, Pierleoni, and Crescenzi, to acquire papal power by placing their own particular candidates on the throne, are graphically recorded. In the process, popes were mutilated and murdered. To be further entrenched within the papal domain, some families such as the Fieschi, Piccolomini and della Rovere had two

of their members elected to the throne. Three of the Medici popes were related, and to insure Medici influence in Rome and consequently throughout Italy, Lorenzo de' Medici, called "the Magnificent," married his daughter Maddalena to Franceschetto Cibo, the son of Pope Innocent VIII (Giovanni Battista Cibo). He was the first pope to openly acknowledge that he had children. Certainly the Borgia popes, Callistus III and Alexander VI, both of whom appointed numerous Spanish relatives and friends as cardinals to weight the College of Cardinals in favor of selecting a Spanish pope — preferably a Borgia — were bent on creating a hereditary papacy. In fact, for a period of time Pope Alexander VI's son Caesar Borgia was a cardinal, and it was believed that he would succeed his father. But Caesar resigned the cardinalate.

The interrelationships of these families to each other, their impact on the history of the church and their intricate role in the establishment of a papal royalty are some of the strands of the history traced in this study. Interwoven in this fabric is another strand: a strong and serious reaction within the Holy See itself to papal nepotism. The despoiling of the Papal States for the gain of papal relatives had its own consequences: the church thereby placed itself squarely as a temporal power and lost the essence of its being, its spiritual and religious domain. The story draws to a close as those church territories in Italy are lost to the popes after almost 1,500 years. In their absence emerges a new papacy, one with a renewed spiritual quality that has affirmed the current reverency of the bishop of Rome of today. This is a story — never before completely told — of the 2,000-year-old church and of the development of papal dynasties since the church's early history.

CHAPTER ONE

In the Beginning— The First 1,200 Years

I: The Stage Is Set

Before Peter the Apostle (originally named Simon) joined Jesus Christ as one of Christ's disciples, he was a married man. Legend has it that he had children. Jesus bestowed upon Simon the appellation *petros*, or "rock":

> And I tell you, you are Peter, and on this rock I will build my church, and the powers of death shall not prevail against it. I will give you the keys of the kingdom of heaven, and whatever you bind on earth shall be bound in heaven, and whatever you loose on earth shall be loosed in heaven.

It was these words from the Holy Scripture (Matt. 16:18–19) that formed the basis for the papacy. The word "papacy," which is of medieval origin, is derived from *papa*, "pope" (meaning "father"), and is used as the title for bishops. And it was the bishop of Rome who was to assume the title of pope. The Roman bishop's role in the church, certainly one that would come as a surprise to Peter the Apostle, was to evolve and to expand, giving the bishop of Rome enormous spiritual, jurisdictional and political powers. The beginnings of the office were quite simple. It has been reported that Peter and Paul themselves placed this office on St. Linus (ca. 67–76), who was the first bishop of Rome, but tradition has given that honor to Peter the Apostle.

The successors of Peter the Apostle and St. Linus in the third century began to affirm their primacy or supreme authority over the univer-

sal church. They claimed that, because Peter was first among the Apostles, they were first among the bishops having preeminence over doctrinal and judicial matters. Stephen I (254–57) espoused the view that he was the successor of Peter, citing the relevant verses from the sixteenth chapter of Matthew, and thus holder of special prerogatives. Later, Damasus I (366–84), claiming to be the direct successor of Peter, focused on Rome as "the apostolic see." Celestine I (422–32) used much the same reasoning to affirm his exclusive rights over the entire church, including the eastern bishop of Constantinople, who was viewed as a rival. Leo I (440–61), called "the Great," expressed the view that the universal authority of the church, derived from Christ who placed it in the hands of Peter, was carried on by the bishops of Rome. They had inherited that role from Peter, who was first among the Apostles. The bishop of Rome was thus the "primate of all the bishops." The support for this claim was no less than that this supremacy had been established by Jesus Christ. In 495, Gelasius I was the first pope to proclaim that the bishop of Rome was the "vicar of Christ" and had received his spiritual authority from God. And in slightly more than a hundred years, Boniface III (607) had the emperor officially declare that the See of St. Peter was head of all the churches. This was Boniface's attempt to thwart the bishop of Constantinople's claim as "ecumenical patriarch" of the church. Eventually papal supremacy as proclaimed by the bishop of Rome would lead to a permanent schism between the Latin and Greek churches.[1]

The Church, however, from its earliest times suffered from another problem: the election of two or more popes at the same time. Rivalry between various factions and schismatic groups often resulted in the election of more than one bishop of Rome. Later it was determined that these schismatically elected popes would be known as "antipopes." These included Hippolytus (217–35), Novatian (251–58), Ursinus (366–67), Eulalius (418–19) and others. This split regarding papal leadership continued and became exacerbated during the Middle Ages — when antipopes created separate ruling spheres for themselves and their adherents — but the tradition of rival papacies had already been established during the early part of the church's history.

The papal power, which would be transformed into the papal monarchy so prevalent in the late Middle Ages and early Renaissance, was acquired after years of struggle. During the early years of the church, the bishop of Rome was in fear for his life as the Roman emperors and government sought to destroy both the church and its adherents — especially persecuting its ministers. Persecutions and executions were widespread. Popes went into hiding, and some, such as St. Telesphorus (ca. 125–36), St. Fabian (236–50) and St. Sixtus II (257–58) were martyrized. During a religious ceremony on August 6, 258, the soldiers of the Emperor Valerian came upon the bishop of Rome, Sixtus II, seated on his episcopal chair. He and his congregation were in the cemetery of Praetextatus, where they felt safely hidden from the authorities. This error was fatal. Sixtus II was beheaded on the spot, as were his deacons.[2] Less than one hundred years after this inauspicious event, the status of the Roman church and its bishop changed drastically. Miltiades' reign (311–14) saw the easing of restrictions on the church; and the Convention of Milan, in February 313, restored to the church properties that had been taken from it earlier in the century.

The emperor Constantine the Great (306–337), who embraced Christianity only on his deathbed, had during his lifetime become committed to Christianity, extending to its members the right to practice their religion freely and openly. And Constantine was extremely generous to the bishop of Rome, and he donated property for the Basilica Constantiniana, later St. John the Lateran. Other benefactions included the building of the basilicas of St. Peter and St. Paul. It is through Constantine and his policy of toleration that the Roman Empire was transformed into a Christian state.

In the years to follow, the church advanced and prospered, acquiring vast estates in Italy, Gaul, North Africa, Dalmatia and Sicily. The bishop of Rome was Stephen II (752–77) when the Papal States were established in 756. It was he who asked Pepin III, king of the Franks, to protect the Holy See from the Lombards. They had been menacing Rome. Pepin came to Stephen II's assistance, defeating the Lombards. To the apostle Peter and his successor Stephen II, caretaker of the Holy See, Pepin presented the Duchy of Rome, Emilia, Ravenna, Rimini, Pesaro, Fano, Ancona and Senigallia, a vast area in the center of Italy that became known as the Papal States, or States of the Church.

Located north of the Neapolitan frontier (which became the Kingdom of Naples), south of Tuscany, Lombardy and Veneto, the States of the Church varied in size during succeeding centuries. In the eleventh century only the area around Rome remained under the jurisdiction of the Holy See. Later, the size of the Papal States was to increase — especially under the pontificate of the warlike pope Julius II.

The initial acquisition of territory in the eighth century was to climax with Charlemagne, who restored vast territories to the papacy under Pope Hadrian I (772–95), a member of the powerful Conti (Comites) family, and Pope Paschal I (817–24), who was pledged continued support by Louis I, successor of Charlemagne, guaranteeing the Apostolic See with the possession of the Papal States. But there was a hefty price to pay for the pope's reliance on the Frankish emperors. Louis I's son Lothair went to Rome in 824 and set forth an agreement between the empire and the Papal States. One of the provisions determined that papal elections would be jointly and cooperatively conducted by the clergy along with the people of Rome. The choice was then to be approved by an imperial legate after taking an oath of loyalty to the emperor. In succeeding periods the Roman Senate often played a role in the selection process, but almost always the emperors had to approve the bishop-elect. This procedure lasted until the election in 1057 of Pope Stephen IX, who did not seek the approval of the emperor. But control of the papacy by the emperor did not end then; future emperors — including Frederick I (ca. 1123–90) and Frederick II (1194–1250) — continued to influence papal elections.

Even the earlier Byzantine emperors had exercised their rights to approve the bishop of Rome. In 625 Pope Honorius I was confirmed by the exarch, governor and representative of the emperor. The exarchate, which exercised the power of confirming the pope, ended in 751. The papal historian Horace Mann is of the opinion that "where the State interferes to any considerable extent in the freedom of episcopal elections, fatal is the result first to that liberty which the Church needs to fulfill its glorious destiny, and then to the religious good of the people. For the State will always look for men who will be its creatures, rather than for men who will be most fit to work for the spiritual needs of the people."[3]

The earliest bishops of Rome had simply been elected by the Christian community in Rome. Many were of Greek extraction — St. Sixtus I (ca. 115–25). Telesphorus (ca. 125–36), Hyginus (ca. 136–40), St. Eleutherius (ca. 175–89), St. Anterus (235–36), Sixtus II (257–58) and others. St. Zacharias (741–52) was the last of the Greek popes. A few of the early popes came from Syria, Africa, Sicily, Sardinia and regions of Italy such as Campania and Tuscany. The first Latin pope was St. Victor (189–99), and most of the popes after that date were Roman. Even those who were not Roman were selected from the Roman clergy so that during the first thousand years the Bishop of Rome and the papacy were controlled by Roman bishops elected by Romans, primarily by the Roman clergy.[4] We shall soon see how the

Romans abused this power; in reaction to feuding Roman families, the emperor Henry III proposed (and then imposed) four popes — Clement II (1046–47), Damasus II (1048), Leo IX (1049–54), and Victor II (1055–57).

In an attempt to curtail the interference of both the Roman aristocracy and the German emperors on nominating popes, Pope Nicholas II (1059–61) reserved the election of the bishop of Rome to cardinal-bishops, and Alexander III in 1179 established the Sacred College of Cardinals. They — the cardinals — possessed the exclusive right to choose the pope.

The change in the election of the supreme head of the church evolved over 1,200 years. During this same period the church developed its stance on celibacy. In the early church there was a goodly number of celibate clergy. Celibacy was considered superior to marriage. Spiritual perfection was to be sought without the distractions of sex and worldly possessions. The ecumenical Council of Nicaea proposed a law of celibacy for the clergy in 325, but at that time there was general agreement with the Egyptian bishop Paphnutus who sought to regain the church tradition that marriage before ordination, but not after, was acceptable.[5] Pope Siricius in 386 ruled in favor of the law of celibacy for bishops, priests and deacons; succeeding popes — Innocent I (401–417), Leo I (440–61) and Gregory I (590–604) — enforced clerical celibacy, obviously unsuccessfully. In the history of the papacy, many of the popes themselves were the sons of priests, among them Damasus I (366–84), Boniface I (418–22), Anastasius II (496–98), Agapi(e)tus I (535–36) and Marinus I (882–84). Theodore I (642–49) and Boniface VI (896) were sons of bishops. Pope Felix III (483–92) was not only the son of a priest but he himself had been married and was a widower with two children. Pope Gregory I, called "the Great," (590–604) was descended from one of Felix's offspring.[6] Hadrian II (867–72) had been married before his ordination, but his wife and daughter were alive when he ascended to the papacy. During a sacking of Rome, his daughter was raped, and she and her mother murdered.[7] It was only during the pontificate of Gregory VII (1073–

85), who decreed and vigorously enforced a ruling against clerical marriage, that celibacy became the rule for all priests. He demanded that princes and laity refuse to be served by members of the clergy who were incontinent. That policy has prevailed in the church to the present day.

As we have seen, some bishops of Rome married, and there was a definite tendency begun in this early period of the church for the bishops of Rome to be blood relations to one another. Anastasius I (399–401) was the father of Innocent I (401–417); Silverius, son of Hormisdas (514–23), served as bishop of Rome from 536 to 537; Pope Constantine (708–709) was probably the brother of Pope Sisinnius (708). Likewise, Stephen I (752–57) was succeeded as bishop of Rome by his brother Paul I (757–67), both being members of the wealthy and influential Roman family, the Orso/Orsini (Bobo/di Bobone). That family was to provide three other popes for the church — Celestine III (1191–98), Nicholas III (1277–80) and Benedict XIII (1724–30). Several members of the Roman Anici family, including Felix III (483–92), Agapi(e)tus I (535–36) and Gregory I (590–604) also became Bishops of Rome.[8] Hadrian I (772–95) and Hadrian III (884–85) belonged to the Conti family of Tusculum. That family established a papal dynasty and considered the papacy to be their own private domain, as shall be explained. And Stephen IV (816–17), Sergius II (844–47) and Hadrian II (867–72) all belonged to the same Roman family.

Members of aristocratic Roman families were often brought up in the Lateran Palace, including those individuals who later became Stephen II, Paul I and Stephen IV. These precedents for selecting members of the same Roman family as Supreme Pontiff had thus been established early in the history of the church and had continued even under the Sacred College of Cardinals. Popes often nominated members of their own families as cardinals, who in turn selected other members of the same family to succeed the previous pope. This practice had become a fairly common one during much of the first 1,200 years of the papacy, as shall be illustrated.

The Macabre — The Cadaver Synod

It was during the Middle Ages that the papacy was to sink to abysmal depths — a time fueled by Roman families fighting for control of the Holy See. In 891 the Roman Formosus had been elected pope. Threatened by Duke Lambert (Lamberto) of Spoleto, whom he had been forced to crown as emperor, Pope Formosus appealed to Arnulf, king of the East Franks (d. 899) for assistance. Arnulf came to the aid of the Holy See, and he was rewarded by the pope. Arnulf was proclaimed emperor. The successor of Pope Formosus was Stephen VI (896–97), who was pressured to conduct a trial of Formosus by Duke Lambert and his mother Ageltrude, wife of the Emperor Guido II of Spoleto, a great grandson of Charlemagne. Mother and son were furious that Formosus had crowned Arnulf as emperor and sought revenge on the deceased pope. The body of Formosus was disinterred, and a mock trial was held. The dead Formosus, dressed in his papal garments, was placed on a throne. A courtroom with witnesses and assembled guests had been set up for legal action and judgment. A deacon submissively answered the charges for the deceased pontiff in a trial for which the results had already been prescribed. Enraged that her son has not been declared emperor, Ageltrude followed the proceedings of the trial with particular attention. She wanted and was determined to obtain revenge.

The political influence exerted by Lambert and his mother resulted in the anticipated guilty verdict. Formosus was found culpable of such crimes as perjury and covetous conduct. As punishment, all his acts were declared to be null and void. The vestments of Formosus were removed, three of his fingers — those used to bless — were cut off, and his body was thrown into the Tiber.[9] This was Lambert and his mother's victory over the dead; however, the Roman populace found Stephen's actions abominable, and Stephen himself was deposed, jailed and strangled. The succeeding popes tended to be either partisans of the humiliated Formosus or of his persecutor Stephen. Theodore II (897) was one of the former. He had the body of Formosus — whose body was fished out of the Tiber — solemnly reburied in St. Peter's.

Upon the death of Pope Theodore II (897), the Formosans and the anti–Formosans elected two separate popes: John IX, a supporter of Formosus, and Sergius, bishop of Cere and a foe of Formosus. John IX (898–900) received the approval of Emperor Lambert of Spoleto; during his reign, John IX annulled the pronouncements made against Formosus at the "Cadaver Synod." Four years after John IX's death, Sergius (Pope Sergius III — this time with the assistance of the army of Duke Alberico I of Spoleto — gained the papacy. Sergius III (904–911) had backed Pope Stephen VI and had even participated in the trial of the dead Formosus. Sergius, who hated Formosus, again condemned the deceased pope. Sergius was also a vicious man, who seized the papacy by force of arms and had the two previous popes strangled.

II: The Early Papal Dynasties

The Family of Teofilatto
(Theophylact or Theophylactus)

In Rome Sergius III was supported by Senator Teofilatto, who had attained imperial power in Rome, and his wife, the Senatrix Teodora (Theodora). Their family were to be the creators of popes for almost one hundred years. Teofilatto had come to Rome from Tusculum, a hilltop city near Rome and may have been a cousin of Sergius, who was related to the counts of Tusculum.

Teofilatto was a man who collected titles, serving as *magister militum* (commander of the militia), *vestararius* (head of the papal administration), treasurer of the Holy See, consul and *dominus urbis* (lord of Rome). He and Teodora dominated the temporal power of Rome and the Holy See. This was accomplished in a most unusual way. To the north of Rome was Alberico I, duke of Spoleto, an ambitious ruler. He was a soldier of fortune, an adventurer, possibly of French origin, who had led his men

into battle for the cause of Guido II of Spoleto, later to be emperor. Guido had named him marchese of Camerino. In 897 Alberico had killed Guido IV of Spoleto and united Spoleto with his own territory, Camerino, to become the most powerful ruler in central Italy. Since his territory was in the very heart of the Italian peninsula, it became tied with the adjacent areas — those held by the pope, the Papal States. Alberico wished to exert his influence on Rome and the Holy See, and his opportunity came when Sergius, allied with Teofilatto and Teodora, asked for his assistance. All three Romans acted jointly when the papal throne was vacant and the Formosians were fighting among themselves. They asked: Would he — Alberico — with his army come to Rome and place Sergius on the Apostolic throne? The duke was anxious to move into the Roman political arena. He advanced on Rome, and in 904 he made his candidate, Sergius III, pope.

Sergius III was to reign as Supreme Pontiff until 911. Upholding the legality of the Cadaver Synod, he stipulated that the decrees and clerical appointments of Formosus were invalid, and members of the clergy ordained during the time of Formosus had to be readmitted into the priesthood. He was supported in these decisions by his military commander, Teofilatto. Violence became the basis of their power. In order to be secure in their domination of the papacy, Teodora and Teofilatto may well have encouraged Sergius to become sexually involved with their young and beautiful daughter, who might have been only fifteen years of age — the yet-to-become notorious Marozia.[10] From this liaison was born a son, the future pope John XI. This particular charge was written by Liutprand of Cremona (ca. 922–72), who chronicled those times. However, his accounts are disputed by Mann: "His (Sergius III's) illicit intercourse with Marozia rests chiefly on the word of a careless, spiteful relator (Liutprand) of indiscreet gossip."[11] Soon after the death of Sergius III, Marozia was married to Alberico I; it was the object of her parents to insure the protection of the Teofilatto family interest by being related to this powerful ruler. Alberico's military force thus became intricately linked to

TABLE I: HOUSE OF TUSCULUM (ALBERICHI, CRESCENZI, COLONNA)

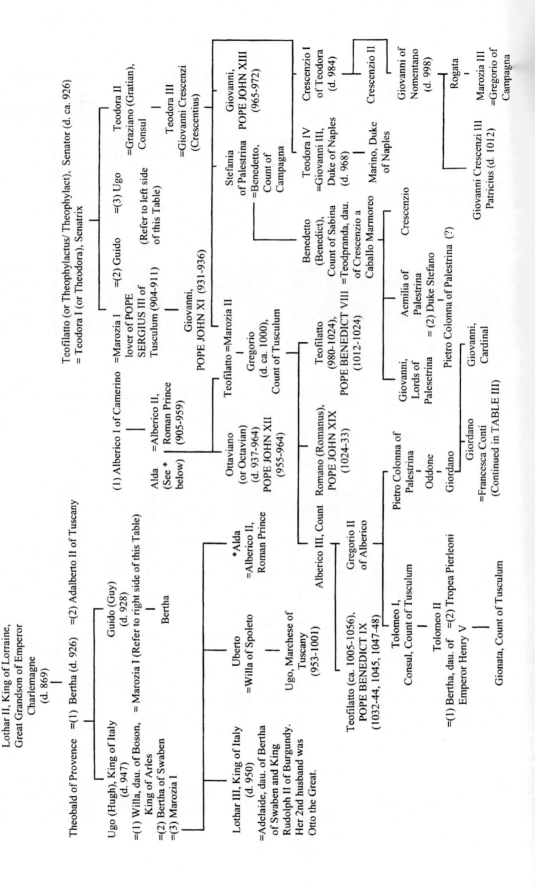

the papacy and the domination of Rome. In 914 he brought about the election of Pope John X (914–28).

TEODORA (THEODORA)

Pope John X also owed his election specifically to the family of Teofilatto, which supported his candidacy. He was the reputed lover of Teodora, Teofilatto's wife.[12] According to Liutprand, who had served as a confidential secretary and diplomat to leading figures of the time (mainly Berengar II, king of Italy, and the Emperor Otto I), Teodora gave the papal tiara to her "favorites." "Captivated by his handsome appearance," Teodora "compelled John to sin with her repeatedly," declared Liutprand. Again Mann defends Teodora by stating that Liutprand was "not a reliable source."[13]

While beautiful, Teodora was also consumed by vices; Liutprand wrote: "scortum impudens ... romanae civitatis non inviriliter monarchiam obtinebat" (shameless whore ... she exercised power on the Roman citizenry like a man). But another historian, Eugenio Vulgario, proclaimed that Teodora "was filled with genuine virtues."[14] So one must decide whether there is any basis for Liutprand's accusations. There is little question that Teodora was the monarch of Rome and was called "serenissima vestaratrix" (*serene highness*). What is also known for sure is that she was the mother of Marozia, Teodora II and Sergia (named after Pope Sergius III, whom the family of Teofilatto obviously admired). She also had another son: Teodora's name along with that of her husband and Sergius III were mentioned in a hymn sung in the Church of St. Maria in Rome to commemorate a miracle that the Virgin had performed on the couple's paralytic little boy. No other mention is made of the boy. The extended family of Teofilatto and Teodora, including those of the House of Tusculum and the Alberichi, are shown in Table I.

As we have seen, Teodora was largely responsible for the election of popes Sergius III and John X, who may have been her lover. John X (914–28) was an energetic and creative pope who, during the early stages of his

pontificate, enjoyed the blessing of Teofilatto and family. Early in his administration he was able to bring together the military forces of the southern Italian states, King Berengar of Italy, Duke Alberico I of Spoleto and the emperor of the West against the Saracens who were invading Italy. They were defeated at the Battle of Garigliano (August 915). In that same battle the army of Rome was commanded by Teofilatto. John X succeeded in establishing good relations with both the Greek Church and the German emperor. Unfortunately for John X, his protectors — Teofilatto, Teodora, King Berengar I (an old friend) and Duke Alberico I — had all died by 925, and he found himself in need of protection from the growing influence of Marozia, who sought greater power for the Roman aristocracy, which she represented. She felt that her family's pivotal position in Rome had been slowly taken away by a strong pontiff, John X, and she was not about to let that happen.

MAROZIA

Born around 890, Marozia had married as her first husband the Duke of Spoleto, Alberico I. In her youth she had taken a lover, purportedly Pope Sergius III, and a son had been born of this union around 906.[15] As mentioned earlier, the relationship between Marozia and Sergius is recorded by Liutprand, but it has been disputed.[16] It is not known when Marozia married Alberico I, and her relationship with Sergius, encouraged by her parents, may have been adulterous. Four children were born of her marriage to Alberico: Duke Alberico II, Sergius (later bishop of Nepi), Constantine and a daughter. While her parents and husband were alive, her power in Rome was assured; but upon their deaths, Marozia felt threatened by Pope John X. (Liutprand also accused Marozia of having "illicit intercourse" with this pope as well.)[17] The pope, in turn, wanted to free himself from the influence of the Roman aristocracy, especially of the family of Teofilatto.[18] After all, it was Teofilatto and Teodora who not only had nominated the popes, but who had ruled the government. In an attempt to assert his independence, Pope John X formed an alliance with Hugh, king of Provence (d. 947), who wished to make himself king of Italy. Such an agreement was made in Mantua in 926. But Marozia was not to be outmaneuvered in this struggle for papal dominance. In 925 she married Guy, marchese of Tuscany, another influential Italian ruler who was the half brother of Hugh. Like his brother, Guy was a descendant of the royal house of Charlemagne of the Carolingians, or Carlovingian, Dynasty (see Table I). Guy loved his beautiful wife Marozia and also loved power. He had at his disposal a military force that could help execute Marozia's schemes. Together they moved on Rome, which at that time was governed by Roman consul, the Marchese Peter, brother of Pope John X. Peter had received the consular position after the death of Alberico I.

The pontificate of John X was now drawing to a close. Guy's troops entered Rome. As the pope watched, Peter was "cut to pieces" by Guy; John was imprisoned in a dungeon in the Castle Sant' Angelo, and soon after (in 928) Guy suffocated him with a pillow.[19] Marozia was now in full command of Rome. She was ennobled with the titled "senatrix" and "patricia," and with her husband, she ruled Rome in effect, placing three popes on the papal throne — Leo VI (928), Stephen VII (929–31) and her own son John XI (931–35), who was only in his early twenties when elected. John XI became a tool to be used by his mother.

When Guy of Tuscany died in 929, Marozia did not wish to remain a widow for long. Needing a new power base, she quickly offered her hand in marriage to King Hugh of Provence. In 932 the marriage was performed in Castle Sant' Angelo, blessed by Pope John XI. After the marriage Hugh was to receive the imperial crown. It was the culmination of Marozia's aspiration of supreme power. She would become empress.

But during these festivities the unexpected was to happen. Hugh became increasingly arrogant, treating the Roman nobility with contempt. Further, this marriage between in-laws (Hugh and Guy were half brothers), prohibited by the church, had profoundly offended the

moral sense of Rome. It had also infuriated Marozia's son Alberico II, who had been informed that his new stepfather intended to blind him so that he would not become a rival to the imperial throne. As the festivities progressed, Marozia asked her son to pour some water for Hugh to wash his hands. In the process some water may have spilled — Hugh, claiming that his stepson had shown disrespect, slapped Alberico's face.[20] Alberico left the castle and called upon the Romans to revolt against this alien who was married to his mother and was to become lord of Rome. The Romans responded, attacking and seizing the castle in December 932. Hugh barely escaped and fled the city.

Even though he was to threaten Rome from time to time, Hugh was thenceforth to play an inconsequential role in the history of Rome, dying in 947. The consequences for Marozia of this popular revolt of the Romans were even more devastating. She was handed over to Alberico II, her son, who imprisoned his mother in the dungeons of Castle Sant' Angelo to disappear from history. Her domination of Rome had come to an abrupt end. Marozia died in obscurity before 937.

ALBERICO II

Marozia was succeeded by her son Alberico II. In 932 he was proclaimed lord of Rome (*Princeps Atque Senator Omniun Romanorum Patricius*). His absolute rule for over twenty years was generally beneficial to Rome. He brought tranquility to the city by ruling it with a firm hand. He permitted his half brother the pope to exercise nominal sovereignty but denied the papacy a role in the politics of the state. John XI continued his religious functions, administering sacraments and officiating in ecclesiastical ceremonies. It has been said that Alberico II treated him as a personal lackey who did only what he was told. Pope John XI had become a puppet, "a man without authority, destitute of all worldly dignity."[21] It was Alberico who ruled, and under every government pronouncement was written "Alberico, thanks to God, humble prince and senator of all the Romans."[22] John XI was to die in December 935, after being pontiff for four years. The next four popes — Leo VII (936–39), Stephen VIII (939–42), Marinus II (942–46) and Agapi(e)tus II (946–55) were all the creations of Alberico II. Since they were indebted to him personally for their elections, they generally did as he directed; when they did not, as was the case of Stephen VIII, they were disposed of. Stephen VIII was put into jail, mutilated, so disfigured by partisans of Alberico "that he could not appear in public" and died from these inflictions.[23]

POPE JOHN XII

After twenty-two years, Alberico II, prince of Rome, senator and patrician, was aware of his own impending death. He had come to the realization that "the separation of the temporal power from the Papacy in Rome was impossible for any length of time" and decided to reunite the two. On August 31, 954, he was brought to the Basilica of St. Peter. With him were the Roman nobility and clergy. As he lay dying he made them promise to elect — upon the death of the reigning Pope Agapi(e)tus II — his son Octavian, who was seventeen years of age. When Alberico died, Octavian became the ruler of Rome, and a year later, upon the death of Agapi(e)tus, he became Supreme Pontiff as John XII (955–64). When Octavian became pope, he was probably only eighteen years of age. And he is considered the second pope "who changed his name on his election to the pontifical throne." The first pope to change his name was John II in 533. John II, as a priest, had been known as Mercury, but this was considered a pagan name and hence the change.[24] John XII's reign was one of vacillation and dissipation. He sought the protection of both the Emperor Otto I and Berengar, king of Italy. This displeased Otto who called a synod and had John deposed.

During his reign as pope, John lived a life of debauchery. The Lateran Palace, residence of the pope, became a bordello.[24] His life was extremely remote from any ecclesiastical interest. He lived as a lord of the times; had numerous lovers and mistresses, plundered the papal treasury for gambling and behaved in a way which forced the emperor to admonish him, urging him to change his way of life. The accusations made against John included these: "You should know ... therefore that not just a few, but all, laity and clergy, have accused you of homicide, perjury, sacrilege, incest with some of your female relatives and two sisters ... that you have toasted the devil, and gambled with dice, while playing thusly you have evoked Zeus, Venus and other demons." The names of several women were named specifically in the indictment. After this trial, a new pope, Leo VIII, was elected; but within a short period, John returned in triumph to Rome and rid the city of his rival. His life of dissipation ended when he was still in his twenties. Supposedly he had a stroke while in bed with an adulterous wife named Stefanetta; another account has the pope being thrown out of a window by the betrayed husband.[25] The date of his death is given as May 14, 964.

The Family of Crescenzi (Crescentii or Crescentius)

As a result of his disastrous experience with John XII, the emperor Otto I, who had become the protector of the papacy, insisted that no pope could be elected without the consent of the emperor. Otto had sought the election of Leo VIII, but the Romans wanted and elected Benedict V in 964. Otto placed a siege around Rome and the city surrendered. Leo VIII was again placed on the papal throne, and Benedict V was degraded. His papal garments were removed, Leo VIII whacked the papal scepter over Benedict's head and the scepter broke; Benedict was exiled.

But there was no harmony in store for the papacy: a new family was to shake Rome. That family was the Crescenzi. Individual members of this family, like the Teofilatto, were called *Princeps Atque Omnium Romanorum Senator*.[26] Giovanni Crescenzi had married the niece of Marozia. Her name was Teodora III; thus this family — the Crescenzi — were descended from

Teofilatto and Teodora (see Table I). All of the Crescenzi children — Giovanni (later Pope John XIII), Crescenzio I of Teodora, Stephania, Teodora IV and Marozia II — were to play a role in the selection of the popes until the beginning of the next century.

The Crescenzi belonged to the Roman aristocracy, which wished to control both the papacy and the Roman government. It was part of their birthright, as had been shown by Teofilatto, Marozia and Alberico II, but now the Holy Roman emperor (Otto I and his successors) wanted to play a role, too, and had already selected Leo VIII to be their instrument. The next pope, John XIII (965–72), has been reputed to be the son of Giovanni Crescenzio and Teodora III. John XIII had been bishop of Narni and had found favor with the Emperor Otto I, who approved his appointment in 965. Soon after, there was an insurrection in Rome, and the pope, who for a while was imprisoned, received the military assistance of the emperor and the Crescenzi family, including that of the duke of Naples, who was married to a Crescenzi, Teodora IV. John XIII became more and more indebted to the emperor and to the Crescenzi. He favored the interests of this family — it was, after all, his own — and bestowed on Stephania, his sister, the fiefdom of Palestrina and on her son, Benedetto, the fiefdom of Sabina. The Crescenzi family thus gained a dominant position in Rome from the favoritism shown by Pope John XIII.

After John XIII's death in 972, Benedict VI (973–74), supported by the emperor, was elected pope, but one of Teodora III's sons, Crescenzio I of Teodora (d. 984), had a candidate of his own, the deacon Franco. Unfortunately for Pope Benedict, Otto I died, and the new emperor, Otto II, was not able to help him retain the papal miter. Soon after, in June 974, Crescenzio I instigated a revolt and captured and strangled Benedict, placing Franco as pope.[27] Franco took the name Boniface VII, but he was quickly deposed — at least temporarily — when the imperial forces quieted the revolt and restored order. Crescenzio I of Teodora escaped punishment for his part in the

insurrection against Benedict VI. He went to a convent, S. Alessio, where he lived his remaining years in tranquility.[28] His creation, Boniface VII, had as pope "stripped St. Peter's of its treasures.[29]

A new pope, Benedict VII, was consecrated in 974. He was related both to Alberico II and to the Crescenzi family and enjoyed the support of the Roman aristocracy and the emperor. However, the succeeding pope, John XIV (983–84) only had imperial approval; thus, when the emperor was away, Giovanni II Crescenzi, surnamed Nomentanus (d. 998) and son of Crescenzio I of Teodora, had the pope seized, placed in Castle Sant' Angelo, beaten, "his eyes torn out" and deposed.[30] In August 984 Pope John XIV was poisoned. Almost immediately, the former pope Boniface VII reappeared and claimed the papacy, but these were violent times and he may have been assassinated. He had become extremely unpopular. His dead body became an expression of the Romans' dislike. His clothing was removed, and he was dragged through the streets of Rome, to be thrown at the feet of the equestrian statue of Marcus Aurelius.[31] He was stomped upon, and spears were thrown into the nude cadaver.

Giovanni II Crescenzi, called Nomentanus (d. 998), instrumental in the selection of popes, became patrician in 985 and served as the political ruler of Rome. He approved of the next pope, John XV (985–96). At the ascent of this new pope, Giovanni II had his brother Crescenzio II receive the city of Terracina. Soon after, John XV became a virtual prisoner of Giovanni II Crescenzi, and the pope fled from Rome seeking the help of the emperor. When John XV died, the emperor Otto III appointed his cousin Bruno as Pope Gregory V (996–99). Bruno, son of Duke Otto of Carinthia, was a great-grandson of the emperor Otto I. Bruno's nephew was the emperor Conrad II.

Conrad II not only had an uncle who was a pope, he was also the cousin of a pope, Leo IX, and his wife's niece Beatrice was married to the brother of a pope, Stephen IX. Conrad II's son, grandson, and great grandson (Henrys III, IV,

V) were all emperors. Henry V's sister Agnes (d. 1142), mother of twenty-two children, was the mother of the emperor Conrad III and grandmother of the emperor Frederick I Barbarossa. Frederick I's son was the emperor Henry VI and his grandson, the emperor Frederick II (see Table II). They were the renowned members of the Hohenstaufen family, which will be described in more detail later because of its conflict with the papacy.

Needless to say, there were a host of popes who were closely related to the imperial houses. Gregory V was one of these royal relatives; by this appointment, Otto III wished to have greater control over the papacy and at the same time diminish the power of the Crescenzi family. Otto III was crowned emperor by his cousin Gregory V and then left Rome. The Romans resented the installation of a foreign pope, and Giovanni II Crescenzi again seized power. Pope Gregory was exiled, and John Philagathos, known as the antipope John XVI, was placed on the papal throne by Giovanni II. Otto III returned to Rome, restored Gregory V as rightful heir of St. Peter and seized Giovanni II Crescenzi, who was beheaded after two months of resistance at the Castle Sant' Angelo.[32] As for the antipope John XVI, Giovanni's appointment, his fate was far more horrible. John XVI was seized by the imperial forces, blinded and then disfigured. His hands, tongue, nose, lips were severely maimed. He was placed on an ass and paraded throughout the city. Finally there was a trial in which he was officially condemned and imprisoned in a monastery where he died in 1001.

Upon the death of Pope Gregory V, the emperor appointed the next pope, to be known as Silvester II (999–1003). He was from France, born in Auvergne. Again the Romans revolted against a foreigner as pope. When Otto III died, Giovanni III Crescenzi, son of Giovanni II Nomentanus, became governor (*patrician*) of Rome. Giovanni III served as the ruler while Silvester concerned himself solely with spiritual matters. Giovanni III nominated the next popes: John XVII (1003), John XVIII (1003–1009), and Sergius IV (1009–1012). For all practical purposes, the rule of the Crescenzi

family ended when both Giovanni III and his creation Pope Sergius IV died within one week of each other in 1012.[33]

The Counts of Tusculum and Other Descendants of Teofilatto

By contrast, the power of the descendants of Teofilatto was to continue. As we have described, Alberico I, marchese of Spoleto, and his infamous wife Marozia, daughter of Senator Teofilatto, had a son Alberico II, who ruled Rome with impressive firmness. Alberico II married Alda, daughter of his stepfather, Hugo of Burgundy. (It should be noted that another account has him married to Stephania Colonna of S. Eussac.) Alberico II's son Octavian was made pope — the licentious John XII (955–64). Alberico II had other children who became the counts of Tusculum, a stronghold near Rome. One son, a count of Tusculum, had married Marozia II Crescenzi, his cousin. They were the parents of Gregorio, a count of Tusculum who died around 1012. This count was thus a direct descendant of Marozia I, daughter of Teofilatto and Teodora, as well as of Teodora III, wife of Giovanni Crescenzi and granddaughter of Teofilatto and Teodora (see Table I). Gregorio was the embodiment of Roman nobility, descended from those members of the aristocracy who had controlled the papal throne for over one hundred years. Obviously the family was not interested in losing that control.

Gregorio, Count of Tusculum, was another who represented the Roman aristocracy and their resentment of assertion of authority by the German emperors. Gregorio had received the title *Praefectus Navalis* (Naval Commander or Prefect). With the almost simultaneous death of both Pope Sergius IV and the Roman patrician Giovanni III Crescenzi in 1012, Gregorio of Tusculum saw an opportunity for advancing his branch of the family. He succeeded in placing his son Teofilatto (named for his ancestor) on the papal throne as Pope Benedict VIII (1012–24). He first had to battle his cousins the Crescenzi, who had named a certain Gregory (known as Gregory VI, antipope

TABLE II: POPES FROM IMPERIAL HOUSES

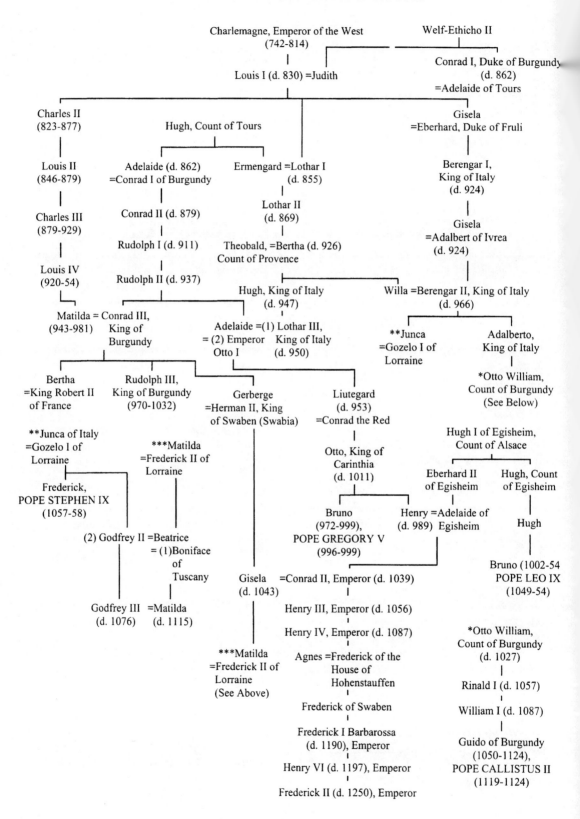

in 1012) to the papacy. Gregorio of Tusculum made his brother Romanus "senator" to direct the actual civil government of Rome. Benedict VIII strengthened the papal military forces and regained land for the papacy. Upon Benedict's death, the pontifical scepter went to his brother Romanus, who became known as Pope John XIX (1024–34). He was not a member of the clergy and had probably obtained this office through bribery. He placed his brother, the consul Alberico III, in a position of power within the Roman Church.

Alberico looked at the papacy as the private property of the Tusculum, or Alberichi (descendants of Alberico II), family, so that when his brother John XIX died, he used whatever means at his disposal — mostly money — to enthrone his son, also named Teofilatto, as Supreme Pontiff.[34]

The counts of Tusculum were trying to make the position of Roman pontiff hereditary. When Teofilatto, son of Alberico III, became pope, he was known as Benedict IX (1032–44, 1045, 1047–48). He was all of twelve years of age (that young age has been disputed, and some sources say that he was in his twenties).[35] He was for sure a layman and lived in the style of his great-great uncle Pope John XII. The historian Gregorovius concluded that "with Benedict IX the papacy hit the bottom of moral decadency. Conditions in Rome during this period probably seemed worse than that of the period of John XIII, and perhaps, would surpass in horror the period of the Borgias."[36] Benedict was considered by future historians to be a crook and an assassin. Gregorovius went on to say, "It seemed as if a demon from Hell in the disguise of a priest occupied the chair of Peter and profaned the sacred mysteries of religion by his insolent courses. Protected by his brother Gregory, who ruled the city as Senator of the Romans, he led unchecked the life of a Turkish Sultan in the Lateran Palace. He and his family filled Rome with robbery and murder. All lawful conditions had ceased."[37]

The Romans revolted against Benedict's dissolute life, as well as against the Tusculum's family's heavy handed control of Rome. The pope was deposed. Pope Silvester III of the

Crescenzi family became pope in 1045, but within a few months Benedict was to return. In less than a year after his return, he was to abdicate to Pope Gregory VI (1045–46). With popular support and bribery, Benedict returned again for a short time (1047–48), but he was soon forced to retreat to the family estate in Tusculum. There Benedict died around 1055.

The scandal created by Benedict IX, who had reigned as pontiff on three separate occasions, caused the emperor Henry III to nominate four popes to the papal throne — Clement II (1046–47), Damasus II (1048), Leo IX (1049–54) and Victor II (1055–57). Victor was succeeded by Stephen IX (1057–58). Four of these popes — Clement, Leo, Victor and Stephen — were from German nobility. Clement was the son of the lords of Morsleben and Hornburg. Leo was the son of Hugh, Count of Egisheim-Dagsburg, and a cousin of the emperor Conrad II, whose mother Adelaide was also of the Egisheim-Dagsburg family.[38] Victor (Gebhard von Dollnstein-Hirschberg) was the son of Hartwig, Count of Calvi in Swabia. Stephen, a direct descendant of Charlemagne, was related to many of the European royal families (see Table III). Stephen's brother, Duke Gregory II of Lorraine, had married Beatrice, widow of Duke Boniface of Tuscany and niece of Gisela; Gisela was married to Emperor Conrad II and was mother of Emperor Henry III. This was a period of time when the German emperors themselves wanted to exert influence over the popes. They placed into the papal office members of the imperial families. In spite of this tendency on the part of the German emperors, the Roman nobility tried to place their own candidates on the throne.

When Stephen IX died in 1058, Gregorio II of Tusculum, brother of the pope Benedict IX, had a relative of his made pope, to be called Benedict X (1058–59). Considered an antipope, Benedict X was excommunicated, jailed, tried and degraded. Gregorio II of Tusculum (d. 1064) may well have been the father of Pietro who settled in the hills and established the Colonna dynasty that was to impact upon the papacy for hundreds of years.[39] The origins of the Colonna family, however, are debatable. Pompeo Litta is not sure if Pietro Colonna was the son of Gregorio II, Count of Tusculum and nephew of Pope Benedict IX, or the son of Aemilia of Palestrina, granddaughter of Stephania Crescenzi of Palestrina (see Table I). Aemilia supposedly married twice: first Agapitus Conti and then Duke Stefano of Germany. A study by Pompeo Colonna, *I Colonna dalle Origini all'Inizio del secolo XIX*, places the family as direct descendants of the counts of Tusculum.

The Pierleoni Family

During this period, when the counts of Tusculum and the Crescenzi family ruled Rome and pushed their candidates onto the papal throne, there emerged other rival Roman families who were to share in the pope-making process. The next centuries were to see the rise of the Savelli, Caetani, Frangipane (sometimes spelled Frangipani) and Pierleoni families. Sometimes they were locked together as allies, and often they fought against one another. Some of these families provided members who attained the hierarchical position of Supreme Pontiff; others, like the Frangipane, became the power behind the election of candidates for the papal throne.

Certainly the Pierleoni were without parallel in the history of the papacy. They were descended from Baruch, a Jewish banker who, with his son Leone (Leo), converted to the Roman Catholic Church. When baptized, he took the name Benedictus Christianus. The Pierleoni family were the bankers and financial advisors of numerous popes. Baruch was probably married to a member of the Frangipane family and apparently had another son [Giovanni Graziano] (a translation of the Jewish name Yochanan. Giovanni Graziano had become a priest and served at the monastery of St. Mary on the Aventine and as archpriest of St. John of the Latin Gate. As a member of the distinguished Pierleoni family, he would have been acquainted with the Roman aristocracy. He was the godfather of the profligate Pope

Benedict IX, who served as pope on three different occasions. Desirous of marrying his beautiful cousin, Benedict confided in Giovanni Graziano that he would like to abdicate. Graziano, of a wealthy family, is reported to have paid Benedict about 2,000 pounds of silver to leave the papacy; in his turn, Graziano, who was in his seventies, assumed the papal throne in 1045 and took the name Gregory VI. It is possible that Gregory VI wished to rid the papacy of Benedict, who had brought the Roman See to such a low ebb. Certainly, the Romans hailed Gregory VI's election, believing that he would reform an office that was in dire need of change. But soon after this election, he was accused of buying the papacy from Benedict IX and was deposed in 1046.

Gregory was sent to Germany, accompanied by his chaplain Hildebrand, who was a Pierleoni or otherwise related to the deposed pontiff.[40] One source comes to the conclusion that Hildebrand was the son of Leo, brother of Giovanni Graziano, while another believes him to be the son of Leo's wife's sister and thus a nephew by marriage. What is known is that Hildebrand was very close to Graziano, whose great wealth was bequeathed to Hildebrand upon his death.[41]

Graziano's genealogy is somewhat in dispute. Another source places him in the Stefaneschi family. Duke Hildebrand (d. 975) of the Stefaneschi had a son Hildebrand, a monk, whose son became Pope Benedict VI. He wore the papal miter for a short time, from 973 to 974, and was murdered. The monk Hildebrand had a sister Costantia, wife of Duke Gregorio; their son Gratianus, husband of Teodora (Theodora), was the father of Pope Gregory VI (Giovanni Graziano).[42] There is some confusion here as Teodora, daughter of Senator Teofilatto, is listed in other sources as the wife of Consul Gratianus, and because Teodora and Gratianus's daughter married into the Crescenzi family, the maker and breaker of popes. It is even possible that the Stefaneschi and Pierleoni are part of the same family. What is known for sure is that the Stefaneschi were cousins to the Crescenzi, Alberichi, Savelli, Annibaldi (Conti) and Papareschi. Pope Innocent II (1130–43), born Gregorio Papareschi, belonged to that family.

There is no doubt that the Roman (or Lazio) families such as the Orsini, Colonna, Savelli, Gaetani, Frangipane, Pierleoni, Crescenzi and Stefaneschi were related by common ancestors and intermarriage. The Pierleoni and Frangipane families were related, both being of the ancient Latin gens Anicia Augusta. The Frangipane may indeed have been descended from the Pierleoni. The Conti (and in turn the Colonna family, which is believed to have been directly descended from the Tusculum Conti or Alberichi families) are also of the Latin gens Anicia. Zazzera in his history of the Conti family says that they were of the Roman house of Augusta Ottavia.[43] The Crescenzi married into prominent families like the Gaetani. Crescenzio Gaetani, descended from both the Crescenzi and Gaetani, was the father of Gaetana, wife of Orso Orsini, and his grandchildren included Giacoma, wife of Pietro de Pierleoni; Margherita, wife of Oddone Colonna; and Matteo Rosso Orsini, father of Pope Nicholas III. These interrelationships can be seen in the genealogical tables for the Orsini during this early period (although the genealogy differs in various sources).[44] While exact genealogy during this early period is a matter of conjecture, it is clear that members of these few families were consistently placed on the papal throne for an extensive period of time (see Tables IIIa and IIIb).

Thus, while it is not possible to know the exact parentage of Pope Gregory VI (Giovanni Graziano), that pope, like many others during this period, was definitely related to these papal families. Current research indicates that Gregory VI was a member of the Pierleoni family. It is also likely that Hildebrand, the future Pope Gregory VII, was a member of this family.

Both Hildebrand and his ostensible uncle were vitally concerned about reforming the church. Because of his exceptional brilliance and determination, Hildebrand had become the chancellor and treasurer of the Roman Church, and later the secretary of state within the Roman Curia of Pope Leo IX (1049–54), establishing himself as the leading figure in Rome. He became the trusted advisor of succeeding popes — Stephen IX (1057–58), Nicholas II (1058–61), who appointed Hildebrand an archdeacon, and Alexander II (1061–73). The election of these three popes was due to the influential force of Hildebrand, and he guided these "reform popes" during their administrations. They were popes who opposed simony, especially the paying for ecclesiastical advancement and appointments; they were against priestly marriage and concubinage; and they were keenly aware of the dangers of lay investiture, whereby churches (or dioceses) were given to clergymen by lords, princes, kings and others who were not officially designated members of the church.

Hildebrand had been a popemaker, and he was a reformer, seeing the need to modify the church in the aftermath of such popes as Benedict IX and in the midst of the general corruption that had permeated the church. And so, in 1073, Hildebrand was to be acclaimed as Pope Gregory VII (1073–85) — the pontiff of reform who fought the investiture policies of Emperor Henry IV. Pursuing a policy of papal supremacy over the temporal power of princes, Gregory VII opposed the imperial appointment of clergy to churches and offices. When the emperor appointed bishops to Milan, Spoleto and other sees in Germany, Gregory VII excommunicated him. At Canossa, the emperor Henry IV stood in the snow and asked for forgiveness, and while Gregory forgave him, the struggle between emperor and pope continued.[45] Henry eventually retaliated by driving Gregory out of Rome, and Gregory was to die in Salerno in 1085.

During Gregory's pontificate, the emperor had the archbishop of Ravenna elected a pope under the name Clement III (1083–1100), but he is considered an antipope. The Pierleoni family was successful in removing him from Rome in 1098. The legitimate popes during that period, Victor III (1086–87) and Urban II (1088–99) continued to promulgate Gregory's reforms. The succeeding pope, Paschal II (1099–1118), after being imprisoned by the

TABLE IIIa: TEN GENERATIONS OF THE ORSINI FAMILY,
SHOWING RELATIONS TO OTHER ROMAN ARISTOCRATIC FAMILIES (CA. 1100–1450) (continued from TABLE I)

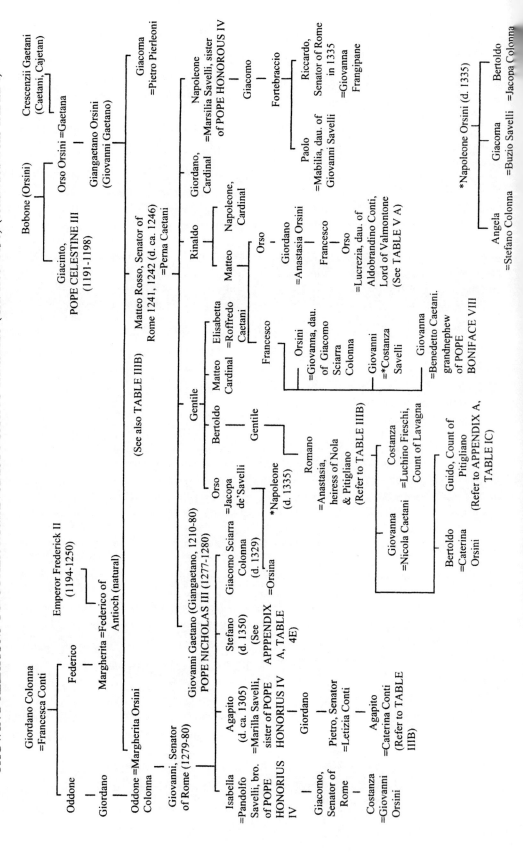

TABLE IIIb: TEN GENERATIONS
(continued from IIIa; for further information on the Colonna, Orsini, Savelli and Caetani families, refer to TABLES 1, 2, 3 and 4)

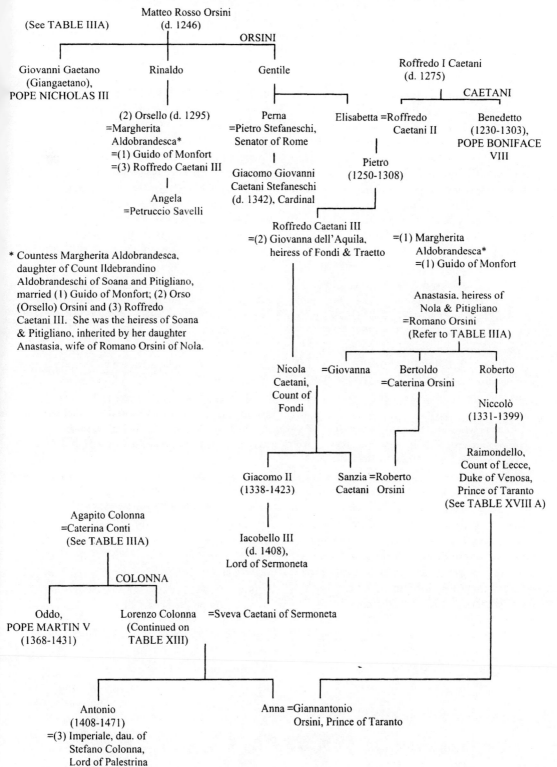

(See TABLE IIIA)

Matteo Rosso Orsini
(d. 1246)

ORSINI

Giovanni Gaetano
(Giangaetano),
POPE NICHOLAS III

Rinaldo

Gentile

Roffredo I Caetani
(d. 1275)

CAETANI

(2) Orsello (d. 1295)
=Margherita
Aldobrandesca*
=(1) Guido of Monfort
=(3) Roffredo Caetani III

Perna
=Pietro Stefaneschi,
Senator of Rome

Elisabetta =Roffredo
Caetani II

Benedetto
(1230-1303),
POPE BONIFACE
VIII

Giacomo Giovanni
Caetani Stefaneschi
(d. 1342), Cardinal

Pietro
(1250-1308)

Angela
=Petruccio Savelli

Roffredo Caetani III
=(2) Giovanna dell'Aquila,
heiress of Fondi & Traetto

=(1) Margherita
Aldobrandesca*
=(1) Guido of Monfort

* Countess Margherita Aldobrandesca,
daughter of Count Ildebrandino
Aldobrandeschi of Soana and Pitigliano,
married (1) Guido of Monfort; (2) Orso
(Orsello) Orsini and (3) Roffredo
Caetani III. She was the heiress of Soana
& Pitigliano, inherited by her daughter
Anastasia, wife of Romano Orsini of Nola.

Anastasia, heiress of
Nola & Pitigliano
=Romano Orsini
(Refer to TABLE IIIA)

Nicola
Caetani,
Count of
Fondi

=Giovanna

Bertoldo
=Caterina Orsini

Roberto

Niccolò
(1331-1399)

Giacomo II
(1338-1423)

Sanzia =Roberto
Caetani Orsini

Raimondello,
Count of Lecce,
Duke of Venosa,
Prince of Taranto
(See TABLE XVIII A)

Agapito Colonna
=Caterina Conti
(See TABLE IIIA)

Iacobello III
(d. 1408),
Lord of Sermoneta

COLONNA

Oddo,
POPE MARTIN V
(1368-1431)

Lorenzo Colonna
(Continued on
TABLE XIII)

=Sveva Caetani of Sermoneta

Antonio
(1408-1471)
=(3) Imperiale, dau. of
Stefano Colonna,
Lord of Palestrina

Anna =Giannantonio
Orsini, Prince of Taranto

emperor Henry V, capitulated to his demands to invest bishops and abbots. He was considered a traitor by those — including the Pierleoni family, now headed by Petrus Leonis, son of Leo — who supported reform and stood against the dictates of the Holy Roman Emperor.[46]

In 1118 Gelasius II (1118–19) was elected in a conclave of cardinals. It was conducted — as it is today — in secret, and the Romans rioted, desiring greater input in papal selection. Gelasius II's reign started when he was apprehended by Cencio (Cencius) Frangipane and his soldiers. Frangipane supported Henry V and the imperial faction against the papacy.[47] Cencio brutally treated the newly elected pope — "seized the aged pope by the throat, threw him on the ground, assailed him with blows, gashed him with his spires, dragged him along by the hair."[48] Cencio also punished the cardinals, and dragged Gelasius II in chains back to Rome and had him imprisoned in the Frangipane fortification. The Pierleoni family had the pope released. Soon after, as he was saying mass, Gelasius was again attacked by the forces of the Frangipane. This time Gelasius II decided to flee from Rome. He settled and died in Cluny, France.[49]

In the meantime the emperor had proclaimed Gregory VIII as pope, but he is considered an antipope. When Callistus II (1119–24), the successor of Gelasius II, was elected, he imprisoned Gregory VIII for life. Gregory was also punished publicly in Rome, being placed on the rear end of a camel and paraded through the city as the citizenry jeered and threw objects at him. Callistus II was a son of the count of Burgundy, closely related to the imperial as well as the French and Castilian royal families and descended from Charlemagne (see Table II). He was able to bring about a peaceful solution to the investiture issue, making peace with the emperor in the Concordat of Worms in 1122.

The election for pope that followed the death of Callistus II was a turbulent one, fought between the Frangipane and Pierleoni families in 1124. The Pierleoni wished to elect Cardinal Teobaldo Boccadipecora, who became known as Celestine II (1124) and reigned as

pope for two days. He was opposed by the Frangipane. As "Te Deum" was being sung as part of the solemn ceremony to consecrate Celestine II as pope, the Frangipane troops entered. They severely beat the new pope, who was forced to resign. He died a few days later from his injuries. In his place was elected Honorius II (1124–30), the Frangipane candidate for the papacy. Under Honorius the church was influenced by his chancellor Aimeric Frangipane, who had helped to put the pope on the throne. When Honorius died, his body was secretly buried.[50] Immediately, without the knowledge of the Roman populace, the Frangipane brought together some cardinals and, in a furtive session, elected the next pope, Innocent II (1130–43). The other cardinals and the Pierleoni family were furious at this clandestine election, and they assembled and elected Cardinal Pietro Pierleoni, the son of Petrus Leone. He took the name Anacletus II (1130–38), but is considered an antipope. Anacletus II had wide support, however, as well as the Pierleoni family's wealth. He controlled Rome with Pierleoni soldiers and was recognized as pope by King Roger II (d. 1154) of Sicily who is said to have married a Pierleoni, sister of Anacletus.[51] Upon the death of Anacletus, the schism between Innocent II and Anacletus II ended, and the Pierleoni family paid the pope homage. But the Pierleoni family now waited for their turn to influence the papacy.

It came quickly. When Pope Lucius II (1144–45) was made pontiff, he appointed Giordano Pierleoni, brother of Anacletus II, as patrician of Rome. In trying to regain Rome during an insurrection, Lucius was felled by stones used as weapons. Hit on the head by a rock, the pope died soon after in 1145. His successor was Eugene III (1145–53), who was the last pope of the reform movement started by Hildebrand Pierleoni both as papal advisor and as pope himself. At this point in the history of the papacy, the Pierleoni family for all practical purposes ended its dominant role in the selection of the Supreme Pontiff. Tropea Pierleoni, daughter of Petrus Leone, married Tolomeo II (d. 1153), consul of the Romans and a count of Tusculum; he was the nephew of Pietro (Peter)

Colonna, whose family made a marked impact on the papacy for the next several hundred years.[52]

During the second half of the twelfth century, new issues and problems were coming to the forefront. Eugene III (1145–53) was followed by a Roman, Anastasius IV (1153–54), and then by the only English pope, Hadrian IV (1154–59). It was during the latter's pontificate that the papacy came into conflict with the emperor Frederick I Barbarossa (d. 1190), who wished to proclaim imperial supremacy over Italy and the papacy. Upon Hadrian's death, Alexander III (1159–81) was elected, and the conflict between pope and emperor ignited into a mammoth fire. As Alexander was being enthroned, a group supporting the emperor burst into the meeting. Cardinal Ottaviano Monticelli, later to become the antipope Victor IV (1159–64), grabbed the papal mantle from Alexander and put it on his own shoulders. Alexander succeeded in grabbing it back, but in the confusion he placed it on backwards much to the laughter of the assembled group. This incident was followed by a riot;[53] the pope was crowned elsewhere. During his long rule Alexander III was confronted constantly by the Emperor Frederick I and by four successive pro-imperial antipopes — Victor IV (1159–64), Paschal III (1164–68), Callistus III (1168–78) and Innocent III (1179–80). Alexander III, both a strong and a courageous pope against odds maintained the independence of the church against the forces of the empire. But Rome had become hostile to the popes, and Alexander had to leave the city because of anti-papal feelings. The next three legitimate popes — Lucius III (1181–85), Urban III (1185–87), and Gregory VIII (1187) — were forced to live away from Rome.

Urban III belonged to a noble family from Milan, the Crivelli. His sister Cassandra married Giovanni Castiglione, and their son Goffredo da Castiglione became Pope Celestine IV in 1241 for a few days. This pattern of selecting members of the same family as Supreme Pontiff was one that was to continue with the families of Urban III's and Celestine IV's successors.

The Conti Family Dynasty (Part One)

In 1187 Paolo Scolari of an aristocratic Roman family was elected pontiff, taking the name Clement III (1187–91). Clement made peace with the emperor Henry VI by granting him the imperial crown. Clement III was related to the Conti family, which was to establish its own papal dynasty. Clement, who was thus connected to powerful Roman families, made members of these families cardinals and gave the College of Cardinal "a strongly Roman character." Upon Clement's death, there were eighteen Roman cardinals, three-fifths of the College. The next pope after Clement III was Celestine III (1191–98) of the Roman Orsinis. That family was to become the arbitrator for the selection of popes for hundreds of years. Celestine "clearly had no intention of reducing the Roman aristocratic predominance established by his predecessor. The motive for creating this Roman predominance was political; the purpose was to make Rome a secure refuge for the papacy at a time of growing tension between papacy and empire."[54]

The century ended with the election of Pope Innocent III (1198–1261), who was a direct descendant of the Conti, the counts of Tusculum. The father of Innocent III (Lotario dei Conti) was Trasimondo, Count of Segni; his mother was Claricia of the Scotti family. Trasimondo was the grandson of Gregorio, brother of Pope Benedict IX (Teofilatto Conti). Innocent III was a nephew of Pope Clement III, who had made him cardinal in 1190. One authority states that the Conti family gave the papacy thirteen popes.[55] From the tenth to the eighteenth centuries, Conti popes included Sergius III, John XI, John XII, Benedict VII, Benedict VIII, Benedict IX, John XIX, Innocent III, Gregory IX, Alexander IV, Innocent XIII and two antipopes Benedict X and Victor IV. Hadrian I and Hadrian III were also members of this family[56] (see Table IV).

As will be discussed further in Chapter Two, Pope Innocent III was generous to his brother Riccardo and his family, as well as to the family of his sister, who married Pietro Annibaldi. Pietro's son Annibaldo the Elder was a senator

TABLE IV: CONTI FAMILY (DICOMIS, COMIS) OF TUSCULUM, SEGNI, VALMONTONE and POLI*

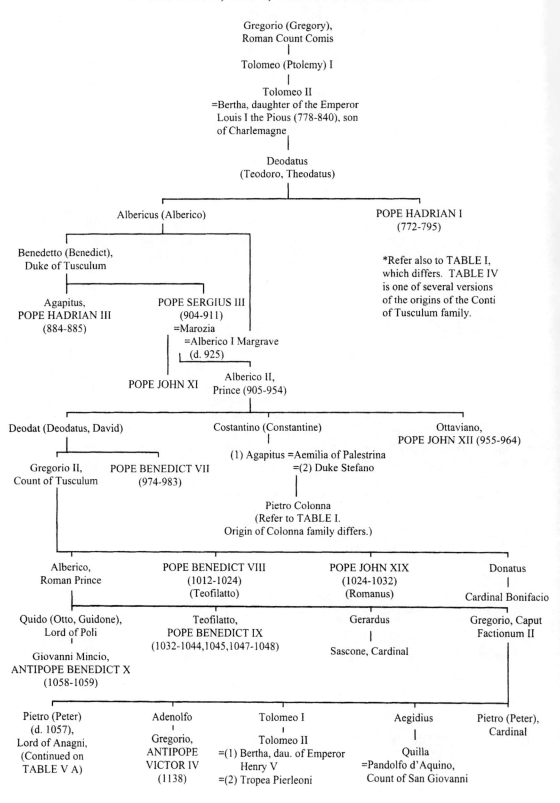

Gregorio (Gregory),
Roman Count Comis

Tolomeo (Ptolemy) I

Tolomeo II
=Bertha, daughter of the Emperor
Louis I the Pious (778-840), son
of Charlemagne

Deodatus
(Teodoro, Theodatus)

Albericus (Alberico)

POPE HADRIAN I
(772-795)

Benedetto (Benedict),
Duke of Tusculum

*Refer also to TABLE I,
which differs. TABLE IV
is one of several versions
of the origins of the Conti
of Tusculum family.

Agapitus,
POPE HADRIAN III
(884-885)

POPE SERGIUS III
(904-911)
=Marozia
=Alberico I Margrave
(d. 925)

POPE JOHN XI

Alberico II,
Prince (905-954)

Deodat (Deodatus, David)

Costantino (Constantine)
(1) Agapitus =Aemilia of Palestrina
=(2) Duke Stefano

Ottaviano,
POPE JOHN XII (955-964)

Gregorio II,
Count of Tusculum

POPE BENEDICT VII
(974-983)

Pietro Colonna
(Refer to TABLE I.
Origin of Colonna family differs.)

Alberico,
Roman Prince

POPE BENEDICT VIII
(1012-1024)
(Teofilatto)

POPE JOHN XIX
(1024-1032)
(Romanus)

Donatus

Cardinal Bonifacio

Quido (Otto, Guidone),
Lord of Poli

Giovanni Mincio,
ANTIPOPE BENEDICT X
(1058-1059)

Teofilatto,
POPE BENEDICT IX
(1032-1044,1045,1047-1048)

Gerardus

Sascone, Cardinal

Gregorio, Caput
Factionum II

Pietro (Peter)
(d. 1057),
Lord of Anagni,
(Continued on
TABLE V A)

Adenolfo

Gregorio,
ANTIPOPE
VICTOR IV
(1138)

Tolomeo I

Tolomeo II
=(1) Bertha, dau. of Emperor
Henry V
=(2) Tropea Pierleoni

Aegidius

Quilla
=Pandolfo d'Aquino,
Count of San Giovanni

Pietro (Peter),
Cardinal

TABLE Va: CONTI OF SEGNI, VALMONTONE and POLI (continued from TABLE IV)

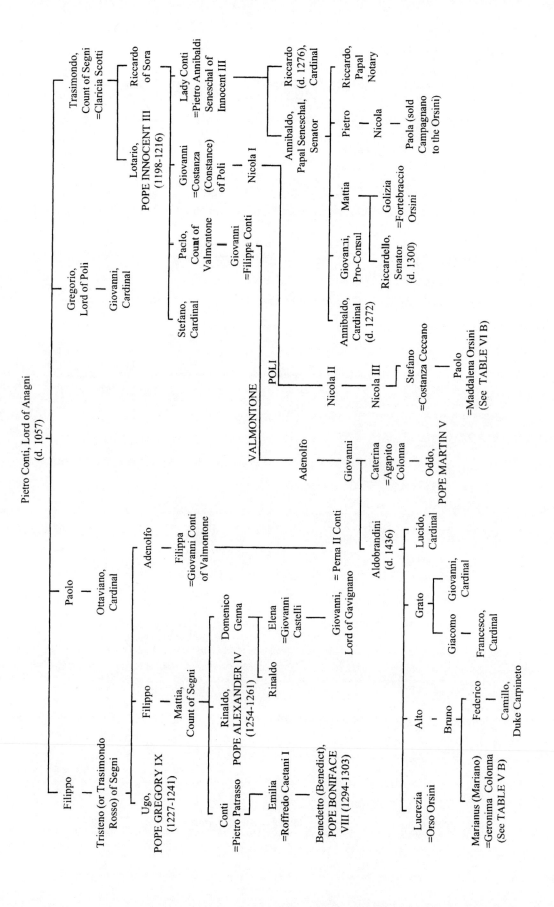

TABLE Vb: CONTI OF SEGNI, VALMONTONE and POLI
(continued from TABLE Va)

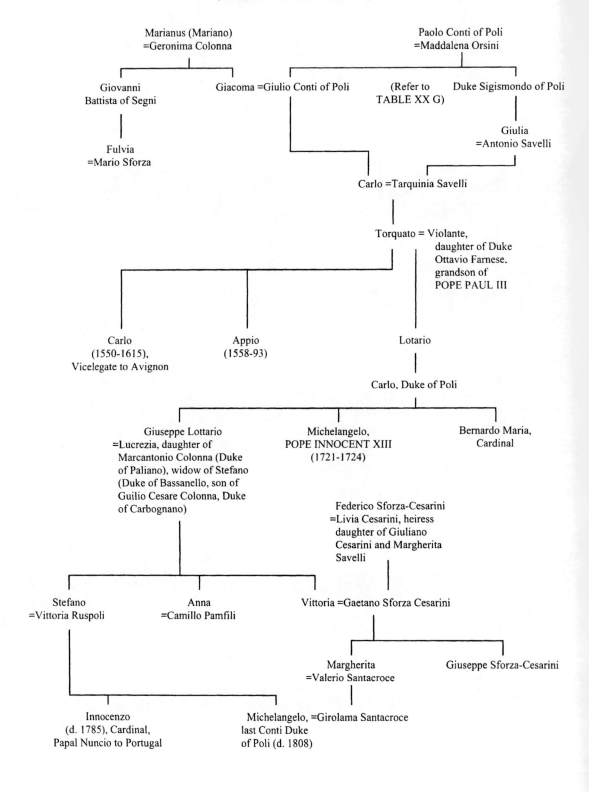

and papal seneschal, another son Riccardo (d. 1276) was elected a cardinal and the other two sons, Pietro and Trasimondo, also became senators. Annibaldo the Elder's son Giovanni Annibaldi (d. 1300) was a proconsul; two other sons were Annibaldo (d. 1272), a cardinal, and Riccardo, a papal notary. The power granted to the Annibaldis permitted them, in effect, to rule Rome and the Papal States. Two cousins of Pope Innocent III, Ugo and Rinaldo Conti, were later to serve as popes Gregory IX (1227–41) and Alexander IV (1254–61). Alexander's grandnephew was Pope Boniface VIII (1294–1303), son of Emilia Conti and Roffredo I Caetani. From 1198 to 1303, these four related Conti (and Caetani) popes reigned a total of forty-eight years. Papal authority rested in the hands of the Conti family primarily because the Conti popes appointed so many Roman relatives and friends to the cardinalate, which insured their elections (see Table Va).

The Conti, in addition, consolidated their power by marrying into the Roman aristocracy — specifically, into the Colonna, Orsini, and Caetani families. In order for the family not to lose its wealth, it was sometimes necessary for different branches of the Conti family to intermarry. Giulio Conti of Poli married his cousin Giacoma Conti of Segni and Valmontone, and their son, in turn, married the heiress Tarquinia Conti. Thus the family continued to remain counts and dukes of Poli. It was this branch of the family that produced yet another pope, Innocent XIII (1721–24), Michelangelo dei Conti of Poli. While Pope Innocent XIII made his brother Bernardo (d. 1730) a cardinal

in 1721, he limited his benefices. Bernardo headed the Grand Penitentiary, an office that dealt with penance, absolution, confession, and similar matters. Innocent XIII's pontificate was a short one and not as glorious as that of other members of his family. The Conti family of Poli became extinct at the beginning of the nineteenth century when another Michelangelo Conti died. The family had a palazzo near the Fontana di Trevi.

Duke Giuseppe Conti of Poli, another brother of Pope Innocent XIII, married Lucrezia, the daughter of Marcantonio Colonna of the family of Martin V. Pope Innocent XIII's grandfather Lotario had married Claire Orsini, of the family of Nicholas III; his great grandfather Torquato had been the husband of Violante, daughter of Ottavio Farnese, grandson of Pope Paul III; Innocent's great-great-grandfather Giulio had married Tarquinia, daughter of Giulia Conti and Antonio Savelli of the family of Pope Honorius III (1216–27). Giulia Conti was the daughter of Sigismondo Conti of Poli. Pope Innocent XIII's niece Vittoria married Gaetano Sforza-Cesarini. These families represented papal dynasties.

The last Conti duke of Poli died in 1808, and the Sforza-Cesarini family inherited the Conti estate. Salvatore Sforza-Cesarini sold Poli and Guadaguolo to Giovanni Torlonia in 1820 for 73,582 scudi and 80 baiocchi.[57] (For additional information on this family, refer to Chapter Three on the Farnese Dynasty and see Tables 5a and 5b in Appendix A.)

CHAPTER TWO

The Papal Families at the Close of the Middle Ages, 1200–1471

The Conti Family Dynasty (Part Two)

The climax of the medieval papacy was to be reached with Pope Innocent III (Lotario dei Conti, 1198–1216). He referred to himself as the "Vicar of Christ" on earth and claimed to rule with divine authority. His goal, according to an authoritative source, was "the enforcement of papal rule in the church and in the world."[1] Temporal power became subjected to the will of the pope, and when the emperor Henry VI died in 1196, Innocent proclaimed his successor to be Otto IV, whom he later deposed in favor of Frederick II, son of the emperor Henry VI and Constance of Sicily.

Constance (1154–98) was the posthumous daughter of King Roger II of Sicily. When her nephew King William II, without heirs, was near the end of his reign, Constance was regarded as the next in line to the wealthy Sicilian kingdom. According to Dante, Constance had been in a convent, from which Henry VI took her. They were married on January 27, 1186. The papacy was naturally frightened by this marriage because it would unite southern Italy and Germany. In 1194 Constance and Henry VI had a son, the future emperor and king of Sicily, Frederick II (1194–1250). In 1197 Frederick II's father died, and in the following year his mother did likewise. She placed him under the guardianship of Pope Innocent III. Frederick II was to create serious problems, as many predicted, for future popes.

One of the crowning achievements of Innocent's brilliant reign was the twelfth Ecumenical Council, held in November 1215 (the Fourth Lateran Council) and attended by more than seventy patriarchs and archbishops, around four hundred bishops and eight hundred abbots, numerous ambassadors from the European states and the personal presence of Emperor Frederick II.[2] Innocent III was to die a year later on July 16, 1216.

It has been said that the selection of Innocent III had been conducted in a manner whereby the cardinals balloted in secret and, thus, that it was the first conclave in history. The cardinals had unanimously elected Lotario Conti. During his reign he aggrandized members of his family: Cousin Giovanni Conti (d. 1231) became cardinal in 1200 and chancellor of the church in 1205; cousin Ottaviano Conti (d. 1231) was appointed a cardinal in 1206; and cousin Ugo/Ugolino Conti, later pope, also became a cardinal in 1206; Innocent's brother Riccardo became lord of Poli, Guadagnolo and Valmontone, Count of Sora; and Riccardo's son Stefano (d. 1254) was appointed a cardinal-deacon in 1216.[3]

The Conti family produced forty cardinals, seven prefects of Rome and five senators — even King Philip Augustus of France called himself a blood relative of the Conti family.[4] The importance of the role of cardinals in the process of papal selection became increasingly apparent.

Ugo (Ugolino) Conti, son of a count of

Segni,[5] was elected pope in 1227 and took the name Gregory IX; like his relative Innocent III, he was a champion for the rights of the Holy Church. His reign was one of conflict with the emperor Frederick II, whom he excommunicated several times. Gregory IX died in 1241 as the emperor's troops encircled Rome; he may well have been close to one hundred years old. Gregory too bestowed favors on his family. He placed the red hat of the cardinalate on his nephew Rinaldo in 1227 (later to be Pope Alexander IV), as well as on his relatives Niccolò Conti (d. 1239) in 1228 and Riccardo Annibaldi (d. 1276) in 1238.[6] The three sons of Riccardo Conti, Innocent III's brother, were to received special positions: Paolo became proconsul of Rome in 1138, Stefano was made a cardinal-priest in 1129 and Giovanni was appointed senator in 1139. Paolo was the ancestor of the dukes of Segni and counts of Valmontone. The heiress of this family, Fulvia, daughter of Giovanni Battista Conti, married Mario Sforza, Count of Santa Flora in 1548, and their descendants, the Sforza-Conti-Cesarini family, acquired the titles of Duke of Segni and Count of Valmontone.[7]

As we have just noted, Pope Gregory IX's nephew Rinaldo became Pope Alexander IV (1254–61). He was an inept pope for his time. Pope Alexander served as the guardian of Conradin, the heir to the Kingdom of Frederick II, but sought to place other royal families on the Sicilian throne. He was thwarted in this attempt by Manfred (d. 1266), the illegitimate son of Frederick II. Manfred and Conradin were the last of the royal house of Hohenstaufen, to which the emperors Frederick I, Frederick II and Henry VI belonged. Alexander IV had wished to annihilate the powerful Hohenstaufen family, especially Frederick II and his "viperish offspring,"[8] which had, according to the pope, disturbed Italian and church affairs. The next two popes, Urban IV (1261–64) and Clement IV (1265–68), accomplished this objective by engaging Charles, Count of Anjou (1226–85), brother of King Louis IX of France, to free Italy and Sicily first from Manfred and then from Conradin. Manfred was killed by French forces in 1266, and

two years later, Conradin, defeated in battle, was captured and beheaded. Unfortunately for the church, the papacy had now made Charles of Anjou as powerful as the Hohenstaufen once were.

The Fieschi Family

The Fieschi were a prominent Genovese family that gave the church two popes, many cardinals and hundreds of other members of the Roman Catholic clergy. Caterina Fieschi of Genova (1448–1510) was a saint, canonized in 1737. Members of the Fieschi family married into many noble Italian families. The Fieschi united with the Grimaldi, from which the princely house of Monaco is descended, against another important Genoa family, the Doria. The first Fieschi pope — Sinibaldo, who took the name Innocent IV (1243–54) — followed Celestine IV (1241), successor to Gregory IX. Sinibaldo was the son of Hugo, Count of Lavagna. To distinguish cardinals from other clergy, Innocent IV initiated the "distinguished sign of the red hat."[9] During his pontificate (in 1245) he deposed Frederick II as emperor, noting that, as the successor of St. Peter, the pope had the spiritual authority to control temporal matters. Even though Frederick died in 1250, Innocent IV still had to contend with Frederick's children.

Like other dynastic popes, Innocent was generous with his relatives. His nephew Alberto was appointed captain of the papal military forces. Another nephew Guglielmo (William), who died in 1256, became a cardinal and papal legate; still another nephew, Ottobono, became a cardinal in 1251 and was elected pope as Hadrian V in 1276 for a few months. Hadrian V died before being crowned. Hadrian V's sister Beatrice married Tommaso II of the House of Savoy, Lord of Piedmont and Count of Flanders; thus the Fieschi family were related to the major sovereigns of Europe (see Table VI).

At the same time, the Fieschi family retained power in Genoa by allying with the French Prince Charles of Anjou. This was the

TABLE VI: FIESCHI, VISCONTI, SAVOY, GENEVA AND ROGER FAMILIES

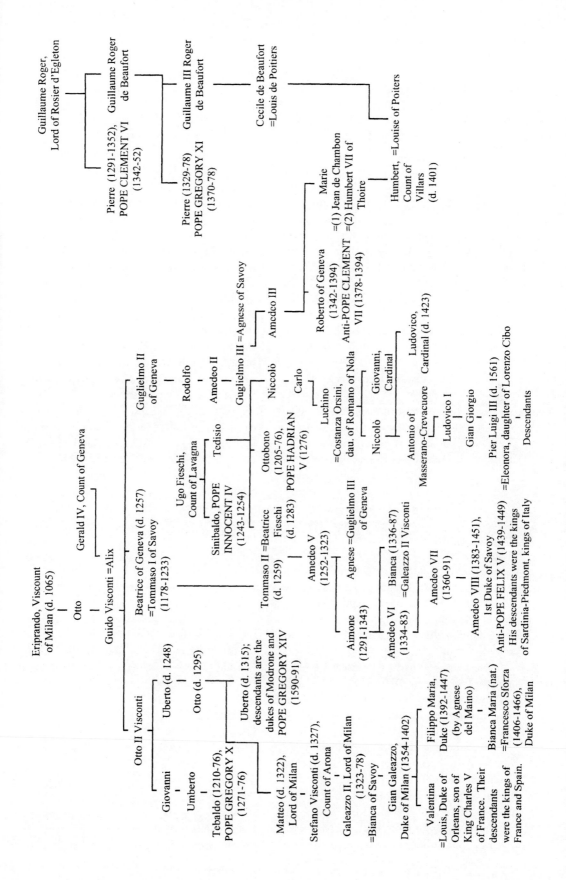

same Charles who in 1265 was made king of Sicily and Naples by Pope Clement IV. After Clement's death it took almost three years to elect a papal successor and that was only after the cardinals were threatened with starvation. After the death of Hadrian V, the political power of the Fieschi declined.

Unlike the many Italian families that came to Rome as members of the pope's clan, the Fieschi returned and remained in Genoa. Members of the family were counts of Lavagna, Torriglia and Savignone. In conflict with the Dorias in Genoa, the Fieschis were defeated in the plot against them in 1547, and the family's power came to an end. The Torriglia and Lavagana branch of the family, from which the Fieschi popes were descended, is extinct.

The Visconti Family

In 1271 Tebaldo Visconti became Pope Gregory X (1271–76), successor of Clement IV. The Visconti family was to become the rulers of Milan, and members of that family married into the Fieschi family. Pope Gregory X was the great-grandson of Otto II Visconti from whose son Uberto the lords and dukes of Milan are descended.[10] Uberto's grandson Matteo (d. 1322) became the first Visconti lord of Milan. Matteo's brother Uberto (d. 1315) was the ancestor of the dukes of Visconti-Madrone. The mother of Pope Gregory XIV belonged to this family. And the contemporary film director Luchino Visconti (1906–1976) is also a member of this family. Other branches of the Visconti family exist into the present.

Otto II Visconti had a sister Beatrice who married Tommaso (d. 1189), Count of Savoy, and it was their son Tommaso II (d. 1259) who married Beatrice Fieschi, the sister of Pope Hadrian V (1276).

Later, other members of the Visconti family were to marry into the Fieschi family. Isabelle Fieschi was the wife of Luchino Visconti (1292–1349), the lord of Milan from 1339 until his death. (She probably poisoned him.) Isabelle was the mother of Luchino Novello, who was excluded from ruling because it

appeared that Lord Luchino Visconti was not his father. Luchino, son of Matteo (d. 1322), first Lord of Milan, was a direct descendent of Uberto Visconti and a cousin of Pope Gregory X. Milan was now grabbed by Luchino's three nephews — Galeazzo II, Bernabò and Matteo. The ducal branch is descended from Galeazzo II Visconti.

Galeazzo's brother was the infamous Bernabò Visconti (1323–85), who ruled a vast area from Milan to Brescia. His ambition was to expand his territory, and he went from one war into another, invading papal fiefs and in turn being excommunicated by Urban V (1362–70), one of the Avignon popes. In order to maintain peace in northern Italy, Urban V promised to pay 500,000 florins to Bernabò, but within a short period of time this lord of Milan was back to his inherent bellicosity. Renowned for his barbarism and excessive cruelty, Bernabò lived by instituting severe laws and penalties for his subjects, and his atrocities spread general terror in Italy. His grand passion was the hunt, and he zealously killed wild boars. He even punished a youth "because the boy had dreamed of killing a boar."[11] Bernabò kept 5,000 dogs. He had numerous children: seventeen legitimate and at least twenty illegitimate. His death came in the same spirit as he had lived. In 1385 Bernabò was surprised and captured by his nephew Glan Galeazzo Visconti, who was also his son-in-law. He was imprisoned in the *castello* of Trezzo and probably murdered.

Gian Galeazzo took control of Milan, becoming its first duke. His daughter Valentina (d. 1498) married Louis, Duke of Orléans, son of King Charles V of France, and she became the ancestor of numerous French kings, including Henry II, Henry III and Francis I, whose sister Margaret was the grandmother of the first Bourbon king of France, Henry IV (see Table VI). Henry IV (1589–1610) was the ancestor of the kings of France, Spain, Portugal, Italy, Naples and Sicily; the dukes of Parma; the present kings of Belgium and Spain; the grand duke of Luxemburg; several Holy Roman emperors; the emperors of Austria; the present prince of Liechtenstein; the dukes of

Wurttemberg; and the royal house of Bavaria. Gian Gazleazzo's granddaughter Bianca Maria was to marry the condottiere Francesco Sforza, who was named duke of Milan along with his descendants. These descendants married into the ducal and papal families of Italy, including the Farnese and Orsini.

While none of Bernabò's children obtained the reins of government, they married into the great families of Europe. His daughter Caterina was the wife of Gian Galeazzo Visconti, and his granddaughter was the aforementioned Valentina. Bernabò's daughter Maddalena married Friedrich of Bavaria, whose daughter Elisabeth was the wife of Friedrich I, the Hohenzollern king of Brandenberg whose descendants were the kings of Prussia and kaisers of Germany. Maddalena and Friedrich's daughter Agnesse married Francesco Gonzaga of Mantua; Agnesse and Francesco's descendants were the dukes of Mantova as well as Holy Roman emperors. Maddalena and Friedrich were the forebears of the kings of Denmark, Sweden and Poland. Another daughter, Antonia, wife of Eberhard IV of Wurttemberg, was the progenitor of the House of Wurttemberg; daughter Elisabeth (Elisabetta) married Ernest of Bavaria, and their descendants were the dukes of Bavaria; yet another daughter, Taddea, was wife of Stephen III of Bavaria, and they were ancestors of the Bourbon kings of Spain and France, as well as of the kings of Scotland and the present royal family of England.[12]

Verde (d. 1365), Bernabò's oldest daughter, was united in marriage with Duke Leopold III of Hapsburg. She was the ancestor of the Hapsburg emperors of the Holy Roman Empire, the emperors of Austria, the kings of Spain (including the present reigning monarch), the Bourbon dukes of Parma, the Hapsburg grand dukes of Tuscany, the Bourbon kings of the Two Sicilies, the dukes of Wurttemberg and the present claimants to the thrones of Italy and France. Verde's granddaughter Margherita married Duke Friedrich II of Saxony, whose descendants were members of the royal house of Saxony and produced kings of Prussia, kaisers of Germany and kings and queens of Greece and the Netherlands. Descended too

from Duke Friedrich and Margherita was the House of Saxe-Coburg-Gotha, which includes kings of Portugal, kings of Belgium and kings of Bulgaria. Queen Victoria's mother and her husband were members of that family. Descended from Queen Victoria and Albert, Prince Consort, is Queen Elizabeth II of England; King Olaf of Norway; Constantine, former king of Greece; Michael, former king of Romania; Alexander, Crown Prince of Yugoslavia; King Carl XVI Gustaf of Sweden; Margrethe II, Queen of Denmark; and Kira, a claimant to the throne of Russia.[13] The royal house of Saxony is also related to many of the princes of smaller German states including Saxe-Meiningen and Saxe-Altenburg. Elector Friedrich August I (1670–1733) of Saxony, similar to his lustful ancestor Bernabò Visconti, "kept a harem of beautiful women and when he died left 354 bastards."[14] One of his illegitimate children was Maurice, Comte de Saxe, the distinguished military leader, who was recognized by his elector father. Maurice was the grandfather of Amandine Aurore Lucie Dupin (1804–76), who wrote under the pseudonym George Sand. She was among the many distinguished descendants of the Visconti family of Milan, to which Pope Gregory X belonged. It should be clear that the Visconti family of Milan are the ancestors of numerous royal houses of Europe and that they were directly related to many of the princely as well as papal houses in Italy, such as the Medici and the Fieschi.

The two popes who followed Gregory X reigned for only a few months, in 1276. They were Pope Innocent V and Pope Hadrian V of the Fieschi family, a cousin of the Visconti. When Hadrian died in 1276, he was followed on the papal throne by a Portugese, Cardinal Pedro Juliani (Petrus Hispanus, that is, Peter of Spain), who assumed the name John XXI (1276–77). John XXI, a scholar, had a study built for him where he spent most of his time. He left matters of state in the hands of Cardinal Giovanni Gaetano Orsini, who was soon to become the next pope. Pope John was killed when the ceiling of his study caved in on him. Orsini, his successor, was known as Pope Nicholas III (1277–80).

The Orsini Family Dynasty (Part One)

The Orsini family[15] was represented in the papacy with at least five popes: Stephen II (752–57), who was the founder of the Papal States; his brother Paul (757–67), who defended these states from the king of Lombardy; Celestine III (1191–98), who saw the Papal States threatened by the emperor Henry VI; and popes Nicholas III (1277–80) and Benedict XIII (1724–30), about whom we will learn more later. Pope Eugene (Eugenius) II (824–27) was also supposed to be a member of the Orsini (Bobo-Orso or Bobone-Orsini) family (see Table 1a in Appendix A).

In 1191 Giacinto Orsini, son of Petrus Bobo, was elected to the pontifical throne. He became Celestine III (1191–98) and was extremely generous to members of his family, presenting them with church lands and titles. His grandnephew Matteo Rosso, son of Giangaetano Orsini, Lord of Vicovaro, became the lord of Mugnano, Monterotondo, Galeria and S. Angelo in 1195. Later, in 1241, he was appointed senator of Rome (the chief of the government) and valiantly defended Rome against the emperor Frederick II and his Roman allies, the Colonna family. The Orsini, belonging to the Guelph party, supported the Roman papacy and committed their fortune against the Ghibelline (imperial) party of the Colonna. The slogans at the time were "Orsini for the church" and "Colonna for the people." The rivalry between these two families was to last for generations and will be delineated as the history of papal dynasties progresses. In spite of this conflict, however, both families frequently intermarried, often for political advantages. Marriage with other papal families helped them to retain their own base of power and their territorial possessions.

Cardinal Giovanni Gaetano Orsini was the son of Matteo Rosso Orsini, the senator of Rome, and was elected in 1277 to become Pope Nicholas III (1277–80).[16] Giovanni Gaetano's election had been opposed by the supporters of King Charles of Sicily and Naples because, as the leading statesman for John XXI (1276–77), Gaetano had been instrumental in blocking the political ambitions and advancement of King Charles.

During the pontificate of Nicholas III, there was a consistent policy to establish the independence of the Papal States from foreign domination. He wished to reduce the power of King Charles in favor of papal authority. He persuaded Charles not to seek a position as senator of Rome in 1278, but rather had himself appointed for life. He then had King Charles resign his position as imperial vicar of Tuscany. Nicholas III favored King Rudolph of Hapsburg as emperor because Rudolph had withdrawn the imperial claims for Romagna, which then firmly rested within the Papal States.

Like his Orsini predecessors, Nicholas III was much engaged with enlarging those states. The boundaries established by him were to last until 1860, when these territories were incorporated into the kingdom of Italy. He resided in the Vatican Palace, the first pope to do so. Previously, the popes had inhabited the quarters of the Lateran Palace. He died suddenly in 1280, but not before he had showered his relatives with possessions and offices.

His nephew Bertoldo Orsini became count of Romagna, and another nephew Orso Orsini was given a splendid palace at Soriano. Matteo Rosso Orsini (1230–1305), son of Gentile, a brother of Nicholas III, was created a cardinal and became the most influential member of the Sacred College of Cardinals during the reign of his uncle. Nicholas' sister Mabilla (d. 1294), married to a Frangipane, was the mother of Latino Malabranca (d. 1294). Malabranca was appointed a cardinal by his uncle in 1278 and served as pontifical legate to Bologna in 1278 and to Florence in 1280. In 1294 Cardinal Malabranca helped to secure the election of Pope Celestine V. Nicholas named his brother Giordano to be a cardinal in 1278. He permitted another brother, Matteo Rosso, to become senator of Rome, and in 1279 this office was divided between Giovanni Colonna and Pandolfo Savelli. The Colonna and Savelli families were both of noble Roman origin and were closely related to the Orsini by marriage and political ties.

The Orsini family's fortunes were to prosper long after the death of Nicholas III. Napoleone

(d. 1342), son of Rinaldo, who was the lord of Monterotondo and a brother of Nicholas, was appointed as a cardinal in 1288. He was to play a decisive role in the history of the church at the close of the thirteenth century. The descendants of another brother of Pope Nicholas III, Napoleone (family names were often repeated in succeeding generations), became the dukes of Bracciano and Gravina (by Pope Eugene IV in 1435) and counts of Tagliacozzo. The descendants of yet another brother, Gentile, lord of Magnano, were the future lords of Nola and Pitigliano. Likewise, Francesco, son of Matteo, another brother of the pope, received the castles of Poggio di Corese and Comunanza in 1297. He became senator of Rome, along with Stefano Colonna, in 1302. The Orsini family wrestled for power in Rome and for influence within the Holy See for hundreds of years, as will be recorded, and other family descendants will be described in the second and third parts of the Orsini's history.

Nicholas III is remembered as the pope who espoused nepotism, the first pope that deliberately and overtly initiated a policy (according to Pompeo Litta) of depriving the church of its property and wealth to enrich his own family. Because of simony and nepotism, Dante placed him in Hell. Upon his demise, the cardinals were to select a new pope in the city of Viterbo. At the papal conclave, Giordano (d. 1297), brother of Nicholas III, did all he could to impede the election of a pope who favored King Charles of Sicily and Naples. For his obstinacy, he was imprisoned, along with his nephew Cardinal Matteo Rosso. Both being confined in prison, the Orsini interests were absent in the election. Thus, to King Charles' delight, a Frenchman became pope, taking the name Martin IV. The Romans never accepted him, and so the pope did not reside in Rome. His actions were in opposition to Nicholas III, his predecessor. Pope Martin's policy was to place "the universal church at the service" of the French.[17]

First, Martin appointed King Charles as senator for life, so that Charles, in effect, ruled the Papal States. At the request of the king, the pope excommunicated the Byzantine emperor Michael VIII, destroying the possibility of a union between the eastern and western churches. Of the first seven cardinals that Martin IV created, four were French. Martin's reign was a disaster for the papacy since he permitted its domination by the French king of Sicily. But King Charles was hated by the Sicilians, who rebelled victoriously against him (in 1282) and offered the crown to Peter III of Aragon. Martin IV died shortly after the death of King Charles in 1285.

The Savelli Family (Part One)

Giacomo (James) Savelli was of a noble Roman family related to both the Orsini (his brother Giovanni married Giacoma Orsini and his sister Marsilia married Napoleone Orsini) and the Colonna (his brother Pandulfo Savelli married Isabella Colonna and his sister Mabilia married Agapito Colonna). He was now elected pontiff[18] (see Table 2a in Appendix A). He was a grandnephew of Pope Honorius III (1216–27) and took the name Honorius IV (1285–87). The Savelli family had had a long association with the papacy — Pope Gregory II (715–31) had probably been a member of this family. As a cardinal, Giacomo Savelli had made provisions for his family, obtaining the territories of Castel Savello, Castel Gandolfo, Castrum Faiolae, Castrum Arignani as well as Palombara, Scrofano, Albano, Castelleone and Monteverde. The family also received two hereditary positions — marshal of the church and custodian of the conclave.

Honorius took the title of senator but made his brother Pandolfo his deputy. Order was restored in Rome. Under his regime, Sicily was under the control of the House of Aragon, and King Peter III was succeeded by his son James who was crowned king of Sicily in 1286. The following year Pope Honorius IV died. He was followed by Nicholas IV (1188–92).

An Abdication

Pope Nicholas IV was partial to the Colonna family, appointing Giovanni Colonna to be senator. Upon his death, the rival factions among twelve cardinals divided into three partisan groups and debated for over two years. The Colonna cardinals and their allies, the Orsini cardinals and their allies and the French cardinals could not agree upon electing a pope to satisfy their diverse goals. It was Cardinal Latino Malabranca of the Orsini family who recommended the selection of the scholarly hermit Pietro Angeleri da Morrone, who was duly elected in 1294 and took the name Celestine V. He reluctantly accepted the mantle. He became the instrument of King Charles II (son of Charles of Sicily), who ruled the Kingdom of Naples. He had Celestine V appoint seven French cardinals. Weak and ineffectual, the pope soon began to think of abdicating as Supreme Pontiff and consulted Cardinal Benedetto Caetani about his proposed resignation. Cardinal Caetani assured him that this was canonically permissible. Celestine V abdicated, and soon after Cardinal Caetani assumed the papacy as Pope Boniface VIII. The new pope imprisoned Celestine, who died in 1296, two years after his abdication. In the history of the church, Celestine V was one of only five popes who renounced the papal throne.

The C(G)aetani Family

There were two Caetani popes, but many others were descended from this noble family in Campagna. One branch, Caetani (also spelled "Gaetani," from the town of Gaeta where the family originated) produced popes Gelasius II (Giovanni Caetani of Gaeta, 1118–19) and Boniface VIII (Benedetto Caetani of Anagni, 1294–1303). The Caetani were related to other noble Roman families, including the Conti of Segni and the Orsini. The father of Pope Nicholas III (Giovanni Gaetano Orsini) had married Perna Gaetani and was the great-grandson of Gaetana Gaetani. Boniface VIII was the son of Roffredo I Caetani and Emilia Conti of the House of Patrasso di Alatri; Emilia was the niece of Pope Alexander IV of the Conti family (see Table 3a in Appendix A).

As mentioned previously, Boniface became pope by advising his predecessor Celestine V to abdicate. Celestine only wanted to return to the quiet peace of his monastery, but Boniface, fearing a schism, sent the former pope to a remote prison. When told of this decision, Celestine cursed Boniface: "You have entered like a fox [referring to how Boniface attained the papacy]. You will reign like a lion — and you will die like a dog."[19] These were prophetic words.

Boniface reigned like an emperor-pope. He immediately came into conflict with King Philip IV of France over the taxation of church property. He also came into contention with the rich Colonna family, which occupied the castles of Zagarolo as well as the city of Palestrina. Boniface favored the Orsini family, to whom he was related. In 1297 Francesco Orsini, son of Matteo and nephew of Pope Nicholas III, received the castles of Poggio di Corese and Comunanza. Further, he was made senator of Rome in 1302.

Boniface indulged his own family, the Caetani, with enormous wealth. His brother Roffredo II (d. 1296), who had married Elisabetta of the Orsini family — a niece of Pope Nicholas III — was made the count of Caserta. This title was then conferred upon his son Pietro II (d. 1308), who became the marchese della Marca and enlarged the possessions of the family in the Marittima and Campagna. He also secured the fortresses of Capo di Bove and the Torre delle Milizie in Rome. Boniface not only made three of his nephews — Benedetto II Caetani (d. 1296), Iacopo Tommasi (d. 1300), and Francesco Caetani (d. 1317) — cardinals, but he conferred upon them vast estates in the Marittima and Campagna. The children of Pietro II (d. 1308) — Roffredo III and Benedetto III — were also amply provided for. Roffredo III had married the heiress of Fondi and Traetto, and Benedetto III (d. 1327) obtained the confiscated feudal lands of the Aldobrandeschi family. Boniface also appointed his relatives to significant positions in the church. Benedetto III was made head of the church estates (patrimony) in Tuscany. The grandnephews of Boniface and their descendants acquired some two hundred fortresses and castles, mostly between Rome and Naples. They included Anagni, Carpineto, Ceccano, Filettino, Marino, Ninfa, Pofi, Ripi, Sermoneta, Sezze, Sgurgola, Trevi, Vallecorsa in the Marittima and Campagna, as well as Alife, Atina, Calvi, Fondi, Maranola, Piedimonte, Sperlonga, Vairano in the Kingdom of Naples. Boniface was not only the emperor-pope of the church, he was certainly the emperor-pope of nepotism. And the descendants of his brother Roffredo II retain much wealth, property and titles — even today. The family acquired 139 fiefdoms, seven dukedoms and the principalities of Altamura, Cassero, Piedimonte and Teano.

There are several branches of the family including (in the twentieth century) those that hold the titles Prince of Piedimonte, Duke of Laurenzana and Count of Alife, as well as the Caetani who carry the titles Duke of Sermoneta (conferred on the family by Boniface VIII), Prince of Teano, Duke of San Marco, Marchese of Cisterna and Lord of Bassiano, Norma, Ninfa and San Donato.[20] A descendant of Roffredo II, Onorato II Caetani, Lord of Sermoneta, was the father of Giovanna who married Pier Luigi Farnese. They became the parents of Pope Paul III (Alessandro Farnese, 1534–49). Onorato II had three sons, Niccolò, Giacomo and Guglielmo. Pope Alexander VI Borgia decided to confiscate the property of the Caetani in Sermoneta in 1499. He had Niccolò's son strangled. Giacomo, Protonotary Apostolic, was arrested and died in prison. Guglielmo (d. 1519) escaped, and upon the death of Pope Alexander VI, Sermoneta was restored to him by Pope Julius II, in 1504. Descended from Guglielmo were numerous cardinals — Niccolò (d. 1585), Enrico, Bonifacio, Antonio II and Luigi (d. 1642), the last of the Caetani cardinals. Guglielmo's great-grandson Onortao IV, brother of Cardinal Enrico (1550–99), married Agnesina, sister of General Marcantonio Colonna. Onorato was captain general of the pontifical infantry at the battle of Lepanto, and for his services to the papacy he was proclaimed first duke of Sermoneta by Pope Sixtus V.

In the early 1700s the Caetani of Sermoneta began to share the financial difficulties that became prevalent for the Roman aristocracy at that time. Their Palazzo al Corso, the fiefs of S. Felice and Cicero and the Lago di Paola were sold. The fortunes of the Caetani were restored with Michelangelo II (1804–1882), thirteenth Duke of Sermoneta. Wisely administering and frugally economizing what was left of the Caetani patrimony, he restored the Caetani to a new position of wealth and power in Italy. He was minister of the police in 1848; he presented to the king the results of the Roman plebiscite to unite with the kingdom of Italy; and he became a deputy in the parliament. Michelangelo was a Dante scholar, writing several books on the subject; he was also a friend of several renowned men — Sir Walter Scott, Stendhal, Balzac, Liszt and Chateaubriand.

His son Onorato (1842–1917), fourteenth duke, was president of the Royal Geographic Society, mayor of Rome, Italian deputy, minister of foreign affairs in 1896 and then an Italian senator. Onorato's sister Ersilla (1840–1925) was a scholar and writer of Roman antiquity. Leone Caetani (1869–1935), Onorato's son and fifteenth duke, married Vittoria Colonna, daughter of the Duke of Paliano. Leone too served as a deputy in the Italian parliament. His life was devoted to the study of Islam, and among his many works on the subject was *Annali dell'Islam*, published in 1904, a history of Islam's origins and its primordial roots. He donated the Caetani Library to the Accademia del Lincei and established the Caetani Foundation for the study of Muhammadanism. This branch of the Caetani family are dukes of Sermoneta, princes of Teano, marquises of Cisterna and lords of Bassiano, Norma, Ninfa and San Donato. Leone's brother Roffredo Caetani was the last duke of male descent; he died in 1961. There are other branches of the family as well, including those of Gaetani dell'Aquila d'Aragona, princes of Piedimont, dukes of Laurenzana, counts of Alifie.[21]

Many of the territories to which the members of Caetani family had obtained the above titles had been secured seven hundred years ago by their illustrious benefactor Boniface VIII. Pope Boniface VIII established the Caetani as one of the most important noble families in Italy along with the Orsini, Colonna, Savelli and Conti, with whom they intermarried. He not only enhanced his own family, but he was ruthless in using violence to destroy others.

In 1297 he had 200,000 gold florins transported by mule so that he could obtain another fiefdom for his nephew Pietro. Stefano Colonna plundered this caravan carrying the pope's gold, and Boniface was infuriated. Even though the gold was returned, Boniface demanded that Stefano be brought to the pope to be reprimanded and that papal troops be placed in those territories controlled by the Colonna. The family refused to comply with these requests, and two Colonna cardinals — Giacomo and his nephew Pietro — were excommunicated and deposed. Later, all members of the family were excommunicated. The Colonna were placed under a siege by papal forces. Their property was confiscated; their crops were destroyed; the peasants on their land were sold into slavery. Pretending he would pardon the family, Boniface had the leaders of the family come to him and beg forgiveness. While he held them in his power, he had the Colonna stronghold of Palestrina completely destroyed. Colonna territory became the possession of the Caetani. The Colonna were now forced to flee Italy for other lands. Some, such as Sciarra Colonna, went to France where he sought to secure financial aid from the French King Philip IV, who had been called a heretic by Boniface. King Philip had arrested and imprisoned the bishop of Pamiers. Now he had also harbored the Colonna family. Boniface sought revenge. He wrote a papal bull, which he was about to issue, excommunicating the French king.

Boniface had emphasized during his regime the supremacy of the church over temporal kingdoms and, in 1302, had issued his final proclamation on that issue. It was entitled *Unam sanctam* on the rights of the Roman pontiff. He wrote "Porro subesse Romano Pontifici omni humane creature declaramus, dicimus et diffinimus omnino esse de necessitate salutis." (We declare, affirm, define that every human creature is totally subject to the Roman Pontiff by necessity for their salvation.)[22] The

supremacy of the church is established in his next words: "Ecclesia, manu regum et militum, sed ad nutum et patientiam sacerdotis."[23] The church is paramount; the temporal sword (a metaphor used by Boniface), as far as the church is concerned, can be employed by the hands of kings and soldiers — but only with the approval and acceptance of the clergy.

The response of the French to the dictates of Boniface was swift. When King Philip IV heard that he was about to be excommunicated, he had his counselor Guillaume de Nogaret draw up charges against the pope. The pope was roundly condemned for heresy, simony, nepotism and a variety of other charges, including one emphasized by the Colonna family — that Boniface had murdered Pope Celestine V and illegally obtained the papal crown.

Sciarra Colonna and Guillaume de Nogaret were not interested in the mere utterance of idle words. They decided on a plan of attack. Financed by the French king, they returned secretly to Italy with a military force. While Boniface was relaxing in his hometown of Anagni, his palace was seized, the papal treasures sacked, and the pope captured by Colonna and de Nogaret in a surprise assault.[24] Boniface had been abandoned by his family members, his guards and his servants. Dressed in papal attire, with the tiara on his head, seated on his throne, the lone pope met Sciarra Colonna, who wished nothing better than to kill him. Colonna took out his dagger, but was prevented from murdering Boniface by de Nogaret, who had decided to bring the pope back to the French King — if not in chains then in disgrace. Boniface screamed at them: "Here is my neck; here is by head."[25] Nogaret slapped the pope with his iron glove and demanded that Boniface resign, but the pope preferred, as he told them, to die "for the faith of his lord Jesus Christ."[26]

Boniface was ill treated, scorned and insulted especially by Sciarra Colonna, who had seen his family and territory systematically ruined. Colonna and de Nogaret conferred as to what to do with the pope; suddenly after three days the citizens of Anagni stormed the papal palace and freed Boniface. Sciarra and de Nogaret escaped. In the meantime, Boniface VIII had been permanently traumatized.

The pope returned to Rome, but he was a defeated man: broken physically and emotionally, the shadow of the omnipotent pope that he was. He died on October 11, 1303. The ominous words of Celestine V had been fulfilled, and the memory of the reign of Boniface VIII was to have a lasting impact on the church.[27]

Boniface VIII had envisioned himself as an emperor-pope, an advocate of the church's dominance over earthly princes. The papal tiara was raised from one to two or three crowns, symbolizing the pope's emphasis of his supremacy over spiritual and temporal matters. For his family, the pope, using the funds from the treasury of the Holy See, created a vast dominion which the Caetani family secured for centuries. Boniface VIII thus epitomizes the flagrant nepotism and ruthlessness of the absolute pontifical power that was to flourish during much of the Renaissance and Baroque periods.

The French Papacy in Avignon

Boniface VIII was succeeded by a loyal supporter who was called Benedict XI (1303–1304); he had taken this name from his predecessor, whose actual name was Benedetto (Benedict) Caetani. While Pope Benedict XI rescinded the excommunication order placed on the Colonna family by Boniface, he did not reinstate the Colonna cardinals. Their lands thus were not restored, which resulted in violent confrontations between the two families in Rome — to the extent that the pope felt it safer to leave that city for Perugia. The war between the Colonna and the Caetani was to last for twenty-four years; ultimately the Caetani were able to retain absolute hegemony in Campagna and the Marittima during the fourteenth century. The pontificate of his pro–Boniface pope, Benedict XI, was to last less than a year, for he died on July 7, 1304.

During the conclave of 1304–1305, which lasted eleven months, the French cardinals were supported by the anti–Boniface group in the Sacred College. Cardinal Napoleone Orsini (1263–1342), son of Rinaldo (a nephew of Pope Nicholas III), hated the depotism of Boniface even though he himself, like the rest of the Orsini family, had initially supported the pope against the Colonna family. Cardinal Orsini became devoted to the French cause and king (who had given him a pension of 1,000 florins annually). At the conclave of 1304–1305, he sided with the French in advocating the election of Bertrand de Got of a noble French family. Bertrand took the name Clement V (1305–1314). In 1309, under pressure from the French king Philip IV, Clement V dramatically moved the papal court to Avignon, France, where it remained until 1377. Seven French popes reigned from Avignon. This period became known as the "Babylonian captivity." The papacy's stay at Avignon represented the domination of the popes by the French kings; it was a reaction to the intransigency of Roman pontiffs like Boniface VIII who had given the French so much difficulty.

Clement V was kept under the control of the French king, who demanded that there be a trial of the deceased Boniface VIII to condemn his actions against Philip IV. This trial, which never took place, obviously had a precedence — the famous "Cadaver Synod" of 897 against Pope Formosus. Even though the trial was tactfully postponed, the pope was forced to reappoint the Colonna cardinals and pay the family for losses suffered under Boniface; he exonerated Guillaume de Nogaret for his role in attacking Boniface and went so far as to issue a bull lauding Philip IV for assaulting the dead pope. He had, in short, become a puppet in the hands of the French King.[28]

Similar to the previous Roman popes, especially Nicholas III and Boniface VIII, Clement V was a nepotist. He placed large areas of land into the hands of his family; he made five of his relatives (including four nephews) cardinals, and his nephew Bertrand became viscount of Lomagne and d'Auvillars and marquis de'Ancona. The pope then bestowed 300,000 florins on the viscount of Lomagne for leading a crusade and gave 200,000 florins to relatives and friends.[29]

Clement V also helped to deplete the papal treasury, which luckily was placed on a more secure footing by his successor John XXII (Jacques Duèse/d'Euse), who was frugal with himself but generous with relatives. It took more than two years (1314–16) for John to be elected. During those years Cardinal Napoleone Orsini tried using all the means at his disposal to prevent the election of John XXII. Napoleone had come to the conclusion, in spite of his previous assent to move the papacy to Avignon, that the Holy See should not be permanently established there. The authority and wealth of the church — which had so benefited the Roman nobility — must return to Rome. Upon John's election, Napoleone would come into conflict with the new pope at every turn.

After Clement V died and after the cardinals could not agree on a successor, moving bands of Gascons, led by Raimond Guilhem de Budos, a nephew of the late pope, menacingly threatened the Italian members of the conclave. Contentious groups rode through Avignon chanting "Death to the Italian cardinals. Death to the Italian cardinals. We want a pope."[30] They obviously meant a French pope, which the Italian cardinals — including Napoleone Orsini, Giacomo Stefaneschi and Francesco Caetani — were opposed to. Finally the cardinals agreed to elect Jacques Duèse as pontiff.[31] He became John XXII (1316–34). As pope, he carried family affection and esteem for his compatriots to excessive heights."[32] He made his brother Pierre the viscount of Caraman and presented him with 60,000 gold florins.[33] Material goods and church offices were given to all his kin; in fact, "all those who were connected closely or distantly with the Duèse family" became the benefactors of the pope's largess.[34] Five nephews were appointed to the purple; others were granted bishoprics; his nieces married into the prestigious Argmagnac, Poiters and Auvergne families. John XXII was followed on the Avignon throne by Benedict XII (Jacques Fournier, 1334–42), who unlike his predecessor avoided pomp and warned his nephew not to come to Avignon as he would receive no benefits from the pope.[35]

On the other hand, Benedict's successor,

Clement VI, was probably the most extravagant of all the Avignon popes. Clement, whose name was Pierre Roger, was the son of the lord of Rosier. In 1333, as archbishop of Rouen, he had provided the money for property to be secured by his brother Guillaume II Roger, and as pope he paid 62,000 florins to acquire additional territory for this same brother, who took the title Count of Beaufort.[36] Clement made his brother Hugues and several of his nephews cardinals. The pope's nephew Guillaume de la Jugie served as his principal advisor and confidant.[37] Clement provided handsomely for his relatives. Cardinal Hugues acquired over 1,500,000 gold florins with over ten million francs in gold.[38] "Guillaume Roger II {another brother} received an annual stipend of 1,000 florins from the Apostolic Camera."[39] Guillaume II had thirteen children, and they were to "reap many advantages from Pierre's success."[40] Two of Guillaume's sons, Nicholas and Guillaume III, were to marry heiresses, another son Jean became archbishop of Narbonne and another, Pierre II, was appointed a cardinal and became Pope Gregory XI.

Clement VI lived as a worldly prince. The Avignon court was one of luxurious living. Visitors marveled at the priceless furnishings: rare tapestries, gold goblets, ornate clothing and furs. Lavish festivities and banquets occurred with great frequency. Prelates and guests enjoyed all the riches that life could afford.[41] As an Avignon pope, Clement VI was obliged to the king of France. Between 1345 and 1350, 592,000 florins and 5,000 crowns were advanced to Philip VI by the papacy.[42] It has been estimated that, from 1345 to 1360, during the pontificates of Clement VI and his successor, Innocent VI (1352–62), the French kings received 3,500,000 florins.[43] It is no wonder that King Philip VI made Guillaume, the favorite brother of Pope Clement VI, the baron of Alais.[44] When Clement died, the cardinals selected Clement's own brother Hugues to become pope, but he refused.[45]

Clement VI was followed by Innocent VI (1352–62), who in turn was succeeded by Urban V (1362–70) and then by Gregory XI (1370–78). Of the seven Avignon popes, all were to be French-born. For the most part, they ruled from Avignon very much in the same way popes had ruled from Rome — they had learned that nepotism was a way of life. Clement V (1305–1314), John XXII (1316–34) and Clement VI (1342–52) lavished papal moneys and gifts on relatives and fellow countrymen; at the same time, because of the status of the papacy, the families of the popes received royal benefices, titles and property from the French sovereign.[46] And following the pattern of the Roman nobility, nephews of the popes became pontiffs. Clement VI was the uncle of Pope Gregory XI (1370–78), who like Clement was named Pierre Roger (of Beaufort; see Table VI). When Gregory was elected in 1370, six of the seventeen or eighteen cardinals belonged to members of the Roger family.[47] While in power during the fourteenth century, twenty-four members of the Roger family were appointed cardinals and another twenty-four were bishops or archbishops.[48]

There was also a continuation of simony on the part of many of the Avignon popes. When John XXII was elected, he bestowed 100,000 florins on those cardinals who had voted for him. Benedict XII did the same; Clement VI gave 108,000 florins; Innocent VI gave 75,000 florins; and Urban V gave 40,000.[49] It would appear that the cardinals were paid for their votes. Further, of the cardinals created by the Avignon popes, thirteen were Italian, five Spanish, two English, one Genovan and 113 were French.[50] The French royal house had insisted on shaping the College of Cardinals so that it had a distinctly French flavor.[51] In turn, their puppets, the Avignon popes, strengthened the predominate role of the French clergy in the College just as the Roman popes had previously dominated it with Roman and Italian appointments.

The Romans begged most of the Avignon popes to return to the eternal city, but during much of this time there was anarchy in Rome, and the popes were frightened to return. Benedict XII fortified Avignon, and Clement VI enlarged the Avignon palace, which made the Romans fearful that the papacy would be retained in France. Innocent VI often expressed the desire to return, and his successor, Urban V, the pope who had unwisely paid off Bernabò Visconti, Lord of Milan, to maintain peace in northern Italy, reluctantly did go back to Rome — even though there was much opposition from the French cardinals and the French royal family — and stayed there for three years (1367–70). He decided to return to Avignon in 1370 despite a concerted Roman effort to keep him in the city. He died a few weeks after returning to France.[52]

The papal tiara now fell on Gregory XI. Responding to the appeals of St. Catherine (Caterina) of Siena, Gregory returned the papacy to Rome. Later insurrections in that city forced him to leave for nearby Anagni, the home and birthplace of Boniface VIII, who had originally served as the motivating force for taking the papacy to France. After a little more than a year in Italy, Gregory XI was dead; upon the riotous insistence by the Romans, an Italian pope Urban VI (1378–89) was elected.

The Babylonian captivity had lasted for less than seventy years, and the French popes had never had the opportunity to develop and foster papal dynasties as had been so conspicuous in Rome. Yet in that period, two of the popes were closely related — Clement VI and his nephew Gregory XI. It can only be supposed if the popes had remained in Avignon that numerous French families, ennobled by the papacy, would have emerged to control the papal throne.

As it were, the families of the Orsini and Colonna — who had remained in Rome during the Avignon papacy — fought for power in that city and, since they had much to lose with the tiara in France, were most adamant in demanding the popes return to Rome. While the popes remained in France, the Colonna often fought bloody battles with their ancient rivals the Orsini and Caetani, and at other times they joined forces with them against a common adversary. Stefano Colonna, the Elder, (d. 1350) wished to recover the family's former territories that the Caetani had obtained from Boniface VIII. In 1306 he became senator of Rome with Gentile Orsini, but the feud between these two families resumed in 1309.

Stefano's brother Sciarra, the Colonna who had captured Boniface VIII and caused the pope to destroy the Colonna's fortifications, also served as senator of Rome in 1312, 1313 and 1328.

In that last year, 1328, Sciarra crowned Louis IV the Bavarian as emperor, much against the wishes of Pope John XXII in Avignon. Louis opposed the policies of that French pope and accused John of heresy. Louis went so far as to name Pietro Rainalducci, a Franciscan, as pope. Rainalducci took the name Nicholas V (1328–30). Considered an antipope, he reigned for a short period. In 1329 Nicholas held a mock trial at the cathedral in Pisa. He had a straw puppet made of John XXII, dressed in pontifical regalia. At the trial John was duly condemned, but during the following year Nicholas V was forced to surrender to John and appeared before him as a penitent with a halter around his neck. He admitted to being a schismatic pope and was confined by John in Avignon until his death in 1333.

During the Avignon captivity, the situation in Rome moved into a state of anarchy. The popes in Avignon attempted to have the Orsini and Colonna share power in the city in order to avoid the frequent battles that reduced Rome, after 1331, to a state of terror. Bertoldo Orsini, son of Poncello and grandnephew of Nicholas III, became senator of Rome in 1342, jointly with Stefano Colonna the Younger (d. 1347). Bertoldo's brother Giordano was appointed senator of Rome with Stefano Colonna the Younger in 1337, and in 1344 with Giovanni Colonna. The Colonna family had returned to Rome after Boniface's death and helped to restore the family's fortune and to reaffirm its power in that city.[53]

But the conflict between these two families did not cease. The Roman citizenry in an attempt to curb the excesses of these noble families had formed a popular party, and in 1343, a messianic popular leader, Cola (Nicola di Rienzo, 1313–54) appeared on the scene. At first he was supported not only by the popular party but by the pope as well — Clement VI in Avignon made him notary of the Roman civic treasury. Cola envisioned a new Roman Empire, a return of Rome's ancient glory. On

May 19, 1347, he addressed a multitude from the Campidoglio (the Capitol), which was the seat of government. By acclamation, Cola was able to proclaim a series of laws against the nobles, and he assumed dictatorial rights for himself, taking the title of tribune. At that time it was written: "Nicholaus, severus et clemens, libertatis, pacis justiciaeque tribunus, et sacre Romane Reipublice liberator" (Nicola, stern and merciful, the tribune of freedom, peace and justice and the liberator of the Sacred Roman Republic).[54] He decided to unite the Italian cities by establishing a national parliament, and he set in motion steps to elect a Roman emperor of Italy. Pope Clement VI now tried to stop Cola's plans, and this time the pope was joined by members of both the Colonna and Orsini families, who allied themselves against him. On November 20, 1347, in a battle outside one of the gates of Rome, Porta S. Lorenzo, these united forces were defeated by Cola. Three Colonnas including Stefano Colonna the Younger, and an Orsini were killed.

Cola's triumph did not last long, for the nobles once again formed an alliance against him. Meanwhile the pope, fearful of losing Rome, issued a bull naming him as a heretic. In that same year, Cola was forced to resign. Cola di Rienzo was not unaware of the forceful presence of the Roman aristocracy, and he himself had hoped to marry Francesca, the daughter of Giordano Orsini — but his aspirations never materialized.[55] At first Cola fled to Prague, but eventually he was sent to Avignon where during a trial he denounced, according to Litta, the prodigality of the ecclesiastical benefices given to the Roman noble families who used these moneys for war. Cola was found guilty and imprisoned.

With Cola out of the way, the Roman families again resumed their struggles for power. Giordano Orsini in 1351 was made senator, but he was not to the liking of the Romans and was removed. At this point the papal vicar wished to assume the reins of government for the pontiff. He was immediately expelled by Jacopo Savelli, aided by the Colonna. And "anarchy became the life of Rome."[56] In 1352, Giordano commanded the Roman militia; he was also elected senator in 1353, but was not able to function in that capacity.

Cola di Rienzo was now permitted by the new pope Innocent VI (1352–62) to return to Rome. He was enthusiastically received and was made tribune. But the Colonna family simply would not stand for this intruder. Riots broke out afresh. Cola attempted to subdue a crowd by speaking to them, but a fire was set and objects were thrown at him. Disguised, he tried to hide, but was discovered and killed. His body was exposed for several days in the Piazza San Marcello before it was burned.

Pope Innocent VI was determined to restore law and order to Rome. Under the military and political leadership of the Spanish cardinal Gil di Albornoz (d. 1367), the pope was successful. Albornoz's military actions permitted Urban V's three-year sojourn in Rome from 1367 to 1370. As previously mentioned, it was Urban's successor, Gregory XI, who brought the papacy permanently back to Rome in 1377.

Avignon Ends and a New Era of Italian Popes Begins

At Gregory XI's death, an Italian pope, Urban VI (1378–89), came to the throne. He was a violent man, and probably his unexpected election — due to threats made by a clamorous Roman citizenry insisting on an Italian pope — had unhinged his mind. Cantankerous and unreasonable, Urban VI forced the French cardinals to flee Rome. In exile they asked the pope to abdicate — to which he did not assent. Cardinal Roberto of Geneva (1378–94) was now proclaimed pope (he is now considered an antipope) and took the name Clement VII (see Table VI). Roberto was a member of the Visconti family, related to the House of Savoy (his grandmother was Agnese of Savoy) and to the crown heads of Europe. His nephew Humbert of Villars (d. 1401) married Louise of Poitiers whose wife Cecile de Beaufort was a niece of Pope Gregory XI.

Thus — with the ascent of Roberto of Geneva as antipope Clement VII — began the Great Schism in which two or three popes simultaneously existed for a period of forty years (1378–1417). Clement VII reigned from Avignon, and was recognized by France, Savoy, Naples and Scotland. The other nations, including Germany and England, accepted Urban VI. Clement VII was to be succeeded by the antipope Benedict XIII (1394–1417). When Benedict XIII was deposed, the Great Schism came to an end.

Throughout the schism, Urban VI's mental state of health continued to deteriorate. Fearing a plot against him, he imprisoned six cardinals, five of whom were later murdered. He himself was probably poisoned.[57] As a result of misrule, the Papal States were again in ruins and confusion. His successor Boniface IX (1389–1404) tried to improve these adverse conditions.

In accordance with Roman tradition, the popes of this period espoused the principles of nepotism. In 1380 Urban VI went so far as to depose Queen Giovanna (Joanna) of Naples in a vain attempt to place an unworthy nephew on the throne of that kingdom. Urban's nephew Francesco Prignano, Prince of Capua, was married to Orsina of the Gravina branch of the Orsini family, which wished to secure a new foothold with the return of the papacy to Rome.[58] Pope Boniface IX made his relatives, the Tomacelli, lords of various cities including Pontecorvo, Sora and Orvieto. While Boniface IX did not bring the Great Schism to an end, he did establish his own supremacy in Rome; Germany, England and southern Italy also remained loyal to him. He increased taxes and sought money by any means, becoming known for both his nepotism and avidity. His brother Giovanni Tomacelli married Agnesella, sister of Cardinal Antonio Caetani and daughter of Giacomo II of the family that had produced Pope Boniface VIII.

The following pope, Innocent VII (Cosimo Migliorati, 1404–1406), indulged his unpopular nephew Ludovico Migliorati, who had murdered eleven members of a Roman delegation sent to the pope for a discussion. The populace rebelled, and the pope, barely escaping with his life, fled from the city. Ludovico received a slight reprimand from the pope, who soon thereafter made his nephew the lord of Ancona and Fermo. [59]

The election of Innocent VII had created the usual furor between the Colonna and the Orsini. The Orsini had taken over the Campidoglio from a brother of the deceased pope, Boniface XI; at the same time, the Colonna demanded a return to democratic practices. Both family groups were, of course, interested in having a pope selected who would confer papal favors — money, land, position — on them. They were accustomed to these kinds of gifts.

When new popes were elected and new papal families emerged in Rome, the older aristocracy would marry into these families to secure the papal privileges or benefits given to these new families by the pope. Boniface IX's brother Giovannello Tomacelli had a daughter Caterina who married Andrea Matteo Acquaviva, Duke of Atri. Their son Antonio (d. 1415) married Maria, daughter of Raimondello Orsini, Duke of Taranto, and their grandson Giulio Antonio married Caterina Orsini, daughter of Giannantonio of Taranto, whose son Gianbernadini married Giovanna (Joanna), daughter of Onorato Caetani, Count of Fondi.[60] Pope Innocent VII was the son of Gentile Migliorati of Sulmona. The pope's brother Antonio was the father of the infamous Ludovico, the murderer, and of Gentile who married Elena, daughter of Carlo Orsini of Bracciano. Their descendants were to marry into other papal families. It was in this way that Italian nobility became, not only related to each other, but at the same time related to many of those who had placed the papal tiara on their heads.

The Dynasty from Venice

Other than the French popes at Avignon, the tendency had been to elect the pontiff from either Rome and its vicinity or southern Italy, often from the kingdom of Naples. Urban VI had been born in Naples; Boniface IX had been born in Naples; and Innocent VII had been born in Sulmona in the Abruzzi.[61] However, a new trend was to commence in the 1400s, when the papacy was often to be occupied by popes selected from northern Italy — Pisa, Florence and Venice.

The republic of Venice had been governed by doges, their serene highnesses, selected from noble Venetian families. Venice was thus an oligarchy. It was a state that had developed impressive maritime capabilities. In 1381, with the Treaty of Turin, Venice terminated its long war with its rival republic Genoa. Venice became master of the seas and began to expand on the mainland of Italy during the administration of Doge Francesco Foscari (1423–57). It was during this period of time, when Venice claimed its right as a world power, that three popes, all related, should be elected from that city. The first Venetian pope was from the Correr (or Corraro) family, one of the aristocratic Venetian clans.[62]

Angelo Correr took the name Gregory XII (1406–1415). He was elected on the condition that he would resign when the antipope Benedict XIII (1394–1417) at Avignon renounced the papacy; at such time, a new pope would be elected by the joint cardinals from both Rome and Avignon. The election of Gregory XII was thus an attempt to end the Great Schism. Before his election, Gregory XII had also promised not to name any cardinals during his reign — an attempt to foster a settlement with Benedict XIII. However, negotiations with the antipope came to naught, and in 1407, Gregory created four new cardinals, two of them nephews. The family of Gregory was now determined to keep him as Supreme Pontiff and not to make any agreement with Benedict XIII.[63]

Feeling betrayed, most of Gregory's cardinals deserted him and joined four of the Avignon cardinals in arranging a council at Pisa, which in June 1405 declared that both Gregory and Benedict were schismatics; consequently, both pontiffs were deposed by the council, and a new pope, Alexander V (1409–1410), called the "Council Pope," was selected. Alexander received recognition from France, England, Bohemia, Prussia and much of Italy. At this junction in church history, three popes were ruling in effect since none resigned — Gregory XII, Benedict XIII and Alexander V. In 1410 Alexander was succeeded by John XXIII (1410–15), but there was no reconciliation. Finally, Gregory, supported by Naples, Hungary, Bavaria and the German king, Rupert, resigned at the Council of Constance on July 4, 1415. Antipopes John XXIII (Baldassare Cossa), whose career had included piracy and the seduction of hundreds of women, and Benedict XIII were deposed. The Great Schism had come to an end. The cardinals were now united and ready to elect one pope. For his cooperation, the cardinals at the council named Gregory, the former pope, bishop of Porto. He died in 1417.

During his rule, Gregory XII appointed two of his nephews from Venice as cardinals. They were Cardinal Gabriele Condulmer (son of his sister Bariola Correr and Angelo Condulmer) and Cardinal Barbarigo (son of his sister Caterina Correr and Bartolomeo Barbarigo). A relative, Gregorio Correr, was named protonotary apostolic and from 1411 to 1464 he served as patriarch of Venice. [64]

In 1431 Gabriele Condulmer became Pope Eugene IV (1431–47). At first, he fought primarily against the Colonna family, which had occupied papal territory. Difficulties with the Roman citizenry caused him to move the papacy to Florence, where he stayed from 1434 to 1443. His main intent was to strengthen the papacy and to diminish the power of ecclesiastical councils such as the one that had deposed his uncle Gregory XII.[65] He was at odds with the Council of Basle (1431–49), which deposed him in 1439. In his place elected Amedeo (Amadeus) VIII, Duke of Savoy, who took the name Pope Felix V (1439–49). Felix is considered an antipope, the last of the antipopes in the history of the church. He was related to the antipope Clement VII (1378–94), Roberto of Geneva, and to all the major royal families in Europe (see Table VI). Receiving very little backing, Felix abdicated in 1449 and served as cardinal bishop of Sta. Sabina, dying two years later.

Eugene IV made one nephew, Marco, the governor of Bologna; another, Francesco Condulmer, the pope made a cardinal; still another,

Pietro, son of Polissena Condulmer and Niccolò Barbo, the pope made a cardinal at the age of twenty-three in 1440. Litta specifically notes that Polissena Condulmer, daughter of Angelo Condulmer and Bariola Correr, was the niece of Pope Gregory XII, the sister of Pope Eugene IV, the mother of Pope Paul II (Pietro Barbo) and the grandmother of cardinals Marco Barbo, Cardinal Zeno and Cardinal Giovanni Michiel, who were the offspring of Polissena's other children.[66] Cardinal Marco Barbo was known for his magnificent library; Cardinal Zeno belonged to a prominent Venetian family; and Cardinal Giovanni Michiel became papal legate in 1485 and served as an advisor to future popes. He was liquidated by the Borgias.

Like his uncle and granduncle, Paul II (1464–71), distrusted church councils, and even though he was supposed to hold one during the first three years of his pontificate, he did not. He is known for closing the Roman academy, for abolishing the college of abbreviators, composed of scholars, and for imposing a tax on corporations. He lived lavishly, loved carnivals and entertainment. Litta writes that Paul II was "generally hated," and his memory, honored by few, was denigrated by posterity, even beyond reason.[67] When Paul II died in 1471, the Venetian dynasty came to an end. Future generations of the Zeno family would marry into the Barberini family, a papal dynasty during the Baroque period.

The Colonna Family (Part One)

Martin V (1417–31), the unifying pope who was elected to bring the Great Schism to an end, was a member of the Colonna family. While Martin is listed as the only member of that family to become pope, some sources indicate that Marcellinus (296–304), Sixtus III (432–40) and Stephen IV (816–17) were also members of this illustrious Roman family.

According to some sources, the Colonna were descended from Gregorio II, Count of Tusculum, brother of Pope Benedict IX (1032–48). As we have seen, the counts of Tusculum gave at least seven popes to the Holy

Church and were the descendants of Marozia, Senatrix of Rome (926–32) and her first husband, Alberico I. The progenitor of the House of Colonna was Tolomeo or Pietro, who took his name from the Trajan column, assuming the appellation *de Columna*. He lived between 1060 and 1120.

Pompeo Litta is not sure of the Colonna ancestors. Perhaps they were descended from Duke Stefano (Stephan) who came from Germany in 1135 and his wife, the Countess Aemilla of Palestrina. Aemilla was a granddaughter of Stephania Crescenzi, granddaughter of Marozia's sister Theodora II. Others express the opinion that Pietro's wife was a member of the House of Tusculum and that his son Oddone inherited Tusculum as a result. Oddone, it is said, married a niece of Pope Honorius II (1124–30), who had restored Palestrina to Pietro Colonna after it had been sacked by the Romans.[68]

Pietro Colonna (Pietro della Colonna) was important in his own right and was referred to, in 1078, as a count and a Roman counsel. He succeeded in obtaining Palestrina, which remained the stronghold of the Colonna family, even after being destroyed by Boniface VIII in 1297. It was during the lifetime of Pietro's son Oddone that the Colonna fortress of Palestrina was again attacked in 1143 by an angry Roman populace. It was set afire in 1187 and again was returned to the Colonna family; however, Oddone was probably dead by this time. As we have seen, the family was often involved in conflicts with the papacy, as were other Roman aristocratic families — the Orsini, Savelli, Conti, Caetani, Crescenzi and Frangipane. The Colonna, as did these other noble families, had their own tribunals to adjudicate civil and criminal cases. They also had their own impressive fortresses and their own armies, which engaged in wars and insured the peace and placed many a pope of their choice on the papal throne. They were powers to be reckoned with by the Apostolic See.

The Colonna family had close ties to the church. Oddone's son Giovanni became the first Colonna cardinal in 1192, and his grandson, another Giovanni, was made a cardinal in 1216 by Honorius III (1216–27) of the Savelli family and played a significant role during the pontificate of Pope Gregory IX (1227–41). The Savellis and Colonnas were allies against the Orsinis and the Caetanis. The great nemesis of the Colonnas was, of course, Boniface XIII, who confiscated their castles, burned Palestrina, excommunicated all the Colonnas up to four generations and forced the family into exile. But as we already know, Sciarra and his brother Stefano Colonna regained the family fortune. It was their brother Agipito's great-great-grandson Oddo who became Pope Martin V. Thus, by the start of the fifteenth century, the Colonnas were in power.[69] Martin was the son of Agapito and Caterina Conti, of the Valmontone branch of the Conti family, which was descended from a brother of Pope Innocent III (see Tables 4a and 4b in Appendix A).

Litta declares that Martin V's election was immediately and universally approved.[70] His own virtuous life, his surname, the solemnity of his election and the desire for peace after forty years of schism all contributed to his initial popularity. His reign was spent in settling a dispute between Queen Giovanna (Joanna) II of Naples and her enemies, in aggrandizing the house of Colonna, and in reneging on his promise to implement the reforms recommended at the Council of Constance.

Using military force to regain the Papal States, he successfully reorganized them and, in the process, generously provided for his relatives.[71] The pope's brother Lorenzo Onofrio (d. 1423) received the territories of Ardea, Marino, Genazzano, Rocca di Cave, Capranica, S. Vito, Olevano and Frascati. In 1419 Queen Giovanna II, a friend and ally of Martin, named Lorenzo Onofrio as the count of Alba in Abruzzi. Lorenzo Onofrio was married to Sveva, daughter of Jacobello Caetani, Count of Fondi, of Boniface VIII's family. Lorenzo's brother Giordano was made the duke of Amalfi and Venosa and prince of Salerno by the queen. Martin had given him Sipicciano in the diocese of Bagnorea, which he sold to the count of Anguillara, proceeding then himself to buy Monterano and sections of Supino from the same count. Martin V made the Colonnas the recipients of Marsico, Nettuno, Astura, Bassanello in the valley of the Tiber, Soriano, Paliano, Pietra Porzia, Rocca di Papa, and Serrone — as well as other lands too numerous to mention.[72]

To advance the status of the Colonnas, Pope Martin V tried to arrange fortuitous marriages between members of his family with heiresses or members of other illustrious noble families. For example, he tried to have his nephew Antonio marry the heiress Giovanella Ruffo di Calabria so that Antonio would obtain the marquisate of Cotrone. It is believed that this marriage did not take place because it was decided that the girl was too young. A contract had also been signed for Martin's niece Caterina to marry Filippo Maria Visconti, Duke of Milan, but it was never fulfilled. This matrimonial alliance had been proposed to insure better relations between the papacy and Milan. In another case, Catherine's sister Anna had been promised to the son of the Montone family of minor nobility, but she was forced to marry Giannantonio Orsini, prince of Taranto, for political reasons.

Lorenzio Onofrio Colonna, the pope's brother, and his wife, Sveva Caetani, had three sons — Odoardo, Antonio and Prospero. Odoardo became lord of the county of Celano. Antonio not only inherited vast possessions from his father and uncle, given to them by Martin, but when the pope died in 1431, he stole the papal treasures accumulated by Martin to conduct a war against the Turks.[73] Antonio also appropriated for himself precious objects collected by the pope. It was necessary for the next pope, Eugene IV, with the help of the envious Orsini, to battle Antonio for years. Eugene wanted the valuable treasures taken from the Holy See, as well as the lands of Soriano, Genazzano, Rocca di Cave and Marino.[74] The castles of the Savelli and Colonna were taken and destroyed. Palestrina, principal fortress of the Colonna, surrendered on August 18, 1436. Only when Eugene IV died in 1447 was Antonio able to live in peace, marrying as his third wife Imperiale, daughter of another Stefano Colonna. Antonio had at least ten children, several of whom were illegitimate. Prospero,

Antonio's brother and Lorenzo's youngest son, was made a cardinal by his uncle in 1426, amassed an impressive library and was considered first among the cardinals. He crowned three popes: Nicholas V, Callistus III and Pius II. The role of the Colonna family was to be a decisive one for the next several hundred years, and the glories of that family were to both wane and be revitalized. In the eighteenth century one branch of the family was to marry with the heiress of the Barberini dynasty, and that branch was called Colonna-Barberini (see Tables 4f and 4g in Appendix A).

When Martin V died, Cardinal Parentucelli became Nicholas V (1447–55). He was a compromise candidate for the papacy, being elected primarily because the Colonna and Orsini cardinals and their adherents had assumed antagonistic positions in the conclave toward one another. In spite of the attempt made by Prospero Colonna, a leading candidate to become pope, his efforts and those of his family were not realized. The Colonna, similar to their Conti ancestors, would have liked to have established a hereditary papacy; they had numerous family members made cardinals for that purpose. Nicholas was able to restore peace to Rome and immediately established a conciliatory attitude toward the Roman nobility. He restored the Colonna possessions to Antonio Colonna and did the same for the Savellis. Stefano Colonna also received permission to rebuild Palestrina on the condition that the town would not be fortified.

The historian Pastor exclaims that "bloodless restoration of peace and order to the States of the Church must ever be viewed as one of the chief glories of the Pontificate of Nicholas V."[75] When Frederick of Hapsburg was crowned as emperor of the Holy Roman Empire in 1452, Nicholas V had the Colonna and Orsini families welcome him and participate in the ceremony.[76] The pope was a patron of the Renaissance in art and literature and founded the Vatican Library. Here was a man of many accomplishments who was able to diffuse the warlike rivalry generated by the Roman aristocracy. He was, moreover, one of the few popes who escaped the Roman tradition of nepotism.

Nicholas V was followed by Callistus III (1455–58) of the Borgia family, whom we shall discuss in Chapter Three. Callistus III, in turn, was succeeded by Pope Pius II.

The Piccolomini Family of Siena

In 1458 Enea Silvio Piccolomini from Siena became Pope Pius II (1458–64). In the conclave, he was able to unite Colonna and Orsini cardinals and their allies to vote for him. Prospero Colonna was the deciding vote. Soon after his election, he nominated Antonio Colonna, Prospero's brother, to be prefect of Rome, with the right of succession for the position being given to his eldest son.

During the pontificate of Nicholas V, the Turkish sultan Muhammad II had conquered Constantinople, in 1453. Pius II spent most of his pontificate trying to organize a crusade against the Turks. In 1464 he traveled to Ancona to meet the forces that he would personally lead in a crusade against the Sultan's army. When the Venetian galleys, which were to serve as a naval convoy, appeared in the harbor, Pius died.

Although Pius was a sincere and noble pope with exceptional insights — envisioning a united Christian Europe — he was inclined to favor his relatives and Sienese compatriots. He named a relative, Alessandro de Miraballi-Piccolomini, as prefect of Frascati; his closest advisor was Gregorio Lolli, the son of his aunt Bartolomea; and the children of his sister Caterina were ennobled and became Piccolomini di Sticciano. Caterina's daughter Antonia married Pietro Sticciano, and their great-grandson Enea married Vittoria Piccolomini, great-granddaughter of Giacomo Piccolomini, a cousin. Enea and Vittoria's grandson was Ottavio (1600–1656), the illustrious imperial general in the Thirty Years War. Ottavio was proclaimed duke of Amalfi and prince of the Empire for his defense of Austria. His grand-nephews inherited the dukedom of Amalfi.

Pope Pius II was also generous to the children of his sister Laudomia, who married

Nanni Todeschini and took the surname Piccolomini. Their four children were Francesco (Francis) (1439–1503), Antonio (d. 1493), Giacomo and Andrea Todeschini-Piccolomini. When only twenty-one years of age, Francesco Todeschini-Piccolomini was made an archbishop and cardinal by his uncle Pope Pius II. In 1503 he was elected pope and took the name Pius III after his uncle. But he was seriously ill and died ten days after his coronation.[77] Francesco's brother Andrea Todeschini-Piccolomini married Agnese Farnese, aunt of Pope Paul III, and their son Alexander became the husband of Francesca Conti of that ancient Roman family. Giacomo Todeschini-Piccolomini married Camilla Monaldeschi the grandniece of Pope Martin V. Giacomo was given the territory of Camporsevoli. His great-grandson, Giacomo, Duke of Montemarciano, married Isabella daughter of Nicola Orsini, Count of Pitigliano. Their son Alfonso (d. 1591), was deprived of his fiefdom by Pope Gregory XIII and became a notorious bandit. Antonio Todeschini-Piccolomini was made governor of the Castel Sant' Angelo in Rome by his uncle. He commanded the pontifical troops in defending the king of Naples and married the king's daughter, receiving the titles Duke of Amalfi and Lord of Celano.

Piccolomini descendants married into other papal dynasties. One of Antonio's daughters, Maria, married Francesco Orsini, Duke of Gravina, and became an ancestor of Pope Benedict XIII. The Orsini family of Gravina exists at the present time (see Table 1e in Appendix A). Andrea's son Alfonso and his descendants became the counts of Celano.[78] Alfonso's great-great-great-great-grandson Giuseppe (d. 1733) married Ann, daughter of Pompeo Colonna.[79]

Two of the principal branches of the family are extinct — the Todeschini, which included Antonio, Duke of Amalfi, descended from the pope's sister Laudomia, and the Piccolomini of Sticciano, which produced the distinguished general and prince Ottavio Piccolomini, also a duke of Amalfi (1600–1656, descended from the pope's sister Caterina.

CHAPTER THREE

The Renaissance Popes and Their Families, 1471–1565[1]

I: The della Rovere and Cibo Families

The della Rovere Family Dynasty

Francesco della Rovere was elected pope following the reign of the Venetian Pope Paul II (1464–71), successor to Pope Pius II (1458–64) of the Piccolomini family. Francesco, born into a poor family from Cella (near Savona, Liguria), took the name Sixtus IV (1471–84). Before his election the Romans demanded that church benefices in Rome should be conferred only upon Romans. Cardinal Battista Orsini had gathered his brothers and relatives in the neighborhood of Rome to pressure for his own election to the papal throne "whether by fair means or foul."[2]

In spite of the Orsini quest for papal power, Francesco della Rovere persuaded Orsini, along with two other influential cardinals — Rodrigo de Borgia and Francesco Gonzaga — to elect him, and they were duly rewarded. Orsini became treasurer of the Holy See; Gonzaga received the diocese of St. Gregorio; and Borgia received the Abby of Subiaco.

Sixtus was a Renaissance pope who constructed new churches, widened the streets of Rome, decorated the Sistine Chapel, founded the Sistine Choir and enlarged the Vatican Library. Above all, he enlarged the pockets of his avaricious and unworthy relatives (see Table VII). He made six of his nephews into cardinals and generously provided for other nieces and nephews. In 1472 Leonardo, son of Bartolomeo della Rovere, brother of the pope, became the city prefect and received the fiefdom of Sora and Arpino, which had been the property of the church. Leonardo was one of Pope Sixtus IV's favorite nephews. In 1473 he married Giovanna, daughter of King Ferdinando of Naples. The king adopted him into the family of Aragon and made him grand constable of Sicily, as well as duke of Sora and Arce, and he received the territories of Fontana, Arpino, Santopadre, Brocco, Casalmeri, Isola, Isoletta and Castelluccio. At the same time the pope gave Leonardo an enormous amount of money loaned to him by the apostolic chamber so that his nephew would appear "magnificent," worthy of being related to the pope. Sixtus gifted Leonardo's wife Giovanna with precious jewelry and a large sum of money. Leonardo himself died a year later in 1475.[3]

Giuliano and Bartolommeo, two of the sons of the pope's brother Raffaello, entered the clergy. Sixtus conferred upon Bartolommeo (d. 1495) the bishopric of Massa. Sixtus made Giuliano della Rovere into a cardinal and named him the "Archbishop of Avignon and of Bologna, Bishop of Lausanne, Contances, Viviers, Mande, and finally of Ostia and Velletri, and Abbot of Nonantola and Grottaferrata, heaping benefice after benefice upon him."[4] Thirty years later, Giuliano was to become a pope himself, taking the name Julius II.

TABLE VII: DELLA ROVERE FAMILY

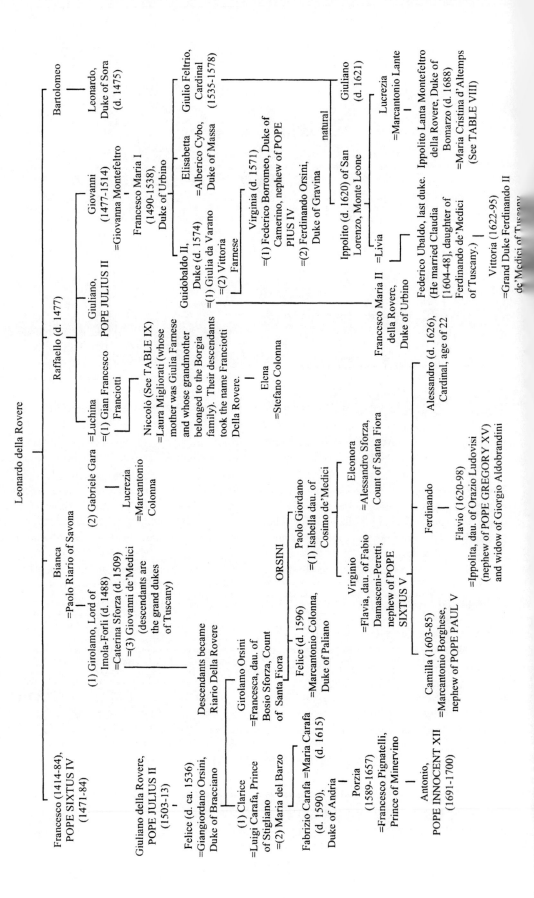

Julius II had four nephews named to the purple, and seven other della Rovere family members were appointed bishops.[5]

Giuliano had another brother, Giovanni, who went to learn the art of war from Federico of Montefeltro, Duke of Urbino. Giovanni was an excellent student. He also married Federico's daughter Giovanna in 1474. Upon their marriage, Giovanni was given by his uncle the Vicariate of Senigallia, as well as the Vicariate of Mondavio and the lands of Mondolfo, S. Costanza, Orchiano, Poggio S. Giorgio, Montemaggiore and Monterado. When Leonardo della Rovere died, Giovanni was made prefect of Rome with the rights of having his oldest son succeed him. Meanwhile, the king of Naples conferred upon him the title of Duke of Sora and Acre, with the same rights as that of his predecessor, Leonardo. Giovanni, who ruled the territory of Senigalla, was much loved by his subjects. He died in 1501.[6]

One of Pope Sixtus IV's sisters, Luchina, married Giovanni Basso, who became the marchese of Bistagno and Monastero. Of their children, Girolamo (d. 1507) became a cardinal in 1477, Antonio was the marchese of Cisterna; Bartolomeo was the count of Bistagno, and Maria married Antonio Grosso (della Rovere). Antonio Grosso della Rovere's great-granddaughter Clemenza was the wife of Giovanni Giorgio, grandson of Bartolomeo della Rovere, Count of Bistagno, and their descendants are the marchese of Montaleone, Bistagno, Monastero, di Castelletto Ussone and di Roccaverano.

Another of the pope's sisters, Bianca, married Paolo Riario, and their daughter Violante married Antonio Sansoni; Violante and Antonio were the parents of Cardinal Raffaele Riario Sansoni. Bianca's son Pietro Riario was named a cardinal at the age of twenty-five. Pietro held the archbishopric of Florence, the patriarchate of Constantinople, the Abbey of S. Ambrogio and other bishoprics. He received a yearly income of over 60,000 golden florins. He lived like a prince, had numerous servants, dressed himself in "garments laden with gold" and "adorned his mistress from hand to foot with costly pearls." Pietro was much loved by his uncle Sixtus IV and was considered first among the cardinals. The pope gave him complete control of the papal treasury. At the age of twenty-eight, he died from his own excesses. By the time of his death in 1474, he had squandered over 300,000 golden florins.[7]

Pietro's brother Girolamo Riario became the lord of Imola and Forlì, marrying Caterina Sforza, the legitimized, natural daughter of the duke of Milan, Galeazzo Maria. In 1488 when her husband Girolamo was assassinated, Caterina Sforza was determined to retain control of her states for her son Ottaviano, even though the conspirators against her threatened to kill her children.[8] At one point during the ensuing battle, she lifted up her dress to her enemies and exclaimed that she still had the ability to make more.[9] Indeed she did have another child later in her remarkable life. In 1496 she married a third husband, Giovanni de' Medici, and thus was the grandmother of the ruler Cosimo I of Tuscany and the ancestor of the Medici grand dukes.

Girolamo Riario and Caterina Sforza founded the House of Riario-Sforza, which gave three cardinals to the church: (1) Alessandro (1543–85), Patriarch of Alexandria, who was legate to Perugia and Umbria, and prefect of the Tribunal of Justice of the Holy See: (2) Tomaso, who became a cardinal in 1830 and served as camerlengo, or papal treasurer, and (3) Sisto (1810–77), Archbishop of Naples, who restored seminaries, founded a library and was renowned for his charities. The Riario-Sforza family which lost Forlì and Imola to the papacy, settled first in Bologna and then in Naples. In 1620 Ferdinando Riario-Sforza, a descendant, was created a duke and count of the empire; later members of the family took the titles Marchese of Corleto, Duke of S. Paolo and Prince of Ardore.

Girolamo, the founder of the Riario-Sforza princely house, had been given the fiefdom of Imola by his uncle Pope Sixtus, who had paid 40,000 ducats for it. Lorenzo de' Medici, who ruled Florence at that time, protested the acquisition of Imola by Sixtus IV. As a consequence, Girolamo, a vicious and vile ruler, persuaded Sixtus to support what is known as the Pazzi Conspiracy of 1478. It was a plan to murder Lorenzo and his brother Guiliano de' Medici. The plot failed, though Giuliano was killed. The architects of the conspiracy and the agents of the della Rovere (Archbishop Francesco Salviati, his brother and his nephew) were strung up; their bodies fell among the crowd and were torn to pieces. Sixtus IV promptly excommunicated Lorenzo and pursued a war against Florence from 1478 to 1480. It was during this period that Girolamo Riario became commander-in-chief of the church's military forces. Sixtus now encouraged Venice to go to war against Ferrara and Naples, allies of Florence and the Medici. As the war continued (1481–83), the ancient feud between the Colonna and the Orsini was again ignited. Virginio Orsini, urged on by his friend Girolamo Riario, joined by Count Niccolò Orsini, Giordano Orsini and Giacomo and Andrea de' Conti against the Savellis and Colonnas. Prospero and Fabrizio Colonna, both great-grandnephews of Pope Martin V, fought bravely against the Orsini. The Colonna palaces were again plundered, and Lorenzo Oddone Colonna was taken prisoner, tortured and beheaded in the Castel Sant' Angelo.[10]

Pope Sixtus was to die in 1484. His death may have been hastened by the fact that the Italian princes and states in Italy had forced the pope into making peace. It was upon the pope's death that Caterina Sforza seized the Castel Sant' Angelo in an unsuccessful attempt to influence the selection of the next pope.

Sixtus IV's nephew Giuliano della Rovere, who was also a warmonger, became Pope Julius II (1503–1513). Known as the warrior pope, or "the Terrible," he actually led soldiers into battle. At sixty-four years of age, in 1506, Julius took the field in full armor to win and obtain Perugia and Bologna. In 1512 he included Parma, Piacenza and Reggio Emilia into the Papal States, strengthening Italy and quelling its domination by foreign powers. Pastor comments about the pontificate of Julius II when he notes that "ever since the 8th Century the Popes, besides being Vicar of Christ, had also been temporal princes." Julius II was "one of the greatest [of the popes] since Innocent III," the inspirational pope of the Conti family.[11]

Julius II was a Renaissance pope, who encouraged such artists as Bramante, Raphael, and Michelangelo. The pope had Michelangelo paint the ceiling of the Sistine Chapel; persuaded Raphael to do the frescos in three rooms of the Vatican; and had Bramante design various Vatican buildings, including the initial model for the new Basilica of St. Peter.

Julius II was not as generous to his relatives as his uncle Pope Sixtus IV had been. Guicciardini, the historian and author of *The History of Italy*, wrote of Julius that "without neglecting his relations, he never sacrificed the interests of either the State or the Church to them, or carried his nepotism beyond due bounds."[12] Julius made his nephew Francesco Maria, son of Giovanni della Rovere, the prefect of Rome and gave him the Vicariate of Pesaro, which was the only portion of the papal states that Julius ever withdrew from the direct rule of Holy See.[13] He gave his consent that Guidobaldo of Montefeltro adopt Francesco Maria, nephew both of Julius II and of the last Montefeltro ruler, to succeed to the dukedom of Urbino. The line of della Rovere dukes or Urbino, prominent in Italy history, was to become extinct in 1631. Julius was also extremely kind to the children of his sister Luchina. She married Gianfrancesco Franciotti, patrician of Lucca, as her first husband. All of her children from both this marriage and her next were adopted by Julius II and carried the name della Rovere. Her son Agostino was appointed archbishop of Trebisonda; Galeotto, another son, was bishop of Luca, Cremona, Benevento, Vicenza and Padova and was made a cardinal and vice-chancellor of the church by his uncle; and Niccolò, her third son by Franciotti, a valorous man of war, obtained the lordship of S. Angelo of Todi, Monticelli, Frascatello, Soriano, Gallese, Castellaccia and Suvera. Niccolò married Laura, daughter of Orsini Migliorati, great-great-grandnephew of Pope Innocent VII. Their son Giulio had two daughters: Elena, wife of Stefano Colonna of Palestrina, and Lavinia, wife of Paolo Orsini of Lamentana.

Luchina's second husband was Gabriele Garra (or Gara) of Savona. Her three children from this marriage were Sixtus, who in spite of the fact that he was illiterate, became a cardinal in 1508 (in this capacity, writes Litta, he functioned only in that he received a hefty income) and the bishop of Lucca, Benevento, Vicenza, Padova and Cremona; Lucrezia, to be noted later; and Raffaele, who married Niccolosa Fogliani, the heiress of Fermo.[14] Raffaele and her two children were killed in 1501 by orders of the Borgias. All the possessions of Niccolosa's went to Marcantonio Colonna, who had married Lucrezia, the sister of Raffaele and Cardinal Sixtus. Marcantonio was a direct descendant of Lorenzo Colonna (d. 1305) and the great-grandnephew of Pope Martin V.[15]

Of all the members in his family, Pope Julius II was probably the least generous to his own children, all of whom were born before he became pope. They were Giulia, Clarice (wife of Agnolo Del Bufalo) and Felice.[16] Felice was Julius II's illegitimate daughter by a woman named Lucrezia Normanni, who later became the wife of Bernardo De Cuppis, (Cupis or Coppi) of Montefalco. Julius according to Litta, "was never kind to her," and, primarily because it was in his best interests, he had Felice married to Giangiordano, son of Gentil Virginio Orsini, Lord of Bracciano and vice-chancellor of the palace.[17] Her dowry was 15,000 ducats, and the wedding was privately celebrated in 1504. This was not a happy marriage as her husband, the widower of the daughter of King Ferdinando of Naples, was an old, unsympathetic man. Further he continually taunted Felice about her humble origin — the bastard daughter of a pope.[18] As her father Julius II lay dying in February of 1513, he received a deathbed request from Felice. She asked that he name her (maternal) half brother Guido da Montefalco as a cardinal. Julius refused.[19] In 1521 Felice bought from Cardinal Innocent Cibo the land of Galera and leased part of the Abbey of S. Saba; in the same year she bought from Cardinal Franciotto Orsini the fiefdom of Palo in the dioceses of Porto, Collevago and Garigliano. She governed Farfa from 1513 to 1519. She wrote her will in September 1536 and probably died shortly thereafter.[20] Her descendants married into the prominent families of that time — the Colonna,

Sforza, Borghese, Gonzaga and Appiani.[21] Her Orsini offspring became the dukes of Bracciano, which family became extinct in 1699. Other members of the della Rovere family — the descendants of the nieces and nephews of Sixtus IV and Julius II — were to marry into papal families including the Orsini, Farnese and Cibo and into ducal dynasties such as the d'Este, Medici and Gonzaga. The della Rovere name will reappear in succeeding generations of families of future popes.

Through the female line, the name appears in the twentieth century with the Lante Montefeltro della Rovere family. The Lante family originated in Pisa. Michel del Lante was chancellor of that republic, and his son Pietro (1335–1403) was created the marchese of Massa. A descendant, Marcantonio Lante, married Lucrezia della Rovere in 1609, and the della Rovere name was added to that of Lante. Lucrezia was a direct descendant of the first della Rovere duke of Urbino.

Francesco Maria I della Rovere (1490–1538), Duke of Urbino, and nephew of Pope Julius II, had a son Guidobaldo, who succeeded him as duke and married as his second wife, Vittoria Farnese (d. 1602), granddaughter of Pope Paul III. Another son, Giulio Feltrio (1535–78), was nominated as a cardinal at the age of thirteen, receiving the cardinal's ring in 1560. He had two illegitimate children: Ippolito (d. 1620) and Giuliano (d. 1621), legitimatized in 1572 by Pope Pius V. Ippolito became the marchese of San Lorenzo, and his daughter Lucrezia married Marcantonio Lante; that family assumed the name Lante Montefeltro della Rovere (after the heiress Giovanna Montefeltro, wife of Giovanni della Rovere). Marcantonio and Lucrezia had a son, Ippolito Lante Montefeltro della Rovere (d. 1681), who became the duke of Bomarzio in 1645 and married Maria Cristina, daughter of Pietro of Altemps (of the family of Pope Pius IV) and Angelica de' Medici. Maria Cristina's mother, Angelica, was the daughter of Cosimo, natural son of Giulio (d. 1600), natural son of Duke Alexander de' Medici and Angelica Malaspina, a nun. Duke Alexander of Florence was the son of Pope Clement VII (1523–34).

TABLE VIII: LANTE MONTEFELTRO DELLA ROVERE AND MEDICI FAMILIES

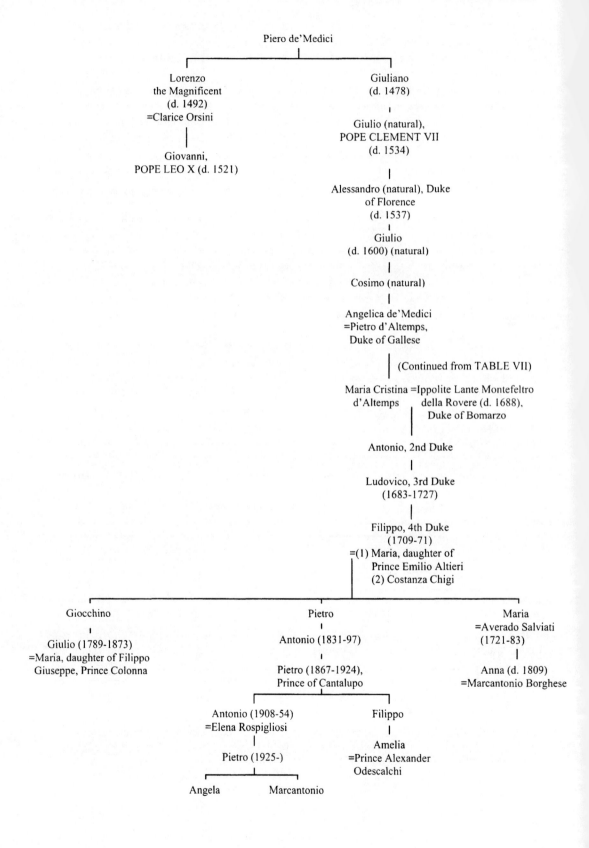

Piero de'Medici

Lorenzo
the Magnificent
(d. 1492)
=Clarice Orsini

Giovanni,
POPE LEO X (d. 1521)

Giuliano
(d. 1478)

Giulio (natural),
POPE CLEMENT VII
(d. 1534)

Alessandro (natural), Duke
of Florence
(d. 1537)

Giulio
(d. 1600) (natural)

Cosimo (natural)

Angelica de'Medici
=Pietro d'Altemps,
Duke of Gallese

(Continued from TABLE VII)

Maria Cristina =Ippolite Lante Montefeltro
d'Altemps   della Rovere (d. 1688),
                  Duke of Bomarzo

Antonio, 2nd Duke

Ludovico, 3rd Duke
(1683-1727)

Filippo, 4th Duke
(1709-71)
=(1) Maria, daughter of
Prince Emilio Altieri
(2) Costanza Chigi

Giocchino

Giulio (1789-1873)
=Maria, daughter of Filippo
Giuseppe, Prince Colonna

Pietro

Antonio (1831-97)

Pietro (1867-1924),
Prince of Cantalupo

Maria
=Averado Salviati
(1721-83)

Anna (d. 1809)
=Marcantonio Borghese

Antonio (1908-54)
=Elena Rospigliosi

Pietro (1925-)

Angela   Marcantonio

Filippo

Amelia
=Prince Alexander
Odescalchi

Duke Ippolito and Maria Cristina's great grandson Filippo (1709–1771) first married Maria Altieri of the family of Pope Clement X and then married Costanza Chigi of the family of Pope Alexander VII. One of Filippo's grandsons, Giulio (1789–1877), was the husband of Maria Colonna; one of Giulio and Maria's great-great-granddaughters, Amelia, married Prince Alessandro Odescalchi (b. 1921). Prince Alessandro of Palazzo Odescalchi in Rome was descended from a sister of Pope Innocent XI. The present duke, Pietro (b. 1928), is the son of Duke Antonio Lante Montelfeltro della Rovere and his wife Elena Rospigliosi, whose family produced Pope Clement IX[22] (see Table VIII).

The Cibo (Cybo) Family

Giovanni Battista Cibo became Pope Innocent VIII (1484–92), the successor of Pope Sixtus IV. He gained the papacy through the intervention of Cardinal Giuliano della Rovere, nephew of the previous pope, and by signing statements promising various bequests and favors to the voting cardinals previous to his election. Assuming the papal throne, he had Cardinal della Rovere reside in the Vatican as his chief advisor and made della Rovere's brother Giovanni into the captain general of the church. Innocent VIII also soon assigned his own brother Maurizio Cibo as governor of Perugia, and Maurizio's son Lorenzo was created a cardinal. Innocent's accomplishments as pope were few: his administration was filled with ecclesiastical abuses, and he sold papal offices to the highest bidder.[23] When Innocent was dying, he was given human blood to restore his life. The blood was taken from three young boys who died as a result; Innocent, who before his death had often gone into deep trances so that he appeared dead, finally succumbed on July 25, 1492.[24]

As a young man, Giovanni Battista Cibo had led a licentious life in Aragon and had two illegitimate children, Teodorina and Franceschetto. Teodorina Cibo married Gherardo Usodimare of Genoa; their children included Alarino, Peretta and Battistina. Their son Alarino (d. 1586) took the surname Cibo from his mother's family.[25] Teodorina's daughter Peretta married Alfonso del Carretto as her first husband and, as her second, the renowned admiral Andrea Doria (1466–1560), Prince of Melfi.[26] Peretta, wife of Alfonso del Caretto, had two sons. One of them was Giovanni I (d. 1535) whose descendants continued the del Caretto family; the other son, Marcantonio, had a daughter Zenobia who married Giovanni Andrea Doria (1539–1606), Prince of Melfi, heir of Admiral Andrea Doria. Giovanni Andrea and Zenobia were the great-great-grandparents of Giovanni (Gian) Andrea IV Doria, husband of the heiress Anna Pamfill whose descendants Doria-Pamfill-Landi are delineated elsewhere. Teodorina and Gherardo Usodimare's other daughter, Battistina, married Luigi of Aragon, son of King Alfonso II of Naples. The marriage between Luigi of Aragon and Battistina was short-lived; she died soon after, and he became a priest and then a cardinal.[27] Battistina is mentioned as being an escort at Lucrezia Borgia's wedding to Giovanni Sforza on June 12, 1492, and thus frequented the papal court even after her grandfather the pope had died.[28]

Franceschetto Cibo, Innocent VIII's son, was the husband of Maddalena de' Medici, the daughter of Lorenzo de' Medici, ruler of Florence. The marriage proved to be an unhappy one as Franceschetto was rude, uncultured, corrupt and greedy. Innocent VIII acknowledged him openly as his son and attended his wedding.[29] This was the first time in the history of the church that the son of a pope was publicly recognized.[30] The pope made his son into the count of Anguillara and governor of the church. Franceschetto led a life unbecoming "the son of the pope. He paraded the streets at night with Girolamo Tuttavilla, forced his way into the houses of the citizens for evil purposes, and was often driven out with shame." Moreover, he was a compulsive gambler, losing as much as 14,000 ducats in a single night. When his father was ill, Franceschetto attempted to seize the papal treasury for his own benefit; when his father died in 1492, Franceschetto realized that he was so unpopular that he had to flee from Rome. He went to Florence to seek the protection of his brother-in-law Piero (or Pietro) de' Medici. Wisely, Franceschetto sold his land in Romagna (given to him by his father) to Virginio Orsini for 40,000 ducats. As a result, Virginio Orsini became the lord of Cervetri and count of Anguillara.[31] The selling of this territory, which was considered to be papal land, was eventually disputed by the succeeding pope Alexander VI.[32]

Franceschetto Cibo and Maddalena de' Medici had six children: (1) Innocenzo, (2) Ippolita, (3) Eleonora, (4) Caterina, (5) Giambattista and (6) Lorenzo. Innocenzo Cibo (1491–1550), Archbishop of Genoa and papal legate to Bologna, was made a cardinal by his uncle Pope Leo X in 1513. Ippolita married Roberto di Sanseverino, Count of Caiazzo. Eleonora became a nun, and Caterina (1501–1557) married Giovan Maria Varano, Lord of Camerino. After her husband's death, Caterina tried to retain Camerino for her daughter Giulia, wife of Guldobaldo della Rovere, Duke of Urbino, but she was deposed and lived in Florence.[33] Giambattista Cibo (1501–1552) was the bishop of Marseilles. Lorenzo Cibo (1500–44) married Ricciarda Malaspina, heiress of the earldom of Massa and Carrara.

Lorenzo and Ricciarda's oldest son Giulio (1515–48) was in conflict with his mother since he wished to rule Massa. He was also unhappy in his marriage to Peretta Doria, sister of Giannettino and cousin of the famous admiral Andrea Doria. Disillusioned, he became involved in an unsuccessful plot to capture Genoa. Denounced by his mother, he was captured, tried, tortured and decapitated. Giulio's brother Alberico I (1529–1623) was more fortunate. He took the name Cibo Malaspina and was proclaimed the prince of the Holy Roman Empire and marchese of Massa by the Emperor Charles V.[34]

Alberico's daughter Lucrezia married Ercole Sfondrati, Duke of Montemarciano, heir of Pope Gregory XIV (1590–91), whose family will be delineated later in the book. Alberico's son Alderano (d. 1605) was the husband of Marfisa d'Este; their grandson Alberico II became the first duke of Massa. Duke Alberico II's brother Alderano (1613–1700) became a cardinal in 1648, and under Pope Innocent XI he was papal secretary of state and then legate to Urbino and Ferrara. Alberico and Alderano's sister Veronica (1611–87), the great-great-great-granddaughter of Innocent VIII, was the wife of Giacomo Salviati, Duke of San Giuliano. She killed her husband's lover and, placing the deceased's head in a basket, sent it to her husband.

The last Duke of Massa of the Cibo-Malaspina family, founded by Alberico I, was Alderano. He died in 1731, leaving a daughter Maria Teresa, wife of Duke Ercole III (1727–1803), son of Francesco III d'Este, Duke of Modena.[35] They had only one child, a daughter, Maria Beatrice d'Este (1750–1829) who married Ferdinando of the Hapsburg family, Archduke of Austria, and their descendants became the d'Este-Hapsburg dukes of Modena. Duke Ercole III d'Este (1727–1803) was the great-grandson of Lucrezia Barberini and her husband, Duke Francesco I of Modena (1610–58).[36] The Barberinis were yet another papal dynasty during the Baroque period (see Tables 4f and 4g in Appendix A). The descendants and members of papal families often married into such ducal families as the d'Este and even into such royal families as the Hapsburgs.

II: The House of Borgia

In 1455 a seventy-seven-year-old cardinal, Alfonso de Borja (or Borgia) was elected pope because the Colonna and Orsini factions wanted an elderly, compromise candidate. He took the name Callistus III (1455–58). Borgia was from Aragon and was one of the few Spanish prelates to attain the papacy. He had served as bishop of Valencia and had become a cardinal in 1444. He devoted his three years on the papal throne to forming a crusade against the Turks, selling precious works of art and even dispersing the Vatican Library in order to raise moneys for this cause. Borgia allied himself with the Colonna family and sent papal forces against the Orsini to recover fortresses that he considered to be property of the church.

Probably Callistus III is best known for his excessive nepotism and for ushering the Borgia onto the historical stage. Callistus' sister Caterina married Juan Mila, who was named the baron of Mazalanes. Their son Luis Juan was made the governor of Bologna by his uncle in 1455 and became a cardinal. The pope's other sister Isabella married Jofré Lanzol de Borja, a cousin. Isabella and Jofré's two sons, Pedro Luis and Rodrigo, benefited from their papal uncle, who bestowed upon them ample gifts. Pedro Luis became the captain general of the church's militia in 1456. Later he was to become the governor of Terni, Narmi and Todi, vicar-general of Benevenuto and Terracina, and duke of Spoleto. In 1457 he was made prefect of Rome. The pope was so ambitious for his nephew that he invaded Naples with the intent of putting Pedro Luis on the throne of that kingdom. Rodrigo became notary of the Apostolic See and at the age of twenty-five was named a cardinal. He became vice-chancellor of the Holy See in 1457 and retained that position for over thirty years, accumulating a vast sum of wealth. Rodrigo Borgia was later to use that wealth to buy the papacy.

The pope's nephews were overbearing and insolent toward the Romans; as Callistus III was dying, Pedro Luis fled from Rome, fearing reprisals from the Orsini family as well as from others in the city who hated the "Catalans." This was the name given to the Spanish relatives and friends who received lucrative church positions by the Borgia pope.[37] When Pedro Luis died in 1458, Pope Pius II (1458–64) conferred the office of prefect of Rome on Anthonio Colonna with the right of succession to his eldest son.

Rodrigo has been called a "serpent who in his boundless ambition and pestiferous perfidity, and with all his examples of horrible cruelty and monstrous sensuality and unheard of avarice…, had envenomed the entire world."[38] Pope Pius II had castigated Rodrigo when he was a cardinal in 1460 for attending an orgy where there was "licentious dancing" and the "allurements of love."[39] Rodrigo was elected pope in 1492 and attained the office through simony. For their vote in the papal conclave, he offered Cardinal Ascaniu Sforza the office of vice-chancellor, the castle at Nepi and 10,000 ducats; Cardinal Orsini was to receive Monticelli and Soriano and the bishopric of Carthegena; Cardinal Colonna was to receive the Abbey of Subiaco and the surrounding villages; Cardinal Savelli was to receive the Civita Castellana and the bishopric of Majorica; and so forth.[40] By purchasing votes, Rodrigo was elected and became Pope Alexander VI (1492–1503).

Alexander VI was a man of the flesh; he had many mistresses and several illegitimate children. His papacy was one of "unabashed nepotism," and it was a reign whereby state and church property became the property of members of the Borgia family.[41] To his son Caesar, who early in his career had seemed destined for an ecclesiastical career, the pope gave the bishopric of Valencia. Juan (Giovanni, John), son of Galceran (d. 1503), Alexander's uncle, had been made cardinal in 1492. He lived in the Vatican and was a close advisor of the pope. Juan, Jr. (1474–1500), son of Jofré Lanzol y de Borja, the son of Juana, who was the pope's sister, became the bishop of Melfi in 1494 and a cardinal two years later. He served as papal legate to Perugia, Spoleto, Bologna and Romagna. Juan, Jr., was closely allied with Caesar Borgia, the pope's son. Juan, Jr.,'s brother Pedro Luis (1480–1511) was also named a cardinal in 1500. Francesco (1441–1511), who was known as the son of Alexander's uncle Juan de Borja — but who was more likely the son of Pope Callistus III — was born in Valencia. He was named a cardinal by his cousin Alexander VI when he was sixty years of age and was named treasurer of the Holy See, the bishop of Teano and the archbishop of Cosenza. Pope Julius II, enemy of the House of Borgia, deprived Francesco of all of his titles in 1511. Francesco died from apoplexy that same year.[42]

Alexander VI's other children included Pedro Luis (1458–88), born in Spain, who was a soldier and fought for the king of Aragon (later known as King Ferdinand the Catholic of

Spain). The king had Pedro Luis betrothed to his cousin Maria Enriquez and created him the duke of Gandia. After Pedro Luis died, his brother Juan (Giovanni) inherited the dukedom of Gandia and proceeded to marry Maria Enriquez.

Juan was one of several children born to Cardinal Borgia (before he became pope) and his mistress Vannozza Catanei.[43] (It has been disputed as to whether Juan or his brother Caesar were the oldest of the children born of this liaison — a question complicated by the fact that, while Caesar was certainly the son of Vannozza, he may not have been fathered by Borgia at all.[44]) Juan and Maria Enriquez had two children: Juan II, third Duke (1494–1543), whose children will be described later, and Isabel (1495–1557), the abbess of the Poor Clares at Gandia. Juan also became the duke of Sessa, acquired the principality of Terracina and received such titles as Duke of Benevento and Lord of Pontecorvo (1497). He was created a papal legate of the church's patrimony and served as captain general of papal forces.[45]

Juan was much loved by his father Pope Alexander VI, who was devastated when he was mysteriously murdered on the night of June 14, 1497. There were many suspects — such as the Orsini family, who hated the Borgias and might have plotted Juan's death, and Cardinal Ascanio Sforza of another influential family (the rulers of Milan), who was also an enemy of the pope. But the person most likely to have killed Juan, according to the general consensus at the time, was his own brother Caesar. Immediately after his son's death, Pope Alexander was inconsolable and decided to reform his life; he actually began to instill meaningful church reforms, especially against simony about which he was an expert. But this period of repentance was short-lived, and Alexander VI resumed his old, lascivious ways. It was reported that three years after his murder, the ghost of Juan, Duke of Gandia, appeared in the Castle S. Angelo "moaning fearfully." His murderers were never apprehended, and his brother Caesar now became the pope's favorite. The pope said that Caesar "was more dear to him than anyone on earth."[46]

Besides Pedro Luis, Juan and Caesar, the pope had at least six other children. They were Lucrezia (1480–1519), about whom we will hear more: Goffredo (1481–1516; Giovanni (1498–1548), called the "Infante Romano"; Rodrigo (1502–1527); Isabella (1467–1541), married to Petro Mattuzzo; and Jeronima (1470?–1483), married to Gianandrea Caesarini. The pope's son Goffredo (Jofre) married twice. His first wife was Sancia of Aragon, daughter of King Alfonso II of Naples who created his son-in-law the prince of Squillace, count of Cariati and protonotary of the Kingdom of Sicily.[47] His second wife was Juana de Mila of Aragona, and they had four children. Their son Francesco Borgia, second Prince of Squillace, married into the Piccolomini family and had a son Giovanni Battista, third Prince, father of Pietro Borgia, fourth Prince. One of Pietro's daughters, Anna, married her distant cousin Francesco Borgia of Gandia; another daughter, Giovanna, married Michele Antonio Orsini of Gravina.

Pope Alexander's son Giovanni, the "Infante Romano," was born in 1498.[48] He was created the duke of Nepi in 1501 and a year later the duke of Camerino. Giovanni was deposed in both dukedoms when his father died in 1503 and spent much of his life trying to regain the rights to these lost titles. He died before 1550, when most of his famous Borgia relatives were already dead and could do nothing for him. Giovanni, the "Infante Romano," may actually have been the illegitimate son of Lucrezia Borgia and her lover Perotto. This is suggested by two papal bulls issued by Alexander VI: one indicating that Caesar was the father (rather than the brother) of Giovanni and the other that the pope himself was the boy's father. Certainly Lucrezia treated Giovanni like a son, and after she married Duke Alfonso I, Lucrezia took Giovanni to Ferrara, the dukedom of her husband.[49]

Caesar Borgia

Certainly the most notorious of Alexander VI's children was the infamous Caesar Borgia

(1475–1507). In his youth Caesar had been headed for a career in the church. Already in 1491 he was bishop of Pamplona, and a year later he became the archbishop of Valencia. Caesar's prospects of becoming a cardinal were stymied by the fact that he was a bastard. In order to resolve this problem, a canonical tribunal was held which declared that Caesar was the legitimate son of one Domenico of Arignano (the first husband of la Vannozza), enabling him to receive the red hat in 1493. Subsequently, his father, the pope, appointed him governor of Orvieto in 1495 and legate to Naples two years later. It was in the year 1497 that his brother the duke of Gandia was murdered. His death influenced Caesar's decision to leave the church (August 17, 1498). Afterwards, he became a papal legate to the court of King Louis XII of France. He brought with him the pope's bull to annul the king's marriage. In gratitude the French king made Caesar the duke of Valentinois, and Borgia became known as Duke Valentino.

After being rejected by King Federigo of Naples as an appropriate spouse for the king's daughter — the king objected on the grounds that Caesar was merely the "son of a priest"[50] — Caesar married Carlotta d'Albret, sister of the king of Navarra, in 1498. The d'Albret family were closely related to the French and Spanish royal houses, and Carlotta's grandniece Jeanne d'Albret (1528–72) was the mother of the first Bourbon king of France, Henry IV.

On the night of Caesar Borgia's marriage, he asked for an aphrodisiac, but received "laxative pills instead," forcing him to spend much time in the privy.[51] From this marriage Caesar and Carlotta had a daughter Luisa (1500–1553), who first married Louis de Tremouille and then Philip, Lord of Bourbon-Busset. By her second husband, Luisa had six children — one of whom, Claude, succeeded as the lord of Bourbon-Busset and married Marguerite de Rochefoucauld. Luisa's descendants, the House of Bourbon-Busset, was to thrive and exists through the present time.

The House of Bourbon-Busset was descended from Louis of Bourbon (1428–82), who married Catherine d'Egmont in 1464.

Louis of Bourbon had been destined for the priesthood and received Holy Orders in 1466, becoming the bishop of Liege one year later.[52] The marriage was opposed by the French king Louis XI (1461–83), who proclaimed it null and had Louis and Catherine's three children declared illegitimate. The descendants of the union thus became ineligible for the French crown. Louis and Catherine's oldest son, Pierre, married the heiress of Busset in Auvergne; it was their descendants who first took the name Bourbon-Busset. Pierre's son Philip married Luise Borgia, and their descendants married into numerous noble French families — in one case to a princess of Polignac. The Bourbon-Busset family divided into three main branches: counts of Busset, counts of Chalus and counts of Lignieres. All these branches have had representative members into the twentieth century.

By allying himself with a French princess, Caesar Borgia could move under the aegis of the French king Louis XII (1498–1515), who supplied him with an army. Caesar's military ambitions were also advanced by his father, the pope, who was now politically tied to French policies. Alexander VI generously supported his son with financial resources, as well as with the power and influence of the papacy, to promote Caesar's military campaigns. Caesar now proceeded to conquer Romagna in north central Italy on the pretext that he was bringing that region back under the church's control. In 1499 his army took Imola and Forlì from the Riario family. Although Girolamo Riario, the nephew of Pope Sixtus IV, was dead by 1499, Forlì was valiantly defended by his wife Caterina Sforza. Upon her defeat, she was taken to Rome in chains and imprisoned in the Castel Sant' Angelo. The pope now named Caesar *gonfaloniere* of the church. At this time, in order to get increased revenue for Caesar's military expeditions, the pope appointed twelve new cardinals, selling the cardinalates for the highest price.[53] In 1500 Duke Valentino again set out to subdue Romagna. As Caesar approached with his army, many lords fled to avoid a belligerent confrontation and defeat. Lord Pandolfo Malatesta hurriedly left Rimini, and Lord Giovanni Sforza did the same from Pesaro. However, the city of Faenza, inspired by its young leader Astorre Manfredi III, fought against Caesar. When Faenza finally surrendered, Caesar promised to spare Astorre's life. The ruler was taken back to Rome and also placed in Castel Sant' Angelo, and there he was molested. (Litta notes that Astorre had a "beautiful body."[54]) He was strangled and thrown into the Tiber.[55] Caesar's cruelty would become legendary.

For his military successes, Caesar was named the duke of Romagna by the pope. His next campaign — wholly instigated and sustained by his father, the pope — included the sacking of Capua. Many women were captured when Capua was taken, and Caesar selected forty of the most beautiful women for himself.[56] Valentino then went on to take Camerino, ruled by Lord Giulio Caesar Varano, which when conquered was given to the pope's four-year-old son Giovanni, "l'Infante Romano." Varano was captured, and he too was killed in prison. Finally Caesar seized the dukedom of Urbino, ruled by Guidobaldo of Montefeltro, who barely escaped. Urbino was a conquest necessary for Caesar to become master of Romagna, and he now proclaimed himself the duke of Urbino.

It was at the apex of his success that the Orsini, along with Caesar's own captains (Vitellozzo Vitelli and Oliverotto da Fermo) and others, decided to rid Italy of the ruthless Caesar. They began to fear this tyrant — who like a dragon was devouring one by one the Italian states and their rulers — and they were all afraid of becoming yet other victims. At first they were successful, defeating Caesar's papal forces; but when the French promised additional military aid to subdue these enemies, the conspirators asked for Caesar's forgiveness. He seemingly accepted their repentance, inviting them to his home for the purpose of reconciliation. Upon their arrival, all were arrested. Vitelli and Oliverotto were strangled immediately; Francesco Orsini, Duke of Gravina, and his cousin Paolo Orsini were strangled soon after.[57] Likewise, members of the Orsini family in Rome were arrested by the pope. Cardinal

Battista Orsini, old and blind, was poisoned (on February 22, 1503), and the Orsini property was confiscated by papal forces.

Meanwhile, Perugia and the Citta of Castello fell to Caesar, and Romagna was now politically organized by Borgia. On June 24, 1503, to inaugurate the first session of the supreme court, a festive public ceremony was held in which Caesar appeared in a triumphal carriage designed to simulate that of Julius Caesar and Cleopatra. Caesar Borgia often alluded to himself as the new Caesar, comparing himself to that famous Roman. On his sword was written: *Cum Nomine Caesaris Omen*—"The name of Caesar carries an omen"— foretelling his becoming a powerful ruler.[58]

Caesar, now ready to demonstrate this power, planned to conquer Siena, Pisa and Florence. In the midst of these plans, his father became ill after dining at the villa of His Eminence Adriano Castellesi, the cardinal of Corneto, on August 5, 1503; Pope Alexander VI died thirteen days later. The historian Guicciardini explains how goblets of poisoned wine had been prepared by the pope and Caesar to kill the cardinal in order to confiscate his wealth. It was reported that "Valentino had prepared certain flacons of wine infected with poison, which he consigned to a stewart unaware of the plot, commanding him not to give them to anyone. But by chance it happened that the Pontiff, before the dinner hour became thirsty as a result of the overwhelming heat and asked that some drink be brought him, and because the supplies for the dinner had not yet arrived from the palace, the stewart, who believed that the most precious wine had been set aside for his keeping, gave the Pope that wine to drink which Valentino had sent ahead; and that Valentino while his father was drinking, began similarly to drink of the same wine." The pope and his son Caesar had previously engaged in such murders; the death of a cardinal meant that church benefices, property and riches were restored to the church — or better, into the hands of the pope. Alexander VI and his son had thus "frequently and habitually made use of poison" to kill off enemies, "but also because of their wicked greed to despoil the wealthy of their possessions, both amongst the cardinals and other members of the court, heedless of the fact that they had never been harmed in any way by these people." In April of that same year Caesar had already poisoned, with the help of his cousin Cardinal Pier Luigi Borgia (1471–1511), the rich Venetian cardinal Giovanni Michiel in the Castel Sant' Angelo. They had also liquidated the cardinals of Capua and Modena.[59]

Controversy surrounds the pope's death. As noted, it has been rumored that poisoned wine meant for Cardinal Adriano de Corneto was taken by mistake by both the pope and Caesar. On the other hand, the historian Sanuto claims that Cardinal Corneto paid the carver of poisoned sweetmeats, originally meant to kill the cardinal, to give the food instead to the pope and his son.[60] Other sources report that it was not poison but a malady that killed the pope. In any event soon after eating with the cardinal, Alexander VI and Caesar became violently ill. Caesar confessed "that although he had formerly often anticipated all the difficulties that might result from his father's death and planned all the remedies against such troubles, it had never occurred to him that he also might happen to be impeded by a dangerous illness at the same time."[61] Since Borgia was incapacitated, he was forced to leave Rome as the papal conclave met to elect a new pope. As a result, a compromise between the French and Spanish cardinals was reached whereby Pius III, Francesco Todeschini-Piccolomini, was elected. Pius reconfirmed Caesar's church positions (such as *gonfaloniere*, which Alexander VI had bestowed upon his son) and permitted Borgia to return to Rome on October 3, 1503. Fifteen days later, Pius III was dead, and the arch-rival of the Borgias, Giuliano della Rovere, emerged as the leading candidate for the papacy.

No longer sustained by the power of the papacy, all of Caesar's plans to rule Italy were destroyed. He could no longer keep control of those areas he had seized. Urbino, Rimini, Pesaro, Falenza and Forlì soon freed themselves from his yoke. Moreover, the Orsinis united with the Savelli and Colonna families against

Caesar, who was down to a military force of only 650 men.[62] The success of Caesar's enemies was the direct result of the death of Pope Alexander VI. Without the pope, Caesar was nothing.

In desperation, Caesar sought the help of the family rival — the potent candidate for the pontificate, Guiliano della Rovere — who promised Caesar that if he were elected pope Borgia would remain standard-bearer of the church and retain all his possessions.[63] In return Caesar promised that the Spanish cardinals would vote for him in the conclave. Once elected pope, Julius II had no intention of keeping his word, and Caesar was forced to flee. The Borgia prince was arrested, returned to Rome, liberated, imprisoned again — until he finally escaped to the kingdom of Navarra, where he died fighting to capture the castle of Viana on March 12, 1507.

It is not known how many illegitimate children Caesar begot. One son Gerolamo was living in Ferrara in 1545, probably protected by his cousins, the children of Caesar's sister Lucrezia, whose husband was the ducal ruler. Gerolamo married as his second wife Isabella Pio of Capri and had two daughters. Caesar also had a illegitimate daughter named Camilla Lucrezia (1502 –1573). She was the abbess of S. Bernardino in Ferrara.[64]

Lucrezia Borgia

Lucrezia Borgia (1480–1519), Caesar's younger sister, became a political instrument in the hands of the pope and her brother, both of whom reportedly — and probably erroneously — were her incestuous lovers.[65] To please her father, she had been married by proxy to Don Gasparo de Procida, son of the count of Aversa in Spain. She was not yet twelve years of age. When her father assumed the papal throne in 1492, he promptly annulled her marriage to Procida, and one year later he had her marry Giovanni Sforza, Lord of Pesaro. This was a political union created to gain the friendship of the Sforza family rulers in north and central Italy.[66] When the pope wished to ally himself with the king of Naples, he annulled Lucrezia's marriage to Sforza in 1497 and had her marry Alfonso, Duke of Bisceglie, the son of King Alfonso II of the Aragonesi family that ruled Naples. They were united in an elaborate ceremony.[67]

Soon after Caesar allied himself with France, the enemy of the Aragon dynasty in Naples, the duke of Bisceglie was forced to flee from Rome, leaving his pregnant wife. To comfort Lucrezia, the pope named her governor of Spoleto, Foligno and Nepi. Her husband returned to Rome just before the birth of their son Rodrigo. Favoring French policies against the Aragonesi family in Naples, Caesar decided to assassinate his brother-in-law, who was brutally attacked in the piazza of St. Peter's. He was gravely wounded, and it was while recovering from his wounds that he was slain in his own bed in the papal apartments by Caesar's agents on August 18, 1500.[68] A year later, when the dukedom of Sermoneta was seized by the Borgias, it was given to Lucrezia and later bestowed upon her son Rodrigo. Sermoneta was the stronghold of the Caetani family, which had secured it two hundred years earlier by their benefactor Boniface VIII.[69]

In that same year, Alexander VI planned Lucrezia's marriage to Alfonse d'Este (later to become Duke Alfonso I), son of the duke of Ferrara, who at first opposed the marriage — the reputation of the Borgias had circulated throughout Italy. Eventually, fearing reprisals from the pope, from the almighty Caesar Borgia and from his ally France, the duke of Ferrara consented to the marriage. Her dowry was fit for a princess — "100,000 ducats in cash and many other gifts of the greatest value."[70] There were numerous festive occasions, first in Rome and then in Ferrara to celebrate this marriage. Lucrezia was first escorted to the Porta del Popolo in Rome by all the cardinals, the governmental officials and ambassadors. Later, when she entered Ferrara in a triumphal procession on February 21, 1502, dressed in magnificent finery and jewels, she graciously moved through the applauding crowds.[71] She was quite beautiful and, in spite of having three previous husbands, was only twenty-two years of age.

It was in Ferrara, separated from her father and brother, that she flourished as her own person. She became a patron of arts and literature — Ariosto, Cardinal Bembo, Titian and Dosso Dossi were all in her court. She won the love of both her husband — who in 1505 became the duke of Ferrara — and the populace of his dukedom. She was a "faithful and loving wife," charitable and an advocate of the poor. She did not involve herself in the politics of the country, but centered her life around her family and the education of her children.[72] She also found solace in religion, frequently going to a monastery for contemplation and praying "for the sins of this our era." She fervently mourned the death of her father and her brother Caesar.[73] Lucrezia was only thirty-nine years of age when she died during a miscarriage in 1519.

During her seventeen years of marriage to the duke of Ferrara, Lucrezia was often pregnant, fragile and sickly. She and Duke Alfonso I had five children: (1) Ercole II (1508–1559), her eldest son, who married Renée (Renata), the daughter of King Louis XII of France; (2) Eleanora (1515–75) who became a nun; (3) Francesco (1516–78) who was named the marchese of Massalombarda and had two natural daughters, Bradamante and Marfisa; (4) Alessandro (1511–16) who died young; and (5) Ippolito (1509–1572) who became the archbishop of Milan when he was ten years of age and cardinal in 1539. Similar to his mother, Ippolito encouraged poets and artists, and as governor of Tivoli, he constructed the famous Villa d'Este. His greatest aspiration, however, was to become pope, and he was prepared to pay for that office; but it was not to be his. He had a natural daughter Renata who married Ludovico II Pico, Lord of Mirandola.[74] Ludovico II and Renata were the parents of a daughter Ippolita and a son Alessandro I. Ippolita became the wife of Alfonso Piccolomini, Duke of Montemarciano, who became the infamous bandit. Ippolita's brother, Alessandro I Pico (d. 1637), married Laura, daughter of Cesare d'Este, Duke of Modena, and Virginia de' Medici. Alessandro I and Laura's daughter Fulvia was the wife of Alberico II Cibo, descendant of Pope Innocent VII.

Alberico II's great-granddaughter Maria Teresa, heiress of the Cibo family, married Ercole III d'Este, Duke of Modena. This d'Este family was descended from Duke Alfonso I, husband of Lucreazia Borgia, and his mistress Laura Dianti. Maria Teresa and Ercole's daughter Maria Beatrice (1750–1829) was the heiress of the d'Este family. She was the wife of Archduke Ferdinando of Austria, and their descendants became the Hapsburg-d'Este dukes of Modena. The last duke's niece married Louis III, King of Bavaria, and their numerous descendants, claimants to the Bavarian throne, have Lucrezia Borgia's bloodline.

Duke Alfonso I and Lucrezia Borgia's eldest son, Ercole II, Duke of Ferrara, had several children. Among them were (1) Anna (Anne, d. 1607) who married Francois, Duke of Guise (1519–63) and then Giacomo of Savoy, Duke of Nemours; (2) Alfonso II, Duke of Ferrara from 1559 to 1591, who married the daughter of Cosimo de' Medici, Duke of Tuscany, and then Barbara, the daughter of the Emperor Ferdinard I, and finally Eleonora Gonzaga, the daughter of the duke of Mantua: (3) Lucrezia (1535–98) who will be described later; and (4) Luigi (1538–86) who was destined for the clergy, but detested the religious life. When very young, he received the rich benefices of the diocese of Ferrara, but he fled to France and contemplated marriage with the countess of Saint-Paul. In 1561 Pope Pius IV offered the cardinalate to Luigi, which he accepted; but he dreamed of leaving his life as a cleric — especially when his brother, the Duke Alfonso II, had no children, Luigi thought that he might marry in order to have children and preserve the dukedom for the dynasty. But this never happened. While his character was a rebellious one, he had inherited another characteristic: patron of the arts. He completed the Villa d'Este in Tivoli, begun by his uncle Cardinal Ippolito, he constructed the Palazzo del Diamanti in Ferrara; and he was a patron of the writer Tasso.[75]

Luigi's sister Lucrezia d'Este, named after her grandmother, married Francesco Maria della Rovere II, Duke of Urbino, great-grand-nephew of Pope Julius II, the archenemy of the Borgia family. She separated from her husband in 1574 and returned to Ferrara. When her brother Duke Alfonso II died, she did not wish her cousin Caesar (1552–1628), who was the son of Alfonso (1527–87), a bastard son of her grandfather Duke Alfonso I, to become the duke of Ferrara. Wishing to rule Ferrara, which the church now claimed as its own, Caesar had been excommunicated by Pope Clement VIII. Lucrezia d'Este intervened in this matter with her personal friend Cardinal Pietro Aldobrandini, nephew of the pope. On behalf of Caesar, she came to an agreement with Aldobrandini, and thus with the papacy, whereby Ferrara was to be returned to the church. The pope ended his excommunication of Caesar, permitting him to keep the d'Este art collection, its library and allodial estates.[76] By the Convention of Faenza, in 1598, by which Caesar gave up his rights to Ferrara to the church, he was compensated by becoming the duke of Modena and Reggio, which the d'Este family ruled until 1859. Lucrezia (1535–98) had no children. She saw to it that only the descendants of her grandfather and grandmother, Duke Alfonso I and Lucrezia Borgia, reigned over the city of Ferrara.

Only Lucrezia's sister Anna d'Este had legitimate children. Anna had married the distinguished second duke of Guise, François (1519–63). Their children included Cardinal Louis; Catherine, wife of Louis de Bourbon; Henry, third Duke of Guise, and Charles, Duke of Mayenne. All these children will be subsequently delineated. Anna d'Este's second husband, Giacomo of Savoy, Duke of Nemours (1531–85), had ardently participated with the House of Guise in its religious wars. Their great-granddaughters married into the House of Savoy and the Portuguese royal family. Anna d'Este was known for a disposition equal to that of her grandmother Lucrezia Borgia, and Anna is described as being "the sweet, best, humblest, and most affable princess that one could find, although she showed in her behavior a proud dignity." Anna's husband, the duke of Guise, had a sister Marie who was the wife of King James V of Scotland and was the mother of Mary Stuart, from whom the present royal house of England is descended.

François, Duke of Guise, "le grand Guise," was a military leader who became lieutenant-general of the French kingdom. He was the undisputed head of the Catholic party against the Huguenot forces, which he defeated in battle. Later he was assassinated by a Huguenot. Two of François' brothers, Charles and Louis, were cardinals, as were one of his sons, Louis, and one of his grandsons. His daughter Catherine married Louis de Bourbon, Duke of Montpensier. The male line of Guise became extinct in 1675.[77] Catherine (1552–96) and another of François' sons, Henry, third Duke of Guise, instigated a revolt in 1588 against King Henry III of France. Called "the day of the barricades," the Guises controlled the kingdom. The power of the Guises ended when King Henry had Henry murdered. Consequently, Catherine, the murdered duke's sister, persuaded a fanatic monk, Jacques Clement to stab the king and kill him in 1589 — she was a true descendant of Pope Alexander VI Borgia.

Another of François' sons was Charles, Duke of Mayenne (1554–1611). As head of the Catholic party upon the death of his brother Henry, Charles opposed the proposed designation of Henry of Navarre, who was a Protestant, to rule France. But he eventually reconciled with Henry, who converted to Catholicism and became King Henry IV, the first French Bourbon monarch.

Catherine of Lorraine, daughter of Charles, Duke of Mayenne, and granddaughter of François, Duke of Guise, married Duke Carlo Gonzaga of Mantua. Their daughter Anna Gonzaga (1616–84) first married Duke Henry of Guise, who was the archbishop of Rheins when espoused, and then Edward of the Palatinate (d. 1663), whom she converted to Catholicism. Edward was the son of Frederick V of the Palatinate, the Protestant military leader, and Elizabeth, daughter of King James I of England. Edward's younger sister Sophia married the Protestant Duke Ernest of Hanover. They became the parents of King George I of England, from whom the present English royal family is descended. If Sophia's elder brother Edward had not converted to Catholicism, it is possible that the English throne would have

been held by his descendants. Anna Gonzaga and Edward of the Palatinate's daughter, Anna Enrichetta, inherited the possessions of the Guise family. Anna Enrichetta married Henry-Jules (1643–1709), Prince of Conde, from whom were descended the famous Duke of Enghein, murdered in 1804, and the princes of Conti, the present-day pretenders to the throne of France and Italy and the current kings of Spain and Belgium. All are direct descendants of Pope Alexander VI through his daughter Lucrezia.

Lucrezia Borgia (1480–1519), the daughter of the pope, had another son Rodrigo (1499–1512) by her marriage to the duke of Bisceglie. Rodrigo, named after his grandfather, had received the dukedom of Sermoneta upon its being seized by his uncle Caesar from the Caetani family. At the election of Guiliano della Rovere as Pope Julius II, the dukedom of Sermoneta was taken away from Rodrigo and restored to the Caetanis, in 1504. Other castles confiscated by the Borgias were returned to the Orsini and Colonna families.[78]

Other Borgia Descendants

The only territory that the Borgia family was able to retain in Italy was the principality of Squillace, Calabria, in the kingdom of Naples. Goffredo (1481–1516), son of Alexander VI, and his descendants kept the title Prince of Squillace. In Spain the Borgia family was able to retain the dukedom of Gandia, which was ruled by the descendants of Juan, second Duke (1476–97), the murdered son of the pope. One of Goffredo's daughters, Antonia, married Antonio Todeschini-Piccolomini, Marchese of Delicete, of the family of Pope Pius II; another daughter, Lucrezia, married Giovan-Battista Carafa of the family of Pope Paul IV. The descendants of Lucrezia and Giovan-Battista Carafa include the present-day princes of Roccella and princes of the Holy Roman Empire. A descendant, Gennaro Carafa (b. 1905), Prince of Roccella, was the son of Vincenzo (1870–1918) and Marina Colonna of Paliano (Colonna was the family of Pope Martin V).

Gennaro's grandfather Luigi Carafa married Maria Pignetelli of the family of Pope Innocent XII. Luigi's brother Prince Gennaro (1833–1903) married Clotilde de' Medici, who was the daughter of Marianna Gaetani and Giuseppe, Duke of Ottaiano. Both the Medici and Gaetani families gave several popes to the church.

Juan III, third Duke of Gandia, (1494–1543), son of the second duke and grandson of Pope Alexander VI, had sixteen children—including Francesco de Borja (Borgia), fourth Duke (1510–72); two cardinals, Enrico and Rodrigo; Alphonso, Viceroy of Catalonia; and Pedro Luis, Viceroy of Naples. Francesco Borgia, fourth Duke, married Leonor de Castro, a noble lady from Portugal. They had eight children, including Carlos fifth duke (1530–92). The last male descendant of the Borgia family, Duke of Gandia, was Luis Ignacio, eleventh Duke, who died in 1740.

In spite of the fact that the Borgia family produced such demonic individuals as Alexander VI and Caesar, they had a definite bent toward religiosity, as was shown in the demeanor of Lucrezia Borgia, the pope's daughter and Caesar's sister, and in that of Isabel Borgia (1497–1557), Abbess of the Poor Clares in Gandia, daughter of Juan, the second Duke of Gandia. Moreover, the great-grandson of Alexander VI, Francesco Borgia, fourth Duke of Gandia, was to become a saint. When his wife died in 1546, he entered the order of the Society of Jesus (the Jesuits), becoming the order's third general. A pious, devout man, he stressed a simple monastic life of penance and prayer for the Jesuits and is considered, after Igantious Loyola, the order's "second founder." He was canonized by Pope Clement X in 1671. The great-grandson of St. Francesco Borgia was Gaspard, named cardinal, archbishop of Seville and ambassador of the king of Spain to the Holy See. He died in 1645, disappointed that he had not been elected pope. A great-great-grandson, Francesco (d. 1702), also became a cardinal—as did his brother Carlos (1653–1733), serving in Rome on the Sacred Congregation of Prohibited Books. A distant cousin, descended from a brother of Callistus III's

great-great-great-grandfather, was Cardinal Stefano Borgia (1731–1804), Proprefecture to the Prefecture of Propaganda Fide. He died in Lyons, France, while accompanying Pope Pius VII on his trip to Paris to crown Napoleon. Stefano Borgia established the Borgia Museum of Antiquities in Velletri. The cardinal was known for his simple piety and "his universally sympathetic personality." Stefano's uncle Alessandro was also a cardinal. This Borgia branch of the family were distant cousins of the Borgia popes, but all traced their ancestry to one Sancia Borgia, ca. 1000 A.D.[79]

The impressive spiritual qualities of St. Francis Borgia and some of his descendants is in marked contrast to that of the Borgia ancestor Pope Alexander VI, who has been described as a man "without scruples, without faith, without morals."[80]

The Mistresses of Pope Alexander VI

In his various ecclesiastical offices—bishop, cardinal, and pope—Rodrigo Borgia had numerous concubines. Two of them were Roman matrons—Rosa (la Vannozza) Catanei and Giulia Farnese Orsini.

According to Litta, Rosa Catanei (1442–1518) was the daughter of Ranuccio Farnese, of an illustrious Roman family, but Litta may have confused her with another Farnese lover of Pope Alexander VI.[81] What we know with certainty is that she was born of Roman parents in 1442 and was married three times, first to Domenico of Arignano in 1474, second to Giorgie de Croce of Milan in 1480 and third to Carlo Canale of Mantua in 1486.[82] Rosa, whom the Romans called "la Vannozza," was the celebrated and acknowledged mistress of Rodrigo Lanzal de Borja, the nephew of Pope Callistus III, who obtained his uncle's surname Borja (in Spanish; Borgia in English).

Litta writes that "captivated by the beauty and exquisite arts of this courtesan"—who had made a "career of seduction"—Rodrigo Borgia had an "unbridled lust" for Vannozza. "The holiness of the tiara, which Rodrigo assumed under the infamous name of Alexander VI in

1492, did not extinguish this fire."[83] Litta is probably confusing la Vannozza with Guilia Farnese, "la Bella," who became the pope's mistress after 1589; la Vannozza, after her third marriage in 1586, ceased to be the pope's lover. Previous to being Cardinal Rodrigo Borgia's concubine, Vannozza had been the lover of Cardinal Giuliano della Rovere, who became Pope Julius II, and Caesar Borgia may have been their son.[84] In the 1470s Vannozza became the mistress of Cardinal Rodrigo. Depending on Caesar's paternity, she had either three or four children by Borgia — Caesar in 1475, Juan in 1476, Lucrezia in 1480 and Goffredo in 1481.[85] The names of her children were inscribed on her tomb.[86] Vannozza lived in a villa in Rome on the Piazza Branca, very close to the palace of the cardinal, now known as Palazzo Sforza-Cesarini.

In 1494, the king of France Charles VIII, at war with Pope Alexander VI, invaded Italy and occupied Rome. It was during this period of time that it was feared Vannozza might be taken prisoner by the French king. When warned about the invading French, la Vannozza is depicted in her villa taking care of her children and her household. The French soldiers invaded her most personal rooms, hurling insults to those who tried to protect her. She survived this invasion of her privacy and was unhurt.[87]

Three years later, on July 14, 1497, Vannozza had a dinner attended by two of her children, the duke of Gandia and Cardinal Caesar. They had a pleasant evening conversing together. It was after the dinner that the duke disappeared and was found murdered. Litta depicts Vannozza as being "the mother of the victim and the killer," assuming that Caesar was responsible for the death of his brother.[88] Guicciardini claims that Caesar killed his brother because "Gandia occupied a greater place than himself in the love of Madonna Lucrezia, their common sister." He accuses the two brothers and their father, Pope Alexander, of all competing "for the love of Madonna Lucrezia."[89]

There is little to report about the later years of Vannozza. Certainly she was replaced sometime after 1489 by "la bella Giulia" as the pope's lover. It is said that before la Vannozza died, she made "reparation for her sins by her piety."[90] She gave assistance to churches and hospitals.[91] She died on November 26, 1518, a year before the death of her only daughter, Lucrezia. She was seventy-six years of age.

La Vannozza probably lost the love of the energetic pope because of her age and because of his desire for a younger woman. In September 1500, Paolo Capello wrote, "The pope [Alexander VI] is now seventy years of age; he grows younger every day…"[92] And it may have been his new love Giulia Farnese, "Giulia Bella," (1474–1524), daughter of Pier Luigi Farnese, who helped to rejuvenate him. According to Litta, Pier Luigi was the brother of Rosa "la Vannozza," but Litta was probably confused about Rosa's family origin.[93]

There is also some confusion by Litta as to whom Giulia Farnese married. She was the wife of Orsino Orsini Migliorati, even though some sources state that her husband was Orsino Orsini, but Litta finds this to be unlikely and proposes other candidates from the Orsini family, all of which are equally unlikely.[94] Orsino's father was Ludovico Orsini Migliorati, Lord of Bassanello, who took the cognomen "Orsini." Ludovico's mother was Elena Orsini, the daughter of Carlo, Duke of Bracciano, of the family of Pope Nicholas III, and the wife of Gentile Migliorati, nephew of Pope Innocent VII. Ludovico's wife was Adriana del Mita, the grandniece of Pope Callistus III, the first Borgia pope and uncle of Alexander VI. The interrelationships of these papal families is uncanny (see Table IX).

Adriana del Mita Migliorati, grandniece of Pope Callistus III and cousin of Pope Alexander VI, was the pope's confidante. She assisted in the intrigues of her cousin Pope Alexander VI up to the moment of his death. In all the bacchanals of the Borgias, Adriana figures among those who were the first to be invited. She took care of some of the pope's children, being responsible for the education of Lucrezia Borgia. She accompanied Lucrezia to Ferrara in 1502 for Lucrezia's wedding. She was also the mother-in-law of Giulia Farnese Migliorati, and it was through her that Giulia met the

TABLE IX: BORGIA (BORJA) AND MIGLIORATI FAMILIES

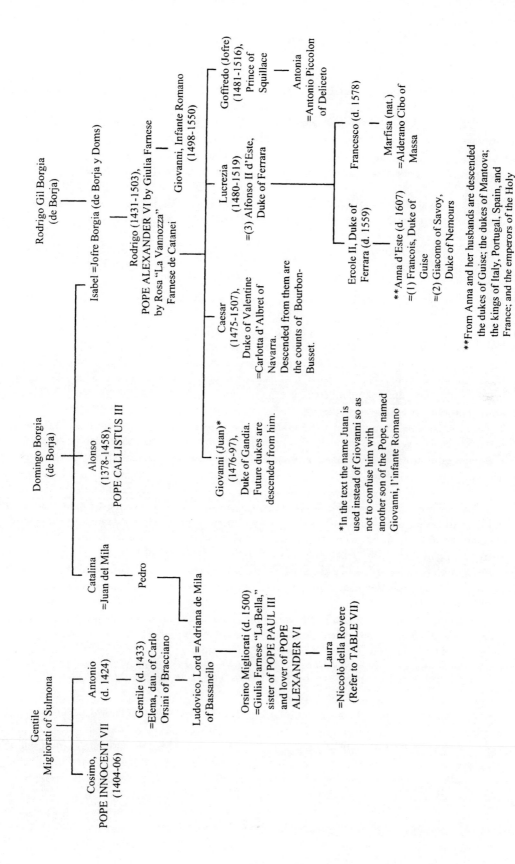

*In the text the name Juan is used instead of Giovanni so as not to confuse him with another son of the Pope, named Giovanni, l'infante Romano

**From Anna and her husbands are descended the dukes of Guise; the dukes of Mantova; the kings of Italy, Portugal, Spain, and France; and the emperors of the Holy Roman Empire.

pope and became his lover. Adriana encouraged the notorious and shameful adultery between the pope and Guilia.[95]

Known throughout Rome for her extraordinary beauty, Giulia was called "la Bella" in the pontifical court. Alexander VI had many concubines, and Giulia was certainly one of his favorites. She was often seen with the pope. In 1493 in the papal court, a splendid dinner was arranged by the pope. Litta refers to it as a bacchanal; it was attended by Alexander VI, the cardinals and Lucrezia Borgia, but most conspicuously by Giulia Bella. After the dinner there were presentations of lewd comic scenes. It was in that year that Giulia persuaded the pope to make her brother Alessandro a cardinal. Consequently, Alessandro Farnese (later Pope Paul III) became known as the "petticoat cardinal." At the marriage of Lucrezia Borgia to Giovanni Sforza, Lord of Pesaro, celebrated on June 12, 1493, five hundred members of the Roman nobility were invited to the great Sala Reale. In attendance were the pope and Giulia Bella. She is also mentioned as being present at a banquet given in the apostolic palace (October 1502) for five hundred courtesans. The pope, cardinals and many prelates were all present. It is believed that Giulia's likeness can be found in the frescoes by Pinturicchio (Bernardino di Betto di Biago) in the Borgia apartments. She apparently was the model for the Virgin Mary holding Jesus in her arms. Facing her is the pope, depicted as praying on his knees.[96]

In 1494, when the French army invaded Italy, Giulia and her mother-in-law were captured outside of Rome and ransomed personally for 3,000 ducats by the pope himself. They were described as being "the heart and eyes of the pontiff."[97] Giulia may have had several children by the pope, including Rodrigo, "l'Infante Romano," Duke of Nepi, born in 1498, and Laura, born 1492, who was officially the daughter of Orsino Orsini Migliorati and his wife, Giulia Farnese-Migliorati. (Litta declares that "her father, in fact, was the pope," whom she closely resembled.[98]) Giulia lived with her husband in Rome near Monte Giordano; but

Orsino spent most of his time away from Rome. For his compliance, permitting Giulia to be with the pope at his will, Orsino received the fiefdom of Carbognano. He died in 1500 and was the last Migliorati male.

Giulia was already a widow in 1506 when her daughter Laura married Nicolò della Rovere, whose descendants were called Franciotti-della Rovere. Pope Julius II, Nicolò's uncle, wanted Laura's rich inheritance — wealth accumulated by the Orsinis, Miglioratis and Borgias — and so he married her to Nicolò and Laura's daughter Elena married Stefano Colonna, Lord of Palestrina, and brought Carbognano and Bassenello to that branch of the Colonna family.[99] Their descendants retained the titles of Prince of Carbognano and Duke of Bassanello; a member of this family married the heiress of the Barberini family. Their descendants, the Barberini-Colonna di Sciarra, are divided into two main branches: the princes of Carbagnano and the princes of Palestrina.

Giulia wrote out her will in 1524, leaving her estate to her daughter Laura. She requested to be buried in the church on the island of Bisentina near the tombs of her Farnese ancestors. And while she was the subject of much scandal, especially during the pontificate of the Borgia pope, she found favor with his enemy and successor Pope Julius II after Alexander's death, primarily because her daughter married into the della Rovere family.[100] The intermarriages between these two papal dynasties, often as much at odds as the Orsini and the Colonna, connected them in succeeding generations, combining the fortunes of one papal family with another — and then another — assuring the fortunes of them all.

And the Spanish Borgia family was connected to other papal families by the closest of familial ties. One of Alexander VI's illegitimate daughters, Isabella (1467–1541), married Pietro Matuzzi and became a Roman matron. Her granddaughter married into the Pamfili family, becoming the grandmother of Giambattista Pamfili, who became Pope Innocent X (1644–55). That pope was a direct descendant of Pope Alexander VI.[101]

III: The Medici and Farnese Families

The Medici Family Dynasty

He was one of Italy's most illustrious princes, and yet he was not a prince. He was Lorenzo de' Medici, called "the Magnificent," who for all practical purposes ruled Florence as a hereditary, uncrowned monarch.

The members of the Medici family, who came to Florence in the twelfth century, became bankers and merchants and extended their power into the political arena. Giovanni de' Medici the Elder (1389–1464), who was extremely wealthy, instituted a senate of one hundred loyal supporters in the Florentine republic and used it to rule the city.[102] He is known as *pater patriae* (father of his country). After Giovanni de' Medici's death his son Piero (1416–69) ruled over Florence; Piero's son was Lorenzo the Magnificent (1449–92). Lorenzo recorded that "on the second day after my father's death, the leading men of the city and the state came to my house to condole with me and at the same time to request that I assume charge of the city and the state as my father and grandfather had done before me."[103]

As *capo della citta* ("head of the city"), Lorenzo de' Medici was an absolute lord, if not a tyrant, of the so-called *republic* of Florence — Florence, wrote Guicciardini, "could not have had a better tyrant or a more pleasant one. His natural inclinations and goodness gave birth to an infinite number of good results."[104] In 1469 he married Clarice Orsini of that aristocratic Roman family, which had given the papacy Nicholas III. She was a direct descendant of Rinaldo, Nicholas III's brother. Her grandmother was Lucrezia Aldobrandino Conti of the lords of Valmontone, whose family was descended from a brother of Pope Innocent III. Lorenzo and Clarice had several children: Piero II (or Pietro); Giovanni, Maddalena, Lucrezia, Contessina and Giuliano. (Refer to Table XXc in Chapter Six.)

While Lorenzo ruled Florence, he displeased the Pazzi family, and Pope Sixtus IV (1471–84)

and his nephew Girolamo Riario, as we may recall, had helped to plan the Pazzi Conspiracy of 1478 to liquidate the Medicis as rulers of Florence. Even though Giuliano, Lorenzo's brother, was killed, the plot failed and Lorenzo was spared. The members of the Pazzi family and the archbishop of Siena (one of the conspirators) were brutally murdered. In retaliation, Pope Sixtus IV excommunicated Lorenzo. Although the pope was supported by King Ferdinando I (also known as Don Ferrante) of Naples in this action, Lorenzo courageously went to the king of Naples and secured a peaceful settlement, thus thwarting the bellicose ambitions of the papacy.

While Lorenzo ruled Florence, his aim was to secure peace and tranquility in Italy. Upon his death in 1484, Sixtus IV was succeeded on the papal throne by Giovanni Battista Cibo, who took the name of Innocent VIII (1484–92). Innocent upset Lorenzo's plan for peace by going to war with the king of Naples; but here again, in 1486, Lorenzo was able to resolve the conflict and conclude an agreement between the pope and the king. Lorenzo now felt the need to establish an even greater accord with the papacy so that it would follow a general policy to insure harmonious relations between the Italian states. And in an effort to realize this goal, he married his daughter Maddalena to Franceschetto Cibo, son of Pope Innocent VIII in 1488 (see Table X). The pope, in turn made Lorenzo's thirteen-year-old son Giovanni into a cardinal. And so peace came to Italy until Lorenzo died in 1492 at the age of forty-three. "The goodness of this man was extraordinary and never equalled in Florence...," concluded Guicciardini.[105]

In his lifetime it had become apparent to Lorenzo that the key to a tranquil Italy depended on the Roman pope, who controlled the Papal States, and it was his intent to influence the papacy by playing a role in selecting the Supreme Pontiff. Soon after his son Giovanni became a cardinal, Lorenzo wrote to him saying that "much depends on the personality and example of a Cardinal. If the Cardinals were such as they ought to be, the whole world would be the better for it, for they

TABLE X: CIBO, MEDICI, FARNESE AND SFONDRATI FAMILIES (continued from TABLE VIII)

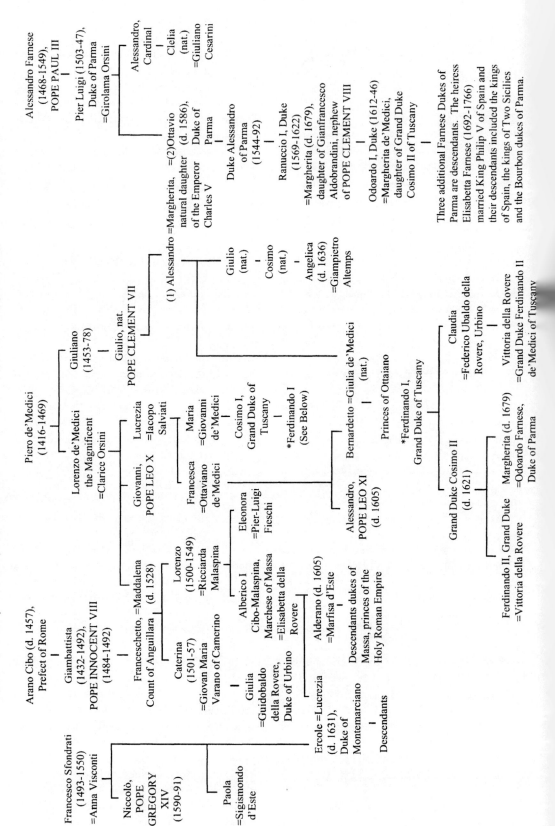

would always select a good Pope and thus secure the peace of Christendom."[106]

In 1513 Giovanni de' Medici was elected pope, following the death of Pope Julius II (Giuliano della Rovere). He assumed the name Leo X (1513–21). His was a reign governed by family interests and by the advancement of the Medicis throughout Italy. His brother Giuliano, who lived a life of extravagant debauchery, married Filiberta of Savoy, sister of Louisa, the mother of King Francis I of France. Giuliano was named captain general of the church in 1515 as well as the lord of Parma, Piacenza, Modena and Reggio. He became ill and died soon after, at which point the son of Leo X's brother Piero (d. 1503), who was named Lorenzo after his grandfather, was made supreme commander of the papal troops. Under Lorenzo's leadership, papal forces conquered Urbino, and Duke Francesco Maria della Rovere, nephew of Pope Julius II, was forced to flee.[107] The pope now made Lorenzo, the duke of Urbino, and soon after Lorenzo was married to Madeleine de la Tour d'Auvergne of the royal house of Boulogne, niece of King Francis I of France.[108]

Leo's relatives were the recipients of numerous other favors. Duke Lorenzo's sister Clarice (d. 1528) was married to Filippo Strozzi, who was appointed receiver-general of the papal exchequer. Fraceschetto Cibo (d. 1519), husband of the pope's sister, Maddalena, was made the governor of Spoleto. Franceschetto and Maddalena's son Innocenzo was made a cardinal in 1513 and archbishop of Genoa in 1520. Giovan Maria da Varano, the husband of daughter Caterina, was created the duke of Camerino. Giovan Maria was also presented with the city of Senigallia, and in 1520 made prefect of Rome. The husband of Ippolita, another daughter, was given the land of Colorno in Parma. Giovanni, the son of Leo's sister Lucrezia and her husband Jacopo Salviati, became the bishop of Fermo and then a cardinal. Niccolò Ridolfi, the son of another sister of Pope Leo, Contessina, was also made a cardinal by his uncle; Niccolò's brother, Piero, became governor of Spoleto after the death of his uncle Franceschetto Cibo. Luigi Rossi, the

son of Lorenzo the Magnificent's illegitimate sister Maria, also received the red hat.[109] Pope Leo's principal advisor became Cardinal Giulio de' Medici, who was the natural son of Giuliano, the murdered brother of Lorenzo the Magnificent. During the papacy of his cousin, Giulio was appointed the archbishop of Florence, cardinal and vice-chancellor (in 1517).

Leo lived like a Renaissance prince, and his expenses were excessive. He maintained a spacious hunting lodge and a magnificent papal court, where lavish dinners were held for hundreds of guests, opulent music festivals were hosted and plays were presented. Leo encouraged the works of Michelangelo and Raphael and continued the construction of St. Peter's, which had been started by his predecessor Pope Julius II. He also shouldered the cost of ruling Florence and of keeping a sizeable military force. Above all he kept his many relatives living in opulence. In order to obtain money, Leo borrowed heavily, sold the cardinalate and arranged for the selling of indulgences — payment for the remission of sins. [110] Buying indulgences became a business whereby agents purchased the right to sell indulgences throughout Europe, especially in Germany. Much of this money never even went to the church. The pope "gave his sister Maddalena the emoluments and exactions of the indulgences of many parts of Germany."[111] To protest the selling of indulgences and other church abuses, Martin Luther posted his ninety-five theses of grievances against the church on October 31, 1517. Leo unsuccessfully dealt with this reform movement, which led to open rebellion and the Protestant Reformation.

Leo was beset by other concerns as well. During this same period, Alfonso Petrucci, Cardinal of Siena, planned to assassinate the pope. But when Cardinal Alfonso's plot was discovered, he was deprived of the cardinalate and "secretly strangled in prison." Freeing himself of insurgents in Rome, Leo concentrated on wars and political strategies outside of his domain.[112] Upon Leo X's death on December 1, 1521, his sister Lucrezia Salviati ransacked the Vatican in order to pilfer its most precious possessions.[113] The greed of the family had become insatiable.

From 1522 to 1523, the Supreme Pontiff was a "foreigner" from the Netherlands. He took the name Hadrian VI. Subsequently, no other non-Italian pope would reign in Rome until the current pope John Paul II from Poland, elected in 1978. Hadrian's vice-chancellor was Cardinal Giulio de' Medici, cousin of Leo X. Hadrian was pope for only a year.

Giulio was the illegitimate son of Antoinetta del Cittadino and Giuliano (d. 1478), brother of Lorenzo the Magnificent. He was born posthumously and was raised in the household of his famous uncle. Leo X had him legitimized so that he could become a cardinal and ultimately a pope. At the conclave of 1523, it was Cardinal Pompeo Colonna (1479–1532) who cast the deciding vote in favor of Giulio.[114] Giulio became Pope Clement VII (1523–34); as a reward for his support, Cardinal Colonna received the Riario palace in Rome and the office of vice-chancellor.

At first, Clement VII supported the emperor Charles V, but he soon allied himself with the French king Frances I, who would be defeated by Charles at the Battle of Pavia on February 24, 1525. Furious at the pope's pro–French position, Charles V invaded Italy and sacked Rome in May 1527. Thousands of Romans were killed, and the pope was besieged in Castel Sant' Angelo. Clement VII surrendered and agreed to a humiliating treaty; he gave up Piacenza, Parma and Modena and paid the emperor 400,000 ducats.[115] Clement became a captive of the emperor for seven months. It was during this period of time that the city of Florence rebelled against Medici rule and declared itself a republic.

Clement VII and Charles V were reconciled, and the pope crowned the emperor in Bologna on February 27, 1530. In that same year, Charles promised to reconquer Florence for the Medici family, and the pope and Charles reclaimed that city for the House of Medici. Clement now made Alessandro de' Medici (his illegitimate son by a Nubian slave) into the first duke of Florence.[116] Thus the government remained in the hands of the papacy. Wishing to secure harmony with both the king of France and the Holy Roman emperor, Clement

married Lorenzo de' Medici's great-grand-daughter Caterina (the legitimate daughter of Lorenzo, Duke of Urbino, and Madeleine de la Tour d'Auvergne) to the French king's son. Caterina was to become the queen of France, wife of King Henry II. Clement himself performed the marriage ceremony.[117]

Clement's absorption in political matters and in advancing his family prevented him from dealing with the serious religious crises that prevailed in Europe in the sixteenth century. During the Protestant Reformation of this time, much of Germany and England were lost to the church. Pressured by the emperor Charles V, the pope defiantly refused to grant King Henry VIII of England a divorce from Catherine of Aragon (1485–1536), the emperor's aunt.

During his pontificate, Clement VII concerned himself primarily with the affairs of his family and with Florence.[118] His cousin Ippolito, who was the son of Giuliano, Duke of Nemours (the youngest son of Lorenzo de' Medici), had been appointed the governor of Florence in 1524 and then cardinal; in 1532, he had been nominated vice-chancellor of the church. Clement made his own debauched, illegitimate son Alessandro into the duke of Florence, keeping the legitimate heir, Lorenzino, of a cadet branch of the Medici family, from assuming any power. The pope appointed his cousin Cardinal Innocenzo Cibo regent of Florence when the duke needed to meet with the emperor in 1532. Upon the death of Clement VII in September 1534, family rivalries became evident.[119]

Duke Alessandro's tyrannical administration in Florence was an unpopular one, and there was a movement to place Cardinal Ippolito on the ducal throne. Ippolito was poisoned soon after, in 1535. To sustain himself as duke and to gain the support of the emperor, Alessandro married Margherita, the illegitimate daughter of Emperor Charles V. He and Margherita had no children, but Alessandro's own illegitimate children included the Admiral Giulio (d. 1600), Porzia and Giulia, wife of Bernardetto de' Medici, the brother of Pope Leo XI.[120]

Lorenzino de' Medici, who was descended from a brother of Cosimo *pater patriae*, became

his cousin Duke Alessandro's constant compan-
ion in a life devoted to orgies and whoring. But
while he was an ostensible friend and accomplice, he was also Alessandro's rival. Lorenzino
had become jealous of the power that had been
given to an illegitimate member of the Medici
clan. On the night of January 5, 1537, when
Alessandro was returning from a nighttime visit
with the wife of Leonardo Ginori, with whom
the duke was enamored, Lorenzino lured Alessandro to his home and there in hand-to-hand
combat killed him. The assassination brought
Florence into a state of turmoil. Lorenzino
claimed that he wanted to return Florence to
its old republican form of government. At this
juncture, it was the hope of Cardinal Innocenzo
Cibo, whose mother was Lorenzo the Magnificent's daughter, to become the next ruler of
Florence, but Cosimo de' Medici, descended
from a brother of Cosimo *pater patriae* as well
as from Lorenzo the Magnificent, emerged as
the leading de' Medici contender to govern
Florence[121] (see Table X). Cosimo was the son
of Lorenzo's granddaughter Maria Salviati.

Duke Cosimo (1519–74) assumed power by
defeating those that opposed him and by
viciously slaying hundreds of prisoners — as
well as anyone else he considered his enemy.
Cosimo I thus emerged as a forceful ruler of
Florence and was proclaimed the grand duke of
Tuscany in 1569. His granddaughter Maria de'
Medici married King Henry IV of France,
founder of the Bourbon dynasty. Cosimo's
descendants married into the major royal families of Europe (the Bourbons of France, Spain
and Parma and the Hapsburgs of Austria), into
prominent ducal families in Italy (the Gonzaga
of Mantua and d'Este of Modena) and into
papal dynasties (including the della Rovere and
Farnese). The last grand duke of the Medici
family was Gian Gastone, who died in 1737.
Gian Gastone had married Anna Maria,
daughter of the duke of Saxony-Lauenburg and
niece of Maria Benigna, wife of the great general Ottavio Piccolomini (d. 1656). The
Saxony-Lauenburgs belonged to a princely
German family related to the kings of Russia,
Denmark, Sweden and England.

Lorenzo de' Medici (1449–92), the progenitor of Medici greatness, was the father of a
pope, Leo X; the father-in-law of a pope's
(Innocent VIII) son; the uncle of a pope,
Clement VII; and the great-grandfather of a
pope, Leo XI. His descendants include the present king of Spain, the Grand duke of Luxem-
bourg, the prince of Liechtenstein, the king of
Belgium and the present representatives of the
royal houses of Austria, Bavaria, Italy, Bulgaria,
France and Portugal. From the Medici are
descended many of the princely houses of Italy,
including those of Prince Borghese, Prince
Aldobrandini and Prince Boncompagni-
Ludovisi.

The Medici family were to produce other
popes. Lorenzo the Magnificent's daughter
Lucrezia had married Iacopo Salviati, and they
had three children: Giovanni Salviati who was
a cardinal; Maria (d. 1543) who married Giovanni de' Medici and was the mother of Grand
Duke Cosimo I; and Francesca Salviati who
married Ottaviano de' Medici (d. 1546), a distant cousin descended from a brother of the
great-grandfather of Cosimo *pater patriae*. The
children of Francesca Salviati and Ottaviano
de' Medici were Bernardetto, husband of Giulia
de' Medici (the illegitimate daughter of Duke
Alessandro of Florence, whose descendants
became the dukes of Sarno and princes of
Ottai[j]ano) and Alessandro (1535–1605).
Alessandro was elected pope as Leo XI in 1605,
but served for only twenty-seven days. Pope
Leo XI, therefore, was a great-grandson of
Lorenzo the Magnificent and a first cousin of
Duke Cosimo I of Florence.[122] The Medici
dukes of Sarno and princes of Ottai(j)ano cur-
rently reside in Naples.

Another Medici pope was Pius IV
(1559–65), whose actual name was Giovanni
Angelo de' Medici of Marigano. It was often
the opinion of scholars that this Medici was
not related to the Medici of Florence, but
Pompeo Litta claims that Pope Pius IV and his
family were descended from Giambuono de'
Medici, a distant cousin of Cosimo *pater
patriae*.[123] This branch of the Medici family
will be delineated later in this chapter.

The Farnese (Farnesi) Family

A month after Pope Clement VII, a Medici, died on September 25, 1534, a member of the Farnese family, Alessandro, was elected Supreme Pontiff as Pope Paul III (1534–49). Clement had played a game of allying first with the emperor, then with the French king, then again with the emperor. He had witnessed the sack of Rome in 1527; had seen the spread of Protestantism in Europe and had left the papacy in disarray. Paul III, who had been educated in the home of Lorenzo de' Medici, the Magnificent, learned from his predecessor's mistakes. He was a shrewd diplomat who worked to insure neutrality between France and the empire.[124] Alessandro Farnese, in the years before ascending to the papacy, had been created a cardinal in 1493 by Pope Alexander VI Borgia, whose mistress at that time was Alessandro's sister Giulia.[125] Similar to Alexander VI, Paul III had several illegitimate children whom he indulged. Ironically, it was this same Paul III who keenly saw the need to place into motion the Council of Trent — which was to deal with doctrinal matters, clerical discipline and church abuses. He was also eager to combat heresy and thus approved the establishment of the Roman Inquisition.

As a Renaissance pope, he had enriched the Vatican Library, restored the University of Rome, persuaded Michelangelo to finish the fresco of "the Last Judgment" in the Sistine Chapel and to complete the designs for the new St. Peter's Basilica. He had also begun the construction of the Farnese Palace and the renovation of structures on Capitoline Hill and had strengthened the fortifications in Rome and the Papal States.[126] Paul, who was descended from a military family, fully realized the need to establish a strong defense system for protection.

The Farnese family of Pope Paul III was a distinguished one from Tuscany. It had extensive holdings southwest of Lake Bolsena — where, on Isola Bisentina, the family mausoleum was erected — between Peruga, Orvieto and the sea. Ranuccio Farnese, the pope's grandfather, was a condottiere (the captain of a band of mercenary soldiers) who had lead his

military forces into battle to defend the papal states. Pope Martin V had made Ranuccio a senator in 1417; and, by giving valuable assistance to Pope Eugene IV, Ranuccio had received a host of fiefdoms, including Cassano, Canino, Latera, Montalto and Valentano.[127] He acquired wealth and territory, establishing the power base for the Farnese family in both Rome and the Papal States. Ranuccio's children included Rosa "la Vannozza," mistress of Rodrigo Borgia (Pope Alexander VI): Gabriele, husband of Lella Orsini, daughter of the count of Pitigliano; Eugenia, wife of Stephano Colonna, Lord of Palestrina; and Pier Luigi, husband of Giovannella Caetani, a daughter of the lord of Sermoneta.[128] The Farnese family was thus related to the aristocracy of Rome, being connected to the Orsinis, Colonnas and Caetanis.

Alessandro Farnese was the son of Pier Luigi Farnese and Giovannella Caetani. His sister was Giulia, the lover of Pope Alexander VI Borgia; his brother Angelo became the husband of Lella Orsini; and his brother Bartolomeo inherited Montalto, a family fief. While a cardinal, Alessandro kept a mistress — probably more than one — and had at least four children, whose names were Pier Luigi, Paolo, Ranuccio and Costanza. There may have also been another daughter, Lucrezia. (Litta is not sure if Lucrezia was the daughter of Alessandro or of his brother Bartolomeo). Pier Luigi and Paolo were legitimatized by Pope Julius II on July 8, 1505.[129] Ranuccio's "deed of legitimation" was issued by Pope Leo X in 1518.

As for the mistresses of Cardinal Alessandro, Litta reports that Farnese had loved a certain Ruffina, a Roman aristocrat. Another source indicates that her given name was Lola. Others have thought that his beloved was from the Bernieri family of Parma. It is said that the cardinal sent his lover to have her baby in Rome, where Pier Luigi Farnese was indeed born on November 19, 1503. Pastor presents similar information about the mistresses of Paul III. Pastor's documents show that one of Cardinal Alessandro Farnese's mistresses belonged to the aristocracy and that she lived in the cardinal's house in the Arenula section of Rome. It appears that his daughter Costanza's mother was from Bolsena. She was probably born of a different mother from her brothers, and she was not legitimatized.[130]

Regarding Alessandro's other two children, Ranuccio (d. 1529) and Paolo, Litta states that Ranuccio (who was very dear to the pope) married Virginia Pallavicino and that Paolo died soon after 1527. In 1513 Cardinal Farnese reformed his private life, giving up his mistresses and devoting himself to the church and his children. It was Pier Luigi and Costanza who were to receive the most benefits when their father became pope in 1534, and it was their descendants who were to marry into so many prominent royal and noble European families.

Pope Paul III was devoted to Pier Luigi in spite of his son's immoral conduct. No one would dare suggest that the pope should reprimand his son. The pope centered much of his life on providing gifts and favors to Pier Luigi and Pier Luigi's children, Ottavio (d. 1586), Cardinal Alessandro II (d. 1589) and Orazio (d. 1553). Much of what happened during the pontificate of Paul III revolved around the activities of his son and grandsons.

At the age of sixteen, Pier Luigi married Gerolama, daughter of Lodovico Orsini, Count of Pitigliano. Pier Luigi became a soldier of fortune, much like that of his great-grandfather, and he joined the imperialist forces and participated in the sack of Rome, robbing and taking a substantial amount of precious items. Pier Luigi engaged in several military campaigns for personal gains before his father was elected Supreme Pontiff. Litta described Pier Luigi in these terms: "and it was this Pier Luigi, completely dissolute, with advanced syphilis, drunkard, debauchee, libertine, son of the Pope, [who] became the most potent personage in Rome."[131]

When Farnese became the pope, one of his first acts was to name both his fourteen-year-old grandson Alessandro II Farnese and his fifteen-year-old grandson Guido Ascanio Sforza (son of the pope's daughter Costanza) as cardinals and to bestow rich benefices on them. During the reign of Paul III, Pier Luigi was to

assist his father in papal military campaigns, and Cardinal Alessandro II was to serve skillfully in diplomatic undertakings to keep the military forces of the king of France and the emperor away from the Papal States. Alessandro II maintained a state of peace and cooperation between the Kingdoms so that the Council of Trent could constructively take place.[132]

The pope duly rewarded his grandsons. Cardinal Alessandro II received the bishoprics of Parma, Avignon and Tours, and with his wealth he constructed the church of Gesù in Rome and an impressive villa in Caprarola. Guido Ascanio Sforza became papal legate to Bologna and Romagna, treasurer of the Holy See and patriarch of Alexandria. With his fortune, he commissioned Michelangelo to do the chapel of the Assumption in the Basilica of Santa Maria Maggiore.[133]

The pope also rewarded Pier Luigi, appointing him as *gonfaloniere* (standard-bearer) of the church in Italy, the duke of Castro and other territories and the count of Pitigliano. With money from the Apostolic Camera, Nepi was purchased for Pier Luigi in 1538. And on February 27, 1538, the Emperor Charles V made the pope's son the marchese of Novarra, which brought Pier Luigi an income of 15,000 scudi annually. The fiefdom of Cervara was purchased for him from the Savelli family, as well as Capo di Monte, Visenzo di Tesco, Pignena, Mozano, Pianzano, Arlena and Civitella. The Vatican then sold Valerano, Corchiano, Fabbrica, Borghetto and Acquasparta to the duke.[134]

But Pier Luigi was not content. He wanted to rule a principality — a sizeable domain — and he thought that Milan might become his state. But the emperor only considered giving Milan to Ottavio, Pier Luigi's son and the husband of the emperor's daughter. Ottavio had already been given Camerino, which the pope had confiscated from the Varano family and presented to his grandson. Finally in 1545, when Charles V decided to cede Parma and Piacenza (which was considered to be part of the state of Milan) to Ottavio, the pope established it as a dukedom, a vassalage of the Papal States, for his son Pier Luigi. To appease Ottavio, the pope proclaimed him the duke of Castro and the captain of the Church; at the same time, Nepi and Camerino were returned to the church; and Pier Luigi was to pay 9,000 ducats in gold to Rome for this transaction. The emperor, however, would not ratify this papal bull.[135]

In any event, Pier Luigi turned all of his attention to making Piacenza into a ducal city. His accomplishments were truly impressive — apparently the position of duke made him become more noble in his pursuits. The senate building and the stairs of the public palazzo were redone. He brought order to the area, created an effective administration and judicial system and worked to improve the region's agricultural and industrial production. He also built an impressive citadel to fortify the city. The duke insisted that the nobles abandon their castles to live in the city and become part of the ducal court. To achieve this end, he usurped the castles of the Pallavicini, Sforza, Gonzaga and other noble families.[136] Not surprisingly in the process, Pier Luigi incurred the ire of the Parmesan aristocracy. He made many enemies as he asserted his "territorial authority."[137] A plot was soon hatched to destroy the duke.

The imperial governor of Milan, Don Ferrante Gonzaga, had been in contact both with the emperor Charles V, who had never recognized Pier Luigi as the duke of Parma and Piacenza and with conspirators in Piacenza who hated the duke. The emperor agreed to Gonzaga's plan to retake the dukedom and rid the city of Pier Luigi Farnese, but at the same time he demanded that the life of the duke be spared. This cabal, instigated by Gonzaga, involved Camillo and Alessandro Pallavicini, Agostino Landi, Gianluigi Confalonieri and Giovanni Anguissola, who were all of local nobility. The duke was completely unaware of any plot against him. After they had lunch on September 10, 1547, as Pier Luigi and Anguissola were going to the duke's chamber, Anguissola stabbed him with a dagger, while the other conspirators subdued the guards. To show the populace that the duke was actually dead, the conspirators threw the bleeding corpse of Pier

Luigi from a window into a trench below, and the murderers screamed "Liberty for our Country." Two days later, imperial forces led by Gonzaga took Piacenza, but the emperor Charles V also wanted Parma. Pier Luigi's son Ottavio refused to accept the loss of either city. In order to prevent the occupation of Parma by imperial forces, the pope had the governor general of the church, Camillo Orsini, take possession of it.[138]

To pacify the emperor, Paul III decided to have Parma and Piacenza returned to the church, revoking the Farnese dukedom, and to compensate Ottavio with the lordship of Camerino — but Ottavio rejected this proposal. The pope was furious at his grandson's disobedience, especially after he learned that his trusted other grandson, Cardinal Alexander II Farnese, his namesake and advisor, was Ottavio's accomplice in the plan not to relinquish that territory. The pope called for his grandson, the cardinal, to come to his chamber. "Brief was their conversation," writes Litta, "but terrible. It soon became a quarrel and when his indignation reached its climax, Paul III ripped the beret from the head of the cardinal and threw it on the floor. The emotions that the eighty-year-old pontiff felt were such that being out of breath he collapsed."[139] He was helped up and immediately put to bed. The upheaval caused by the ingratitude of his family brought about the pope's death. But before dying, he ordered that Parma, which was in the possession of papal forces under Camillo Orsini, be delivered over to Ottavio.[140]

Paul III was a pope who had achieved remarkable heights. His accomplishments to maintain the peace between the French and the Holy Roman Empire and his ability to convoke and steer the Council of Trent testified to Paul's being "magnanimous." As a nepotist, however, he was equally magnanimous, and he was certainly not without his faults. During his reign, for example, there were astrologers in the papal court whom he relied on. Both the pope and Pier Luigi were extremely superstitious. At one point Pier Luigi had consulted an astrologer who predicted, basing his analysis on the conjunction of Jupiter and Saturn, that he would live to be seventy years of age and die a natural death.[141] It would have been equally difficult for Paul III's astrologer to foretell what would happen to the dukedom of Parma and Piacenze when the old pope died.

After the death of Paul III, a close colleague, Cardinal Giovanni del Monte, was elected as Pope Julius III (1550–55) after a ten-week conclave. Upon his accession to the pontifical throne, he permitted Ottavio Farnese the right to claim Parma, and Ottavio, the second Duke, entered that city on February 22, 1550. Still, the emperor remained firm against the Farnese acquisition of that territory, offering Ottavio the state of Camerino in its stead. Since Ottavio was still the standard-bearer of the church, the captain general of the church and a vassal of the Holy See, he was not in a position to negotiate with a foreign power; but he did not want to exchange Parma for Camerino. The duke also knew that he needed military assistance to combat the forces of Charles V. He felt compelled to seek assistance from Henry II, King of France. Two parties went to war — the duke of Parma, joined by France, and the emperor, joined by Pope Julius III.[142] At the conclusion of the war, an accord was reached whereby Charles V reluctantly recognized Ottavio Farnese as duke of Parma.

Wisely, Ottavio worked to heal the breach with his enemies, the emperor and the pope — his aim was to secure Piacenza as well. In this effort, Ottavio sent his representatives to speak to Philip II, King of Spain, son of Charles V, about this matter. Ottavio was helped by his wife, Margherita. Margherita was the half sister to Philip II, and she had helped her brother govern Flanders from 1559 to 1568. (Margherita has the distinction of being the illegitimate daughter of the emperor Charles V; the wife first of Alessandro de' Medici, Duke of Florence and illegitimate son of Pope Clement VII; and then the wife of Ottavio Farnese, son of Pier Luigi Farnese, son of Pope Paul III). Later, Ottavio's son Alessandro (1545–92), the third Duke, became one of the king's principal generals, serving Spain in its military campaigns in the Netherlands. The assistance thus rendered by Ottavio Farnese's relatives placated Philip II,

and in 1556 he finally ceded Piacenza to Ottavio. The duke's tenacity had been well-served, and he brought an orderly government to both Parma and Piacenza.[143]

In 1552, when Pope Julius III waged war against Ottavio, he forfeited the rich benefices of Cardinal Alessandro II Farnese (Ottavio's brother) and Cardinal Ranuccio Farnese (1530–65) (Ottavio's son), and he deposed Orazio Farnese (brother of Ottavio and husband of Diana, the natural daughter of King Henry II of France) as the duke of Castro.[144] When Pope Julius lost the war, the Farnese cardinals resumed their positions of eminence in the church, and Castro was returned to Orazio who died soon after in 1553.

The Farnese family gave eight dukes to Parma and Piacenza, and the family played a vital role as a major papal dynasty. The last Farnese duke died in 1731, and the dukedom was inherited by his niece Elisabetta Farnese (1692–1766), who married King Philip V, the first Bourbon king of Spain. Their descendants, through separate branches of the family descended from the two sons of Philip and Elisabetta, became kings of Spain and dukes of Parma and Piacenza. Elisabetta Farnese, a direct descendant of Pope Paul III, became the ancestor of the present king of Spain, King Juan Carlos (who is eight generations removed from this Farnese queen), the present ruler of Luxemburg, Grand Duke Jean, and the current pretenders to the throne of Portugal, Austria, France, Bulgaria and other royal houses. The Farneses married into such prominent Italian dynasties as the della Rovere (dukes of Urbino) and the d'Este (dukes of Modena) (see Table X).

The Farnese and Sforza Families

The Farnese family of Parma and Piacenza had numerous cousins who belonged to the Sforza family. Pier Luigi Farnese's sister, Costanza, married Bosio II Sforza, Count of Santa Fiora. Bosio was related to the Sforza dukes of Milan; in fact, his great-granduncle was Francesco Sforza (1401–1466), the first Sforza duke of Milan. Bosio II (d. 1535) was named by his father-in-law, Pope Paul III, as captain of the guard. Paul III by his bull of May 14, 1534, extended vast privileges to the descendants of Bosio and Costanza, including fiefdoms in Lombardia and Emilia such as the marquisate of Proceno.[145] Of their eight children, two were cardinals: Guido Ascanio (1518–64) and Alessandro (1534–81); four were military leaders: Sforza (1520–75), Carlo (1524–71), Marco (1530–91) and Paolo (1535–97); and two married into prominent noble families: Francesca, wife of Girolamo Orsini, and Giulia, wife of Sforza Pallavicino.[146]

A life within the Catholic hierarchy had been sought by two sons of Bosio II and Costanza Farnese. Guido Ascanio Sforza, their oldest son, played a significant role during the pontificate of his grandfather. His brother Cardinal Alessandro Sforza served as the bishop of Parma (1530–73) and was an authoritative member of the Council of Trent. He was proclaimed cardinal in 1565, papal legate to Bologna and Romagna and then legate to all the pontifical states to root out robbery. His powers were such that he was called "vice pope."[147]

Another son Sforza (1520–75), a military captain, obtained the earldom of Castel S. Giovanni and the marquisate of Castell'Arquato from his cousin Duke Ottavio Farnese of Parma. Sforza's son Francesco (1562–1624) combined both military and religious careers. He served first as captain general of the military forces fighting in the Low Countries with his cousin Alessandro Farnese, third Duke of Parma. Then, in 1583, Francesco Sforza was appointed a cardinal by Pope Gregory XIII, becoming the bishop of Albano, and then of Frascati, and later becoming legate to Romagna.[148] His sister Costanza (d. 1617) was the wife of Giacomo Boncompagni, son of Pope Gregory XIII. Their descendants were plentiful and will be enumerated under the Boncompagni Dynasty.

Sforza's brother, Mario Sforza (1530–91), Count of San Fiora, married Fulvia Conti, the heiress of Giambattista, the last Count of Segni of the Conti family (which had given the papacy Pope Innocent III). Mario and

Fulvia had a son Federico (1548–81) who became the lord of Segni, Valmontone and Lugnano. Segni and Valmontone had long been the territories of the Conti family, and they were acquired by the Sforzas. Of Federico's three children, his son, Alessandro (1572–1631), was created the duke of Segni in 1585 by Pope Sixtus V;[149] his daughter Ersila married Francesco Colonna, Prince of Palestrina; and his daughter Francesca (1573–1621) was the wife of Alessandro Pallavicino. Francesca and Alessandro were the parents of Pietro Sforza-Pallavicino (1607–1667), who pursued an ecclesiastical career. For the papacy, he served as governor of Iesi, Orvieto and Camerino. In 1659 he was made a cardinal by Pope Alexander VII. Cardinal Pallavicino served as the pope's advisor. He wrote *The History of the Council of Trent*, a highly controversial history of that event.[150]

Alessandro Sforza (1572–1631), uncle of Cardinal Pallavicino, married Eleonora Orsini. Eleonora was the daughter of Paolo Giordano Orsini, Duke of Bracciano, and Isabella, daughter of Grand duke Cosimo I de' Medici. Paolo Giordano Orsini was the grandson of Felice della Rovere, daughter of Pope Julius II. Eleonora's great-grandmother was Maria Salviati, granddaughter of Lorenzo de' Medici, the Magnificent.[151] Eleonora was, therefore, a cousin of the Medici popes, Leo X, Clement VII and Leo XI. She was also a first cousin of Maria de' Medici, queen of King Henry IV, the Bourbon king of France whose descendants became the crown heads of Catholic Europe.

The grandson of Alessandro Sforza and Eleonora Orsini, Federico Sforza (1651–1712), Duke of Segni, married Livia Cesarini, heiress of the Savelli and Cesarini families and their descendants, the dukes of Segni and the counts of Santa Fiora, who acquired the surname Sforza-Cesarini. The Cesarini family had long been associated with the Holy See and were related to Roman nobility. The Cesarinis had given the church three cardinals: Giuliano Cesarini (1398–1444); Alessandro Cesarini, senior (d. 1542); and Alessandro Cesarini, junior (1590–1644). Members of the Cesarini also included Giorgio, apostolic protonotary, and the Marchese Giuliano I (1491–1564), *gonfaloniere* in Rome. The Cesarinis had accumulated much of its wealth from their marriages with the heiresses of the Colonna, Borgia, Farnese, Orsini, Caetani and Savelli families, who brought with them lucrative dowries. (Refer to Tables 5a and 5b in Appendix A).

Livia, who was the eldest daughter of Giuliano Cesarini III, Count of Celano, was slated to be a nun in the order of the Sette Dolori and had become an oblate. Her sister Clerica was expected to inherit the Cesarini fortune; Clerica had married Filippo Colonna, Prince of Sonnino. Federico Sforza seduced the young Livia, forcing her to leave the convent. He married her much to the fury of the Colonna family and their ally King Louis XIV of France. The Sacra Romana Rota, the high tribunal for the Roman Catholic Church, decided in Livia's favor, and her oblate did not impede either her marriage to Sforza or her receiving the Cesarini inheritance.[152]

Livia and Federico's son Gaetano (1674–1727), Duke of Segni, married Vittoria Conti, daughter of Giuseppe Conti of Poli and his wife Lucrecia Colonna. Vittoria was a niece of Pope Innocent XIII. Gaetano and Vittoria's son was Duke Guiseppe Sforza-Cesarini (1705–1744), who was the father of (1) Duke Filippo (1717–64); (2) Duke Gaetano II (1728–76), first protonotary and papal commissioner to Perugia and captain of the pontifical cavalry; (3) Sisto (1730–1802) head of the branch of the family that called itself Sforza Cabrera Bovadilla, Counts of Celano; and (4) Vittoria, wife of Antonio Boncompagni.[153] It was during this time that the Sforza-Cesarini family was considered among the first in Rome and in Italy. They and their Farnese cousins had one thing in common: they all had the same ancestor, a pope, the "magnanimous" Paul III.

The Sforza family illustrates how the aristocracy in Italy lived during the sixteenth and early seventeenth centuries in Italy. It was a period of time for Italian nobility to enter either the military or the clergy. Members of the Colonna, Sforza and Orsini families, and later the Farnese, became the leaders of troops, which sided at various times with the empire,

France, Spain or the Papal States in an ever-revolving fashion and in various combinations as a way to gain power and possessions. As one observer wrote in 1647: "Virginio Orsini was a Spaniard and on his palace he had the arms of the Catholic King. When his son died he became a Frenchman and shortly afterwards a Spaniard once more; at present he is French again — for how long no one knows." Other sons in the same families entered the ecclesiastical life. The aspiration was to be appointed a cardinal and to receive lucrative benefices. The greatest prize of all was the papacy itself. The aristocracy had a further need. In order to sustain wealth, it was necessary to marry an heiress (thus members of the Sforza family of Santa Fiora had married into the Conti and Cesarini families) or to ally by matrimony with wealthy papal dynasties (thus Bosio II Sforza took Costanza Farnese as his wife). It should be further noted that during the seventeenth century these marriages became increasingly important as Italian captains and military leaders were no longer needed, limiting the occupational choices of the Roman barons.[154] The late seventeenth and early eighteenth centuries witnessed a decline among these families, which went into serious debt and had to sell their territories. This period will be explained in succeeding chapters.

One of the great scandals in the Sforza-Cesarini family occurred in 1832 when Duke Salvatore Sforza-Cesarini died, and his sister Anna and her husband Marino Torlonia tried to deprive a younger brother Lorenzo (legitimate son of Duke Francesco and his wife Geltrude de' Conti) of his inheritance. Claiming that the Cesarini estate belonged to Salvatore's next of kin (his older sister), Anna and her husband appealed to the Sacra Romana Rota to keep Lorenzo from receiving any of the Sforza-Cesarini inheritance. In 1854 the Rota decided in Lorenzo's favor so that the entire Sforza-Cesarini inheritance became his, and he was proclaimed duke of Segni.[155] Lorenzo (1807–1866) became both a deputy and senator in the newly created kingdom of Italy. He was a staunch supporter of the policy of Italian independence advocated by Cavour. He married

Lady Caroline Shirley of England and had two sons, Francesco, who became the duke of Segni, and Bosio, Count of Santa Fiora. These titles had been inherited from the Conti and Sforza families, so eminent in Italian and papal history.[156]

The Sforza-Conti-Cesarini family represented the legacy of several papal dynasties — the Conti, the Farnese (which had married into the Sforza of S. Fiora family) and the Savelli (which had united with the Cesarini clan). The heiress of the Cesarini brought the Savelli inheritance to the Sforzas in a matrimonial alliance.[157]

The Sforza-Cesarinis were all descended from a common ancestor, Pope Paul III (Alessandro Farnese). This pope had assisted the fortune of his son-in-law Bosio II's family, the Sforzas of Santa Fiora and for his son Pier Luigi, he had created a dukedom. But he was also the ancestor of another inheritance which affected the church itself. Pope Paul III had numerous descendants who contributed to the hierarchy of the Catholic Church. Descended from him were four Farnese and four Sforza cardinals, including that pope's chief advisors, Cardinal Alessandro Farnese II (1520–89) and Guido Ascanio Sforza (1618–54). Pope Paul's great-granddaughter Violante Farnese was the wife of Torquato Conti of Poli, and they were the forebears of four Conti cardinals, including one Michelangelo Conti who assumed the pontifical throne as Innocent XIII (1721–24). He was the direct descendant of Paul III.

Another great-granddaughter of that pope, Ersilia Farnese, married Renato Borromeo, nephew of Gilberto, brother-in-law of Pope Pius IV. Future generations of that family were to produce four Borromeo cardinals. The grandson of Ersilia and Renato was Cardinal Federico Borromeo (1617–73), who became the patriarch of Alexandria and the governor of Rome (in 1666). He was elevated in 1670 as secretary of state of Pope Clement X (1670–76). These Farnese, Sforza, Conti and Borromeo descendants of Pope Paul III were to attain influential and pivotal positions in the Roman Curia and in church affairs long after the death of Pope Paul III.

IV: The Renaissance Comes to a Close

The del Monte Family

When Pope Paul III died in 1549, there was a conclave that lasted ten weeks and took fifty-two ballots. The pro–French forces aligned with the Farnese cardinals to elect Giovanni Maria Ciocchi del Monte, named Pope Julius III (1550–55). He was the nephew of Cardinal Antonio del Monte, camerlengo in 1514, who had gone with Pope Clement VII to celebrate the marriage of his niece Caterina de' Medici to King Henry II of France.

"The pernicious tradition of the Renaissance Popes was also repeatedly followed by Julius III, in the promotion of his relatives."[158] A cousin Pietro del Monte was made governor of Castel Sant' Angelo. Several nephews — Cristoforo del Monte, Fulvio della Corgna and Roberto de'Nobili — were also nominated cardinals.

Julius III's brother Baldovino received the Borgia apartment as his lodging and then the Palazzo dell'Aquila. He was appointed governor of Spoleto and declared lord of Monte San Savino (which included the territories of Aretino, Gargonza, Palazzuolo, Verniana and Alberoli in Tuscany). Monte San Savino was secured from Duke Cosimo de' Medici. Baldovino was also given the territory of Camerino for life.[159] Baldovino's son Giovanni Battista was named *gonfaloniere* of the church and received the feudal territory of Nepi, but he died in 1552. Thus the male line of the del Monte family became extinct.[160] However, Baldovino's natural son Fabiano had been legitimized in 1552 by the pope, and he became the count of Monte San Savino. Fabiano married Vittoria, daughter of Jacopo Appiani, Lord of Piombino. This marriage was never consummated; and so, after Fabiano's death in 1570, Monte San Savino was returned to the Medici family.[161]

The pope's sister Jacopa was the wife of Francis della Corgna. One of their sons Fulvio was appointed a cardinal and the other, Ascanio, became a marchese and commander of the papal guards. After Ascanio died, his widow Francesca, daughter of Federico Sforza, Count of S. Fiora (related to the Farnese and Conti families), married Alessandro, Marchese Pallavicino of Zibello. Jacopa's sister Ludovica married Roberto de'Nobili; one of their grand-children was a cardinal, and another, Caterina, grandniece of the pope, married Sforza Sforza (1520–75). Their daughter Costanza married the son of Pope Gregory XIII.

One of Julius III's most disastrous exhibi-tions of nepotism occurred when the pope had his brother adopt a certain Innocenzo, a truly contemptible teenager. Innocenzo was the keeper of monkeys that had belonged to del Monte before he became pope. This youth was given the name Innocenzo del Monte, and it was "very probable that he was the son of the pope because so much care and affection for such a depraved person could not be otherwise explained. Julius III even raised him to the car-dinalate, making a mockery of the Sacred Col-lege, and entrusted him with the Secretary of State, just a nominal appointment, as he was in reality unable to deal with the affairs of this position."[162] Julius III promoted Innocenzo as cardinal to St. Zeno in Verona. He became the papal legate to Bologna and was appointed sec-retary of state. He was incapable of serving in that capacity, but pocketed church revenues. He had an income of 12,000 crowns. Inno-cenzo del Monte was nicknamed "Monkey" by the Romans because of his association with that primate. His behavior was often strange and erratic, and he was to routinely embarrass the pope, the Curia, and the church. A later pontiff, Pope Pius IV, jailed him in Castel Sant' Angelo after he had killed two people. His benefices were taken away, and Pope Pius V had him removed as a cardinal. In 1561 he was fined 100,000 scudi. Innocenzo del Monte died in disgrace at the age of forty-six.[163]

Julius III was a pope who enjoyed parties and theatre, and his reign was a frivolous one. He had fought a useless war with Ottavio Far-nese over Parma with great financial loss to the Holy See. While he reconvened the Council of Trent in 1551, it was indefinitely suspended a year later and succeeded in doing very little. This second session established the doctrines of

the Eucharist, confession and extreme unction. It also dealt with the issue of improving the way the members of the clergy conducted themselves.[164]

While he helped to embellish Rome by con-structing S. Andrea della Via Flaminia and the gardens of the Villa Giulio, where he spent much of his time, the city itself was now at the end of the Renaissance period. His was a pontificate that "had left no profound mark" on the church.[165] One of Julius' few accom-plishments was his recognition of the talents of the composer Palestrina, whom he made choir-master of the Cappella Giulia.

After Julius III's death in 1555, Marcello Cervini was elected pope as Marcellus II; but he reigned for less than twenty-two days.

The Carafa Family (Part One)

Rigid, arrogant, intolerant, dogmatic and unfriendly, the intensely disliked Giampietro Carafa, of a noble family in the kingdom of Naples (Two Sicilies), was unexpectedly elected pope in 1555 after the brief reign of Pope Mar-cellus II. Giampietro, who became Pope Paul IV, was inclined to believe that his election was a miracle ignited by the fires of the Holy Spirit. His was a severe regime: placing renewed emphasis on the Roman Inquisition, headed by his friend Michele Ghislieri, whom he made a cardinal; creating the Index of Forbidden Books; and forcing the Jews into Roman ghet-tos. Paul IV was a pope of reform, and he wished to curb the excesses of the clergy — especially the extravagant lifestyle of many car-dinals who had received bountiful benefices. As a result of his dictatorial manner regarding doctrine, he placed the saintly Cardinal Gio-vanni Morone into the prison of Castel Sant' Angelo.

Paul IV's driving hatred for Spain and its Hapsburg rulers brought about a war in which the pope was totally and ignominiously defeated. He was advised and often dominated by his nephew — the corrupt and debauched Cardinal Carlo Carafa, who played a vital role in pro-voking Spain to war. Designated secretary of state by his uncle, Carlo was given the legation of Bologna with a stipend of 8,000 ducats in 1555; the year after he was given control of the government of Ancona and presented with the bishopric of Comminges. The pope also favored another unworthy nephew, Giovanni, Count of Montorio, who also obtained numerous benefits from the pope, including the dukedom of Paliano (which was taken from the Colonna family).

Paul IV was warned about the profligacies of his nephews, but being stubborn and imperial, he refused to listen until their conduct became unbearable even to him. It was then with equal severity that he dismissed them in January 1559 and refused to see them. Repulsed by their excessive abuses of authority, Paul IV exclaimed upon their removal, according to Litta, that "only now can we and should we say that this is the first year of our pontificate!" (*Ora sì, che possiamo e dobbiamo dire del nostro pontificato, anno primo!*) But it was already too late; Paul IV Carafa died in August 1559.[166]

The criminal trials of Cardinal Carlo Carafa and Duke Giovanni Carafa will follow in the discussion of Pope Pius IV.

PIUS IV AND THE CARAFA TRIAL

By using his influence with members of the Curia, Cardinal Carlo Carafa was instrumental in the selection of the next pope — a decision he was soon to regret. Giovanni Angelo de' Medici of Marignano was now elected to the papacy, becoming Pope Pius IV (1559–65). It was often the opinion of scholars that this Medici was not related to the Medici of Florence,[167] but Pompeo Litta claims that Pius IV and his family were descended from Giambuono de' Medici, a distant cousin of Cosimo, *pater patriae*.[168] Pius IV had received permission from Duke Cosimo I de' Medici to use the Medici coat of arms: golden balls on a red field.

Giovanni Angelo de' Medici was one of the many children of Bernardino de' Medici and Cecilia Serbelloni. His older brother was the skilled military leader Gian Giacomo, the Marchese of Marignano (1495–1555), who

married Marzia (d. 1548), a daughter of Lodovico Orsini, Count of Pitigliano. Lodivico's second wife was Vittoria, daughter of Lodovico Frangipane-della Tolfa and Elisabetta Carafa, sister of Pope Paul IV, whom Pius IV succeeded. Lodovico Orsini's sister Lella had married Angelo Farnese, the brother of Pope Paul III (1534–49), and another daughter of Ludovico, Girolama, had become the spouse of Pier Luigi Farnese, Duke of Parma (d. 1547), the son of Pope Paul III.[169]

When Gian Giacomo de' Medici of Marignano married into the Orsini family, it helped elevate the importance of his brother Giovanni Angelo in the eyes of Paul III, who made him the archbishop of Ragusa in 1545 and then a cardinal in 1549. Paul III and Giovanni Angelo became close friends, and both men had illegitimate children. Paul III's children were to play an eminent role during his pontificate, but little is known of Giovanni Angelo's three offspring. One was a son born in 1541 or 1542; he also had two daughters.[170]

Pope Paul III and his protégé, Pius IV, had much in common. They were both keenly aware of the need to bring the church together by reforming it. Paul III established the foundation for the Council of Trent in 1545 in an attempt to modify church abuses. During the pontificate of Pius, that council was brought to a conclusion on December 4, 1563, at its twenty-fifth and final session. The decrees of the council were formally delineated in the papal bull, *Benedictus Deus*, of 1564. These were the principal accomplishments of Pius' reign, and much of his success as Supreme Pontiff was due to his nephew Carlo (Charles) Borromeo (1538–84), son of Gilberto Borromeo, Count of Arona, and Magherita de' Medici, sister of the pope. Carlo Borromeo served as Pius' secretary of state and administered the Papal States.[171]

The pope's love for Carlo was exceedingly strong. He made his nephew a cardinal in 1560 and had him named head of the Abbey of Arona, archbishop of Milan, legate to Bologna, protector of Portugal and Lower Germany and protector of the Franciscans, the Carmelites and other religious orders. His revenue came to 48,000 scudi annually.

Pius was also generous to Carlo's younger brother Federico Borromeo (1533–62), who was made captain general of the church and prince of Oria. In 1560 he married Virginia della Rovere (1544–71), the daughter of Duke Guidabaldo of Urdino, great-grandnephew of Pope Julius II (Giuliano della Rovere), and the duke's wife, Giulia da Varano. Giulia was the daughter of Giovanni Maria da Varano and Caterina Cibo. Caterina was the granddaughter of Pope Innocent VIII (Giambattista Cibo) and the niece of Pope Leo X (Giovanni de' Medici). By marrying Virginia della Rovere, Federico had, of course, compounded the interrelationships between papal families.

Other relatives and friends of the pope also received church positions. All the sons of Gian Pietro Serbelloni, the pope's uncle, were rewarded: Gian Antonio Serbelloni was created a cardinal in 1560, along with Carlo Borromeo; Gian Battista Serbelloni became captain of Castel Sant' Angelo; Gabrio was appointed Captain of the papal guard; and Fabrizio Serbelloni was sent on missions for the pope.[172] Friends also received the pope's largess. In 1559 Duke (later Grand duke) Cosimo I of Florence, who had vigorously supported Cardinal Giovanni Angelo de' Medici in the papal election, was rewarded by the newly elected pope. Pius IV conferred the cardinalate on the duke's seventeen-year-old son, Giovanni.

Pius IV had many relatives to honor with titles and positions. His sister Chiara had married Wolfgang Dietrich von Hohenems, who was appointed governor of the Papal States. The Emperor Ferdinand I had made that family counts of the Empire. One of Chiara and Wolfgang's sons, Mark Sittich von Hohenems (1533–95), became the bishop of Cassano and later the bishop of Constance. In 1561 he too was created a cardinal. Later he served as papal legate at the Council of Trent. From the cardinal's natural son Robert were descended the Altemps (a branch of the family had assumed that name in Italy), who became the dukes of Gallese.[173]

One of the most extravagant pageants in the reign of Pius took place when Ortensia Borromeo married Jacopo Annibale d'Altemps, another son of Chiara and Wolfgang Dietrich von Hohenems. Jacopo Annibale was nominated count of Gallarate by King Philip II of Spain. Ortensia was the daughter of Gilberto Borromeo, Count of Arona, and his second wife. She was a half sister of the pope's beloved nephew Carlo Borromeo. The pope proposed a dowry of 100,000 for Ortensia. To commemorate the wedding, there was a spectacular tournament, which took place at the Belvedere Theatre in 1565 with over 6,000 spectators. Later a banquet and lavish ball for 1,000 guests in an elaborately decorated setting were held for the couple.

The pope's Borromeo nieces — the sisters of Carlo and Federico — also married into prominent families. Camilla (d. 1583) married Cesare Gonzaga, Count of Gustalla, Prince of Ariano; Geronima (d. 1580) became the wife of Fabrizio Gesualdo, Prince of Venosa; and Anna (d. 1582) married Fabrizio, son of Marcantonio Colonna.[174]

The latter, Anna Borromeo, was considered a papal heiress; papal wealth would be her inheritance. Since the treasury of the Holy See had become one of the prime sources of fortifying Italian aristocracy, it is no wonder that Fabrizio Colonna married this girl, only eleven years old at the time. It was obvious to the Colonna family that she should be snatched as young as possible, before some other family received her in matrimony. The Colonnas were anxious for these close ties with the papacy of Pius IV, anticipating as a result of this union that the pontiff would have the church return their family fiefdom of Paliano to them.

The Colonna family had been deprived of Paliano by Pope Paul IV (Giampietro Carafa, 1555–59), who had given it to his nephew Giovanni. Paul had placed the administration of the Vatican in the hands of his other corrupt and immoral nephew, Cardinal Carlo Carafa, who had made a great number of enemies among the cardinals.[175] The Carafa family was hated, and after the death of Carlo and Giovanni's uncle, the pope, revenge was sought.

Thus, it was during the pontificate of Pius IV that Cardinal Carlo and his brother Giovanni Carafa were brought to trial for numerous offenses, including murder. Giovanni had had his pregnant wife Violante d'Alife killed because he believed that she had been unfaithful to him; she had protested her innocence "with her dying breath."[176] Cardinal Carlo Carafa, who knew about the planned murder, was implicated too. The cardinal was also accused of causing a war with Spain that had depleted the papal treasury. Finally, both brothers were charged with high treason. The pope received daily reports of the hearings, which were conducted by biased judges; and even though several cardinals and the king of Spain intervened in behalf of Cardinal Carlo Carafa, the crimes were so heinous that both brothers were found guilty of the charges and condemned to death and their wealth was confiscated. Giovanni was beheaded; Cardinal Carlo, once the powerful ruler of Rome under his uncle, was strangled in his prison cell on March 4, 1561.[177]

Another nephew of Pope Paul IV, Cardinal Alfonso Carafa, Archbishop of Naples and President of the Apostolic Camera, was brought to trial, but he was found innocent of any wrongdoing. Nevertheless, he was fined 100,000 gold scudi. His sister Agnese had once been destined to be the wife of the duke of Ferrara, but when the family's fortune fell so precipitously, she became a nun.[178] The Carafa properties were regained by the church, and Paliano was returned to the Colonna family.[179] Certainly these events and the Carafa verdict made a pronounced statement against the papal nepotism that had been so much in evidence during the previous ninety years under the della Rovere, Borgia, Medici and Farnese popes. The aim of the ecclesiastical court was to bring an end to the creation of principalities, carved out of the papal states, for the pope's relatives.[180] It was this preoccupation with family interests that had prevented any concrete reform within the church.

Even though Pius IV (1559–65) was himself a nepotist, he was fortunate to have selected as his main advisor, and as the principal benefactor of his favors, his nephew Carlo Borromeo, a virtuous prelate who was to be canonized as a saint. While the extermination of the Carafa brothers was to serve as an example of what might happen to power-driven papal relatives, it, of course, did not prevent or stop papal nepotism. In fact, Pius IV exemplified this papal trait. The pope's sister Chiara's descendants became the distinguished Altemps family; his brother Agostino's descendants were the marchesi of Marignano; his Borromeo and Serbelloni nephews and nieces also received benefits — church positions and sizeable dowries.

The Altemps and Borromeo families that Pope Pius IV favored, as well as other families related to the Renaissance popes including the Medici and the Farnese, were to continue an often-repeated pattern.[181] They too were to intermarry with the relatives of the pontiffs who reigned during the Baroque period which followed.

POPE PIUS V AND THE CARAFA EPILOGUE

The successor of the Medici pope was Cardinal "Alessandrino" Michele Ghislieri, who took the name Pope Pius V (1566–72). Soon after his election, Pius V, a loyal and sympathetic friend of Pope Paul IV, had serious reservations about the "tainted" proceedings which had condemned the Carafa brothers. After his own investigation, he ordered the reversal of the Carafa trial, the rehabilitation of Cardinal Carlo's memory and the restitution of the Carafa possessions.[182]

Pius V was known as a reform pope for his zealous ambition to cleanse the church as proposed by the Council of Trent. The Ghislieri family of Bologna, branches of which moved to other sections in Italy, gave the church one pope, two cardinals and seven bishops. Two members of the family were beatified by the church. Pius V (1566–72) was not known for enriching members of his family, who had prospered on their own for centuries in Bologna with governmental and military positions.

The reign of Pope Pius V was thus exceptional. Unlike most of the Renaissance pontiffs, he was not a nepotist. His aim was to purify the church, to make it a holy one. He saw to it that the decrees of the Council of Trent were circulated throughout the world. A reform pope who espoused poverty and purity for himself, he was declared a saint in 1712. This too distinguished him from the other Renaissance popes.

Holy Mother Church had witnessed the tumultuous uncertainties of the Middle Ages. It was beset by warlike factions that ravaged the Papal States and caused havoc for the popes themselves. War reigned through Europe, and the church was threatened from all sides. Within this setting arose the steady hand of favoritism for the relatives and friends of the Supreme Pontiff at the expense of the church. This practice was to accelerate during the Renaissance, contributing to the greatest catastrophe of all, the Protestant Reformation. Increased power was placed within the families of the popes. The Renaissance papacy embellished upon the roots of familial greed sown during the Middle Ages, and the popes established principalities for their kin. The Borgia pope Alexander VI gave Romagna to his son Caesar Borgia; the della Rovere pope, Julius II, sanctioned the acquisition of Urbino for his family; Pope Leo X of the Medici family obtained Urbino for his family (Urbino was to be returned to the della Rovere); Leo's cousin Clement VII made the Medicis the dukes of Florence; and the Farnese pope, Paul III, carved out church territory for his relatives who became the dukes of Parma and Piacenza. Power and avidity ruled the Vatican.

The Baroque popes to follow thus had a rich heritage of papal excess and were in a position to create their own course for family enrichment and to establish their own traditions.

CHAPTER FOUR

The Papal Dynasties of the Baroque Period, 1572–1740

I: From Boncompagni to Ludovisi

The Boncompagni Family Dynasty (Part One)

Cristoforo Boncompagni (1470–1546) belonged to a middle-class family in Bologna. He was a merchant who married into an aristocratic family, becoming the husband of Angela Marescalchi. One of their sons, Ugo, entered the priesthood. He celebrated his first mass in St. Peter's in Rome in 1558 when he became bishop of Vieste. An expert in canon law, he played a strategic role at the Council of Trent (1561–63) and was rewarded by Pope Pius IV, who made Ugo the cardinal of S. Sisto in 1565. Seven years later, he was elected pope. He took the name Gregory XIII (1572–85) and devoted himself to the duties of his office, implementing the Tridentine decrees to insure church reform.[1] Realizing the need for a better-prepared clergy, he established colleges and seminaries for future priests, under the direction of the Jesuits.

Zealous to wipe out Protestantism, Pope Gregory was quick to bless the St. Bartholomew's Day massacre of French Huguenots in 1572. The murder of thousands of Huguenots throughout France and the assassination of the movement's leaders had been instigated by Caterina de' Medici (1519–89), mother of King Charles IX of France and great-granddaughter

of Lorenzo the Magnificent of Florence. Gregory is also renowned for his reformation of the Julian Calendar. Errors in that calendar had become apparent, and it was necessary to drop ten days (October 5–14, 1582) to adjust it for greater accuracy. At the same time, the adoption of the Gregorian Calendar in 1582 provided for leap years every fourth even-year and at century-years that are divisible by four (e.g., 1600 and 2000). It is still the calendar used throughout much of the world.

Gregory's relatives did not interfere in the affairs of state, and when the pope's brother Girolamo went to Rome, Gregory refused to see him.[2] The pope did, however, appoint Girolamo's son Filippo to the cardinalate in 1572 and his son Cristoforo as archbishop of Ravenna in 1578. The pope's nephew Filippo Guastavillani, son of the pope's sister, was made a cardinal in 1574.

Gregory was also very generous to his own son Giacomo (Jacopo), who was born in 1548, before the pope had become a priest. (We know nothing about Giacomo's mother.) Litta gives us a fairly thorough profile of this man.[3] Giacomo was educated in Trent, where his father had served on the council. When his father, in 1572, became pontiff, Giacomo was legitimized; on August 26 of that year, he was nominated to be governor of Castel Sant' Angelo while he finished his studies at the Germanico-Ungarico (German-Hungarian) College. In 1573 he was elected general of the

Holy Church and sent to Ancona to defend the coastal areas against the Turks. In August 1575 King Philip II of Spain, in gratitude to Pope Gregory XIII, named the pope's son captain general of the armies in Lombardy and Piedmont; in the following year Giacomo Boncompagni was registered with his descendants to the rank of nobility in the Republic of Venice. In this designation it was difficult to state publicly the degree of the relationship between Giacomo and the pope; it was finally decided to add discreetly the statement that Lord Giacomo "was a close relative of the pope." (*Jacopo stretto parente di sua santità*). The relationship could not have been closer. The pope's son had already been registered with the nobility of Rome.[4]

In 1577 Alfonso II d'Este, Duke of Ferrara, grandson of Lucrezia Borgia, sold to Giacomo the marquisate of Vignola with the territories of Montefestino and Savignano for 75,000 Roman scudi. By paying 110,000 ducats to the duke of Urbino in 1579, Giacomo also purchased the dukedom of Sora and Arce in the Terra de Lavoro, and soon after he was officially installed by the king of Spain in that position as duke. This jurisdiction in the state of Naples opened the way for the Boncompagni family to be registered with the nobility of that kingdom, and he was nominated as knight of Calatrava and grand chancellor (in 1582). The next year Giacomo paid Alfonso d'Avalos, Marchese of Vasto, the sum of 140,000 ducats to acquire the sovereignty of Arpino and Roccasecca, the birthplaces of Cicero and St. Thomas Aquinas.[5]

The moneys for these acquisitions were provided by Pope Gregory XIII, "who loving his son very much, wished to make him wealthy. The popes in these times had vast sums of money..." gathered from everywhere in Christendom, and much wealth was with Gregory who had the fortune to celebrate a jubilee in 1575, in which hundreds of thousands came to Rome filling the coffers of the church. One of the chief benefactors of this wealth was the pope's son, who usually conducted himself with much wisdom and was considered, after the pope, to be "the first personage of Rome."[6]

Giacomo's eminence waned significantly, however, when he indiscreetly and forcibly liberated one of his servants from jail. Giacomo had presumed that this action would go unpunished, but the pope became enraged by his son's scandalous and heavy-handed behavior. Giacomo was forced to return the servant, who was convicted by judges for murder and executed. Giacomo was rebuked by his father and was forced to flee to Perugia. Only through the intervention of prominent members of the papal court was Giacomo returned to the good graces of his father. They often ate together, and soon after sharing a meal with his son on April 10, 1585, Gregory XIII died quietly and quickly at the age of eighty-four. The new pope, Sixtus V, confirmed Giacomo as general of the Holy Church and afterwards awarded him the governorship of Fermo. Other positions that Giacomo held were given to relatives of the new pope.

The following year Giacomo Boncompagni left the pontifical states, never to return. He went to Sora to quell a feudal disturbance, then to Milan, becoming head of the army. He left Lombardy in 1611 for Isola del Liri near Sora, where he died on June 26, 1612.[7]

More than a military leader, Giacomo was a man of substantial knowledge. He himself assembled all the memoirs of the life of his father and entrusted them to the Jesuits, who published them only in 1742. Giacomo encouraged artists, including Palladio, and writers and philosophers like Francesco Patrizi (1529–97) and Torquato Tasso (1544–95). Palestrina became his musical director. We have a letter from Tasso, who was mentally unstable, written in 1580 to Giacomo from the hospital of S. Anna, in which he recounts his harsh treatment and suffering as a prisoner (Tasso was treated more as a prisoner than as a mentally ill person) and asks Boncompagni to intercede on his behalf to the duke of Ferrara.[8] Tasso was freed in 1586 through the intervention of Vincenzo Gongaza, Duke of Mantua.

In 1576 Giacomo married Costanza (1550–1617), daughter of Sforza Sforza, Count of Santa Fiora. Sforza was the son of Bosio Sforza, Count of Fiora, and Costanza, a daughter of

Pope Paul III Farnese. Their marriage was performed in the Vatican with the assistance of all the Sacred College. Numerous European royal houses sent substantial presents. The official reception was worthy of Giacomo as the son of the Supreme Pontiff.

The descendants of Giacomo and Costanza Boncompagni included two popes as direct ancestors. Among their children were (1) Sforza and (2) Giovanna who died young; (3) Giulia (1586–1622), wife of Giovanni, son of the duke of Bovino;[9] (4) Camilla (1591–1631) who took the name Maria Cecilia and became a Benedectine nun; (5) Ugo (1587–1602) who was Marquis di Vignola; and (6) Gregorio (1590–1628), who assumed the title of Marquis of Vignola after the death of his brother. Gregorio also became the duke of Sora, served in the senate of Bologna, and was nominated captain general of the army in the state of Milan (in 1622). Future members of the Boncompagni family were descended from Gregorio.

The descendants of the Boncompagnis were to marry into later papal dynasties — the Borghese, Ludovisi, Barberini, Chigi, Ottoboni — in order to retain the wealth and honors bestowed upon them. In the course of our study, we will learn more about the offspring of the Boncompagni family as well as other related families which were to emerge as new papal dynasties. The interconnections among these families became such that as members of one papal family married into that of another, they often assumed new surnames as well. The Boncompagni family, for example, would add the names Ludovisi and Ottoboni to their own.

The family of Costanza Sforza (1550–1617), wife of Giacomo Boncompagni, has been delineated in Chapter Three's discussion of the Farnese and Sforza families. Costanza's brother Francesco (1562–1624), the marchese di Varzi, served as a captain general in the army of King Philip II of Spain. He was unexpectedly created a cardinal in 1583 by his sister's father-in-law, Pope Gregory XIII. Wearing the red hat, Francesco participated in nine papal conclaves. As papal legate to Romagna in 1591, he ardently fought the rampages of robbery that were sweeping throughout Italy,[10] assisting Pope

Gregory XIII in his concerted but unsuccessful attempt to bring an end to brigandage in the papal territories.[11]

Giacomo Boncompagni, the pope's son, as commandant of the papal troops, was in charge of protecting the Papal States against banditry. In this effort, he was most notably engaged in pursuing the notorious Alfonso Piccolomini, Duke of Montemarciano, of a family that had produced two popes.[12] Alfonso (d. 1591) was a condottiere, known as the "bandit chief," whose mercenaries engaged in plundering and stealing. His rampaging activities devastated the pontifical states; Alfonso was first excommunicated and deprived of his wealth by the pope, and eventually he was captured and executed.

Robbery as a means of securing wealth was not unheard of among members of the aristocracy. You may recall that in 1297 Stefano Colonna had stolen treasures from Pope Boniface VIII. Later, in 1527, Sciarra and Camillo Colonna, along with Pier Luigi Farnese, had engaged in the sack of Rome. At that time Cardinal Alessandro Farnese, Pier Luigi's father, obtained an amnesty from Pope Clement VII for his son, who had been accused of high treason.[13] But as we move into the seventeenth and eighteenth centuries, it becomes obvious that marriages with heiresses — not brigandage or military conquests conducted by such condottieri as Pier Luigi Farnese, Giangiacomo Medici and members of the Colonna and Orsini families — were the prevalent means to secure additional wealth for these influential papal families.

The Damasceni-Peretti Family
The Orsini Family Dynasty (Part Two)

Felice Peretti (1520–90) was the son of a poor farmer in Grottammare in the region of Marche. His uncle Fra Salvatore had him educated to become a Franciscan in the nearby community of Montalto. A doctor of theology, Felice was appointed vicar-general of the Franciscans and in 1570 was named a cardinal. He was known as Cardinal Montalto. In 1581, during the pontificate of Gregory XIII, Cardinal Montalto's nephew Francesco (son of Camilla Peretti and Giovan Battista Mignucci), who had adopted the name Peretti, was assassinated.[14] The assassin was the powerful noble Paolo Giordano Orsini, Duke of Bracciano, great-grandson of both Pope Paul III (Alessandro Farnese) and Pope Julius II (Giuliano della Rovere). Orsini was the lover of Vittoria Accoramboni, wife of Francesco Peretti. Orsini had decided to rid Vittoria of her husband. Four years later while the conclave in which Cardinal Montalto was elected pope as Sixtus V (1585–90) was taking place, Paolo Giordano Orsini married Vittoria. Fearing that the new pope, a stern advocate of Christian morality, would imprison them, the couple fled to Venice and then to Padua. While they escaped papal authority, Orsini died soon after from an infection, and Vittoria was murdered by assassins hired by the Orsini family.[15]

One of the major aims of Sixtus V was to return law and order to the States of the Church. His predecessor, Gregory XIII, had failed to destroy the wanton brigandage that plagued Italy at that time. Creating a police state and ordering massive public executions of brigands, Sixtus was able to secure peace in the Papal States after a two year period.[16] Pope Gregory had also depleted the papal treasury — which Sixtus remarkably replenished, in spite of the fact that he built many new roads, fountains and hydraulic works; constructed a larger Vatican library; saw the completion of the dome of St. Peter's; approved the necessary repairs to the Quirinal, Lateran and Vatican palaces; and had the obelisks erected in front of St. Peter's.[17] The Eternal City owes much to Sixtus V for bringing it to its magnificent splendor.[18]

Reorganizing the central administration of the church, Sixtus established the number of cardinals at a maximum of seventy and the number of permanent congregations of cardinals at fifteen, divided between administrative and spiritual matters. Known as the "Iron pope," Sixtus did not permit his family to influence the affairs of state, but he was not impartial to their needs.[19] The pope greatly loved his sister Camilla, wife of Giovan Battista Mignucci, and gave her a palace adjoining the church of S. S. Apostoli. Camilla's son was the ill-fated Francesco (d. 1581), and her daughter Maria Felice married Fabio Damasceni. Upon Maria Felice's death, Cardinal Montalto gave her children the name Peretti (and they were known as Damasceni-Peretti). Their given names were Alessandro, Michele, Flavia and Orsina.

Alessandro Damasceni-Peretti, at only fifteen years of age, in 1585, was made a cardinal by his granduncle, the pope. He was given the Villa Bagnaia near Viterbo and the office of vice-chancellor. His brother Michele, at eight years of age, was made captain-general of the papal bodyguard, governor of the Borgo and presented with other honors and possessions. Both Alessandro and Michele were created nobles by the Venetians.[20] Michele married Ann Cesi. The Cesi family had given the church five cardinals, Roman senators, military leaders and a noteworthy natural scientist. The dukes of Acquasparta in Umbria were members of this noble family.

Michele and Ann's only child, Maria Felice (d. 1650), married Bernardo Savelli (1606–1658), Prince of Albano, whose family had given the church at least two popes, Honorius III (1216–27) and Honorius IV (1285–87). Michele Damasceni-Peretti was the principal heir of Pope Sixtus V; therefore, his daughter, Maria Felice, brought the barony of Pescina, the earldom of Celano, the marquisate of Incisa and S. Martino and the principality of Venafro to the House of Savelli.[21] Bernardo Savelli and Maria Felice had two children, Giulio and Margherita. Giulio would marry into the families of future popes Clement VIII (Ippolito Aldobrandini) and Innocent X (Giambattista Pamfili). Margherita became the wife of Giuliano III Cesarini, Count of Celano, and she inherited part of the Damasceni-Peretti fortune from her brother, who was childless.[22] The Cesarini were a noble family with vast territories in Sabina. There were three Cesarini cardinals and several members of the family were marquises who served as *gonfalonieres* of the Roman people.

On March 20, 1589, the two grandnieces of the pope — Orsina and Flavia Damasceni-Peretti — married, respectively, into the Colonna and Orsini families. "They received a dowry of 80,000 scudi, 20,000 scudi as pin money, and precious gifts [such as a diamond ring worth 1200 scudi]. Colonna was given the title Duke of Paliano. When he received the couples the Pope expressed his great joy at having by means of these marriages united the two most important families of Rome...." Sixtus made the husbands of Flavia and Orsina into assistants at the pontifical throne — positions of honor that were given to the Colonna and Orsini families for generations.[23]

Orsina Damasceni-Peretti first married Marcantonio Colonna (d. 1595) and had no children. He was the son of Fabrizio Colonna (1557–80), a direct descendant of Lorenzo, brother of Pope Martin V, and Anna Borromeo, a niece of Pope Pius IV and the sister of St. Carlo (Charles) Borromeo.[24] Orsina's second husband was Muzio Sforza II (d. 1622), Marquis of Caravaggio, great-great-grandson of Duke Ludovico the Moro of Milan and his mistress Lucrezia Crivelli. Muzio was a scholar who established in Milan the Accademia Degli Inquieti, the Academy of the Restless. This branch of the Sforza family terminated in 1717.[25]

Flavia Damasceni-Peretti (d. 1606) was the wife of Virginio Orsini, Duke of Bracciano, the son of the same Paolo Giordano who killed Flavia's uncle Francesco Peretti and then married his victim's widow as his second wife. Virginio's mother was Isabella (d. 1576), the first wife of Paolo Giordano. She was the daughter of Duke Cosimo I de' Medici of Florence; thus Virginio was a cousin of three Medici popes, Leo X, Leo XI and Clement VII. One of his great-grandmothers was Felice della Rovere, wife of Giangiordano Orsini and daughter of Pope Julius II, and another great-grandmother was Costanza Farnese, wife of Bosio Sforza, Count of S. Fiora, and daughter of Pope Paul III.[26] (Refer to Table XI later in this chapter.)

Virginio Orsini and Flavia Damasceni-Peretti had several children, including Paolo Giordano (1591–1656) who married Isabella Appiani, daughter of the prince of Piombino; Camilla (1603–1685), wife of Marcantonio Borghese, nephew of Pope Paul V; Isabella, wife of Cesare Gonzaga, Duke of Guastalla; Alessandro (d. 1626) who became a cardinal at the age of twenty-two in 1615; and Ferdinando (d. 1660), Duke of Bracciano. One of Ferdinando's sons, Virginio (d. 1676), was also created a cardinal. Another son, Flavio (1620–98), and his cousin Ippolito (d. 1699) were the last male members of this branch of the Orsini family, the dukes of Bracciano. Flavio married Ippolita Ludovisi (d. 1674), niece of Pope Gregory XV.[27] The Ludovisi and Borghese families still have a role to play in our history of papal dynasties.

Virginio Orsini, son of the assassin Paolo Giordano and his first wife Isabella de' Medici, had a sister Eleonora. She has already been mentioned in Chapter Three in connection with the Farnese Dynasty; Eleonora was the wife of her cousin Alessandro Sforza (1572–1631), Duke of Segni and great-grandson of Costanza Farnese, daughter of the pope. Alessandro's son Paul II (1602–69) was the father of Federico Sforza (1651–1712), who married the heiress Livia Cesarini; their descendants assumed the name Sforza-Cesarini and were dukes of Segni.[28] Livia Cesarini was the daughter of Giuliano III Cesarini, Count of Celano, and Margherita Savelli. Margherita was the daughter of Bernardo Savelli, Prince of Albano, and Maria Felice Damasceni-Peretti, the great-grandniece of Pope Sixtus V. The children of Federico Sforza (1651–1712) and his wife Livia Cesarini were descended from such distinguished papal families as that of the Orsini, de' Medici, della Rovere, Savelli, Farnese and Damasceni-Peretti. Much of the wealth of the Savelli and Damasceni-Peretti families was inherited by the Sforza-Cesarini, which as noted in Chapter Three, was considered to be one of Italy's first families.[29] The male line of the Damasceni-Peretti family died out early in the seventeenth century.

Pope Sixtus V (Felice Peretti) reigned as Supreme Pontiff for only five years, but his accomplishments were monumental. His successor, Urban VII, became ill the night after his election, and he died before his coronation ceremony. The pontificates of the next two popes, Gregory XVI (1590–91) and Innocent IX (1591), were for short durations and were largely ineffectual.

The Sfondrati Family

Niccolò Sfondrati, who took the name Gregory XIV (1590–91), was the son of Francesco Sfondrati (1493–1550) and Anna Visconti di Madrone. One member of the Visconti family had become pope, Gregory X (1271–76); it was a family that had for centuries ruled Milan and was related to the princely families of Europe. Francesco Sfondrati, a count of the Holy Roman Empire, entered an ecclesiastical career after the death of his wife in 1535. He was made a cardinal in 1544; he ended his career as bishop of Cremona, where the Sfondrati family had originated before moving to Milan.

Niccolò, the son of a cardinal, was an expert in jurisprudence, and in 1583 Pope Gregory XIII (Ugo Boncompagni) made him a cardinal. Niccolò Sfondrati had a brother Paolo, Baron of Valassina and Count of Riviera. He died three years before the elevation of his brother to the papacy. Paolo married Sigismonda d'Este, daughter of Sigismondo, Marquis of S. Martino, related to the dukes of Ferrara.[30]

Although the papacy of Gregory XIV was undistinguished, he advanced the careers of his brother Paolo's three sons: Ercole (d. 1637), Francesco and Paolo Emilio (1561–81). Ercole was created the duke of Montemarciano, becoming captain-general of a papal expedition. He continued his military work under the succeeding popes, Innocent IX and Clement VIII. Ercole's brother Francesco was general of the pontifical galleys and castellan of Castel Sant' Angelo. He was created the marchese of Montafia by his uncle the pope. Paolo Emilio was appointed a cardinal by his uncle and became his secretary of state. He was inexperienced and inept, and quickly alienated the Curia. He favored Spanish policies and sent papal forces to France, opposing King Henry IV.

Ercole married Lucrezia, daughter of Alberico Cibo of the papal family of Innocent VIII (1484–92). Ercole's son Valeriano was an officer for the Spanish in Lombardy, where the Sfondrati family had originated. One of Valeriano's sons became the pious Cardinal Celestino (1644–96). Valeriano's great-grandson Carlo (d. 1788) was the last of the male Sfondrati and upon his death he bequested his surname to his friends the Serbelloni and his possessions to his niece Ricciarda, wife of Alberico Barbiano, Prince of Belgioioso. Ricciarda was the daughter of Teresa Sfondrati (1710–73) and Carlo Filiberto d'Este of St. Martino.[31]

Ercole's Sfondrati brother Francesco, Marchese of Montafia, had a daughter Barbara (d. 1706) who became the wife of Francesco Ferrera di Biella. Their son Francesco Celestino (1691–1765) had children whose descendants perpetuated this noble Piedmontese family. Francesco Ferrero was a cousin of Stefano Ferrero di Biella, who married Maddalena Borromeo, sister of Gilberto (husband of the sister of Pope Pius IV). Francesco Sfondrati's sister Anna became the wife of Ercole Visconti of Saliceto, whose line became extinct in 1716. Ercole Visconti was the great-great-great-grandson of Bernabò Visconti, Lord of Milan (1354–85). Ercole was descended from Bernabò's natural son Sagromoro, who married Elisabetta, princess of Bavaria.[32]

The family of Sfondrati married well, but the male line was short-lived, and it never reached the distinction of other papal families that emerged during the late seventeenth and early eighteenth centuries. The grandeur of the Sfondrati family, even though enhanced by Pope Gregory XIV, whose pontificate was less than a year, was very brief; that family was not able to accumulate the great wealth of other papal families. The pope himself was a man of piety and charity.

Gregory XIV was followed by Cardinal Giovanni Antonio Facchinetti, who took the name Innocent IX and ruled for two months in 1591. And even though his reign was of a short duration, family members united with other papal families. His niece's son Cesare took the name Facchinetti. Cesare's daughter married Francesco Ghislieri of the family of Pope Pius V. Cesare's son Lodovico (d. 1644) was a senator in Bologna; Lodovico's granddaughter Violante (d. 1713) married Prince Giambattista Pamfili of the family of Pope Innocent X.

The Aldobrandini Family

In January 1592 Ippolito Aldobrandini of a noble Florentine family was elected pope, taking the name Clement VIII (1592–1605). Ippolito had been appointed cardinal by Sixtus V in 1585. Like Sixtus, Clement was forced to pursue and execute bandits roaming throughout the Papal States. It has been estimated that in 1595 there were 15,000 outlaws in those states and that "no one was safe from bandits."[33] Clement was a firm supporter of the Inquisition, an ecclesiastical tribunal to suppress heresy. During his pontificate, over thirty heretics were burned at the stake. In 1600 the pope celebrated a jubilee inaugurating the opening of the Porta Santa, or "Holy Door," of St. Peter's.

Clement VIII's reign also marked the decline of Spanish power over the papacy. King Philip II of Spain, who had greatly influenced and interfered with papal elections and decisions, died in 1598. (It has been said that Pope Sixtus V became so incensed with the Spanish ambassador who wished the pope to take action against the French king that it hastened the pope's death.) Meanwhile, Clement recognized King Henry IV, who had converted to Catholicism, as the king of France. Henry IV forged an alliance with the Medici family of Tuscany by marrying Maria de' Medici, daughter of Duke Francesco. By enacting the Edict of Nantes (1590), however, the king had also given the French Huguenots religious freedom and civil rights.

Pope Clement established the Aldobrandini family as one of Rome's most influential dynasties.[34] He had implicit trust in his nephews Cinzio and Pietro Aldobrandini, making them joint heads of the Secretariate of State and cardinals in 1593. The two nephews, however, were extremely jealous of each other and often disagreed — much to the consternation of the

pope.[35] Pietro was to emerge as the primary advisor of the pope — "all orders came from his mouth, and the carrying out of everything was in his hands."[36]

Pietro (1572–1621), son of Pietro Aldobrandini, the pope's brother, was nominated apostolic protonotary, prefect of Castel Sant' Angelo and camerlengo (treasurer of the Holy See). He accumulated enormous wealth and built the spectacular Villa Aldobrandini in Frascati. Pietro was also nominated papal legate to Ferrara and Bologna as well as archbishop of Ravenna.

Cinzio (1560–1610), who was the son of Clement's sister Giulia and Aurello Personeni da Passero (or Passeri), assumed the name Aldobrandini. From his uncle he received the legation of Avignon and was nominated prefect of the Tribunal of Justice (*Segnatura di Giustizia*) for the Holy See. Highly educated and cultured, he was the caring and loving patron of Tasso, whose writings Cinzio inherited at Tasso's death. In 1593 Tasso dedicated his work *Gerusalemme conquistata* (*Jerusalem Conquered*) to Cardinal Cinzio.

Clement VIII was equally generous to Pietro's sister Olimpia (d. 1637) and her husband Gian Francesco Aldobrandini (1545–1601), a distant cousin. Gian Francesco received various positions from the pope. He was appointed governor of Ancona, general of the Church, castellan of the Castel of Sant' Angelo, governor of the Borgo and commandant of the papal guard. In 1612, Clement VIII had Gian Francesco ennobled. He became the prince of Rossano. King Philip III of Spain made him the marquis of Meldola in 1622. His yearly income was estimated to be about 60,000 scudi. Gian Francesco received other benefits from his uncle, including 150,000 scudi to buy land in Emilia. The pope bestowed on Olimpia, 2,000 scudi a month and in 1601 gave her several houses and shops in Monte Giordano.[37] The pope's villa on Via de'Branchi in Rome was presented to Olimpia in 1601, and he also gave her the duke of Urbino's palace in Corso (afterwards known as the Palazzo Doria).

Gian Francesco and Olimpia had many children including (1) Silvestro (or Salvestro)

(1590–1612), (2) Ippolito (1592–1638), (3) Margherita (d. 1646), (4) Elena, (5) Maria, (6) Pietro and (7) Giorgio (1591–1637). In 1603 (1) Silvestro, at the age of thirteen was nominated to be a cardinal; after the death of his father, he was made governor of the Borgo and castellan of Castel Sant' Angelo. Silvestro's brother (2) Ippolito also became a cardinal many years later, in 1621, and then was made camerlengo by Pope Gregory XV, his sister-in-law's uncle. Ippolito was the last living male member of this branch of the Aldobrandini family. His sister (3) Margherita married on December 28, 1599, Ranuccio I Farnese, Duke of Parma and Placenza. Ranuccio was the great-great-grandson of Pope Paul III and the son of the military genius, the pope's namesake, Duke Alessandro Farnese. Margherita and Ranuccio's children were to marry into the d'Este and de' Medici families. (Refer to Chapter Three's discussion of the Farnese dynasty.) Unfortunately Ranuccio and the pope violently disliked each other. Another sister, (4) Elena, was unhappily married to Antonio Carafa, Duke of Mondragone, of the family of Pope Paul IV. It seems that she and her husband, who were spendthrifts, were in "want of money."[38] The last sister, (5) Maria, married Giampaolo Sforza II, Marchese of Caravaggio (d. 1630), but they had no children. A brother, (6) Pietro, Duke of Carpineto (the family had received this title in 1616 from Pope Urban VIII), married Carlotta, daughter of Paolo Savelli (d. 1632). Paolo was also the father of Bernardo Savelli (1606–1658), Prince of Albano and husband of Felice Damasceni-Peretti of the family of Pope Sixtus V. Bernardo and Felice's son Giulio Savelli (1626–1712) was the last male member of his branch of the Savellis (see Table 2b in Appendix A). Giulio married his first cousin Caterina, daughter of Pietro Aldobrandini and Carlotta Savelli. Giulio and Caterina's son Bernardino died in 1672 at the age of nineteen without heirs.[39] Pietro and Carlotta had another daughter Anna, wife of Francesco Maria Cesi (d. 1657), last Cesi duke of Ceri and Selci. They were childless. Pietro's brother (7) Giorgio, Prince of Meldola, Sarsina and Rossano, married Immpolita Ludovisi, niece of Pope Gregory XV;

Giorgio and Ippolita's daughter Olimpia, heiress of the Aldobrandini fortune, first married Paolo Borghese, nephew of Pope Paul V, in 1638, and she then married Camillo Pamfili, nephew of Pope Innocent X in 1697.[40] The Aldobrandini wealth eventually fell to the Borghese family.

The heiress Olimpia Aldobrandini had a son Giovan Battista Pamfili, Duke of Carpineto (d. 1707). Giovan Battista's daughter Olimpia (d. 1751) inherited Meldola and Carpineto. She married Filippo Colonna (1663–1714) of Paliano. By her will, she left all titles to her daughter Agnese Colonna, wife of Camillo, fourth Prince Borghese.[41] Their great-grandson Camillo (1816–1902), son of Francesco Borghese — a direct descendant of Olimpia Aldobrandini — renounced his own name and took the name Aldobrandini (see the following discussion of the dynasty).

At first, Camillo supported the liberal reforms of Pope Pius IX (1846–78), during the period between 1846–48 when the pope seemed to encourage Italian nationalism. Camillo became a member of the state council created by Pius. But as the pope's promises turned sour and he became increasingly conservative, Camillo withdrew from his position in the government. One of Camillo's sons, Pietro (1845–85) had four daughters, the oldest of whom, Maria, married her cousin Antonino (Borghese), Duke Salviati. Camillo's other son, Giuseppe, Prince Aldobrandini, had sons who perpetuated the Aldobrandini name into the twentieth century.[42]

As for Clement VIII's nepotism, historian Pastor writes that his conferring of titles and possessions on relatives "cannot in any way be put on a level with that of the Rovere, Borgia, and Farnese; it was far more limited. The Pope resisted all temptations to give his nephews a principality, and did not in practice do more than had been done by Pius IV and Sixtus V. Nevertheless, from a strictly ecclesiastical point of view, the weakness of Clement VIII for his relatives, which he himself admitted, must be severely blamed."[43]

By 1637, the male line of the illustrious Aldobrandini family had already come to an end. It was only thirty-two years after the death of Pope Clement VIII, in 1648, that Cardinal Bentivoglio wrote in his memoirs: "Where today is the greatness of the Aldobrandini? Where are those five nephews that I often saw in the antecameras of the Pope? They are dead, as is Clement VIII and Cardinal Aldobrandini. The male line is quite extinct; how vain are the hopes of men, and how frail the happiness of this world."[44]

The Borghese Family Dynasty
The Orsini Family Dynasty (Part Three)

As we already know, the great-grandniece of Pope Clement VIII, Olimpia Aldobrandini, married Paolo Borghese. He was the grand-nephew of Pope Paul V (Camillo Borghese, 1605–1621), elected in 1605. The Borghese family were originally from Siena. Camillo's father Marcantonio (1504–1574) left Siena and settled in Rome where he became a consistorial lawyer.

There were numerous similarities between the Aldobrandini and Borghese families and between the policies and administrations of Clement VIII and Paul V, even though the two families were rivals. In matters of policy, Clement VIII enlarged the Index to ban Jewish books; Paul V saw to it that Paolo Sarpi's work *Risposta di un dottore in teologia*, attacking the pope's authority in secular matters, was placed on the Index. Clement persecuted heretics, including the renowned philosopher Giordano Bruno (1548–1600) — who was burned at the stake because of his rejection of Ptolemaic astronomy in favor of Copernican, which placed the planets revolving around the sun. Paul V condemned Galileo Galilei (1564–1642) for his theories, which supported the Copernican concept of the solar system.[45]

As for the administration of the church, Clement entrusted the direction of the Vatican to his cardinal nephew Pietro, who accumulated much wealth and built the impressive Villa Alodobrandini. Likewise, Paul V placed the government of the Papal States in the hands of his cardinal nephew Scipione Borghese, who

constructed the luxurious Villa Borghese in Rome. Both popes were nepotists and enriched their relatives. Cardinal Cinzio Aldobrandini, who had received the affluent legation to Avignon from his uncle Clement VIII was replaced in 1607 by Cardinal Scipione Borghese, who had in turn received it from his own papal uncle.[46] Like Cinzio, who took his mother's surname Aldobrandini, Scipione took the surname Borghese from his mother Ortensia, the pope's sister (Scipione's father was Francesco Caffarelli).

Scipione received many honors from his uncle. He became the archpriest of the Lateran and Vatican basilicas, prefect of the Congregation of the Council, abbot of San Gregorio on the Coelian, librarian of the Roman Catholic Church; he also assumed the offices of grand penitentiary, camerlengo, prefect of briefs, archbishop of Bologna, protector of the Swiss Guard and numerous other ecclesiastical positions. In each of these offices the cardinal received stipends. His income in 1609 was about 90,000 scudi, and by 1612 it had reached 140,000 scudi. With his enormous wealth, he bought the villages of Montefortino and Olevano from Pier Francesco Colonna, Duke of Zagarolo, for 280,000 scudi.[47] The old princely families like the Colonna were beginning to need money, which was now freely flowing in new papal dynasties like the Aldobrandini and the Borghese, but was no longer available to the old Roman nobility.

Cardinal Scipione Borghese and his uncle the pope encouraged the construction of magnificent buildings — the completion of St. Peter's, the Pauline Chapel in Santa Maria Maggiore, the Borghese Palace (now known as Palazzo Rospigliosi) built near the Quirinal and the Villa Pinciana (now known as Villa Borghese). The Borgheses also sponsored the enlargement of the Quirinal Palace, the restoration of the Vatican and its gardens, the restoration of the churches of Victory, St. Crisogono, St. Gregorio and St. Sebastiano and the development of Roman streets and fountains. The cardinal recognized the genius of Giovanni Bernini (1598–1680), whose great works of sculpture were enshrined in the Borghese

Palace. "No other family," reports Pastor, "perhaps, has left so many splendid and lasting monuments of itself in Rome, as the Borghese: churches, chapels, palaces, aqueducts, fountains, streets, villas, and gardens."[48] This was, of course, the height of the Baroque period in Rome.

Paul V was also very close to his brothers Francesco and Giovan Battista. They had an audience every night, and the pope was generous to both. Francesco (d. 1620) was governor of the Borgo and captain of the pontifical guard and later of the church; Giovan Battista (d. 1609) was castellan of Castle Sant' Angelo. By 1609 Giovan Battista had acquired about 300,000 ducats to invest in the purchase of vast properties.[49]

The crown of the Borghese family rested on the pope's nephew Marcantanio (Marc'Antonio, 1601–1658), only son of Giovan Battista. He obtained from the king of Spain the title Prince of Sulmona, which was in the kingdom of Naples. Paul V had purchased this property as well as the territory of Morlupo for his nephew. In 1605 Marcantonio received the title Grandee of Spain and was named an honorary citizen by both Venice and the Republic of Genoa. In 1613 he was presented with the palace in Campomarzio.[50] Six years later he married Camilla Orsini (1603–1685), daughter of Virginio, Duke of Bracciano. Camilla's mother was the heiress of the Damasceni-Peretti family; her grandmother was a de' Medici; her great-grandmother was a Sforza descended from Pope Paul III, and her great-great-grandmother was Felice, daughter of Pope Julius II. (Refer to discussions of the Damasceni-Peretti, the Medici, the della Rovere and the Farnese dynasties; see also Table XI.)

Camilla Orsini and Marcantonio Borghese were married in the Pauline Chapel at the Quirinal Palace. The pope said the mass, and he himself gave them Holy Communion. The following year Marcantonio was made general of the church. The prince of Sulmona, Marcantonio, first Prince Borghese, inherited all the wealth from his father, from his uncle Francesco (who was childless) and from his cousin Cardinal Scipione. Besides their palaces and art treasures, the Borghese family had secured the castles of Vivaro, Vallinfreda, Scarpa and Pratica and the territories of Norma, Olevano, Corneto, Montecompatri, Mentana and Palombara (the last bought for 375,000 scudi and bringing with it the title of Duke), as well as the villas of Mondragone and Tuscolana. The riches of the Borghese family equaled, if not surpassed, that of the Colonna and Orsini families.[51]

Marcantonio's son Paolo (1725–46), who lived to be only twenty-one years of age, dying before his father, married the heiress Olimpia Aldobrandini, great-grandniece of Pope Clement VIII. She brought to the Borghese family the Aldobrandini wealth along with the title Prince of Rossano. Paolo and Olimpia had a son, Giovan Battista (1639–1717), second Prince Borghese, who married Eleonora Boncompagni (1642–95), great-great-granddaughter of Pope Gregory XIII. The descendants of Giovan Battista and Eleonora — and there were many since the Borghese were a prolific family (see Tables 6a–6d in Appendix A) — had in them the blood of three direct papal ancestors: Paul III (Alessandro Farnese), Julius II (Giuliano della Rovere) and Gregory XIII (Ugo Boncompagni); they were also related to other popes who were members of the Medici, Orsini, Aldobrandini and Damasceni-Peretti families.[52] Giovan Battista and Eleonora's grandson Camillo Borghese (1693–1763), fourth Prince Borghese, became the husband of Agnese Colonna, the daughter of the duke of Paliano of the family of Pope Martin V, and their son Marcantonio (1730–1800), fifth Prince Borghese, married the heiress Anna Salviati (d. 1819) of Florence, who inherited the fortune of her uncle Cardinal Gregorio Salviati (d. 1794). Cardinal Gregorio had stipulated in his will that the title of Salviati should be bestowed upon the third son of Francesco Borghese (1776–1839), one of Marcantonio and Anna Salviati's children. Anna Salviati was the daughter of Averado Salviati (1721–83) and Maria Lante della Rovere, daughter of Duke Filippo and Virginia Altieri. Averado's parents were Gian Vincenzo Salviati (1693–1752) and Anna Maria, daughter of Gregorio Boncompagni and Ippolita Ludovisi.

TABLE XI: DELLA ROVERE AND ORSINI FAMILIES
(continued from TABLES VII and 1d)

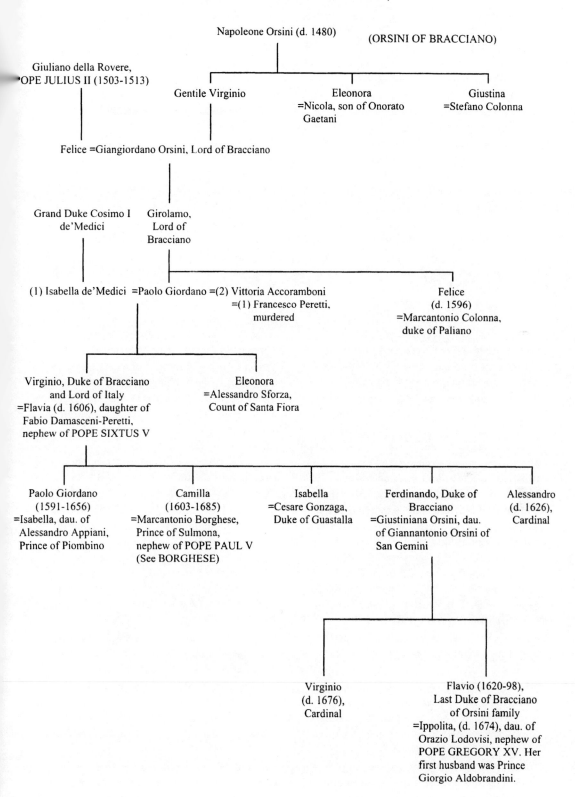

Napoleone Orsini (d. 1480) (ORSINI OF BRACCIANO)

Giuliano della Rovere,
POPE JULIUS II (1503-1513)

Gentile Virginio

Eleonora
=Nicola, son of Onorato
Gaetani

Giustina
=Stefano Colonna

Felice =Giangiordano Orsini, Lord of Bracciano

Grand Duke Cosimo I
de'Medici

Girolamo,
Lord of
Bracciano

(1) Isabella de'Medici =Paolo Giordano =(2) Vittoria Accoramboni
=(1) Francesco Peretti,
murdered

Felice
(d. 1596)
=Marcantonio Colonna,
duke of Paliano

Virginio, Duke of Bracciano
and Lord of Italy
=Flavia (d. 1606), daughter of
Fabio Damasceni-Peretti,
nephew of POPE SIXTUS V

Eleonora
=Alessandro Sforza,
Count of Santa Fiora

Paolo Giordano
(1591-1656)
=Isabella, dau. of
Alessandro Appiani,
Prince of Piombino

Camilla
(1603-1685)
=Marcantonio Borghese,
Prince of Sulmona,
nephew of POPE PAUL V
(See BORGHESE)

Isabella
=Cesare Gonzaga,
Duke of Guastalla

Ferdinando, Duke of
Bracciano
=Giustiniana Orsini, dau.
of Giannantonio Orsini of
San Gemini

Alessandro
(d. 1626),
Cardinal

Virginio
(d. 1676),
Cardinal

Flavio (1620-98),
Last Duke of Bracciano
of Orsini family
=Ippolita, (d. 1674), dau. of
Orazio Lodovisi, nephew of
POPE GREGORY XV. Her
first husband was Prince
Giorgio Aldobrandini.

Marcantonio Borghese and Anna Salviati had two sons; they were Prince Camillo (1775–1832) and Francesco (1776–1839). In 1803 Prince Camillo, Sixth Prince Borghese, married Marie-Paulette (called Pauline), sister of Napoleon I, Emperor of France. Camillo was made duke of Guastalla and served as governor of the French departments of Piedmont and Genova. Fearing a British naval invasion of Rome, he sold to his brother-in-law, the emperor, many of the priceless art treasures of the Borghese family, including two hundred statues of antiquity that Cardinal Scipione had collected at the Villa Pinciana. After Napoleon's defeat at Waterloo in 1815, the Borghese family sought but did not receive restitution. Rather, for these lost treasures they substituted other sculptures and art works that were in their other palaces and country homes.

Camillo and Pauline had no children. Pauline Bonaparte (1780–1821) was most beautiful—even though her ears were deformed and were always kept covered—and overly indulged by her brother, the emperor. She and her husband held a magnificent princely court in Turin from which he governed. She tired of Camillo, however, and left the prince before 1810, returning to Paris. Thereafter her life was one of scandal, and she had many lovers; there was even the rumor of an incestuous relationship with Napoleon. Pauline was separated from her husband until 1825, when she was dying of cancer. Urged by Pope Leo XII, the prince reunited with his wife in Florence before her death.[53] Camillo was to die seven years later and the title of Prince Borghese fell upon Camillo's brother Francesco (1776–1839). Francesco, a general under Napoleon, had tried to restore the Borghese collection of art. His French wife Adelaide La Rochefoucault is remembered for founding a school in Rome for young girls.

As the second son, Francesco had originally taken the title Prince Aldobrandini, as stipulated in the will of Cardinal Ippolito Aldobrandini, who wished to perpetuate the name through the female line—his niece Olimpia having married Paolo Borghese. Upon his brother's death, Francesco took three different titles: Prince Borghese, Prince Aldobrandini

and Duke Salviati. This last illustrious appellation had been inherited from his mother, Anna Salviati, heiress of her family.[54]

Francesco Borghese (1776–1839), seventh Prince Borghese, left each of his three sons with noble titles. His oldest son, Marcantonio (1814–86), was entitled eighth Prince Borghese; his second, Camillo (1816–1902), was Prince Aldobrandini; and his third son, Scipione (1823–92), took the title Duke Salviati, by decree of the Grand duke Leopold II of Tuscany on February 7, 1834. Scipione was named captain of the Roman volunteers by Pope Pius IX, and he fought against Garibaldi. In 1870 Rome was occupied by the Italian forces, and the pope became a prisoner inside the Vatican. Scipione became a founder of the Roman Society, centered on Catholic issues and interests, and was a recognized leader of the Catholic movement in Italy. His daughter Francesca was the wife of her first cousin Francesco Borghese, Duke of Bomarzo (1847–1926), son of the eighth Prince Borghese. Scipione's son Antonio (b. 1855), Duke Salviati, was the husband of his first cousin Maria (Borghese) Aldobrandini, daughter of Camillo (1816–1902). Antonino and Maria had four sons to carry on this branch of the family.[55]

Marcantonio, eighth prince Borghese, had ten children, including (1) Paolo (1845–1920); (2) Giulio (1847–1914); (3) Francesco (1847–1926); and (4) Agnese (1836–1920), wife of Rodolfo Boncompagni-Ludovisi, Prince of Piombino. (1) Paolo, who succeeded his father as ninth Prince Borghese, held many other titles that had been inherited from his aristocratic ancestors, such as Prince of Montecompatri, Prince of Vivaro, Sant' Angelo and San Paolo, Duke of Bomarzo and Prince of Nettuno. Marcantonio's second son, (2) Giulio, took the cognomen of his wife Anna-Maria Torlonia (1855–1901), and their male heirs became princes of Fucino. Giulio and Anna-Maria's son Giovanni (b. 1873) became a senator in the Italian parliament, and their daughter Maria married Lorenzo, Duke Sforza-Cesarini, grandson of Duke Lorenzo (d. 1866) who was declared heir of the Sforza-Cesarini by the tribunal of the Rota. This branch of the Torlonia family will be discussed further on in this section. Marcantonio's third son, (3) Francesco, Duke of Bomarzo, was the husband of his first cousin Francesca Salviati, and they had sons and grandsons to perpetuate this branch of the family.[56]

Paolo, ninth Prince Borghese, was the father of Scipione (1871–1927), tenth Prince, and Livio, (1874–1939) eleventh Prince. Livio's son Flavio Camillo (1902–1980) became the twelfth Prince Borghese, Prince of Sulmona. Flavio Camillo's two sons are Marcantonio, born in 1928, and Camillo, born in 1929.[57] They continue to maintain their status as illustrious members of Roman nobility, related to most of the papal dynasties depicted in this work.

The nineteenth century was a time when many of the old aristocratic families were having financial difficulties. Members of these families were no longer being supported by the papacy, which had been such a lucrative source of financial assistance. These old families were forced to sell many of their possessions. Even the affluent Borghese family was affected. The economic crisis of 1891 forced the Borghese to sell its private art collections and valuable library. The ancestral palace in Rome was sold. Its priceless manuscripts and archives were bought by Pope Leo XIII for 300,000 francs and placed in the Papal Secret Archives.[58] The Borghese collection of statues and paintings, as well as the Villa Borghese, embellished by Cardinal Scipione, were acquired by the Italian government. The Villa Borghese is a principal tourist attraction today in Rome.

The Torlonia Family

As noted previously, Giulio Borghese (1847–1914), second son of the eighth Prince Borghese, married Anna-Maria Torlonia, only child of Alessandro Torlonia (1800–1886 and his wife Teresa Colonna-Doria of Paliano (see Table XII). Among the children of Giulio, who adopted the name Torlonia, and Anna-Maria Torlonia were Maria, wife of Lorenzo Sforza-Cesarini, Duke of Segni; Giovanni, an Italian senator, and Carlo (1874–1947), whose descen-

dants received the titles that had been held by Alessandro Torlonia: Duke of Ceri, Marquis of Romavecchia, Prince of Civitella Cesi and Prince of Fucino.

Alessandro's father Giovanni Torlonia (1755–1829) founded the Torlonia Bank and established the family fortune, acquiring the principality of Civitella Cesi. He was recognized as prince by Pope Pius VII and bought the dukedoms of Poli and Guadagnolo from the Sforza-Cesarini family in 1820. The Torlonia family represented the emergence of a new noble class, entrepreneurs who amassed fortunes and titles.

Besides Alessandro, Giovanni Torlonia also had other offspring, including Marino and Maria Luisa. Marino Torlonia became the duke of Poli and married Anna Sforza-Cesarini. Their son Giulio (1824–72) was the husband of Teresa Chigi-Albani whose mother was Leopoldina Doria-Pamfili; their son Leopoldo (1853–1918) married Amelia Colonna. Giulio and Teresa Torlonia's grandson Alessandro married Maria Luisa, daughter of King Alfonso XIII of Spain. Marino Torlonia's sister Maria Luisa (1804–1883) was the wife of Domenico, Prince Orsini (1790–1874).[59] Members of illustrious papal families such as the Orsini and Borghese were anxious to marry into the Torlonia family so that they could be infused with its fortune; they were no longer being funded by the papacy.

The Ludovisi Family

Through the efforts of Cardinal Scipione Borghese, Alessandro Ludovisi (1554–1623) was elected pope after Paul V (Camillo Borghese). Alessandro, the son of a Bolognese count and the first Jesuit-trained pope, took the name Gregory XV (1621–23). He quickly set about to reform papal elections so that a secret written ballot would determine the winner in the conclave, and he established the Sacred Congregation of the Propaganda of the Faith (1622) to foster the missionary enterprises of the church.[60] And like his predecessors, he loaded his relatives with offices and benefices "in a measure exceeding all bounds."[61]

TABLE XII: TORLONIA FAMILY

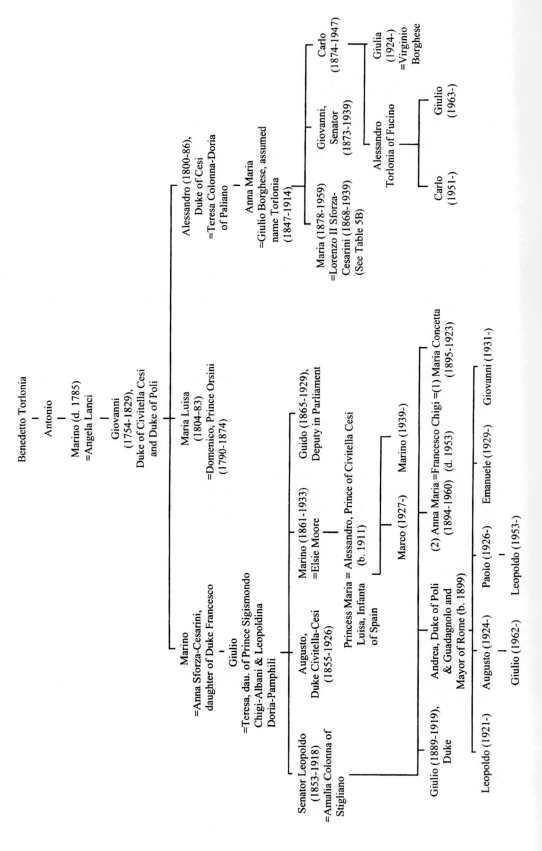

In a period of twenty-nine months — the length of Gregory's reign — the Ludovisi family became one of Italy's richest families. Orazio (1561–1640), the pope's brother, was a senator of Bologna. He was created the duke of Fianco and Zagarolo and was appointed as general of the church.[62] The greatest benefits, however, were reserved for Orazio's son Ludovico (1595–1632), who became a cardinal one day after the elevation of his uncle to the tiara. More than being just the customary "cardinal-nephew," Ludivico became known as *il Cardinal Padrone* (the Cardinal Boss). He was appointed archbishop of Bologna, cardinal of St. Maria in Traspontina and, later, cardinal of St. Lorenzo in Damaso. He was given the prosperous legation of Avignon, which brought him 80,000 scudi annually, and, similar to previous "cardinal-nephews," Ludovico was made camerlengo, receiving 10,000 scudi for that position.

Ludovico built up the family fortune. For 860,000 scudi, he purchased the dukedom of Zagarolo, south of Rome, and the castles of Colonna, Gallicano and Passerano from Pier Francesco Colonna, who was badly in need of money. Ludovico also built the Church of St. Ignatius and several villas, including Villa Ludovisi that he filled with art treasures.[63] Cardinal Ludovico Ludovisi was a humane and sympathetic man who gave freely to the poor and to hospitals. Cardinal Ludovico was also a brilliant administrator and did his uncle the pope credit for having selected so capable an advisor. Ludovico was only twenty-five years of age when he was placed in charge of these offices; he died at the early age of thirty-seven.

Ludovico's brother Niccolò (d. 1664), according to Pompeo Litta, received honors and riches without end.[64] He was appointed castellan of Castle Sant' Angelo and governor of the Borgo. As the nephew of a pope, he was able to make three advantageous marriages. His first wife was Isabella Gesualdo, whose father was Emmanuele Gesualdo, Prince of Venosa. She was the heiress of the principality of Venafro in the kingdom of Naples. His second wife was Polissena Appiani of Mendoza, heiress and princess of Piombino; through this marriage,

Niccolò became the prince of Piombino in 1634. As his third wife, he married Costanza Pamfili, the niece of Pope Innocent X.

Niccolò had an illustrious career. He was a senator of Bologna (first elected in 1640) and commander of the pontifical fleet in the war against the Turks. When the French invaded Piombino, he was able to reconquer it with Spanish help. He was assisted by King Philip IV of Spain, who created Niccolò the prince of Salerno and viceroy of Aragona in 1656 and eight years later viceroy of Sardinia. His son Giambattista (d. 1699) succeeded as prince of Piombino and served as senator of Bologna and viceroy of the Indies. Giambattista Ludovisi's only son died at a young age.

The male members of the Ludovisi family soon died out just like those of the Aldobrandini and Damasceni-Peretti families. Without any male heirs, the family name could not be transmitted except through the female line. In the Aldobrandini family, Cardinal Ippolite had hoped to avoid this dilemma by entrusting his estate to the family of his niece's husband (Olimpia Aldobrandini had married Paolo Borghese) with the stipulation that the second son in that family would take the name Aldobrandini. However, Olimpia and Paolo only had one son. The wealth and property of the Aldobrandini was thus transferred by the female heiresses to the Borghese family, members of which would become Princes Aldobrandini. Five generations later, there were two sons in the Borghese family; the oldest took the title Prince Borghese and the second, Francesco, was known as Prince Aldobrandini. In the case of the Ludovisi, their name was attached to that of the Boncompagni family, which became known as Boncompagni-Ludovisi.

Several of the Ludovisi heiresses made conspicuous marriages. Cardinal Ludovico's sister Ippolita married Giorgio Aldobrandini, Prince of Rossano. Pope Gregory XV officiated at the nuptials in 1621. The bride's dowry consisted of 100,000 scudi. The pope made his nephew-in-law into the prince of Meldola and Sarsina. When a son was born to the couple, Pope Gregory acted as godfather. Unfortunately, this son was to die young, and their daughter Olimpia

(d. 1681) was the heiress of the Aldobrandini fortune, which eventually went to the Borghese family, as has been discussed.

When Giorgio Aldobrandini died in 1637, Ippolita Ludovisi, his widow, married Flavio Orsini, Prince of Nerola and the last duke of Bracciano. They had no children. Flavio Orsini was related to numerous papal dynasties. His aunt Camilla Orsini (1603–1685) married Prince Marcantonio Borghese, and his grandmother was Flavia, one of the heiresses of the Damasceni-Peretti family.[65]

Ippolita had a niece with the same name. This second Ippolita was the sister of Giambattista Ludovisi (d. 1699) and daughter of Niccolò, Prince of Piombino by his third wife, Costanza Panfili. This Ippolita (1663–1733) married Gregorio Boncompagni, Duke of Sora, (1642–1707), great-great-grandson of Pope Gregory XIII. Gregorio Boncompagni's descendants became the princes of Piombino, a title inherited from his wife's family. His twin sister, Eleonora Boncompagni (1642–95), was the wife of Giambattista, second Prince Borghese. Gregorio Boncompagni and his wife Ippolita Ludovisi had four daughters and no sons. One of them, Teresa (1692–1744), married Urbano Barberini, Prince of Palestrina and nephew of Pope Urban VIII; another daughter, Maria (1686–1745), married her uncle Antonio Boncompagni (1658–1731). A dispensation from the church was obtained for Antonio to marry his niece so that the Boncompagni cognomen, and thus the dynasty itself, would continue and hold onto the principality of Piombino.[66] Antonio and Maria had several sons, two of whom married into papal families, the Chigi and the Ottoboni, yet to be discussed. One branch of the Boncompagni family took the surname Boncompagni-Ludovisi-Ottoboni (see Table 7a and 7c in Appendix A). The eldest son of succeeding generations in the House of Boncompagni-Ludovisi would become the prince of Piombino, as well as marchese of Populonia, prince of the Holy Roman Empire, duke of Monterotondo and duke of Sora and Acre. Antonio and Maria's son Gaetano (1706–1777) became the third Prince of Piombino, followed by his son Antonio (1735–1805),

fourth Prince. Antonio's son Luigi (1767–1841) became fifth Prince; Luigi's son Antonio (1808–1883), sixth Prince; Antonio's son Rodolfo (1832–1911), seventh Prince; and Rodolfo's grandson Francesco (b. 1886), eight Prince.

Rodolfo married as his second wife Agnese Borghese, and they had two sons: Ugo-Maria (1856–1935) and Luigi-Maria (b. 1857). Ugo-Maria married twice and then in 1895 entered a religious order, becoming apostolic protonotary and vice-camerlengo of the church. He did not become prince of Piombino. His second wife was Laura (1858–92), daughter of Prince Altieri. Their son Francesco became the eighth Prince of Piombino. At the beginning of this century, Francesco had three daughters and one son Gregorio, born 1910. Francesco's uncle, Luigi-Maria, married Isabella Rondinelli-Vitelli, and their oldest son, Andrea, took the name Boncompagni-Ludovisi-Rondinelli-Vitelli.[67] The Boncompagni-Ludovisi is a contemporary Roman aristocratic family.

II: From Barberini to Corsini

The Barberini Family Dynasty
The Colonna Family (Part Two)

The Ludovisi family were in power for little more than two years. When Pope Gregory XV died, he was followed by Maffeo Barberini, Pope Urban VIII (1623–44). In terms of nepotism, Urban was to outdo the Ludovisi pope — and he had twenty-one years in which to accomplish his family's invasion of Rome.

The Barberini had come to Rome from Florence. Francesco Barberini (1528–1600) was an apostolic protonotary who was quite influential in the Vatican court and became wealthy. Francesco's brother Anton was the father of Maffeo Barberini, who became Pope Urban VIII. Pope Urban VIII held tight reign over the government, and little was done without his knowledge. Throughout his entire reign the Thirty Years' War was fought (1618–48). The Hapsburgs, rulers of Spain and Austria, were engaged in struggles with both the German princes and the Swedish king. France, commanded by Cardinal Richelieu, resisted being encircled by Austria and Spain; the Hapsburgs also threatened the United Provinces of the Netherlands which wished to preserve its independence from Spain. Fearing Hapsburg domination, Urban VIII pursued a pro–French policy.

It was also during his pontificate that Galileo Galilei (1564–1642) wrote *Saggiatore … "Assayer…,"* which was dedicated to Urban VIII, a friend of the astronomer. The pope was delighted. However, in 1632 Galileo published *Dialogo sopra i due massimi sistemi del mondo, Tolemaico e Copernicano (Dialogue Concerning the Two Chief World Systems — Ptolemaic and Copernican)*, his defense of the Copernican theory, which was in conflict with church teaching. As a consequence of this "heretical" work, the pope ordered Galileo to be tried, and he was required to come to Rome, where he was examined by the Inquisition, threatened with torture and confronted with false evidence, forcing him to recant.[68] Instead of imprisonment, Urban VIII placed the sixty-nine-year-old scientist under house arrest, and Galileo was able to continue his studies.

Urban's reign was one of ambiguity. Even though he sought peace between the great powers, his pro–French policy added fuel to the struggle between the Spanish and Austrian Hapsburgs and the French. And even though he encouraged scholars and was pleased with Galileo's dedication, he had his old friend prosecuted and compelled him to condemn his past "errors." And even though Urban permitted his family to acquire enormous wealth from the treasury of the church, he had serious qualms of conscience as he lay dying about the use of papal revenue.[69]

Indeed, the Barberini family was one of contrasts. The pope's brother Antonio (1569–1646), a Capuchin, was made a cardinal (to be known as Cardinal of S. Onofrio) by Urban in 1624. While Antonio held several positions — the bishop of Senigallia, the librarian of the Vatican, the office of Grand Penitentiary — he lived as a simple Capuchin, using his revenues

for charity. When summoned to Rome to become a cardinal, he made the entire journey by foot and lived a life of piety in the eternal city. He helped to build the convent and church of the Cappuccini in Rome and the palazzo of the Propagation of the Faith. On his tomb he instructed to be written: *Hic Iacet Pulvis, Cinis et Nihil* (Here rest dust, ashes and nothing).[70]

Another brother, Carlo, was made governor of the Borgo and general of the Church. With his revenues he bought the castello of Roviano from Otto Colonna, who was much in debt, for 57,000 scudi. From Francesco Colonna, also heavily in debt, Carlo was able to purchase for his family the principality of Palestrina, along with Mezza Selva and Corcollo. The cost was 725,000 scudi. Carlo married Costanza Magalotti, whose brother Lorenzo was named cardinal by Urban VIII in 1624. Lorenzo, who was the secretary of briefs and the archbishop of Ferrara, was a trusted advisor of the pope.[71] Carlo and his wife Costanza Magalotti had three sons — Francesco (1597–1679), Taddeo (1603–1647) and Antonio (1608–1671). These three brothers dramatically illustrate the rise, the fall and the rise of the Barberini family.

Francesco was made a cardinal in 1623 and was given many lucrative offices: legate to Avignon, governor of Tivoli and Ferno, vice-chancellor, archpriest of the Lateran, then of S. Maria Maggiore and St. Peter's (1633), head of the Abbey of Grottaferrata and Farfa and prefect of the Tribunal of Justice. The pope also designated him as his secretary of state, but Francesco had little diplomatic success. He was a somber, melancholy introvert who kept to his studies and collected pictures, cameos and ancient coins. Above all, he used the 80,000 scudi that he obtained annually to build his enormous library, the richest after the Vatican.[72] It contained 10,652 manuscripts, including monastic masterpieces, voluminous correspondences and 31,671 printed works; this library was later acquired by Pope Leo XIII for the Vatican in 1902.

Francesco's younger brother Antonio was made a cardinal at the age of twenty. He was often sent on diplomatic missions by the pope.

He obtained the wealthy abbey of Nonantola and the abbey of Tre Fontane and served as legate at Avignon in 1633; five years later, he was appointed camerlengo, treasurer of the Holy See. Antonio lived in the Palazzo Barberini, built by Bernini, near the *Quattro Fontane*.[73] The palace is now the Galleria Nazionale, a museum holding art works of antiquity. The Barberini had encouraged Bernini, who had been discovered by Cardinal Scipion Borghese. Bernini erected the catafalque in St. Maria in Aracoeli for Cardinal Antonio's father Carlo. The pope commissioned Bernini, as architect and sculptor, to design the baldachin (canopy) over the tomb of St. Peter, the renovation of the Church of St. Bibiana and the Fountain of Triton in Rome.[74] The sepulchral monument to Urban VIII was another of Bernini's masterpieces. The pope's brother, Cardinal Antonio of S. Onofrio, had Bernini restore the facade of the Propagation of the Faith. Bernini represented the epitome of Baroque art, and the Barberini have historically been closely associated with the splendors of his works. To obtain building materials, the Barberini used ancient structures. In 1625 Bernini had the ancient bronze girders of the Pantheon melted down for use as artillery in one of the Barberini's plans for fortification. This inspired the epigram: *Quod non fecerunt barbari, fecerunt Barberini* (What the barbarians did not do, the Barberinis did).[75]

Francesco's brother Taddeo (1603–1647) held many church offices — castellan of Sant' Angelo, captain of the guard, general of the church, governor of the Borgo and finally prefect of Rome. The prefecture had been held by Francesco Maria della Rovere, Duke of Urbino. Upon Duke Francesco Maria's death in 1631, the dukedom of Urbino reverted to the Papal States, and the title of prefect of Rome became vacant. Taddeo devoted his life to the accumulation of wealth. In 1632 his landed property was valued at 4,000,000 scudi. It was rumored that during the twenty-one years of the pontificate of Urban, Taddeo received 42,000,000 scudi and his brother Cardinal Antonio, 63,000,000 scudi.[76] With these vast sums of money, Taddeo had purchased Valmontone,

Pimpinara, Lugnano, Anticoli Corrado, Palestrina and the castle of Corcolle.

In 1627 Taddeo married Anna (d. 1658), daughter of Filippo Colonna, Duke of Paliano. Because the Barberini had acquired the Colonna territory of Palestrina, Taddeo was also declared the prince of Palestrina. The nuptials were celebrated in the chapel at Castel Gandolfo with fourteen cardinals in attendance.[77] Anna devoted herself to works of charity, building a monastery for the discalced Carmelites. Anna was the niece of Marcantonio Colonna (d. 1595), who married Orsina Damasceni-Peretti, grandniece of Pope Sixtus V. Anna's grandfather Fabrizio (1557–80) was the husband of Anna Borromeo, niece of Pope Pius IV; her great-grandfather Marcantonio, Grand Constable, married Felice Orsini, daughter of Girolamo, Duke of Bracciano. Girolamo was the grandson of Pope Julius II (Giuliano della Rovere); Girolamo's wife Francesca Sforza of S. Fiora, was a granddaughter of Pope Paul III (Alessandro Farnese) (see Table XIII and Table 4b in Appendix A). All these papal dynasties were conveniently brought together when Anna Colonna married the nephew of Pope Urban VIII.[78]

In spite of all their wealth, the Barberinis were not satisfied. Cardinal Antonio and his brother Taddeo decided to occupy the papal fief of Castro, which was controlled by Odoardo Farnese, Duke of Parma. It had been given to the Farnese family by Pope Paul III. Thus, in 1641, Castro was captured by the papal forces under the direction of the Barberini brothers, who had formulated and skillfully contrived to conduct this war. Odoardo, who protested, was excommunicated, and the Palazzo Farnese in Rome was sequestrated by the pope. But popular hatred for the Barberinis and their obvious greediness enabled Odoardo to secure support from France, Venice, Tuscany and Modena against the papacy. In 1644, Venice defeated the papal army, almost capturing Cardinal Antonio Barberini himself in the process. Ultimately, Odoardo received absolution and the return of Castro; the pope's treasury, however, had been depleted.[79]

In that same year, Urban VIII died. There

TABLE XIII: COLONNA FAMILY (Continued from TABLE IIIb)

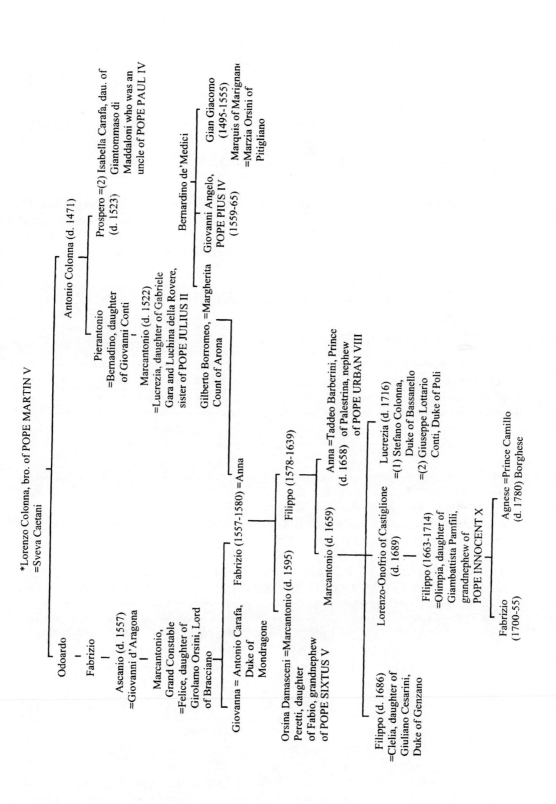

was universal rejoicing in Rome. The Roman nobility, having been excluded from the Vatican, detested the Barberini family; the next pope, Innocent X (Giambattista Pamfili), accused the Barberinis of violating the law by illegally accumulating church wealth. He confiscated their properties, including their palaces, and deposed them in their offices.[80] The three brothers — Cardinal Antonio, Cardinal Francesco and Taddeo Barberini — were forced to flee to France where they were protected by Cardinal Mazarin, who was grateful to their papal uncle for his pro–French policies. In France, Cardinal Antonio became the bishop of Poitiers and the archbishop of Reims. In 1647 Taddeo died in Paris. The family was anxious but unable to return to Rome at that time. Pressured by Mazarin, who sent a French fleet along the Papal States, Innocent X dropped the charges against the three Barberinis and restored their property. The Barberini family returned to Rome triumphantly.[81] The peace between the Barberini and Pope Innocent X was sealed when Taddeo's son Maffeo married Olimpia Giustiniani, Innocent's protégée and grandniece. She was the daughter of Anna Maria Pamfili and Prince Andrea Giustiniani of Bassano. Two of Maffeo's brothers, Carlo and Niccolò, became cardinals. Their sister Lucrezia married Francesco I d'Este, Duke of Modena (1610–58). Their son Rinaldo III d'Este, succeeded as the duke of Modena in 1694; but after only two more generations, the last d'Este duke of Modena, Ercole III, died without sons. Ercole III's daughter Maria Beatrice (1750–1829) married Archduke Ferdinand of Austria, of the royal house of the Hapsburgs.[82] Their son Francesco IV (1779–1846) and grandson Francesco V (1819–1875) ruled Modena. Francesco V was deposed in 1859. His niece, Maria Teresa (1849–1919), the last member of this branch of the d'Este-Hapsburg family, married King Louis III of Bavaria. They had eleven children, and there are many descendants.[83]

Maffeo Barberini and Olimpia Giustiniani had a son Urbano (d. 1722). He married Cornelia Zeno, niece of Pope Alexandro VIII, and they had an only daughter Cornelia (d. 1797).

The vast Barberini fortune was left to her and her husband Giulio Cesare Colonna (1702–1787).[84] This was truly a blessing for the Colonna family. The Colonna had begun to sell their vast estates, bequeathed to them by their papal ancestor Pope Martin V. The Colonna maintained armies, castles and lavish courts, but their income did not keep up with their expenses — especially since the old Roman nobility were often not privy to the monetary flow of the papal treasury now in the hands of a new Roman nobility: the Boncompagni-Ludovisi, the Borghese (Aldobrandidi) and the Barberini. Heavily indebted, the Colonna had begun to sell off their fiefs. You may recall that Pier Francesco Colonna had sold Montefortino and Olevano to Cardinal Scipione Borghese and had then sold the entire dukedom of Zagarolo with the castles of Colonna, Gallicano and Passerano to Cardinal Ludovico Ludovici. Later, Francesco Colonna sold the principality of Palestrina along with the domain of Mezza Selva and Corcollo to the Barberini family.

Fortunate indeed was the Colonna family when Giulio Cesare Colonna (1702–1787) married the enormously wealthy Cornelia Barberini, Princess of Palestrina, who was eleven years of age. The family now assumed the name Barberini-Colonna. Giulio Cesare Colonna (with the blood of the Farnese, della Rovere, Caetani and Orsini families in his veins) and Cornelia Barberini had several children: Urbano (d. 1796), Prince of Carbognano, Duke of Bassanello and Montelibretti, who married Monica Carafa of the family of Paul IV and from whom are descended the Colonna di Sciarra; Vittoria Felice who married Prince Bartolomeo Corsini of the family of Pope Clement XII; Carlo (1735–1819), Prince of Palestrina and Duke of Montelibretti, who married Giustina Borromeo (d. 1815), related to the family of Pius IV (Giovanni Angelo de' Medici) and Clement IX (Giulio Rospigliosi); and Anna Maria who married Duke Filippo Sforza-Cesarini of Segni (1724–64), great-grandson of Federico Sforza-Cesarini (1651–1712), Duke of Segni. (Refer to the discussion of the Farnese dynasty in Chapter Three.) Anna Maria Barberini-Colonna and Duke

Filippo had no children. Carlo (d. 1815) and Giustina's children, from whom are descended the Barberini-Colonna, Princes of Palestrina, were Carlotta who married Augusto Chigi of the family of Pope Alexander VII; Francesco who married Vittoria Colonna, widow of a relative of Pope Clement IX; and Teresa who married the nephew of Pope Pius VII (Luigi Chiaramonti)[85] This family is today represented by the Colonna di Sciarra, or Barberini-Colonna di Sciarra. Enrico Barberini-Colonna di Sciarra (1823–89), Prince of Palestrina, was the last male descendent of this branch; his daughter Maria, who married Marchese Luigi Sacchetti, was authorized by royal decree (ca. 1891) to continue with the name Barberini and the title Prince of Palestrina.[86]

The coat of arms of the Barberini family consisted of three bees, so it was only appropriate, when the Barberini heiress Cornelia married Giulio Cesare Colonna, that so many princely members of papal families sought the hands of their children — drawn as it were to a gigantic honey pot. And so members of the Carafa, Corsini, Borromeo, Sforza-Conti-Cesarini, Chigi and Chiaramonti married into the Barberini-Colonna family. The Barberini fortune was highly desired and helped to sustain the Roman nobility — primarily the Colonna themselves.

The Pamfili Family Dynasty

In contrast to Urban VIII (Maffeo Barberini), his successor Innocent X (Giambattista Pamfili, 1644–55), leaned toward Spain, rather than to France. And when Innocent tried to bring the Barberini nephews (Francesco, Antonio and Taddeo) to trial for using money from the Holy See for personal expenses, including their war on Castro, he was thwarted by both the French monarch and Cardinal Mazarin. The pope was forced to readmit the Barberini family back to Rome. However, his acquiescence to the French did not assist him when he tried to influence the peace treaty to end the Thirty Years' War. In fact the major powers ignored him. The war ended with the signing

of the Peace of Westphalia (October 24, 1648). He complained about this settlement, but his voice was disregarded in the international political arena. During this same period of time, he came into disagreement with Ranuccio II Farnese, Duke of Parma. Ranuccio was not the great political or military leader of his ancestors — Pier Luigi, Ottavio and General Alessandro. He represented the decline of the Farnese family. While the Farnese family still controlled Castro, Duke Ranuccio was heavily in debt. His creditors complained to Innocent X, who was also in need of greater financial resources in order to beautify Rome. When the bishop of Castro was assassinated, Innocent X decided to bring the matter of Castro to a head. In 1649, he sent a papal army to Castro, captured and leveled it to the ground, leaving a column with the inscription "Here Stood Castro."[87] Castro passed to the Apostolic Camera.[88]

As the House of Farnese was waning, the star of the Pamfili dynasty was rising. Members of the Pamfili family, which included Pope Innocent X were direct descendants of Pope Alexander VI (Rodrigo Borgia). (Refer to Appendix B, Part Three.) The Pamfili family had come to Rome from Gubbio. Cardinal Gerolamo Pamfili had assisted his nephew Giambattista, later Pope Innocent X, who was one of the two sons of Gerolamo's brother Camillo. Giambattista's brother Pamfilio had been on diplomatic missions to the court of Ferdinando II, Grand duke of Tuscany, and had served capably as a magistrate. He had married Olimpia Maidalchini (1594–1657). Known as Donna Olimpia, she had brought a sizeable dowry to the Pamfili family; using these resources, she promoted her brother-in-law's career and his election as supreme pontiff. After Giambattista's election as Pope Innocent X, Donna Olimpia "desired to obtain a certain amount of advantage resulting ... from her assistance.[89] Imposing and overbearing, she became the power within the Vatican. To gain access to the pope, it was first necessary to receive permission — from his sister-in-law. She decided who would see the pontiff.

Donna Olimpia became the major influence

on Pope Innocent X. He made no substantial decisions without first consulting her. At first, her son Camillo served as cardinal-nephew, but he resigned the cardinalate in 1647. Donna Olimpia had her seventeen-year-old nephew Francesco Maidalchini made cardinal. Then Innocent X named a distant cousin, Camillo Astalli, a cardinal and gave him the palace of Piazza Navona.[90] The pope intended to have Astalli become cardinal-nephew. Afraid of losing her influential position, Donna Olimpia opposed this appointment; she soon had Cardinal Astalli (also known as Cardinal Pamfili) deposed, in 1649, and sent away from Rome.[91] Donna Olimpia demanded "undivided rule" and insisted on reigning as "absolute mistress in the house" of the pope. It was she who decided who was to receive offices and who made appointments to episcopal sees. A report by Cavalier Giustiniani, written in 1652, stated that "Donna Olimpia Maidalchini is a woman of great spirit, but her sole title to influence is that of a rigid economist. When offices fell vacant at court, nothing was decided without her good pleasure; when church livings were to be distributed, the ministers of the dataria had orders to defer all appointments until, notice having been given to her of the nature of those benefices, she might then select such as best pleased her for her own disposal; if episcopal sees were to be conferred, it was to her that the candidates applied; and that which most effectually revolted every upright mind was to see that those were preferred who were most liberal in giving."[92] She demanded and received gold for her services from those who requested her assistance and sought her influence with the pope.[93] The relationship between Donna Olimpia and the pope was so close that it had been reported that they were lovers, but the historian Ranke maintains: "We may confidently affirm that of all this [sexual intimacy between them], not one word is true."[94]

The real center of power clearly resided with Olimpia during the pontificate of Innocent X. Donna Olimpia was ambitious and greedy — as was aptly demonstrated when Innocent was ill and dying. Before his death, she looted the Vatican and was seen grabbing papal treasures

that had accumulated during the pope's reign.[95] His corpse stayed for three days in a "damp corner of the sacristy and [was] buried in the most simple manner imaginable."[96] "Donna Olimpia declared that she was a poor widow, and that it was beyond her power" to have the body properly interred.[97] The body was finally brought to a local storehouse and placed in a provisional coffin.

Soon after Innocent's death, a new pope was elected. Documents were gathered to bring Donna Olimpia to trial for stealing church property; becoming frightened, she left Rome for Orvieto. There, abandoned by everyone, she died in 1657, leaving 2,000,000 scudi in gold.[98]

The pope's nephew Camillo later erected a monument to Innocent X in the church of St. Agnese.[99] During his reign, in an attempt to beautify Rome, the pope had renovated that church as well as the Villa Pamfili; both were works of Borromini. Pope Innocent X had enlarged and planned new streets for the city and had the fountain of the Quattro Flume (Four Rivers), designed by Bernini, placed in Piazza Navona. He also had Bernini complete the interior of St. Peter's by embellishing the pillars in the longitudinal chapels and the floor of the central nave.[100]

Donna Olimpia's only son Camillo was appointed a cardinal by his uncle in 1644 and served for seven years as cardinal-nephew. His uncle made him general of the church and commander-in-chief of the papal fleet. Further appointments included that of governor of the Borgo and of the fortresses of the Papal States. He became legate to Avignon, supreme superintendent of the Papal States, the head of the abbey of Capua, the prefect of Briefs and the secretary of state for Innocent X. In 1647 he announced that he wished to resign his positions with the church and no longer be a cardinal. He had decided to marry the heiress Olimpia Aldobrandini, Princess of Rossano. She had already been married to Paolo Borghese (1624–46) and was the mother of two children, including Giovan Battista, second Prince Borghese (see the discussion of the Borghese dynasty in this chapter). Donna Olimpia,

Camillo's mother, did not approve of this marriage because her future daughter-in-law's disposition was similar to her own, and they — the two Olimpias — did not get along.[101] Donna Olimpia saw her daughter-in-law as a rival for power, and she convinced the pope to make her son and his new wife live outside of Rome (in Frascati) so that they would not interfere with her domination of the Curia.

Pamfilio and Olimpia Pamfili had three children: Anna Maria, wife of Andrea Guistiniani, whose daughter Olimpia married Maffeo Barberini and whose daughter Caterina married Giulio Savelli; Constanza, who married Niccolò Ludovisi, Prince of Piombino, whose daughter Impolita married Gregorio Boncompagni; and Camillo (d. 1667), who married the heiress Olimpia Aldobrandini. Camillo and his wife had several children, including Anna; Giambattista (d. 1709), Duke of Carpineto; Teresa; and Flaminia. All of these children married into distinguished noble families. They and their families will be discussed separately.

Camillo Pamfili's daughter Anna was the wife of General Giovanni Andrea Doria IV, Prince of Melfi. He was the great-great-grandson of Giovanni Andrea Doria I (1539–1606), who had inherited the title of Prince of Melfi from his famous cousin Andrea Doria, *Pater Patriae* in Genoa. General Doria IV united his fiefs — the principality of Melfi and the marquisate of Torriglia — with those of his wife Anna Pamfili, who inherited the principality of S. Martino and Valmontone from the Pamfili and Aldobrandini families.[102] General Doria had inherited the extensive territories of Borgotaro, Bardi and Compiano from his mother Maria Landi, heiress of Federico Landi. This branch of the Doria family became known as the House of Doria-Pamfili-Landi, distinguished members of Roman nobility,[103] and retained its interests in the papacy long after Pope Innocent X had ceased to be.

Descendants of Anna Pamfili and General Doria include three cardinals: Anton Maria (1749–1821), Giorgio (1772–1837) and Giuseppe (1751–1816), the last of whom was secretary of state for Pope Pius VI and took a political stance that favored Napoleon. In 1767

Giovanni Andrea Doria-Pamfili-Landi, another descendant, married Princess Leopolda (1744–1807) of the House of Savoy-Carignano, to which all the kings of Italy belong. Leopolda was the great-grandaunt of Vittorio Emanuele II, first king of a united Italy. The Doria-Pamfili-Landi family pledged 1,000,000 scudi to the Holy See to help the pope pay the 30,000,000 or so that had been promised Napoleon in the Treaty of Tolentino (February 19, 1797). That treaty, between representatives of Napoleon and Pope Pius VI (1775–99), brought a short-lived settlement between the pope and Napoleon's France, which had invaded the Papal States. By the treaty, the papacy lost considerable territory in the pontifical states as well as the enclave of Avignon and works of art and had to pay the large, aforementioned indemnity.

In the eighteenth, nineteenth and twentieth centuries, the titles of Prince of Melfi and Valmontone and Duke of Avigliano, which had been granted to the Doria-Pamfili-Landi family, had been secured by Prince Giannandrea, son of Giovanni Andrea and the princess Leopolda of Savoy. Giannandrea was succeeded by his son Filippo (1813–76), who was succeeded by his own two sons; Giovanni-Andrea (1843–90) and Alfonso-Maria (b. 1851); the title was then secured by the latter's son Filippo-Andrea Doria-Pamfili-Landi (b. 1886). One of Filippo-Andrea's daughter's Olimpia (presumably named after the infamous Donna Olimpia), born in 1854, married Fabrizio Colonna, prince of Paliano. Filippo-Andrea's sister, Leopoldina Doria-Pamfili-Landi (1811–43) was the wife of Sigismondo, sixth Prince Chigi-Albani, of another papal dynasty that will be discussed later in this chapter.

Camillo Pamfili's only son, Giambattista, married Violante, daughter of Innocenzo Facchinetti and the heiress of Pope Innocent IX (1591). That pope's sister Antonia married Antonio Titta, and she was the great-great-grandmother of Violante. Giambattista and Violante had a daughter Olimpia who married Filippo Colonna (see the subsequent discussion of the Colonna). Filippo and Olimpia's daughter Agnese was the wife of Camillo Borghese, fourth Prince (see the previous discussion of the Borghese dynasty). Giambattista's son Gerolamo was the father of Benedetto who married Teresa (Olimpia) Borghese, Camillo Borghese's sister. This male line of the Pamfili family, which carried the title Duke of Carpineto, ended in 1760.

Camillo Pamfili's daughter Teresa married Carlo Cibo, Duke of Massa, a descendant of Pope Innocent VIII. Teresa and Carlo Cibo had three sons: Alberico (1674–1715), Camillo (1681–1743) and Alderano (1690–1731).[104] Alderano's daughter, Maria Theresa, heiress of the Cibo family, married the duke of Modena, Ercole III d'Este, and they had descendants.[105]

Finally, Camillo Pamfili's daughter Flaminia first married Bernardino Savelli (1653–72) and then Niccolò Francesco Pallavicino, Prince of Civitella. Pallavicino belonged to a noble Genoa family and died in 1709. Flaminia had no children.

The Savelli Family (Part Two)

Bernardino Savelli's grandfather, Bernardino, Prince of Albano (1606–1658), had married Felice, heiress of Pope Sixtus V (Felice Peretti). Their son Giulio Savelli of Rome (1626–1712) first married Caterina Aldobrandini, daughter of Pietro Aldobrandini, Duke of Carpenito. This title was inherited by Olimpia Aldobrandini, wife of Camillo Pamfili, and was given to her son Giambattista (d. 1709), as noted previously. Giulio Savelli's second wife was Caterina Guistiniani, daughter of the prince of Bassano and Anna Maria Pamfili, Camillo's sister and a niece of Pope Innocent X. Giulio was the last male Savelli. His son Bernardino (1653–72) died many years before his father; thus the Savelli family, which had given the papacy at least two popes, Honorius III (1212–27) and Honorius IV (1285–87), ceased to exist.[106]

The Savelli family were of the old Roman nobility and were closely allied with the Orsini family.[107] The Savellis were the hereditary marshals of the Holy Church and the custodian of the conclave. The family had jurisdiction over a tribunal known as the Corte Savella that was suppressed by Pope Innocent X. Similar to other old Roman aristocracy, it had come upon hard times. The Apostolic Camera acquired Castel Gandolfo from the debtor Savelli for only 150,000 scudi in 1596. In 1650 the Savelli were forced to sell Albano to Giambattista, Camillo Pamfili's only son.[108]

Since the Middle Ages, money and valued merchandise had accumulated into associations of depositors, called *monti* (sing., *monte*). These assets were used for commerce and assistance and were often loaned to states and barons at interest. Wealthy families like the Borghese invested in *monti* and received a huge rate of return. Some of the nobles even sold their territories at high prices to papal families and then "invested the proceeds in the papal monti [and] the interest of the *Luoghi di Monte*, drawn without need of exertion, produced a better revenue than could be derived from the most industrious cultivation of the land."[109] Often, barons were unable to pay the interest and, in order to satisfy creditors, were forced to sell their property. In 1596, Pope Clement VIII's "bull of the barons" demanded the redemption of debts by the sale of land, by which the Apostolic Camera acquired Castel Gandolfo so cheaply.

Giulio Savelli's sister Margherita (d. 1690) was the wife of Giuliano Cesarini, Duke of Civitanova. She brought to the family of her husband what remained of the Savelli estates. The Cesarini were a wealthy feudal family whose ancestors included members of the Orsini, Colonna, Gaetani, Sforza and Farnese. Giuliano's great-grandmother Clelia was the natural daughter of Cardinal Alessandro Farnese, grandson of Pope Paul III. The riches of the Cesarini family were inherited by Giuliano Cesarini and Margherita Savelli's two daughters, Clelia and Livia, since the couple had borne no sons.

The Colonna Family (Part Three)

Giuliano Cesarini and Margherita Savelli's daughter, Clelia Cesarini (1655–1735) married

Filippo Colonna (d. 1686). Filippo's brother Lorenzo-Onofrio (d. 1689) — Constable and, later, Viceroy of Naples — was the husband of Maria Mancini, niece of Cardinal Mazarin (Mazzarino) of France who had protected the Barberinis. Maria was a favorite mistress of King Louis XIV; even after she married Lorenzo-Onofrio Colonna, she continued to have lovers. At one point she entered a monastery, but after three years she left, first living in France and then in Italy, where she died in 1717.

The descendants of Filippo Colonna and his wife Clelia Cesarini became the princes of Stigliano and Aliano. (Their descendants will be delineated later; refer to Table 4c in Appendix A.) Clelia's sister Livia (d. 1712) married Federico Sforza, Count of S. Flora, and their descendants took the name Sforza-Cesarini. (Refer to the discussion of the Farnese dynasty in Chapter Three.)

Filippo's brother Lorenzo-Onofrio was the ancestor of a branch of the Colonna family that held the titles Prince of Paliano, Duke of Marino, Prince of Sonnino, Prince of Avella, Duke of Tursi, etc. Lorenzo-Onofrio and Filippo were the sons of Marcantonio (d. 1659), husband of Isabella Gioeni, who was the heiress of Lorenzo, Prince of Castigilione. They were the great-great-grandsons of Marcantonio Colonna (1535–1584), admiral (Captain General), victor of the Battle of Lepanto (1571), Viceroy of Sicily, Grand Constable of the kingdom of Naples, who had received the title Prince of Paliano in 1569. He was the great-great-grandnephew of Pope Martin V. Lorenzo-Onofrio Colonna's son Filippo II (1663–1714) was the husband of Olimpia (d. 1751), daughter of Giambattista Pamfili. Filippo II and Olimpia's daughter, Agnese (d. 1780), married Camillo, fourth Prince Borghese. (Refer to the previous discussion of the Borghese dynasty.) The Paliano branch of the Colonna family, descending through Lorenzo-Onofrio, can be sketched as follows:[110]

Marcantonio Colonna, first Prince
of Paliano (1535–84)
|
Fabrizio (1557–80) married

Anna Borromeo, niece of Pius IV.
|
Filippo I (1578–1639).
|
Marcantonio (d. 1659) married
Isabella Gioeni, heiress of
Lorenzo, Prince of Castiglione.
|
Lorenzo-Onofrio (d. 1689) married
Maria Mancini.
|
Filippo II (1663–1714) married
Olimpia, daughter of Giambattista
Pamfili, grandnephew of Innocent X.
|
Fabrizio (1700–1755)
|
Lorenzo (1723–79)

Lorenzo Colonna (1723–79) was the father of Prince Filippo III (1760–1818), who married Princess Caterina of Savoy-Carignano. They were the parents of two daughters. It was Duke Filippo III who terminated the right of feudal jurisdiction over his territory. His brother Fabrizio (d. 1813) married Bianca Doria, daughter and heiress of Francesco, Duke of Tursi. The titles of Prince of Paliano and Duke of Tursi fell on their son Aspreno Colonna-Doria (1787–1847).[111] His oldest son Giovanni (1820–94), eleventh Prince and second Duke, was succeeded by his son Marcantonio, twelfth Prince and third Duke (1844–1912). Marcantonio had two daughters, one of whom, Vittoria, married Leone Caetani, Prince of Teano. Marcantonio's sister Vittoria, lady in the court of the queen-mother of Italy, was the wife of Francesco Sforza-Cesarini, Duke of Segni. (Refer to Table 4d in Appendix A.)

Giovanni, eleventh Prince of Paliano (1820–94) had a second son Fabrizio (b. 1848), thirteenth Prince of Paliano, who succeeded his brother Marcantonio when he died in 1912. Fabrizio married his cousin Olimpia Doria-Pamfili-Landi (b. 1854). They had four children: Marcantonio (1881–1947), Ascanio, Marozia (a name made famous one thousand years ago) and Margherita. Marcantonio was followed as prince by his son Aspreno (b. 1916), whose eldest son is another Marcantonio (b. 1948).

There are many cousins and descendants of this princely Paliano branch of the Colonna family living today.[112]

Aspreno Colonna-Doria (1787–1847) was also the father of Edoardo (1833–1904), Prince of Summonte. Edoardo's eldest son Luciano married Adele Borghese, daughter of Prince Felix of Rossano, an Italian senator who was the brother of Prince Paolo Borghese (1845–1920).[113]

Filippo Colonna (d. 1689), Lorenzo-Onofrio's brother, gave rise to another existing branch of the Colonna family, the princes of Stigliano and Aliano. As previously mentioned, Filippo married the heiress Clelia (1655–1735), daughter of Giuliano Cesarini. Filippo and Clelia's son Giuliano (1671–1731) acquired the additional title of Prince of Sonnino. The Stigliano and Aliano branch of the Colonna family, descending through Filippo, can be sketched as follows:[114]

Marcantonio (d. 1659) married Isabella Gioeni, heiress of Lorenzo, Prince of Castiglione.

|

Filippo Colonna (d. 1686)
married Clelia Cesarini.

|

Giuliano (1671–1732), Prince of Sonnino
and second
Prince of Stigliano and Aliano

|

Ferdinando (d. 1775), third Prince

|

Marcantonio (1724–96), fourth Prince

|

Andrea (1747–1820), fifth Prince

|

Ferdinando (1785–1834), sixth Prince

|

Gioacchino (1809–1900), seventh Prince
married a cousin Cecilia Colonna, no children.
Ferdinando (1858–1926), eighth Prince,
was the son of Andrea (1820–72),
brother of Gioacchino.

|

Andrea (b. 1885), ninth Prince,
son of Ferdinando.

Andrea Colonna also had a brother Marcantonio (b. 1889). Ferdinando, eighth Prince, had a

sister Amalia (b. 1860), who married Leopoldo Torlonia, Duke of Poli and Guadagnolo.[115] Andrea had a son Lorenzo, born in 1925, tenth Prince of Stigliano, prince of Aliano and marchese of Castelnuovo. [116] Numerous members of this Colonna family presently live in Naples.

The Chigi Family

Pope Innocent X (Giambattista Pamfili) had appointed Fabio Chigi as his secretary of state, and Chigi had represented the Vatican at the congress to end the Thirty Years War. Chigi's grandmother Agnese Bulgarini was related to Pope Paul V (Camillo Borghese). The Chigis were a prominent banking family from Siena. After a conclave that lasted eighty days, Fabio Chigi was elected pope and took the name Alexander VII (1655–67). He was elected primarily for his diplomatic expertise, but as pope his foreign policy — especially with Cardinal Mazarin and King Louis XIV — ended mostly in failure. After his election he had a coffin made "and placed in his bedroom so that on awakening he might be reminded of the vanity of earthly things."[117] This reminder must have lasted for only a short period of time because soon after his accession to the papacy, he began to indulge in nepotism.

It was during Alexander VII's reign that, in 1654, Queen Christina (1626–89) of Sweden, daughter of King Gustavus Adolphus, the defender of Protestantism in northern Europe, abdicated her throne. She had converted to Catholicism. Her entry into Rome "on a magnificent white horse," was one of triumph, and she was received with much honor and curiosity.[118] Alexander VIII served as her sponsor, providing financial support for her and housing her in the Palazzo Farnese in Rome. It was also during his administration that he commissioned Bernini to create the impressive colonnade around the piazza of St. Peter's. As a cardinal he had begun to assemble the Chigi Library (*Biblioteca Chigiana*). The library was placed in the Palazzo Chigi, which faces the Piazza Colonna and Largo Chigi. He was a man of culture, interested in art and literature, and he belonged to a family that had encouraged both.

Pope Alexander VII was descended from Mariano (1439–1504), banker and Sienese ambassador to Pope Alexander VI. Mariano had commissioned the artist Perugino to make the painting of the Crucifixion on the Chigi altar in S. Agostino, Siena. One of his sons was Agostino, called "the Magnificent" (1465–1520). Early in his career Agostino had financially assisted Caesar Borgia in his war enterprises. He became a close, personal friend of Pope Leo X (Giovanni de' Medici) and provided financial assistance for the pope to pursue his extravagances. The pope was a witness at Agostino's wedding.[119] Agostino was named camerlengo; under Pope Leo X, he obtained the contract to manage customs, establishing a commercial relationship throughout Europe. His bank in Rome became prosperous, and he employed over 20,000 workers as his assets reached 800,000 ducats. But more than making money and being a friend of the pontiff, Agostino sponsored writers, including Bembo and Giovio; he had the poetry of Pindaro published (the first Greek book printed in Rome); and he commissioned Raffaelo and Sodoma to paint his villa, Farnesina. He had Raffaelo (Raphael) decorate the chapel of S. Maria della Pace and the chapel of S. Maria del Popolo, which is where Agostino the Magnificent was buried. Agostino the Magnificent's brother Sigismondo (1479–1525) adorned his palazzo with paintings by Sodoma. Sigismondo's great-grandson was Fabio, Pope Alexander VII.

At first, Alexander VII did not want his relatives around the pontifical court, but then he began to indulge them with offices and honors.[120] It is extremely likely that he had witnessed other popes enrich their kin, and, in fairness to his own relatives, he simply did not want his family to be left out of the material blessings that the papacy could supply. Alexander made his brother, Mario, general of the church and superintendent of the Borgo. He had Mario's son Flavio (1631–93) become a cardinal in 1657.

Flavio, who assisted Cardinal Giulio Rospigliosi, the secretary of state, was often sent on diplomatic missions by the pope. He soon accumulated over 100,000 scudi from his ecclesiastical offices. He had Bernini construct a palace for him (today known as the Odescalchi Palazzo) as well as a funeral monument for his uncle in St. Peter's. And he continued to build the Chigi Library's rich collection — started by his uncle the pope — of manuscripts, rare autographed copies and documents, designs and miniature books. Eventually the library became the property of the Italian Government, in 1918; it was donated to the Vatican Library in 1922. A year later, the Palazzo Chigi, where the library was housed, became the home of the Italian Ministry of Foreign Affairs. Fabio's own estate, his wealth and the marquisate of San Quirico, were left to Bonaventura, eldest son of his sister Agnese, wife of Ansano Zondadari. This branch of the family is known as Chigi-Zondadari of Siena; its descendants include cardinals Anton Felice (1655–1735) and Anton Felice (1739–1823) Archbishop of Siena; Angelo Bonaventura (1773–1847), Governor of Siena; and Bonaventura (1841–1908), a senator in the newly established kingdom of Italy.

The pope also showered favors upon another nephew, Agostino (1634–1705), son of his brother Sigismondo. Agostino became castellan of Castel Sant' Angelo. After 1658, when Agostino married Maria Virginia Borghese, daughter of Paolo Borghese and Olimpia Aldobrandini, he received the territories of Ariccia and Campagnano and the Palazzo Aldobrandini in Piazza Colonna. From 1658 to 1662, he received these titles: Prince of Farnese and Campagnano, Prince of the Holy Roman Empire and Duke of Ariccia. The Chigi family of Rome are descended from Agostino. His brother Sigismond (1649–77) became a cardinal at the age of eighteen and was legate to Ferrara. A distant relative of the pope, Antonio Bicci, was made a cardinal as well and also the commander of the papal galleys.

Agostino Chigi and Maria Virginia Borghese had a son Augusto (1662–1744), husband of Eleonora Rospigliosi of the family of Pope Clement IX (1667–69), and a daughter Costanza, who married Emilio Altieri, grandnephew of Pope Clement X (1670–76). Augusto Chigi and

Eleonora Rospigliosi bore a son Agostino (1710–69) who, in 1735, married Giulia Albani (1719–86), grandniece of Pope Clement XI (Giovan Francesco Albani, 1700–1721). In 1712, when the last male member of the Savelli family died, the Savelli titles — Marshal of the Church and Custodian of the Conclave — were bestowed by the pope on Agostino Chigi and his descendants.[121] Agostino's sister Laura (1707–1792) was the wife of Gaetano Boncompagni (1706–1777).

Agostino and Giulia Albani had a son, Sigismondo (1736–1793), who protected the poet Vincenzo Monti. In 1783 Monti dedicated *Sciolti* to him. Sigismondo first married Maria Flaminia Odescalchi and then Maria Giovanna Medici d'Ottaiano. His son was yet another Agostino (1771–1855), whose wife was Amelia Barberini. He was made prefect of Rome under Prince Joachim Murat and was noted for his diary, published in twenty-one volumes, which recorded his life in Rome from 1801 to 1809 and from 1812 to 1855. In 1839, the prefect sold to Abramo Mieli of Rome several villas as well as the Chigi Palazzo in Siena on Via del Casato No. 5.

In 1852 Don Filippo Albani, Prince of Soriano, died and the House of Albani ended. Agostino Chigo, descended from Giulia Albani, now took the name Prince Chigi-Albani. In just a few generations, the Chigi had married into such major papal families as the Borghese, Rospiglosi, Altieri, Boncompagni, Barberini, Odescalchi and Albani.[122]

The present House of Chigi-Albani is descended from Sigismondo (1798–1877), sixth Prince of the Holy Roman Empire and son of Prince Agostino Chigi (1771–1855). He married Leopoldina Doria-Pamfili (1811–43). Their son Mario (1832–1914), seventh Prince, was the father of Ludovico (1866–1951), eighth Prince, who was the father of Sigismondo Chigi-Albani, born in 1894. Sigismondo's eldest son was Agostino, born in 1929.[123]

The Albani (Chigo-Albani) Family

The Albani family–the surname affixed to that of the Roman Chigi family — came from Albania in the fifteenth century.[124] They settled in Urbino and took their surname from their country of origin. Orazio Albani (1576–1653) went to Rome as an ambassador from Urbino and was befriended by Pope Urban VIII (Maffeo Barberini), who made him a senator. His son Carlo Albani (d. 1724) was the Maestro di Camera of Cardinal Franceso Barberini, the pope's nephew. He married Teresa Borromeo. One of Carlo's sons, Giovan Francesco, was elected to the papacy, taking the name Clement XI (1700–1721). This pope, like several previous popes, belonged to families connected with the affairs of the Holy See.

Clement XI's pontificate witnessed the War of Spanish Succession (1701–1714), which resulted in King Louis XIV of France placing his grandson Philip V on the throne of Spain. It was this same Philip who married Elisabetta Farnese, the heiress of the dukedom of Parma and Piacenza. Two of the pope's nephews — Annibale (1682–1751), who was camerlengo, and Alessandro (1692–1779) were appointed cardinals by their prominent uncle. The Albani family gave the Holy See three generations of cardinals, and they exercised a forceful influence on Vatican policies for at least one hundred years after the death of Clement XI.

Cardinal Alessandro Albani was appointed the librarian of the church. A cardinal in 1721, he served as ambassador of Austria in Rome. He was a collector of arts and antique statuary later placed in a Capitoline museum in Rome. He was the patron and friend of Johann Joachim Winckelmann (1717–66), archaeologist and renowned scholar of Greek art and its influence on Roman antiquities. The cardinal placed works inherited from Winckelmann and his own collection of medallions and relics of past civilizations in the Villa Albani on Via Salaria. That villa (Museum of Villa Albani) was to serve as the model for the utilization of other villas as sites for future museums.

Alessandro's nephew Gianfrancesco (1720–1803), Bishop of Sabina, Porto and S. Ruffina, later of Ostia and Velletri, became dean of the Sacred College of Cardinals. With the occupation of Rome by Napoleon's troops in 1797, Cardinal Gianfrancesco fled, going to Venice where he participated in the conclave that elected Pope Pius VII (1800–1823). Gianfrancesco's nephew was Giuseppe (1750–1834), elected to the purple in 1801. He supported the position of the Austrian (Hapsburg) Empire. He held many important offices: legate to Bologna and later to Pesaro and Urbino, librarian of the Holy Church and pro-secretary of briefs. He was a deciding force in the election of Pope Pius VIII (1829–30) and served as his secretary of state. He represented the reactionary faction within the College of Cardinals and was known for his overbearing severity.

Giulia Albani, the wife of Agostino Chigi (1710–69), was the daughter of Carlo Albani and Teresa Borromeo. Carlo was the brother of Annibale (1682–1751), who was appointed cardinal in 1711. Annibale served as papal nuncio to Vienna and helped to secure peace between the Austrian Empire and the German states. He was secretary of records, assistant dean of the Sacred College, bishop of Sabina and then of Porto and S. Rufina. He published the bulls and briefs of his uncle in a work entitled *Pontificale romanum Clementis XI auctoriate recognitum*. The House of Albani became extinct when Prince don Filippo died in 1852, but the branch Chigi-Albani exists to the present day.[125]

In the twentieth century Duke Sigismondo Chigi-Albani, Prince of the S.R.I., Prince of Farnese, Prince of Campagnano, Prince of Soriano, Duke of Ariccia, Duke of Formello, etc., and his son Prince Agostino (b. 1929) headed the family. Sigismondo's father was Prince Ludovico, Grand Master of the S.M.O. of Malta (1866–1951), and Sigismondo's wife was Anna (Borghese) Aldobrandini (1871–98). The present duke is titled Hereditary Marshal and Guardian of the Papal Conclave.

The Chigi family, which has given the church at least five cardinals, also added the name della Rovere so that the family is known today as Chigi-Albani-della Rovere. In 1507 the Chigi family donated property, the Contea della Suvera, to the community of Siena, which gave it to Pope Julius II (Giuliano della Rovere). That property, which had once belonged to the della Rovere family, was given by Julius II to his nephew Niccolò della Rovere.[126] Further the pope was a friend of Agostino Chigi the Magnificent, having dined with him in Rome; the Chigis had also spent 3,000 ducats for rubies for Julius II's papal tiara. In 1509, to show his appreciation for the land and jewelry, the pope granted Agostino, his brother Sigismondo and their descendants both the della Rovere cognomen and its coat of arms.[127]

The wealth of the Chigi family was enhanced by its profitable marriages into other landed and moneyed papal families. Ranking in importance the ten major property owners in Lazio, the region around Rome, in 1840, one report shows that after the Borghese, Torlonia, Boncompagni-Ludovisi and Caetani and before the Doria, Colonna, Rospigliosi, Pallavicini, Braschi and [Sforza] Cesarini was the Chigi.[128] The Sforza-Cesarini had inherited the property of both the Conti and Savelli families. All of these families were closely related, and most had given at least one Supreme Pontiff to the Holy See.

The capital value of the Chigi land in Lazio came to 1,553,922.1 scudi with an income of 35,025.47. Their property was centered in Ariccia, Farnese, Campagnano, Castel Fusano, Formello, Campo Leone, Casaccia, Cesano and Magliano.[129] The family residence is in Rome, rather than in Siena where the family originated.

The Rospigliosi Family

Giulio Rospigliosi, from a military family from Pistoia in Tuscany, was secretary of state for the previous pope, Alexander VII. Elected pope and taking the name Clement IX (1667–69), Rospigliosi was respected by both the French and Spanish and tried to maintain peace between these two nations. The Franco-Spanish War ended in 1668.

Clement IX named his brother Camillo as general of the church in 1667. Five of Camillo's sons — Tommaso, Felice, Vincenzo, Giacomo, and Giambattista — received important church offices. Tommaso (d. 1669) was appointed castellan of Castel Sant' Angelo. Felice (d. 1688)

was named a cardinal in 1673 by the succeeding pope Clement X. His uncle had given him
two abbeys as a source of income. Vincenzo
(d. 1689) was commander of the papal galleys.
In 1669 he was nominated head of all the allied
forces — Venice, France, the Papal States —
against the Turks. Their military expedition
was defeated, and the capital of Crete was lost
to the Venetians. The news of this failure hastened the pope's death. Clement IX is remembered for his "unfailing solicitude for the poor
and the sick as well as his deep piety, [which]
had won for the pope the veneration of the
people of Rome."[130] Giacomo (d. 1684), created
cardinal in 1667, was made legate to Avignon
and Ferrara and prefect of the *Segnatura di
grazia* (Tribunal of the Holy See). Giambattista
(1646–1722) was appointed commander of
the papal guard. In 1658 he was created prince
of the Holy Roman Empire. Ten years later,
Giambattista Rospigliosi acquired the dukedom
of Zagarolo from the Ludovisi family, which
had acquired it from the Colonna. He married
the heiress Maria Camilla Pallavicini(o) in
1670; her dowry included the principality of
Gallicano and the marquisate of Colonna, and
they were inherited by her descendants. Maria
was the daughter of Stefano Pallavicino. Her
first cousin Niccolò (d. 1679) had married
Flaminia (d. 1709) daughter of Camillo Pamfili,
as we have seen. Flaminia and Niccolò had no
children.[131]

Giambattista Rospigliosi and Maria Camilla
Pallavicini had four children: Maria, Niccolò,
Eleonora and Clemente Domenico. Maria married Duke Antonio Salviati (d. 1704); Niccolò
was the husband of Maria Altieri, great-grandniece of Pope Clement X; Eleonora was the
wife of Augusto Chigi; and Clemente
Domenico married Giustina, daughter of Carlo
Borromeo, and they had several sons.

The Colonna Family (Part Four)

Clemente Domenico Rospigliosi and
Giustina Borromeo were the ancestors of
Giulio Cesare Rospigliosi (1781–1859), fourth
Prince Rospigliosi and Duke of Zagarolo, who

married Margherita (b. 1786), daughter of Fil-
ippo Colonna (1760–1818) and his wife
Princess Caterina (1762–1823), daughter of
Prince Luigi Vittorio of the House of Savoy-
Carignano. The Savoy-Carignano family gave
Italy its four kings in the nineteenth and twen-
tieth centuries. Caterina was the sister of
Leopolda, wife of Giovanni Andrea Doria-
Pamfili-Landi. This branch of the Colonna
family also used the name Gioeni to distin-
guish it from other branches. Filippo Colonna
(1760–1818) was the great-grandson of another
Filippo Colonna (1667–1714) whose wife was
Olimpia Pamfili, great-grandniece of Pope
Innocent X. This latter Filippo's daughter
Agnese (d. 1780) had married Prince Camillo
Borghese. The same Filippo's grandfather Mar-
cantonio Colonna (d. 1659) had married the
heiress Isabella Gioeni, daughter of Lorenzo,
Prince of Castiglione. Their great-great-great-
great-grandson Filippo (1760–1818) had no
sons, but one of his daughters, Margherita
(1786–1864), assumed the surname Colonna-
Gioeni in order to permit her to inherit the
Gioeni wealth. (See Table 4d in Appendix A.)

Giulio Cesare Rospigliosi and Margherita
Colonna-Gioeni had two sons, Clemente and
Francesco-Cesare. From the eldest Clemente is
descended the family of Rospigliosi-Colonna-
Gioeni and from the second Francesco, the
branch of Prince Pallavicini Rospigliosi. Both
branches are still in existence.

Clemente Rospigliosi-Colonna-Gioeni
(1823–97), Duke of Zagarolo, Prince of Castiglione, a title inherited from his mother, was
the father of Prince Giuseppe (1848–1913), who
begot Geronimo, Prince Rospigliosi-Colonna-
Gioeni, born in 1907. Prince Giuseppe's
brother Camillo (b. 1850), who served as commander of the papal guard, was the father of a
son Giulio (b. 1907). Since there are male
cousins, the future of the Rospiglios-Gioeni
dynasty seems to be assured.[132]

Giulio Cesare Rospigliosi and Margherita's
second son, Francesco-Cesare (1828–87),
assumed the name Rospigliosi-Pallavicini,
being descended from Giovan Battista Rospigliosi (1646–1722) and the heiress Maria-
Camilla Pallavicini. She brought to the House

of Rospigliosi the principality of Gallicano. Francesco-Cesare's son Uberto (b. 1857) Prince Rospigliosi-Pallavicini, Prince of Gallicano, married Carolina Boncompagni-Ludovisi (1834–1910). They had four children, the youngest of whom was a son, Giulio-Cesare (1871–1941), Prince of Gallicano and Marchese of Colonna. To insure that the Rospigliosi–Pallavicini branch (now listed as Pallavicini in *Libro d'Oro*) would continue, Giulio-Cesare adopted Guglielmo, who took the name Pallavicini in 1937. Guglielmo was the son of Armando, son of Pierre de Bernis, Marchese of Courtavel.[133] Adoption was yet another way of assuring that a noble Italian, papal family's name would survive. It permitted the continuation of the Rospigliosi-Pallavicini family.

The Altieri Family

A month before his death, Pope Clement IX (Giulio Rospigliosi) named Emilio Altieri a cardinal. Emilio's brother, Giambattista the Elder (1589–1654), who had served as bishop of Camerino and later as bishop of Todi, had established the Altieri family in the Holy See when he became cardinal in 1634. Giambattista the Elder is remembered for starting to build the Altieri Palazzo in Piazza del Gesù in Rome. Five months after Clement IX's death, Emilio Altieri succeeded him and took the name of his benefactor, becoming Pope Clement X (1670–76). Born of a Roman patrician family, Clement X had been elected as a short-term, compromise pope. He was almost eighty years old when elected. He often promised the same favors to several different people, forgetting much of what he had done or was about to do. During his reign, he was dominated by Cardinal Paluzzo degli Albertoni, who served as cardinal-nephew. Cardinal Paluzzo took the name Altieri. The cardinal's nephew Gaspare Albertoni, who also called himself Altieri in order to perpetuate that name, married Laura, daughter of Antonio Altieri, brother of Clement X. She was the sole heiress of the Altieri family and its fortune, which was to be accumulated during the pontificate of the Altieri pope.

Cardinal Paluzzo Altieri (1623–98) not only kept disagreeable news away from the aged pope, but he also became the pope's major source of information. The older the pope became, the more indispensable were the services of his cardinal-nephew. The cardinal, omnipotent in his position, easily enriched himself and his family. His nephew Gaspare was made general of the church and castellan of Castel Sant' Angelo. In 1672 the Altieri family was to become princes of Oriolo and Viana and dukes of Monterano. Cardinal Paluzzo Altieri lavishly embellished, extended and completed the Altieri Palazzo, which became the residence of Gaspare and Laura Altieri. Angelo, the father of Gaspare, was appointed inspector of the papal galleys. The cardinal, keenly aware of the need to marry off his nieces (the sisters of Gaspare) to the leading families in Rome, arranged it so that his niece Ludovica Altieri became the wife of Domenico Orsini (1652–1705), Duke of Gravina, the brother of the yet-to-be-elected pope Benedict XIII. Clement X celebrated the Altieri-Orsini nuptials in 1671. Another niece, Tarquinia, became the wife of Egidio Colonna, Duke of Anticoli.[134] Egidio Colonna and Tarquinia Altieri's daughter Tarquinia married Marco Ottoboni, nephew of Pope Alessander VIII; their son Francesco (1684–1750) was the father of Giulio Cesare Colonna (1702–1787), who married Cornelia, the heiress of the Barberini family.[135]

Clement X was far more successful in providing for his family than he was in dealing with matters of state. The pope was virtually ignored by "the Sun King" Louis XIV who confiscated church property and sold it for his own income and who claimed the right to make ecclesiastical appointments. The French ambassador D'Estrées was known to intimidate the aged pontiff, who was often forced to acquiesce to French demands. This octogenarian pope was unable to resolve the problems that confronted the Vatican, and one of his few accomplishments was the construction of a second fountain in front of St. Peter's Square.[136]

As for the Altieri family progeny, Gaspare and Laura had several sons: Emilio who married Costanza, daughter of Agostino Chigi, related to Pope Alexander VII; (2) Gerolamo who married Maria Borromeo, daughter of the noble Carlo Borromeo and his wife Camilla Barberini; Lorenzo (1671–1741); and Giambattista the Younger (1673–1740). Both Lorenzo and Giambattista were cardinals. Emilio and Costanza had a daughter Maria who married Niccolò Rospigliosi of the family of the preceding pope, Clement IX. Descended from Emilio and Costanza was Prince Clemente (1795–1873) who married Vittoria Boncompagni-Ludovisi. One of Clemente and Vittoria's sons was Emilio (1819–1900). Emilio's son Paolo (1849–1901) was the father of Lodovico (1878–1955), who had no issue.[137]

Similar to the Albani family, the Altieri gave four cardinals to the church, thus insuring the family's influence in Vatican circles. Besides the two cardinal sons of Gaspare and Laura, already mentioned, there were Cardinal Vincenzo Maria (1724–1800) and Cardinal Ludovico Altieri (d. 1867), who was a member of a triumvirate of cardinals that brought about order to Rome and the Papal States after the Revolution of 1849 when Pope Pius IX, (1846–78) fled from the Eternal City.

Often such ecclesiastical influence had a price. It can be conjectured that when a goodly number of related males entered the clergy it was detrimental to the continuation of the family's name: since Catholic prelates and other members of the clergy often did not have children, their noble families had fewer males to insure progeny.

The Odescalchi-Erba Family

Pope Clement X (Emilio Altieri) was followed on the papal throne by Benedetto Odescalchi, who reigned as Innocent XI (1676–89). He came from a wealthy commercial family from Como. This pope, as had his predecessor, came into conflict with Louis XIV, who wished to administer vacant church sees in France. Innocent strongly resisted the Sun King's policies to dominate both the pope and church. He was successful in bringing about an alliance with the empire, Poland, Venice and Russia against the Turks, relieving Vienna from them in 1683 and freeing Hungary and Belgrade a few years later. He was aided by his secretary of state, Cardinal Alderano Cibo (d. 1700), brother of Duke Alberico Cibo of Massa.

Innocent's brother Carlo Odescalchi had several children. Among them was Giovanna, wife of Carlo Borromeo of Arona, of a princely family related to several papal dynasties (such as the Medici and the Colonna), and Livio Odescalchi (1612–1713), who was created duke of Ceri. Livio fought against the Turks and received from the emperor Leopold I the title Prince of the Holy Roman Empire. He was granted the dukedom of Syrmia in Hungary and Sava in Slavonia. Livio and his legal heirs were granted extensive privileges over Syrmia — including the rights to coin money and to exercise absolute legal powers and territorial sovereignty, "with the right to erect courts of justice, to employ instruments of torture, and to render justice involving life and death in all cases, civil or other." Livio received numerous other honors and titles. He was proclaimed Prince of Bassano, Marchese of Roncofreddo and Montiano, Count Palatine and Lord of Palo. King Charles II of Spain named him Grandee of Spain. In 1697, Livio was proposed as a candidate for the Polish throne.[138] He did not secure that throne, but in 1696 he acquired the dukedom of Bracciano from the Orsini family. He had no children.

Livio's titles were inherited by Baldassarre, Duke of Bracciano. Baldassarre was the son of Antonio, Marquis of Mondonico, who was the son of Alessandro Erba and Lucrecia Odescalchi, sister of Pope Innocent XI. In 1714 the Odescalchi family received the title "Serene Highness." Baldassarre bought the Chigi family's palace in Piazza S.S. Apostoli in Rome, listed in the *Almanach de Gotha*, as the residence of the Italian branch of the Odescalchi family in the twentieth century.[139] Baldassarre, second Prince Odescalchi, married two sisters, the daughters of Marcantonio Borghese. His children included Maria, wife of Renato Borromeo; Livio Odescalchi-Erba, third Prince, from whom the male line of the family is descended; and Anna Paula (1722–42), wife of

Domenico Orsini (1719–89), Duke of Gravina. Domenico was the grandson of Domenico Orsini (1652–1708) and Ludovica Paluzzo-Altieri, niece of Pope Clement X. Their daughter Giacinta (1741–59) married Antonio Boncompagni-Ludovisi, Prince of Piombino. Antonio Boncompagni-Ludovisi (1735–1805) had a son from his second wife, Vittoria Sforza. That son, Luigi Boncompagni-Ludovisi (B. 1767), married Maddalena, daughter of Baldassarre (1748–1810), fourth Prince, Duke of Ceri, son of Livio Odescaldhi-Erba, third Prince.[140]

Baldassarre, fourth Prince, who founded the Odescalchi Palace in Rome, had a brother Benedetto, a cardinal, who was assigned the diocese of Milan. Odescalchi-Erba descendants have included Cardinal Carlo (1786–1841), Archbishop of Ferrara, Vicar of Rome, who left the cardinalate in 1836 and became a Jesuit. Another descendant, Prince Baldassarre Ladislao (1844–1909), seventh Prince, entered Rome in 1870, liberating it from the papacy. He was a leader in the governmental counsel in Rome and was received as part of a deputation from King Vittorio Emanuele II to the Eternal City. Baldassarre was elected a deputy in the government, representing the center left, and was later a senator of the kingdom (1896). His patriotic leaning did not reflect the conservative administration of the pontiff at the time, Pius XI (1846–78).

Baldassarre's son Innocenzo (1778–1833), fifth Prince, was the father of Livio (1805–1885), sixth Prince Odescalchi (Duke of Syrmia, Price of Bassano, Duke of Bracciano, Marquis of Roncofreddo and Montiano and Count of Pisciarelli), who was the father of Baldassarre Ladislao, seventh Prince, noted above. This Baldassarre's son Innocenzo (b. 1883) eighth Prince, was the father of Livio (b. 1913) ninth Prince.[141] The princely Odescalchi family reside in Rome; however, numerous cousins of the Roman Odescalchi family settled and lived in Roumania and Hungary, where the family had acquired vast estates.

The Ottoboni Family Dynasty

Cardinal Pietro Ottoboni belonged to a family of Venetian nobility. He became pope after the death of Innocent XI (Benedetto Odescalchi) and reigned for only two years, from 1689 to 1691, as Pope Alexander VIII. He tried to improve the relations between the Holy See and King Louis XIV of France. His reign also saw Vatican monetary and military aid being abundantly given to his beloved Venice. He summoned his relatives to Rome and revived the odious forms of nepotism practiced by earlier popes. Since he was quite elderly and had limited time to rule and disperse papal favors, he would laughingly say, "Let us make haste as much as possible for already the twenty-third hour has struck."[142]

His grandnephew Pietro Ottoboni was given the wealthy abbey of Chiaravalle and later the legation of Avignon. He was nominated a cardinal, served as cardinal-nephew and as vice-chancellor and was named *Sopraintendente Generale* of the Papal States. His income was over 50,000 scudi a year. Pietro was a pleasure-loving youth who made merry, enjoying music, the theatre and carnivals. He collected antiques as well as rare books and manuscripts. After his death his library was added to that of the Vatican Library. Antonio Ottoboni, father of Pietro, was made general of the church and commander of the papal troops. The pope's nephew Giambattista Rubini, son of the pope's sister Cristina and Giambattista Rubini, was appointed bishop of Vincenza and was later made cardinal. He was also given the legation of Avignon and became the pope's advisor on matters of state. Marco (1656–1725), a hunchback, son of Agostino (d. 1673), a brother of the pope, served as inspector-in-chief of naval fortifications and the pontifical fleet. The pope purchased the dukedom of Fiano for 170,000 scudi for Marco, who became the duke. Marco was given as his residence the Palazzo Ludovisi in the Corso. Marco first married Tarquinia, daughter of Egidio Colonna and Tarquinia Paluzzo-Altieri, adopted grandniece of Pope Clement X. Marco's second wife was Maria, daughter of Gregorio Boncompagni-Ludovisi, Prince of Piombino.[143]

Marco's sister Chiara was the wife of the Venetian Francesco Zeno; their daughter Cornelia Zeno became the wife of Urbano Barberini.

Marco Ottoboni and Maria Boncompagni-Ludovisi's daughter Maria Francesca (d. 1758), heiress of the Ottoboni family, married Piergregorio Boncompagni-Ludovisi (b. 1709), who then added the name Ottoboni to his own. This branch of the family was then known as Boncompagni-Ludovisi-Ottoboni. Piergregorio was the second son of Antonio Boncompagni-Ludovisi (1658–1731), who had married his own niece Maria Eleonora, daughter of Gregorio Boncompagni (1642–1707) and Ippolita, daughter and heiress of Niccolò Ludovisi. This marriage was arranged to keep the family fortune and the principality of Piombino in the Boncompagni family.[144]

The Boncompagni Family Dynasty (Part Two)

Piergregorio Boncompagni-Ludovisi-Ottoboni's older brother, Gaetano Boncompagni-Ludovisi (1706–1777), Prince of Piombino, had married Laura Chigi of the family of Pope Alexander VII. Gaetano and Laura had several children, including Ippolita (1751–1812), Ignazio (1743–90) and Antonio (1735–1805).

Gaetano and Laura's daughter Ippolita married Abondio Rezzonico, nephew of Pope Clement XIII. Gaetano and Laura's son Ignazio was named a cardinal. Ignazio served as papal legate to Bologna, becoming secretary of state to Pope Pius VI in 1785. The cardinal sought reforms that he found difficult to promulgate, and he resigned that position in 1789. Their son Antonio first married Giacinta Orsini and then Vittoria (d. 1778), daughter of Giuseppe Sforza-Cesarini (1705–1744), Duke of Segni. Antonio and Vittoria's son Luigi, as noted in connection with the Odescalchi family, married Maddalena Odescalchi.

Luigi (1767–1841) and Maddalena Boncompagni-Ludovisi's children included another Antonio (1808–1883); Baldassarre (1821–94), a writer and scholar on the history of mathematics who accumulated a vast library of over 40,000 works; Maria (1813–34), wife of Mario Massimo, Duke of Rignano; Vittoria (1799–1817) who married Prince Clemente Altieri of the family of Pope Clement X; and Costanza who married her cousin Alessandro Boncompagni-Ludovisi-Ottoboni, Duke of Fiano. Alessandro (1805–1831) was the son of Marco, the son of Piergregorio and Maria Francesca. Alessandro (1805–1831) and Costanza Boncompagni-Ludovisi-Ottoboni were the parents of Marco (1832–1909), born posthumously. He became the fifth duke of Fiano and a senator in the Italian kingdom. Since Marco had several daughters, the name Ottoboni and the title of Duke of Fiano was passed on to Augusto Ruspoli, who died without posterity in 1912. Augusto was the son of Costanza (Boncompagni-Ludovisi-Ottoboni) Ruspoli, eldest daughter of the fifth Duke of Fiano.[145] Another daughter of Marco's, Luisa Maria, married Carlo Rasponi. They had a son Cesare who took the name Rasponi-Ottoboni in 1921. The male line of the Boncompagni-Ludovisi-Ottoboni family thus became extinct, while the family of Boncompagni-Ludovisi continues to thrive, even though the members are no longer ruling princes of Piombino.

In effect, Gaetano and Laura's son Antonio (1735–1805) was the last ruling prince of Piombino of the Boncompagni-Ludovisi family. Piombino was lost to the French when Napoleon conquered Italy, but after the Congress of Vienna (1815), Antonio's son Luigi liquidated his interest in the principality of Piombino for 800,000 francesconi (Tuscan silver currency) to the grand duke of Tuscany, who obtained complete control over that state. The Boncompagni-Ludovisi family did, however, retain the title Prince of Piombino.

With the money received from the sale of Piombino in the early part of the nineteenth century, the Boncompagni-Ludovisi family acquired territory near Rome, bought the Palazzo Piombino in Plazza Colonna in Rome and renovated the Villa Ludovisi, constructed by Cardinal Ludovico Ludovisi (1595–1632). The Boncompagni-Ludovisi's precious collection of statuary — much of it collected by Cardinal Ludovisi — was acquired by the National Museum della Terme.

Luigi and Maddalena's son Antonio (1808–1883) fathered Rodolfo Boncompagni-Ludovisi

(1832–1911), seventh Prince of Piombino. Rodolfo married Agnese Borghese, and they were the parents of Ugo (b. 1856) who, late in life, entered the clergy (1895) and did not become prince. Ugo was the father of Francesco Boncompagni-Ludovisi (b. 1886), eighth Prince of Piombino. He was undersecretary in the Department of Finance in the Italian government. In 1929 Francesco became governor of Rome and had several children to succeed to the various titles of that family. His son Gregorio Boncompagni-Ludovisi (1910–88) was the father of Nicolò (b. 1941), the present prince of Piombino. Gregorio's wife was Benedetta Maria Barberini-Colonna di Sciarra, and they had three children, including Nicolò. Gregorio's sister Giulia (b. 1914) married her cousin Giovanni (b. 1911) of the Boncompagni-Ludovisi-Rondinelli-Vitelli branch of the family. They had a son Luigi (b. 1934).[146] Giovanni Boncompagni-Ludovisi-Rondinelli-Vitelli was the son of Paolo (1886–1960), son of Luigi Boncompagni-Ludovisi (1857–1928) who married the heiress Isabella Rondinelli-Vitelli, Marchese of Bucine. Luigi was the son of Rodolfo Boncompagni-Ludovisi (1832–1911), seventh Prince of Piombino, and Agnese Borghese (1836–1920).

The practice of marrying cousins, very common in papal dynasties, was meant to insure inheritances within those same families. The Boncompagnis have added to their own the names Ludovisi, Ottoboni and Rondinelli-Vitelli to distinguish various branches of this papal dynasty. Through marriage, those families have brought considerable wealth to the Boncompagnis. (Refer to tables 7a–7d in Appendix A.)

The Pignatelli Family

Pope Alexander VIII (1689–91) had enhanced the Ottoboni's social and economic position, heightening the desire for other noble Roman and Italian families to intermarry with members of the Ottoboni clan.

The pope that followed, Innocent XII (1691–1700), belonged to the Pignatelli family

of the kingdom of Naples (Two Sicilies). The Pignatellis traced their ancestry back to Agilmondo, Lombardian king, and to the dukes and princes of Benevento. This was a proud and illustrious family. Innocent (Antonio Pignatelli), who was seventy-six years of age when he became pope, established an administration of reform, and his decree of 1692 *Romanum decet pontificem* limited the granting of gifts to family members and stated that only one member of the papal family could be named a cardinal, who could only receive a modest income of not more than 12,000 scudi. Innocent terminated offices such as *gonfaloniere* and captain-general of the church that had often been given, along with sizeable incomes, to relatives of the popes. He attempted to put an end to papal nepotism, which had for centuries despoiled the papal treasury and permitted the families of the popes to attain inordinate powers — much to the detriment of the church.

Pope Innocent VII's mother was Porzia Carafa (1589–1657), a distant relative of Pope Paul IV. Her father Fabrizio Carafa (d. 1590), Duke of Andria, had been killed in what might be called a "classical" scandal of the princely families: Carlo Gesualdo, Prince of Venosa and musical composer, infuriated by his wife Maria d'Avalos' affair with Fabrizio, murdered them both.

Fabrizio had been married to Maria, daughter of Luigi Carafa (1511–76), Prince of Stigliano, his cousin. It was common for Carafas to marry other Carafas, for Pignatellis to marry other Pignatellis and for Carafas, of Neapolitan nobility, to marry Pignatellis, of similar aristocratic lineage (see Table XIV). As intrinsic members of the Italian nobility, the Pignatelli and Carafa families married into prominent papal families, such as the Conti, Orsini, Caetani, Colonna, della Rovere and Borgia. Luigi Carafa, Maria's father, had married Clarice Orsini as his first wife, who was the daughter of Giovan Girolamo, Duke of Bracciano, and Felice, the illegitimate daughter of Pope Julius II (Giuliano della Rovere).[147]

But in many ways the Carafa and the Pignatelli were unlike other papal families. The

TABLE XIV: CARAFA FAMILY

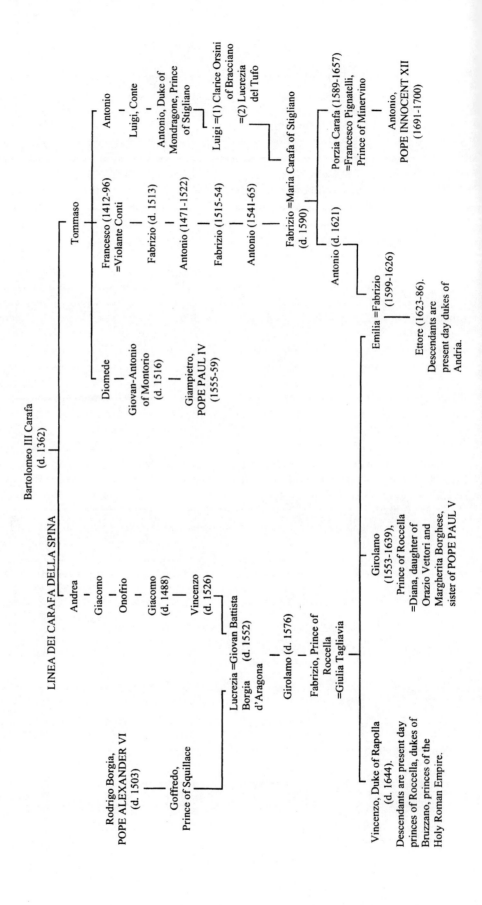

Carafa and Pignatelli families' base of power and the sources of their property and wealth were their feudal holdings in Naples and southern Italy. Other papal families were inclined to focus on, if not to live in, Rome and its region (Lazio). These same families — the Orsini, Caetani, Conti, Colonna, Savelli — had intermarried for centuries and acquired the territory and resources of the Papal States by the bequest of related pontiffs. The Carafa and the Pignatelli tended to marry the heiresses of principalities in southern Italy, mainly in the kingdom of Naples (Two Sicilies.) For example, Camillo Pignatelli, Duke of Monteleone, married Giulia Carafa, who brought in dowry the lands of Tolve, Toja, Cuccaro and Magliano and the jurisdiction for S. Mauro and del Monte Ciurala. Likewise, Caterina Caracciolo, wife of Ettore Pignatelli III, was the heiress of S. Angelo dei Lombardi. Their grandson Ettore IV, Duke of Monteleone, married Giovanna Tagliavia Aragona Cortes; Giovanna was the only daughter of the wealthy Diego, Duke of Aragona, descended from Peter III of Aragon and Costanza (the daughter of King Manfred, son of the emperor Frederick II) and Stefania Cortes, a direct descendant of Hernando Cortes (1485–1547), conqueror of Mexico.[148] Ferdinando Pignatelli, Prince of the Holy Roman Empire, (1689–1767) married his cousin, Lucretia Pignatelli, fourth Princess of Strongoli and Countess of Melissa (1704–1760); these titles went to her husband's family.

The Pignatelli family of Naples, with numerous branches still existing, at one time were the owners of 178 fiefs, 18 counties, 22 marquisates, 16 dukedoms and 14 principalities.[149] At least five cardinals were members of this family.

The Carafa Family (Part Two)

The Carafa family was descended from the Caracciolo family, whose ancestors were Lombard rulers. Gregorio Caracciolo, one of four brothers, assumed the title Count Carafa, and his descendants took that name. His wife was none other than Maria, a member of the Pignatelli family. As has been noted, the Pignatelli and Carafa families were closely related.

Pompeo Litta devotes almost an entire volume to the numerous branches of the Carafa family.[150] Members became the dukes of Forlì, Traetto, Andria, Maddaloni and Nora, princes of Roccella, Belvedere and Stigliano, counts of Policastro, Mondragone and Aliano and marchese of Montesardo and Corato. Ten cardinals were in the Carafa family.[151] This once numerous family has dwindled in the twentieth century to a few members who are princes of Roccella and princes of the Holy Roman Empire and another small branch, the dukes of Andria and Casteldelmonte.

The Carafa married wealthy heiresses, such as Vittoria Pignatelli who brought her husband Girolamo Carafa (1593–1624) 42,000 ducats. Luigi Carafa, fourth Prince of Strongoli, married Isabella Gonzaga, who brought to her husband's family the dukedom of Sabbioneta. To hold family possessions together, it was often necessary for one Carafa to marry another Carafa. Giulia, daughter and heiress of Lelio, Count of Policastro, entered into matrimony with her own uncle Fabrizio Carafa, who received a dispensation from the church to do so. Later, Teresa Carafa, Countess and heiress of Policastro, became the wife of Gennaro Carafa, seventh Prince Roccella.[152]

The Carafa and Pignatelli families benefited little from having a relative become pope (see Paul IV, the Carafa Pope, and the Carafa trial). While Pope Paul IV was generous to his nephews, they lost their possessions when they were condemned to death in 1561. It should be noted that Pope Paul IV had, at the instigation of his nephews, foolishly confiscated Paliano and other territory from the Colonna family and had given it to his nephew Giovanni Carafa, who was made duke of Paliano. Paliano was eventually returned to the Colonna family. On the other hand, Pope Innocent XII (Antonio Pignatelli), who was a firm opponent of nepotism, granted almost nothing to his family. The foundation for the wealth of both the Carafa and Pignatelli families originated, not from papal connections, but with their feudal holdings. This is not to deny that both families on occasion did benefit from papal legacies when they married into such families as the Caetani, Colonna or Orsini. A distant cousin of Pope Paul IV, Giovan Battista Carafa, married Lucrezia Borgia, daughter of Goffredo, Prince of Squillace, son of Pope Alexander VI. Lucrezia's dowry was 10,000 ducats. Another cousin, Antonio Carafa, married Elena, daughter of Giovan Francesco and Olimpia Aldobrandini, niece of Pope Clement VIII. Elena's dowry was 100,000 scudi.[153] The truth of the matter is that money and land obtained by the popes first went into the hands of their immediate families and then into the families of relatives. Eventually, through marriage, some of this inheritance spread into other families, sometimes not even related to papal dynasties. But in the main, as we have seen, this wealth moved from one papal clan into other papal clans, to be concentrated in certain noble families that had attained prominence by having a papal relative.

However, Pope Innocent XII's decree, *Romanum decet pontificem*, stemmed the tide of the papal giveaway. The eighteenth century saw a marked decrease in the nepotism of the previous centuries — but it was not entirely possible to put an end to this papal disease.

Innocent's major reform against nepotistic practices was followed by his diplomatic success with the French king Louis XIV in establishing better relations between the Holy See and France.

The first two popes who reigned at the beginning of the 1700s have been previously described: Clement XI (Giovan Francesco Albani, 1700–1721) and Innocent XIII (Michelangelo Conti, 1721–24).

The Orsini Family Dynasty (Part Four)

In 1724 Pietro Francesco Orsini was elected pope, becoming Benedict XIII (1724–30). He was the son of the duke of Gravina, Ferrante Orsini (1623–60), and Giovanna, daughter of Carlo Frangipane, Duke of Grumo. The Frangipane family was famous for its impact on

the papacy some seven hundred years earlier. Benedict XIII was a pious Dominican with no political experience. When Pietro Francesco Orsini was archbishop of Benevento, he had met Niccolò Coscia who became Orsini's chief advisor as pope. Coscia brought from Benevento a circle of friends who gained important offices and positions in Rome. This was not the nepotism of family so common with previous popes, but it was a new and insidious kind of favoritism of self-serving associates. It had the same effect as the favoritism of relatives: the depletion of church finances.

Pope Benedict placed enormous authority in the hands of his chief minister, Cardinal Niccolò Coscia. Coscia, greedy and power-hungry, enriched himself shamefully, selling church offices and freely accepting bribes for papal favors, so that he pocketed over 2,000,000 scudi for himself. Controlled and isolated by the unscrupulous Coscia, Benedict's administration was a disaster. After Benedict died, Coscia was tried and convicted for his illicit gains. He was deprived of privileges, losing all ecclesiastical benefices. His revenues were sequestrated, and he was fined 100,000 scudi, which was given to charity. Finally, Coscia was imprisoned in Castle Sant' Angelo for ten years.[159] Coscia was released by Pope Benedict XIV (1740–58).

Benedict XIII was the last pope of the one-thousand-year-old Orsini family to play such a crucial role in the history of the church. (Refer to Tables 1a–1g in Appendix A.) The Orsinis had been created princes of the Holy Roman Empire in 1624. In 1718 the family received from Pope Clement XI the title of Roman princes, assistants to the pontifical throne. The Orsini papal dynasty had flourished since the election of Giovanni Gaetano Orsini, who became Pope Nicholas III (1277–80); numerous progeny descended from the pope's brothers, Napoleone, Rinaldo and Gentile. (The family had other branches as well, descended from distant cousins of Nicholas III.)

Nicholas III's brother Napoleone was the forebear of the branch of the family that produced the dukes of Bracciano and the dukes of Gravina — the family of Pope Benedict XIII.

Through intermarriages within the family, though, Benedict was descended from all three brothers, as well as from the Piccolomini, Savelli and Caetani families. Benedict's brother Domenico (1652–1705) had married a grand-niece of Pope Clement X (Emilio Altieri); Domenico's grandson Domenico (1719–1789) married an Odescalchi, heiress of the family of Pope Innocent XI (1676–89), and their daughter had married Antonio Boncompagni-Ludovisi, Prince of Piombino.[155] Filippo Bernualdo (d. 1735), fourteenth Duke of Gravina, son of Domenico (1642–1705) and nephew of Pope Benedict XIII, was given the titles Roman Prince and Prince of the Holy Roman Empire. Filippo's son Domenico (1719–1789), fifteenth Duke and second Prince, was the father of another Filippo Bernualdo (1742–1824); he, in turn, fathered another Domenico (1765–90), whose son was yet another Domenico (1790–1874), fifth Prince. The fifth prince's wife was Maria-Luisa Torlonia (1804–1883) of the important Italian banking family; their son was Filippo (b. 1842), sixth Prince and nineteenth Duke of Gravina. Filippo's son Domenico-Napoleone (b. 1868) was the father of Virginio (b. 1892). The nineteenth duke Filippo's sister, Teresa, married Enrico Barberini-Colonna of Sciarra, Prince of Palestrina (d. 1889), the last male descendant of that branch of the Colonna family. The present-day descendants of Prince Virginio Orsini continue to live at the Palazzo Orsini in Rome.[156]

Pope Benedict XIII's cousins, the dukes of Bracciano, who had also descended on the male line from Napoleone Orsini, had produced Alfonsina (d. 1520), wife of Pietro de' Medici (son of Lorenzo the Magnificent), and Giangiordano, Duke of Bracciano, husband of Felice della Rovere (daughter of Pope Julius II). Their descendants married into such papal dynasties as the Farnese, Medici, Damasceni-Peretti, Borghese and Ludovisi. This Orsini branch of the family, the dukes of Bracciano, became extinct in 1699.

Nicholas III's brother Rinaldo was the fore-father of Clarice, wife of Lorenzo de' Medici. Descended from Clarice and Lorenzo were popes Leo X and Leo XI. Rinaldo's branch of

the family became lords of Monterotondo, and the male line lasted until 1650.

Nicholas III's brother Gentile was the ancestor of the dukes of Nola and counts of Pitigliano. His descendant Nicola, Count of Pitigliano, (b. 1442) was the father of Lella, wife of Angelo Farnese (brother of Pope Paul III), and Lodovico Orsini, whose wife was a daughter of Elisabetta Carafa (sister of Pope Paul IV). Lodovico's daughter Marzia (d. 1548) married the brother of Pope Pius IV, and his daughter Girolama was the wife of Pierluigi Farnese, son of Pope Paul III. The Orsini dukes of Nola ceased in 1528, and the counts of Pitigliano became extinct in 1640.

The intricacies of their relationships and marriages with other papal dynasties — the source of their power and wealth — sustained the Orsini family to the very present. The Orsini branch which produced the dukes of Gravina, as well as Pope Benedict XIII, continues today as a princely Roman family.[157] Their influence penetrated the inner structure of the church and the papacy as can be attested by their continued presence in its history. It was a presence maintained by alliances with other papal families. Given their enormous influence and pivotal historical role, it is ironic to note that the last Orsini pope — Benedict XIII — was so weak a pontiff.

The Corsini Family

The Corsinis were from Florence: they were bankers and merchants who had acquired a vast fortune and had secured territories where they reigned as lords. Filippo Corsini (1578–1636) settled in Rome, where his family and the Medici maintained one of the richest banks in Europe.[158] One of Filippo's sons, Neri (1624–79) entered the clergy, becoming papal nuncio to France, camerlengo and legate to Ferrara. In 1664 he was made a cardinal. His nephew Lorenzo, son of Bartolomeo Corsini (1622–85) also selected an ecclesiastical life, at the age of thirty-three. Lorenzo (1652–1740) had been partially blind since the age of eight and was totally blind after 1732.

Lorenzo was elected pope, taking the name Clement XII (1730–40). During the early part of his pontificate, he brought to trial Cardinal Coscia, who had abused his powers under Benedict XIII. It was during Clement's reign that the dukedom of Parma and Piacenza, a fief of the Papal States, was occupied by Prince Carlo of Spain (also known as Don Carlos de Borbón [Bourbon], later King Charles III of Spain), son of the heiress Elisabetta Farnese. The pope saw those states lost to the Holy See.[159] The pope's foreign policies generally were unsuccessful, but his accomplishments included the beautification of Rome. He had the facade of St. John Lateran completed and the Corsini Chapel, designed by Alessandro Galilei, constructed in that same basilica. He erected the well-known Fontana di Trevi and established the Capitoline museum of antique sculpture. Before becoming pope, Lorenzo Corsini began his collection of books and documents and placed them in his palazzo in Rome on the Circo Agonale. For ten million scudi, Lorenzo had acquired the treasured library of Cardinal Gualtieri (1660–1728) and had enriched it. Lorenzo's nephew Cardinal Neri Corsini (1685–1770) transported this collection, along with a gallery of paintings, to Palazzo dei Riarî alla Lungara. The library, known as *La Biblioteca Corsiniana*, contained many rare and old manuscripts. This palazzo of the Corsini family was acquired by the Italian state in 1883; at the same time, the family donated the library, which served as the foundation of the Royal Academy dei Lincei.

Pope Clement IX's nephews, Bartolomeo and Neri were the sons of his brother Filippo. They were much loved by their uncle, and they benefited from his lofty position. Bartolomeo (1683–1752) was appointed commander of the light cavalry. He became prince of Sismano, grandee of Spain and president of the cabinet of King Carlo (Charles III) in Naples. Neri (1685–1770) was named a cardinal in 1730, becoming cardinal-nephew. He was a poor administrator for the Holy See; rather, he was a scholar who gathered significant works of art and books for the Corsini Library in his palazzo.

Bartolomeo's grandson Andrea (1635–95)

was made a cardinal at twenty-four years of age, serving as bishop of Sabina and vicar of Rome. Andrea's brother Bartolomeo (1729–92) married Vittoria Felice, daughter of Giulio Cesare Colonna (1702–1787) and the heiress Cornelia Barberini (d. 1797). Giulio Cesare and Cornelia had created the Colonna-Barberini family.[160] Bartolomeo had several sons including another Neri (1771–1845) and Tommaso (1767–1856) who were extremely active in the political life of Tuscany. Bartolomeo's son became director of the Department of State (1798–99) for Tuscany and counsellor of state to Paris. He was further honored by being named Count of the Empire. These were turbulent times; France, under Napoleon, had occupied Tuscany as well as most of Italy. After the Bourbon Restoration in 1815, Neri became minister of interior for Tuscany and plenipotentiary at the Congress of Vienna where he was able to obtain the restitution of those art works confiscated by the French during their occupation of Tuscany. He was an avid defender of Tuscan independence, and his life was devoted to benefit the economic and political life of his state. A year before his death, he was president of the cabinet and minister of foreign affairs.

His brother Tommaso served as the ambassador for the grand duke of Tuscany to Bonaparte when the general was in Bologna campaigning to conquer Italy, in 1796. Tommaso went to Paris where he was named senator and count of the empire. He returned to Rome after the Bourbon Restoration and twice became a senator, in 1818 and in 1847. In 1849 there was a popular uprising, and Pope Pius IX (1846–78) was forced to flee from Rome. Tommaso tried to establish a moderate government in Rome, but he refused to join the newly formed Roman Republic and returned to Florence. Upon the pope's return to the Eternal City, Tommaso became a member of the council of the Papal States.

Tommaso's son Andrea (1804–1868), Duke of Casigliano and Prince of Sismano, was appointed a senator in 1845 by the grand duke of Tuscany and later served as the Tuscan minister of foreign affairs, from 1849 to 1856. Andrea's brother Neri (1805–1859), Marchese of Laiatico, was governor of Livorno for several years. In 1848 he was created Tuscan minister of foreign affairs and, some ten years later, took part in the provisional government when the grand duke of Tuscany was deposed. He died just before Tuscany joined the kingdom of Italy. His son Tommaso (1835–1919), Prince of Laiatico, was a deputy in the Italian parliament from 1865 to 1882 and then senator, ending his career as mayor of Florence. He encouraged archaeological digs of Etruscan ruins. In 1883 Tommaso Corsini presented to Italy the Palazzo Corsini in Rome, including the famous Corsini Library.[161]

Tommaso (1835–1919) became the sixth prince Corsini and the fifth Duke of Casigliano. In 1858 he married Anna Barberini-Colonna di Sciarra (1840–1911) of Palestrina. His son Filippo (b. 1873) succeeded as the seventh prince Corsini and became mayor of Florence. He had several sons to continue the dynasty.[162] Tommaso's brother Andrea (1843–95), Marchese of Giovagallo, had a son and several grandsons. The city of Florence remains the residence of the princely Corsinis.

Long after the pope's death, the political activities of the family of Clement XII contributed to Italian independence, and their scholarly endeavors enriched Italy's cultural heritage. The accomplishments of the Corsini pope during his weak administration pale in comparison to the achievements of Corsini family members in the succeeding generations.[163]

CHAPTER FIVE

The Papacy After 1740—
The Modern Period

Surprisingly, it was Prospero Lambertini who, after a six-month conclave, was elected pope after Clement XII, becoming Benedict XIV (1740–58). Open-minded and enlightened, Benedict was able to rectify relations with the European powers that had been so poorly handled by his predecessor. He was truly a man for all seasons — a scholar, a diplomat, a pious person and a humanitarian (calling for better treatment of the Indians in South America). Benedict came from an aristocratic, but modest, family from Bologna. He forbid his brother to come to Rome, and he kept himself entirely free from nepotism. He brought relative peace to the church by his wise and cautious moderation.

When Benedict died, Carlo della Torre Rezzonico, of a wealthy Venetian family, became Pope Clement XIII (1758–69). Rome and the pope were challenged when Portugal, France, Spain and other countries suppressed, and in some cases expelled, the Jesuits in their states. Realizing that the authority of the papacy was the real object of this attack, Clement defended the Jesuits.[1] The pope's nephew Carlo was made a cardinal in 1758, serving as bishop of Porto and secretary of the memorials, but he did not abuse or interfere with the pope's control over church matters.

The pontiff to follow Clement XIII, took the same name, Clement XIV (1769–74) but lacking strength and afraid of France and Spain, he published a brief abolishing the Jesuit order.

This was hardly a constructive achievement as it severely affected Catholic education and missionary work throughout the world. Clement XIV spent the last years of his life fearful that he would be assassinated, and it was rumored that he was poisoned when he died in 1774.[2]

Giovanni Angelo Braschi of a noble family from Cesena, in Romagna, became the next vicar of Christ. The Braschi family was related to the Ghislieri, the family of Pope Pius V.[3] Braschi took the name Pius VI (1775–99). He was inept in dealing with the issues that faced him, and the papacy went into a steady decline. Even the Holy Roman Empire moved to place the church under the authority of the bishops, independent of the pope in Rome.

It was the French Revolution and its aftereffects which dominated the last ten years of Pius VI's pontifical reign. In 1796 Napoleon's army took control of the Papal States and forced the humiliating peace of Tolentino on the pope. It had been negotiated by the pontiff's nephew Luigi Braschi-Onesti. After the Treaty of Tolentino, Cardinal Giuseppe Doria-Pamfili-Landi of the family of Pope Innocent X (Giambattista Pamfili) became the secretary of state for Pius VI. His policy was favorable to Napoleon, but peace between the pope and the emperor was only to be temporary, and Pius was expelled from Rome and forced to flee to Tuscany and then to Valence, France, where he died, but not before leaving plans to hold the next election for pope in Venice.

It was most unfortunate that under Pius VI nepotism again flourished. His nephew Luigi (1745–1816), son of the pope's sister Giulia and her husband Girolamo Onesti, was made the duke of Nemi. Purchasing Nemi had cost the pope 94,000 scudi. Nemi had once been the territory of the Frangipane. The Jesuit estates at Tivoli with a value of 85,000 scudi were also given to Luigi, who annexed Braschi to his own surname to become Braschi-Onesti. Pius VI became the object of great scandal when (for the benefit of Luigi Braschi-Onesti) he declared himself the heir of Amanzio Lepri, priest of the Maltese Order. The inheritance was worth a million and a half scudi and was contested by Lepri's niece. Eventually the pope's nephew Luigi received half of the estate.[4]

When Luigi married Costanza Falconieri, they were presented with 10,000 gold doubloons. Luigi was made prince of the Holy Roman Empire and a Spanish grandee, and he received substantial gifts from the king of France and the king of Sardinia. Conducting himself in an overbearing manner, Luigi "lived in grand style, granting audiences to cardinals and prelates." In 1791, a huge Roman palace, the Palazzo Braschi, designed by Cosimo Morelli, was built for Luigi at a cost of 150,000 scudi. (That palace later became the seat of the minister of the interior and then housed the Federation of Rome of the National Fascist Party; it is presently the Museum of Rome.) Luigi made dishonest speculations in grain, and his greed adversely affected papal finances. When the pope decided to drain the Pontine Marshes near Rome at an enormous expense, the reclaimed land was presented to his nephews, Luigi and Romualdo. Pius VI had already named Luigi's brother Romualdo (1753–1817) as a cardinal. Romualdo was also appointed secretary of briefs and camerlengo. He profited greatly from these positions; but, in contrast to his brother, Romualdo was a pleasant, young man and was liked by everyone.[5]

Pope Pius VI is remembered for completing the Pio-Clementino Museum started by Clement XIV, with its treasure of antique sculpture, much of it collected by Winckelmann and Cardinal Albani. During his reign Pius VI encouraged the French sculptor Canova, who created the pope's sepulchral monument in St. Peter's Basilica. Pius' body had been brought from France to Rome in 1802 by his successor Pope Pius VII (1800–1823).

Pius VII's name was Luigi Chiaramonti, and he too was born in Cesena. In 1804, accompanied by Cardinal Romualdo Braschi-Onesti, nephew of the previous pope, Cardinal Stefano Borgia who died on the trip and other members of the Curia, Pius VII went to Paris to crown Napoleon as emperor. Four years later, Napoleon's troops occupied Rome, and Cardinal Romualdo was expelled from that city by orders of the emperor. The next year France confiscated the Papal States. Pius excommunicated the emperor, who had the pope arrested. In 1810 the other nephew of the previous pope, Luigi Branchi-Onesti (1745–1816) was appointed mayor of Rome by Napoleon, much to the distaste of the people.

Intimidated by the emperor and poorly treated, Pius was forced to sign the Concordat of Fontainebleau, later repudiated, in which he apparently surrendered the Papal States. Fortunately for the papacy, which served as an incentive for the opponents of Napoleon to unite, Napoleon was defeated. With the Bourbon Restoration, Pius returned to Rome. At the Congress of Vienna (1814–1815), the Papal States were given back to the papacy. It was during this same time that Prince Camillo Borghese sought to obtain the art works he had sold to Napoleon, but he failed in this attempt; however, Prince Neri Corsini, Tuscan plenipotentiary at the congress, was able to secure the restitution of art works stolen by the French.

Pius VII reactivated the Society of Jesus, which had been abolished in 1773. He was a pope who tried to modernize the papacy and to renew its prestige; in that he was somewhat successful.

Chiaramonti, the family name of Pius, was one of nobility. Of the five remaining popes of the nineteenth century, all were born into families of Italian aristocracy. Leo XII (1823–29) was a member of the Genga family of Castello della Genga near Ancona. Pius VIII (1829–1830) belonged to the Castiglioni family. His secretary of state was Cardinal Giuseppe Albani of the family of Pope Clement XI (1700–1721). Pope Gregory XVI (1831–46) was of the Cappellari family from Belluno. During his pontificate, Gregory was known to have had a lover. Her name was Clementina Verdesi, the wife of Gaetanino Moroni, a valet in the pope's chamber. Gaetanino became a wealthy man during Gregory's reign as Supreme Pontiff. Clementina earned the reputation as "Puttana santissima" (the holiest harlot).[6]

The mid-nineteenth century was one of nationalistic fervor, and the next pope Pius IX (1846–78), whose actual name was Giovanni Maria Mastai-Ferretti, witnessed the Revolution of 1848. Pius was forced to leave the Eternal City, and the following year Rome was declared a republic. But with the help of French troops, the pope was able to return to the city. Ten years later, the Papal States were taken over by the forces of the Risorgimento (the movement for Italian independence), engineered by the kingdom of Sardinia-Piedmont, and in 1870 Rome itself was occupied. The pope considered himself a prisoner in the Vatican and forbid Italians to take part in the political life of the new kingdom of Italy.

The loss of temporal power placed the emphasis of Pius' reign on spiritual and religious matters. In December 1869 he called the First Vatican Council; in the following year, the doctrine of papal infallibility was proclaimed. It firmly asserted the supremacy of the pope in matters of faith and morals when pronouncements were made *ex cathedra*. Less than a hundred years later, the Second Vatican Council was called by Pope John XXIII (1958–63). It was an attempt to update the church and to set in motion an ecumenical movement. The first council of Pius IX had tended to be a reactionary reaffirmation of church authority, whereas the second was a progressive step forward — preparing the church for the vastly changing contemporary period.

The last pope of the nineteenth century was Leo XIII (1871–1903) of the noble Pecci family. His was a pontificate that focused on social justice, especially via encyclicals and manifestos such as *Rerum novarum* (1891). He is also remembered for opening the Vatican library to scholars.

In the twentieth century the papacy followed a course very much dictated by the past. In contrast to Pope Leo XIII, the next pope Pius X (Giuseppe Melchiorre Sarto, 1903–1914) was born of a very poor family. In 1954 he was canonized a saint. Previous to Pius X, the last pope to be declared a saint was Michele Ghislieri (1566–72), known as Pius V. Both were very spiritual popes, and neither were popes who encouraged nepotism. (Pius V made his grandnephew both a cardinal and his secretary of state, but he did not divest the church of its properties and possessions to enrich his relatives.) After Pius X, the next pope to accept the tiara was Benedict XV (1914–22), born Giacomo della Chiesa of a family of Italian nobility. His father, Marchese Giuseppe della Chiesa, was descended from King Berengar II of Italy, whose family had produced Pope Callistus II (1119–24), and his mother was a Migliorati of the same family as that of Pope Innocent VII (1404–1406).[7] The pope's niece Giovanna married Prince Augosto of the Barberini-Colonna, a descendant of several papal families (see Table XV). Benedict reigned during World War I. Offering a peace proposal that was ignored, the pope could do little to alleviate the sufferings and devastation that occurred during that war. This plan for peace had been drawn up with the capable assistance of the talented clergyman Eugenio Pacelli.

In the conclave of 1922, Camillo Cardinal Laurenti was elected, but he refused to become pope; Achille Cardinal Ratti was subsequently selected. The Ratti family was ennobled, becoming the counts of Desio. As Pope Pius XI (1922–39), he ruled the Vatican during that period when fascism under Benito Mussolini rose to power. In 1929, the Lateran Accord was signed between the pope and Mussolini by which the kingdom of Italy was formally recognized by the Holy See. At the same time, Roman Catholicism was acknowledged as the official religion of Italy, and the Vatican City became an independent state. The lawyer for the Holy See, Francesco Pacelli (1874–1935), served as plenipotentiary for the pope to negotiate this

TABLE XV: DELLA CHIESA FAMILY

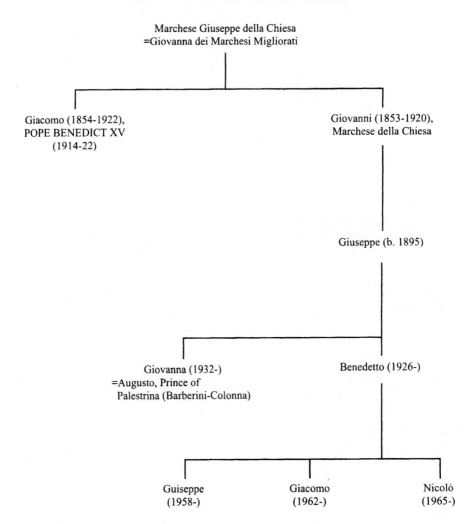

Marchese Giuseppe della Chiesa
=Giovanna dei Marchesi Migliorati

Giacomo (1854-1922),
POPE BENEDICT XV
(1914-22)

Giovanni (1853-1920),
Marchese della Chiesa

Giuseppe (b. 1895)

Giovanna (1932-)
=Augusto, Prince of
Palestrina (Barberini-Colonna)

Benedetto (1926-)

Guiseppe
(1958-)

Giacomo
(1962-)

Nicolò
(1965-)

treaty with Mussolini's representatives. Pacelli's brother Cardinal Eugenio was a close advisor of the pope as well as his secretary of state from 1930 until 1939 when he was elected pope as Pius XII (1939–58).

Pius XII belonged to the Pacelli family of Rome (see Table XVI), long involved with jurisprudence and other matters within the Vatican. Pius XII's grandfather Marcantonio Pacelli (d. 1902) was the founder and editor of *L'Osservatore Romano*, the official Vatican newspaper. He had also served as the Vatican's undersecretary of interior. The pope's uncle Ernesto Pacelli was a key financial advisor to Pope Leo XII,[8] and the pope's father, Filippo,

became dean of the Vatican lawyers. Eugenio Pacelli's own brother Francesco (1874–1935) was the highly regarded attorney whom Pius XII made a marchese with the right for his descendants to inherit the title. Eugenio Pacelli, similar to many of the popes in the seventeenth century, belonged to a family that was in the inner circle of Vatican life.

Pius XII has often been accused of nepotism — somewhat of a different sort from that of the Renaissance period, but nepotism nevertheless. Profiting from the influence of their uncle, three nephews of the pope — Carlo, Marcantonio and Giulio Pacelli — received the title of prince. Carlo and Giulio were among

TABLE XVI: PACELLI AND MONTINI FAMILIES

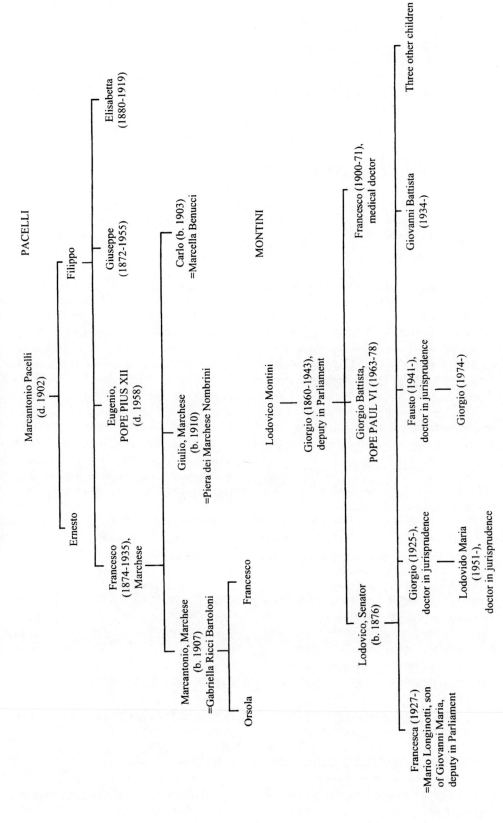

Pius' principal advisers, making top-level decisions and policies.[9] They handled many of the financial holdings of the Catholic Church. It was during the administration of Pius that the Vatican became "one of the largest financial powers in the world."[10] The three Pacelli princes were placed on the boards of Italian companies, companies in which the Holy See had substantial financial investments. It had even been charged that Don Carlo and Don Giulio Pacelli had "made personal gains from Pontifical Aid Organization dealings."[11] By their positions, acquired because they were the nephews of the pope, they gained prestige and enormous wealth.

It was also during Pius' term that one of his staff members had extraordinary control over the pope's actions and activities. That person was Bavarian-born Sister Pascalina. They had met in Switzerland at a convent where he was recuperating from fatigue. The year was 1917. She worked as part of his household staff when he became papal nuncio to Munich and Berlin. He eventually brought her to Rome when he became secretary of state to Pius XI, and she was even to assist him in the conclave when he was elected pope in 1939.

Sister Pascalina has been described as the nun who "rigorously supervised everything, from major decisions to minute details.... His [Pope Pius'] trust in her was complete, and with good reason, for she never once, not even inadvertently, betrayed his confidence." The same historian portrays Sister Pascalina as being "short-tempered, despotic, frightfully outspoken; she ruled the papal household with an iron hand ..."[12] The biographer Paul L. Murphy in his book La Popessa, in spite of the derogatory and inflammatory title, writes sympathetically of Pascalina. She is depicted as demonstrating a forceful personality, but showing remarkable intelligence and insight.

Since the pope suffered from both illness and weariness, she attempted to protect him from the demands of his office, especially those exacted by the cardinals in the Curia. She arranged his appointments, decided who was to see the pope and even interrupted audiences that the pope was having. She determined

"what papers Pius would sign, what order of business, temporal or spiritual, would receive papal priority." Much of what she did was to mitigate the pressures made on the pontiff, who suffered from ill health. She even influenced the pope regarding important appointments, including the selection of "Cardinal Spellman to become Archbishop of the Diocese of New York." Her influence on the pope seemed to know no bounds. She helped Pius with an encyclical entitled "Miranda prorsus," dealing "with the effect upon morals of the movie, television, and radio broadcasting," and they wrote numerous addresses together. Her power over the pope increased as he became older and weaker. Sister Pascalina was a modern day Donna Olimpia Maidalchini, sister-in-law to Pope Innocent X (Giambattista Pamfili, 1644–55). Both women decided whom the pope should see and often determined what the pope should do; but, unlike Donna Olimpia, Pascalina did not seek personal wealth or glorification. The sister was quite remarkable and her talents reached their zenith in World War II. During that war Sister Pascalina played a major role in assisting and saving Jewish individuals who sought Vatican protection. She headed the Pontifical Relief Committee, which shielded thousands of Jewish people in church sanctuaries.[13]

Pius XII, who was the pope during World War II, has often been condemned for not doing enough to protect the Jewish population in Europe and for not standing up to Hitler. After the war, the pope expressly denounced Catholics who voted for communists in Italy, threatening to excommunicate those who were party members or supporters of communist candidates. After Pius died, he was succeeded by John XXIII (Angelo Roncalli), a warm humanitarian. He was the pope of the Second Vatican Council and a cleric who, as an apostolic delegate to Turkey and Greece, had diligently sought to assist in the escape of Jewish refugees in eastern Europe. John's pontificate lasted for less than five years; Cardinal Giovanni Montini was then elected pope in 1963.

It has often been reported that Monsignor Giovanni Montini, who had been an assistant to Cardinal Pacelli, had come into conflict with Pius XII and had been sent away from Rome to Milan in 1954 as a kind of punishment. Montini, who was politically left of center and who vigorously supported the concept of priest-workers, could easily have come into disagreement with Pius XII and the Curia, both of which were deeply conservative.[14] On the other hand, Montini's removal may well have been based on the Montini's criticism of Pius' nepotism and of his handling of church finances.[15] What could have been an even worse black mark is that Sister Pascalina disliked Montini intensely.[16] Even though Montini had worked closely with Pius XII, he was not made a cardinal and therefore could not succeed Pius as pope. Montini had assisted Cardinal Pacelli when he was secretary of state under Pius XI. Later, when Pacelli became pope, he directed internal church affairs. From 1952 to 1954, Montini served as pro-secretary of state. He had been that pontiff's trusted aid for seventeen years.

It was finally John XXIII (1958–63) who raised Montini to the purple. Later, when elected pope, Montini took the name Paul VI (1963–78) and continued the Vatican Council begun by his predecessor. His program was one of implementing the reforms approved by the council. Members of the Montini family had served in the Italian government (see Table XVI).

Popes Pius XI, John XXIII and Paul VI were from the Lombard region in northern Italy. The family of Pius XI became counts of Desio, where Pope Pius XI (Achille Ratti) had been born. Members of the Montini family of Brescia had become distinguished in the law profession and in parliament. Pope John XXIII (Angelo Roncalli), one of thirteen children of a peasant family from Sotto il Monte, a small community near Bergamo, had several brothers who also had large families.

John Paul I (Albino Luciani) of northeastern Italy succeeded Paul VI, but he served as pope for little more than a month before he died suddenly. The present pope, elected in 1978, is John Paul II. Before his election, he was Cardinal Karol Wojtyla of Poland. He was the first non–Italian pope in 455 years. The last such pope was Hadrian VI (1522–23) from the Netherlands. Only the future will tell us if the control of the papacy will return into the hands of Italian families.

CHAPTER SIX

Papal Dynasties and Noble Houses

I: The Italian Houses— A Retrospective

From the earliest history of the Roman Catholic Church, the bishops of Rome were often citizens of Rome: St. Anacletus (76–88), St. Clement I (88–97), St. Alexander I (109–116) and St. Sixtus I (116–25) were all probably Roman. They were the third, fourth, sixth and seventh bishops.

Roman families began to have members elected to the post of bishop of Rome. From the Anici family of Rome (gens Anicia) were elected Felix III (483–92) and his grandson Gregory I (590–604). Agapitus I (535–36), son of Giordianus, a priest, was also a member of this family.[1] Likewise, Pope Stephen V (885–891), son of Marinus, was a member of the same Roman family as Sergius II (844–47) and Hadrian II (867–72).[2] Gregory II (715–31) may have been a member of the Savelli family.[3] Popes Stephen II (752–57) and Paul I (757–67), brothers, were members of the Orsini (Bobo-Orso) family. Hadrian I (772–95) and Hadrian III (884–85) belonged to the Conti family, whose origins were with the Latin gens Octavia and the later Anicia.[4] Marcellinus (296–304), Sixtus III (432–40) and Stephen IV (816–17) were either members or relatives of the Colonna family. The ancestry of the Colonna family indicates that the Latin gens was Julia, then Anicia:

Juli-Juliani-Tertulli
Julii Flavi Anici-Tertulli
Comites Tusculi
Columnenses

This heritage shows that the Colonna family were descended from the counts of Tusculum.[5]

Many of these early pontiffs were members of the Roman aristocracy, such as Stephen I (254–57) of the gens Julia, Vigilius (537–55), Pelagius I (556–61), Gregory IV (827–44) and Stephen V (885–91). It can be presumed that the families of the early popes of Roman aristocracy were probably related by intermarriages. These intermarriages were to continue with such families as the Conti, Colonna, Orsini, Savelli and Caetani—all of the gens Anicia. The Anici were a distinguished Roman family going back to the empire.

In 904 when Sergius III of the counts of Tusculum was elected pope, the Conti of Tusculum, and later of Segni, began their monopoly on the Holy Sea. Teofilatto, consul and senator, his daughter Marozia and her son Alberico II placed their candidates on St. Peter's chair from 911 to 963. Leading Roman families married into the Conti so that for several hundred years the papacy was dominated by that family or its relatives.

Also successful in placing their candidates on the papal throne were the Frangipane, Crescenzi and Pierleoni families. John XIII (965–72) was a member of the Crescenzi family. Leaders of that influential family put antipope Boniface VII (984–85) as well as popes John XV (985–96), John XVII (1003), John XVIII (1003–1009) and Sergius IV (1009–1012) on the papal throne. Subsequently, the Conti of Tusculum faction again assumed power, installing several family members to the papacy: Benedict VIII (1012–24), John XIX (1024–32) and Benedict IX (1032–44, 1045, 1047–48).

A reform movement was ultimately urged by the Pierleonis, who reacted to the political election of the pope, which they felt was detrimental to the church. The Crescenzi, Frangipane and Conti families had placed their candidates on the throne primarily to enhance themselves, not for religious or church reasons. Members of the Pierleoni family became popes as Gregory VI (1045–46), Gregory VII (1073–85) and antipope Anacletus II (1130–38). Prior to becoming pope, Gregory VII, a forceful and powerful member of the church hierarchy, had managed the election of Nicholas II (1058–61) and Alexander II (1061–73).

This was a period of time of considerable conflict and tension between the emperors and the Roman aristocracy. And several popes belonged to German and French royal families and had been nominated by the emperor as in the case of Bruno of Egisheim, who took the name Leo IX (1049–54). His aunt Adelaide of Egisheim was the mother of the emperor Conrad II, whose son was the emperor Henry III. Henry nominated his kinsman Bruno of Egisheim. Adelaide's husband, Count Henry of Spires (Speyer), was a great-grandson of the emperor Otto I; Count Henry's brother Bruno served as Pope Gregory V (996–99), the choice of the emperor Otto III.

The emperors interfered, much to the dismay of the Roman populace, with the election of the popes because they wanted the bishops of Rome to forge policies consistent with the interests of the empire. Henry III had nominated Count Gebhard of Dollnstein-Hirschberg, who became Pope Victor II (1055–57). The next pope, Stephen IX (Frederick of Lorraine), was not only a descendant of Charlemagne, but his uncle was Adalberto, King of Italy. Frederick was a cousin to the Contis, who also claimed descent from Charlemagne. Descended from

King Adalberto were popes Callistus II (Guido of Burgundy, 1119–24) and Gregory X (Tebaldo Visconti, 1271–76).

After the death in 1085 of Pope Gregory VII, who died in exile and who courageously fought against the interference of the emperor, there was again a period of marked struggle. There were four antipopes — Clement III, Theodoric, Albert (Aleric or Adalbert) and Silvester IV — before Gelasius II was elected in 1118.[6] He was from Gaeta and a member of the Caetani family. Soon afterwards, the violent rivalries between the Frangipane and the Pierleoni families ignited again, as they had during the boisterous and tumultuous installations of Pope Honorius II and Celestine (II) in 1124. At this point, the Pierleonis proclaimed antipope Anacletus II and the Conti named antipope Victor IV. Other antipopes, nominated by the emperor Frederick I Barbarossa, were to follow, demonstrating the German emperor's wish to dominate the papacy as it had a hundred years earlier. These German antipopes included Victor IV (1159–64), Paschal III (1164–68) and Callistus II (1168–78). The struggle with the emperor continued into the papacy of Pope Urban III (1185–87).

In 1187 Paolo Scolari was elected Pope Clement III (1187–91). He was Roman and an uncle of Lotario Conti, Pope Innocent III (1198–1216). Upon the death of Clement III, Giacinto Bobo of the Orsini family was elected as Pope Celestine III (1191–98). The Orsini and Conti family were closely related. Table XVII shows how the Conti were intricately connected by marriage to the Colonna, Orsini and C(G)aetani families. As shown in this and previous tables, these families also intermarried with such powerful popemakers as the Crescenzi, the Pierleoni and the Frangipane. In a later period, the Farnese and Medici could claim the Conti as their ancestors. A listing of popes belonging to these families can be found later in this chapter in the discussion titled "The Borghese — Case in Point."

Innocent III (1198–1216) of the Conti family was appointed guardian of the emperor Frederick II, who would play so pivotal a role in the history of Europe. Frederick too was a

TABLE XVII: CONTI, COLONNA, ORSINI and C(G)AETANI FAMILIES

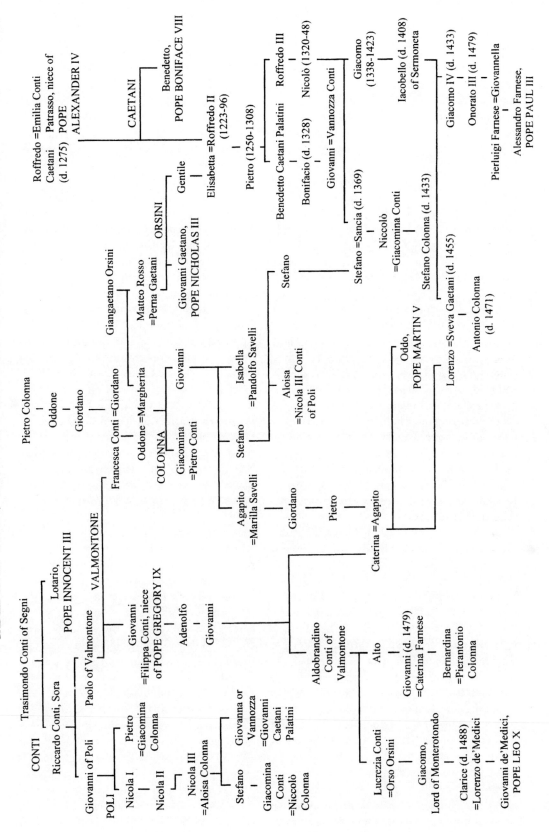

descendant of Adalberto, King of Italy, and of Charlemagne. His great-great-granduncle was Pope Callistus II (1119–24); but in spite of his papal connections, he was a thorn in the side of Pope Gregory IX (Ugo Conti, a cousin of Pope Innocent III), as were Frederick's sons Manfred and Conradin during the reign of Pope Alexander IV (1254–61), another member of the Conti family and a grandnephew of Pope Gregory IX. Frederick II's son Manfred had a daughter Costanza (d. 1302) who married King Peter III of Aragon, and their descendants became the kings of Spain, Sicily and Naples.[7] For a period of time, Spain and Naples were to play a dominant role influencing the Roman papacy. In 1271, Gregory X (Tebaldo Visconti) of an ennobled family from Milan became pope. Popes from the north of Italy and from France at the end of the thirteenth century and during the Babylonian Captivity (1309–1379) were often related to the Visconti of Lombardy and to the Fieschi family of Genova, which gave the church two pontiffs, Pope Innocent IV (1243–54) and Pope Hadrian V (1276). In a later period, Pope Gregory XIV (Niccolò Sfondrati, 1590–91) was descended from the Viscontis. Pope Clement VI (1342–52) and his nephew Pope Gregory XI (1370–78), of the Roger de Beaufort family, were distantly akin to antipope Clement VII (Roberto of Geneva, 1378–94) of the Visconti. The Fieschi and Visconti families also married into the Savoy family which gave the church the last of the antipopes, Felix V (1439–49).

In 1277, Giovanni Gaetano Orsini was elected pope, becoming Nicholas III. His mother was a Caetani. The principal branches of his family were descended from his brothers, Rinaldo, Gentile, Matteo and Napoleone. Members of succeeding papal families frequently married the descendants of these brothers. Innocent III's successor, Pope Honorius III (1216–27) had been a member of the aristocratic Savelli family that also produced popes Gregory II (715–31) and Honorius IV (1285–87) and that would marry into the Orsini family. The Fieschi family also married into the Orsini family. In fact it can be shown repeatedly that as popes emerged from new families, these families were likely to marry into either the Orsini or Colonna families, attaching themselves to the royalty of the papacy.

Two of the Medici popes, Leo X (1513–21) and Leo XI (1605) were descended from the Orsini and Conti families. Besides marrying into the Colonna, Savelli, Caetani, Conti and Fieschi families, the Orsini dynasty married into many other papal families — Farnese, Carafa, Piccolomini, della Rovere, Borgia, Medici, Migliorati, Borghese, Altieri, Boncompagni-Ludovisi, Odescalchi, Dorla-Pamfili, Medici of Marignano, Damasceni-Peretti and Sforza; and was interrelated to most of the others (see Tables 1a–1g in Appendix A).

At the end of the thirteenth century, Cardinal Benedetto Caetani was elected pope. He took the name Boniface VIII and stood for the supremacy of the church over all earthly kingdoms. His mother was a Conti, niece of Pope Alexander IV. The Caetani, along with the Conti (and later the Sforza-Conti-Cesarini, heirs of the Conti), Orsini, Colonna and Savelli, formed the nucleus of the old Roman aristocratic families that constituted the royalty of the papacy. Boniface was responsible for the Babylonian Captivity, whereby the papacy moved to France and was dominated by French popes. When the papacy returned to Rome, however, the tradition of selecting popes from Italian aristocratic families continued: Boniface XI (1389–1404) was a member of the Tomacelli family; Innocent VII was of the Migliorati family, which was to marry into the Borgia, Orsini and della Rovere families.

In the fifteenth century, Venice was to emerge as a world power; the papacy, in turn, responded by electing noble Venetians to the throne of St. Peter. They were Gregory XII (Angelo Correr, 1406–1415), his nephew Eugene IV (Gabriele Condulmer, 1431–47) and his nephew Pope Paul II (Pietro Barbo, 1464–71). Their cousins were the Zenos, who were to marry into another papal family, the Barberinis.

It was Pope Eugene IV who sought to regain church property from the Colonna family. It had been lavishly given to them by Pope Martin V (1417–31), whose reign marked the end of the Great Schism. Martin's family had been connected by marriage to the Caetani, Conti, Orsini and Savelli; Martin perfectly represented the nepotistic tendency and tradition of these Roman families, placing the Papal States and treasury at the disposal of his family. Martin V was the son of Caterina Conti, descended from one of the nephews of Pope Innocent III. His great-great-grandmother was a Savelli, and his brother married a Caetani of the family of Boniface VIII. This marriage is, of course, ironic since it was that pope who tried to destroy the power of the Colonna at the end of the thirteenth century, and it was Sciarra Colonna who slapped Pope Boniface and brought his reign to an end.

Eugene IV was both the nephew and uncle of a pope. The fifteenth and sixteenth centuries were truly family histories for the Vatican. It seemed that papal succession depended on the direct relationship of one pope to another: Pius II (1458–64) of the Piccolomini family had a nephew Pius III (Todeschini-Piccolomini) who became pope in 1503; Callistus III (1455–58) of the Borgia family also had a nephew pope, Alexander VI (1492–1503); likewise, Sixtus IV (1471–84) of the della Rovere family was the uncle of Julius II (1503–13). Pope Leo X (1513–21) of the illustrious Florentine Medicis was followed a year after his death by his first cousin Clement VII (1523–34), and Leo's great-grandnephew was proclaimed Pope Leo XI in 1605.

The mother of Pope Paul III (1534–49) was a Caetani; her ancestor was Pope Boniface VIII's brother. Through his daughter Costanza, Pope Paul III was the ancestor of the Sforza-Conti-Cesarini family, the legitimate inheritors of the Conti family. While there was no Sforza pope, that family allied itself with many of the Roman-Italian papal families of the seventeenth and eighteenth centuries.

The Italian popes of the Conti clan, as well as related families, had common ancestry with most of the royal houses of Europe. The Contis claimed that their ancestor was Tolomeo, who married Bertha, daughter of the emperor Louis I, son of the emperor Charlemagne.[8] Another founder of the Conti (Alberichi) dynasty, Alberico II, married Alda, who also descended

from Charlemagne. The Visconti claimed descent from Berengar II, King of Italy, great-grandson of Charlemagne.[9] During a later period, other papal families, such as the Medici and Farnese, were to continue this tradition, marrying into the kingly Bourbon family of France and Spain. The papal families of the Renaissance period (Borgia, della Rovere, Medici and Farnese) also tended to marry into the older papal dynasties, to intermarry with each other and, later, to marry into newly created papal dynasties like the Boncompagni, Borghese and Aldobrandini.

By the end of the fifteenth century, Spain had emerged as a world power; subsequently it would play a role in Rome. Increasingly, as Spain exerted a powerful influence on the entire Italian peninsula, the families of the popes and the papacy itself sought connections with Spanish royalty: King Ferdinand(o) II of Spain had a natural son Alfonso who became archbishop of Saragossa, and his daughter Juana became the bride of Juan Borgia, Duke of Gandia, grandson of Pope Alexander VI. Ferdinando I, King of Naples, an illegitimate son of the king of Aragon and a first cousin to King Ferdinand(o) II of Spain, had married his children and grandchildren into the papal families so that they became intimately related (see Tables XVIIIa and XVIIIb). One of King Ferdinando's daughters, Maria, was the wife of Antonio Piccolomini, Duke of Amalfi, brother of Pope Pius III and nephew of Pope Pius II; his daughter Giovanna married Leonardo della Rovere, cousin (or brother) of Pope Julius II; his daughter Lucrezia was the wife of Onorato Caetani III of Fonda; yet another daughter, Maria Cecilia, married Giangiordano Orsini, Duke of Bracciano whose second wife was Felice della Rovere, daughter of Pope Julius II. Ferdinando's grandson Luigi was the husband of Battistina Cibo, granddaughter of Pope Innocent VIII. Ferdinando's grandchildren also married into several prominent Roman, papal families; Giovanna was the wife of Ascanio Colonna; Sancia was the wife of Goffredo Borgia, Prince of Squillace, son of Pope Alexander VI; and Sancia's brother Alfonso married Lucrezia Borgia, the pope's daughter.

TABLE XVIIIa: HOUSE OF ARAGON(A), KINGS OF NAPLES

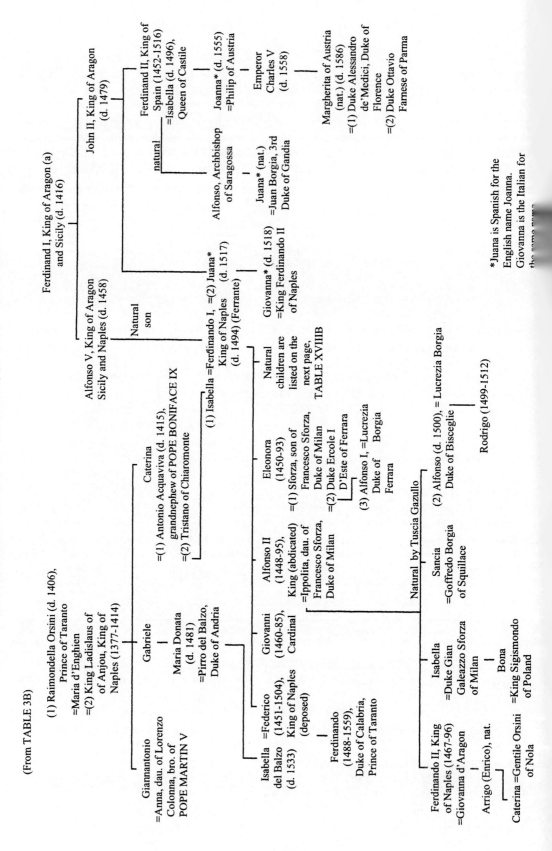

TABLE XVIIIb: ILLEGITIMATE CHILDREN OF KING FERDINANDO I OF NAPLES
(continued from table XVIIIa)

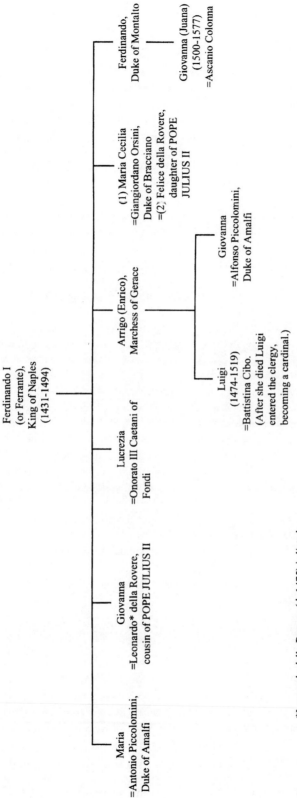

Ferdinando I
(or Ferrante),
King of Naples
(1431-1494)

Maria
=Antonio Piccolomini,
Duke of Amalfi

Giovanna
=Leonardo* della Rovere,
cousin of POPE JULIUS II

Lucrezia
=Onorato III Caetani of
Fondi

Arrigo (Enrico),
Marchess of Gerace

Luigi
(1474-1519)
=Battistina Cibo.
(After she died Luigi
entered the clergy,
becoming a cardinal.)

Giovanna
=Alfonso Piccolomini,
Duke of Amalfi

(1) Maria Cecilia
=Giangiordano Orsini,
Duke of Bracciano
=(2) Felice della Rovere,
daughter of POPE
JULIUS II

Ferdinando,
Duke of Montalto

Giovanna (Juana)
(1500-1577)
=Ascanio Colonna

*Leonardo della Rovere (d. 1475) is listed
as the son of Raffaele della Rovere, brother
of POPE SIXTUS IV (1471-84), by Pompeo
Litta in his *Famiglie celebri italiane*. Litta
assumes that Leonardo is the older brother
of Giuliano della Rovere (POPE JULIUS
II), But it seems that Leonardo was a first
cousin of POPE JULIUS II, and was the son
of Bartolomeo della Rovere, a brother of
POPE SIXTUS IV and Raffaele della
Rovere. Refer to Table VII.

The popes of the early and late Renaissance were inclined to raise their families into the realm of Italian nobility, using their influence with the kings and emperors of Europe to obtain titles for family members. Thus, King Ferdinando I of Naples, who wished to enjoy the good graces of the pope, made Alfonso Piccolomini, nephew of Pope Pius II (and the king's son-in-law), the duke of Amalfi in 1461; the king also had Goffredo Borgia, son of Pope Alexander VI (and another sons-in-law), created the prince of Squillace and the count of Cariati.[10] Another son of Pope Alexander, Juan Borgia, was ennobled, becoming the duke of Gandia in Spain.[11] King Alfonso II of Naples made Juan the prince of Teano in southern Italy. Pope Julius II facilitated the inheritance of the duke of Urbino to his nephew Francesco Maria I; the pope also gave Pesaro to his nephew. Pope Clement VII saw to it that his son Alessandro was made the first Medici duke of Florence, and Pope Paul III had his son Pier Luigi Farnese proclaimed the duke of Parma and Piacenza in 1545. The families thus promoted by papal relatives would emerge as the preeminent nobility of Italy. The Piccolomini family would marry into the Sforza, Farnese, Borgia, Conti, Orsini, Carafa and Colonna families (see Table XIX).

II: The Italian Houses and European Nobility

Papal Families, Their Descendants and Relations

The papal dynasties continue, and thousands of descendants walk this earth even though they may not carry those Medieval and Renaissance surnames. The Conti family (Dukes of Segni, Poli, Valmontone), the royalty of the papacy, is extinct; but intermarriage with the Orsini, Caetani, Sforza and Colonna transmitted the blood of the Conti into those families as well as into succeeding papal families, including the Medici. The enormous power held by later Renaissance popes enabled them to create their own ducal and papal dynasties.

It should be pointed out that the main branches of such families — Visconti (dukes of Milan), Medici (grand dukes of Florence), della Rovere (dukes of Urbino), Cibo (dukes of Massa), Borgia (dukes of Gandia and princes of Squillace) and Farnese (dukes of Parma and Piacenza) — had died out; again, however, through marriage these families have descendants who are members of more recent papal families and of present-day Italian (if not, European) nobility.[12]

The popes and their families were elevated with titles and territories and entered the front ranks of Italian aristocracy. Consequently, members married into the ruling families of Italy — the d'Este, Gonzaga and Savoy — as well as into the royal houses of Europe. While it is not possible to delineate all the nobility of papal descent, a sample through the ages will graphically illustrate their eminence and pervasiveness. It should also be pointed out that several branches of the Colonna, Caetani, Boncompagni-Ludovisi, Borghese, Odescalchi, Corsini and Chigi-Albani exist into the present time.

Those dynasties which married into the Colonna, Caetani and Orsini families were allied to all the old papal families, including the Conti and Savelli, since they were all so intimately related. The Colonna family, as indicated, can boast of being descended from Charlemagne. The lineage of some of the more recent papal families follows.

Visconti

During the Middle Ages, the Visconti family of Pope Gregory X (1271–76), descended from Charlemagne and King Adalberto of Italy, were propelled into prominence in Milan when Ottone Visconti was appointed the archbishop of Milan in 1262 (see Table XXa). Soon after, the Visconti were made lords of Milan, becoming the dukes of that city. Members of the Visconti family would unite with the crown heads of Europe.

By her marriage to Duke Leopold III of Hapsburg, Verde Visconti (d. 1365), a daughter

TABLE XIX: BORGIA-PICCOLOMINI-FARNESE PAPAL FAMILY RELATIONSHIPS

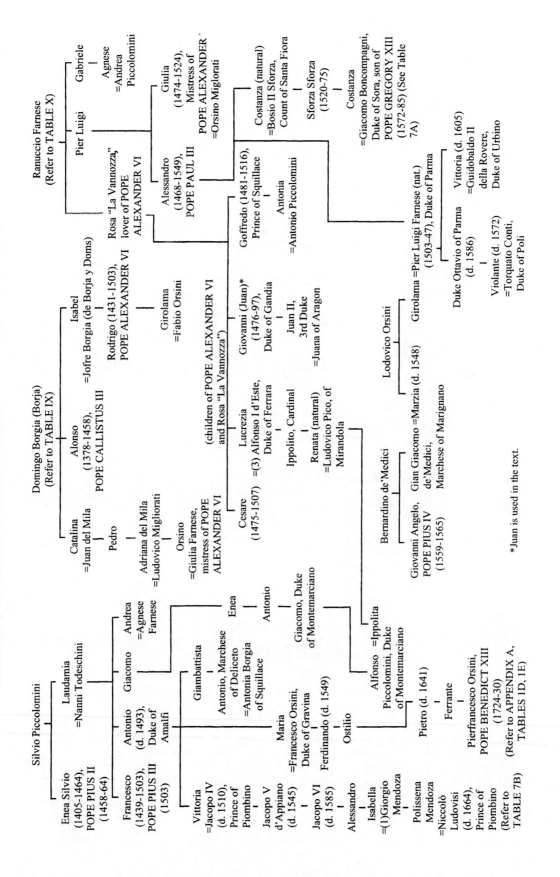

TABLE XXa: VISCONTI, ALBERICHI and CONTI FAMILIES

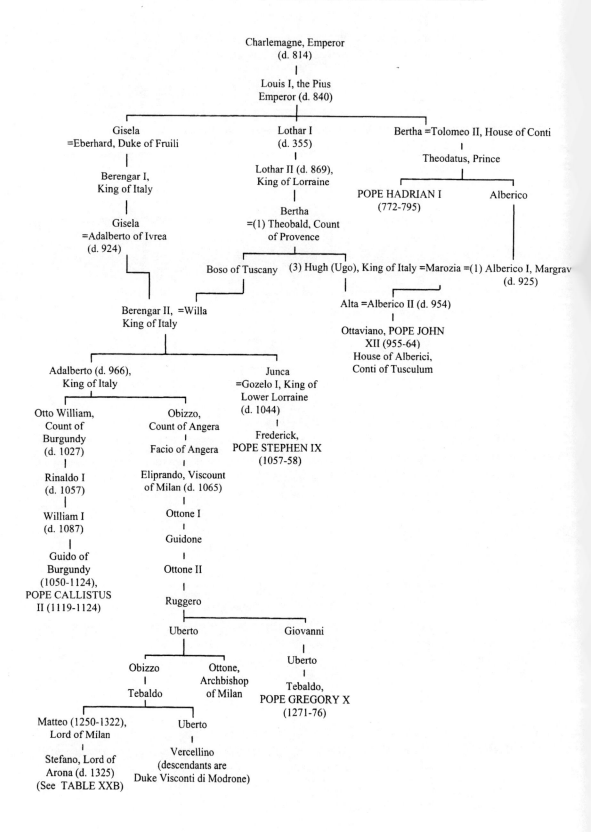

Charlemagne, Emperor
(d. 814)

Louis I, the Pius
Emperor (d. 840)

Gisela
=Eberhard, Duke of Fruili

Lothar I
(d. 355)

Bertha =Tolomeo II, House of Conti

Theodatus, Prince

Berengar I,
King of Italy

Lothar II (d. 869),
King of Lorraine

POPE HADRIAN I
(772-795)

Alberico

Gisela
=Adalberto of Ivrea
(d. 924)

Bertha
=(1) Theobald, Count
of Provence

Boso of Tuscany   (3) Hugh (Ugo), King of Italy =Marozia =(1) Alberico I, Margrav
(d. 925)

Berengar II, =Willa
King of Italy

Alta =Alberico II (d. 954)

Ottaviano, POPE JOHN
XII (955-64)
House of Alberici,
Conti of Tusculum

Adalberto (d. 966),
King of Italy

Junca
=Gozelo I, King of
Lower Lorraine
(d. 1044)

Otto William,
Count of
Burgundy
(d. 1027)

Obizzo,
Count of Angera

Facio of Angera

Frederick,
POPE STEPHEN IX
(1057-58)

Rinaldo I
(d. 1057)

Eliprando, Viscount
of Milan (d. 1065)

William I
(d. 1087)

Ottone I

Guidone

Guido of
Burgundy
(1050-1124),
POPE CALLISTUS
II (1119-1124)

Ottone II

Ruggero

Uberto

Giovanni

Uberto

Obizzo

Ottone,
Archbishop
of Milan

Tebaldo

Tebaldo,
POPE GREGORY X
(1271-76)

Matteo (1250-1322),
Lord of Milan

Uberto

Stefano, Lord of
Arona (d. 1325)
(See TABLE XXB)

Vercellino
(descendants are
Duke Visconti di Modrone)

TABLE XXb: VISCONTI KINGS OF FRANCE, HOLY ROMAN EMPERORS (H.R.E.)

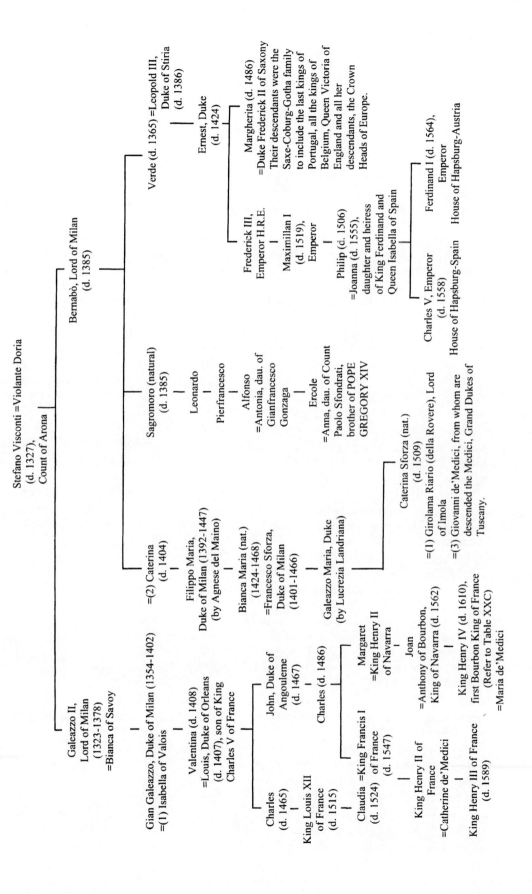

of the lord of Milan, was an ancestor of the Hapsburg emperors of the Holy Roman Empire, the emperors of Austria, the kings of Spain (including the present reigning king), the Bourbon dukes of Parma, the Hapsburg grand dukes of Tuscany, the Bourbon kings of the Two Sicilies, the dukes of Wurttemberg and the present claimants to the thrones of Italy and France (see Table XXb).

Verde's granddaughter Margherita married Duke Frederick II of Saxony, whose descendants were the members of the royal house of Saxony, kings and emperors of Germany, and the kings and queens of Great Britain. Descended too from Duke Frederick II and Margherita was the House of Saxe-Coburg-Gotha, which includes the kings of Portugal, the kings of Belgium and the kings of Bulgaria.[13] Queen Victoria's mother and her husband were members of this family. Descended from Queen Victoria and Albert, Prince Consort, is Queen Elizabeth II of England; King Olaf of Norway; Michael, former king of Roumania; Alexander, Crown Prince of Yugoslavia; King Carl XVI of Sweden; Margrethe II, Queen of Denmark; Constantine, former King of Greece; and Kira, a claimant to the throne of Russia. The royal house of Saxony is related to many of the princes of smaller German states, including Saxe-Meiningen and Saxe-Altenburg. Elector Friedrich August I (1670–1733) had an illegitimate son Maurice, Comte of Saxe. He was recognized by his father and emerged as a distinguished military leader. Maurice was the great-grandfather of Amandine Aurore Lucie Dupin Dudevant (1804–76), who wrote under the pseudonym George Sand.[14]

Verde's cousin Valentina (d. 1498) was the daughter of Gian Galeazzo, Duke of Milan. Valentina married the duke of Orleans, son of King Charles V of France; she became the ancestor of numerous French kings, including Henry II, Henry III and Francis I whose sister Margaret was the grandmother of the first Bourbon king of France, Henry IV, ancestor of the kings of France, the kings of Spain, Portugal, Italy, Naples and Sicily, the dukes of Parma, the present king of Belgium and grand duke of

Luxemburg, Holy Roman Emperors, the emperors of Austria, the present prince of Liechtenstein, the dukes of Wurttemberg and the royal house of Bavaria (see tables XXb and XXc).

The sisters of Verde — including (1) Antonia, (2) Maddalena, (3) Agnese and (4) Elisabetta — also married into distinguished princely houses. (1) Antonia, wife of the count of Wurttemberg, was a forebear of that house. (2) Maddalena married into the Bavarian princely house, and her daughter Elizabeth became one of the ancestors of the Hohenzollern family, the kings of Prussia and kaisers of Germany. (3) Agnese's marriage to Francesco I Gonzaga made her a progenitor of that noble house as well as of the family of Hapsburg-Lorraine. (4) Elisabetta, who became the wife of Ernst of Bavaria, was an ancestor of that ducal house. The Visconti also married into the Sforza families as well as into other noble houses in Italy so that the royal families of Europe were these families' cousins.[15]

A branch of the Visconti family, Visconti di Modrone, dukes of Modrone, marchesi of Vimodrone, continue to live in Milan. Luchino Visconti, the movie director, who made *Rocco and His Brothers* is a member of this family. The mother of Pope Gregory XIV (Niccolò Sfondrati, 1590–91) was Anna Visconti of Modrone.

Cibo

The descendants of Innocent VIII (Giambattista Cibo) through his son Franceschetto and Maddalena de' Medici were not as numerous as those of the Visconti. Pope Innocent found it to be politically advantageous to have his son Franceschetto marry the daughter of Lorenzo the Magnificent. (Refer to Table X.) The pope's great-grandson became the marchese of Massa and assumed the name Cibo Malaspina. The last Cibo Malaspina was the heiress Maria Teresa who married Ercole d'Este of Modena; their daughter Maria Beatrice (1750–1829) became the wife of Ferdinand, Archduke of Austria, and her descendants took

TABLE XXc: THE MEDICI AND THE KINGS OF FRANCE

THE DESCENDANTS OF LORENZO DE'MEDICI, THE MAGNIFICENT (1449-92)

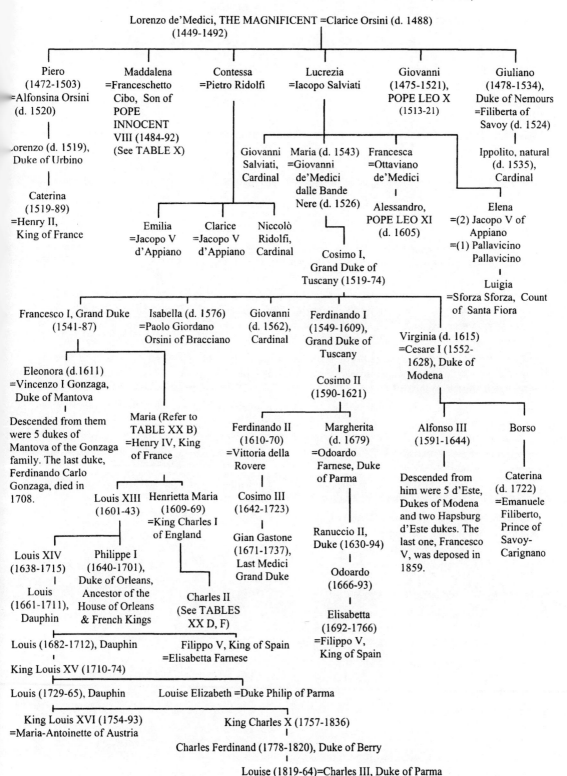

the name Hapsburg-d'Este and were dukes of
Modena. Archduke Ferdinand (d. 1806) was
the son of Maria Theresa (Hapsburg heiress)
and the emperor Franz (Francis) I of the Holy
Roman Empire; his brother was the emperor
Leopold II (d. 1790). These Hapsburgs have, of
course, the blood of the Visconti family. The
last Hapsburg-d'Este, Maria Teresa (d. 1919),
married King Louis III of Bavaria, and the present representatives of that royal house are
Cibo descendants.[16]

Borgia

The descendants of Pope Alexander VI
(Rodrigo Borgia) mostly derive from the pope's
son Caesar Borgia, whose daughter married
into the family of Bourbon-Busset (still in exis-
tence), and from the pope's daughter Lucrezia
Borgia, who married Duke Alfonso d'Este of
Ferrara. Alfonso and Lucrezia's granddaughter
Anna d'Este married into the families of Guise
and Savoy, making her the ancestor of the
Orléans, Conti, Conde and Guise families in
France.[17]

The Borgia family too are related to illustrious members of royalty as a result of the
marriages of Anna de'Este. Anna d'Este's
descendants include the present king of Spain,
the kings of France, Bulgaria and Portugal, the
dukes of Parma, the royal house of Bavaria, the
emperors of the Holy Roman Empire, the
emperors of Austria, the present king of Belgium, the grand duke of Luxemburg, the
prince of Liechtenstein, the royal house of
Wurttemberg, the Italian princely houses of
Doria-Pamfili-Landi and the Rospigliosi-
Colonna-Gioeni (see tables XXd and XXe).

Caesar Borgia's wife Carlotta d'Albret was a
French princess. She was a great-great aunt of
King Henry IV of France, the founder of the
Bourbon royal house. Caesar and Carlotta's
daughter married Philip of Bourbon-Busset,
and their descendants married into French
nobility. One member of the family married a
niece of Louise de Penancoet de Kéroualle, the
infamous duchess of Portsmouth, mistress of
King Charles II of England. Charles and Louise's

son Charles Lennox, Duke of Richmond, is
ancestor of prominent members of English
noble families, including the Lennoxes, Foxes
and Napiers, as well as the dukes of Abercorn
and Bedford, all cousins of the Bourbon-Bussets
(see Table XXg).[18] Charles II was descended
from Lorenzo de' Medici and Valentina Visconti (see tables XXc and XXd).

In more recent times, it should be noted
that Prince Xavier (b. 1889) of the princely
house of Bourbon-Parma married Marie-
Madeleine, daughter of the count of Lignières
of the Bourbon-Busset family. Their son Carlos
Hugo (b. 1930), Prince of Bourbon-Parma, is a
direct descendant of Pope Paul III (Alessandro
Farnese)—since the forebears of the Bourbon-
Parmas were King Philip V of Spain and Elisabetta Farnese—and of Pope Alexander VI
(Rodrigo Borgia). The latter pope's granddaughter Louise Borgia (daughter of Caesar
Borgia and Carlotta d'Albret) is an ancestor of
the Busset-Bourbon family.[19]

Carlos Hugo is a claimant to both the ducal
throne of Parma and the royal throne of Spain.
He claims rights to the Spanish throne from his
Carlist cousins, who insisted on observing the
Salic law that excludes women from succeeding
to the Spanish throne. The present king of
Spain, Juan Carlos, is the great-great-grandson
of Queen Isabella II (1830–1904), whose father
set aside the Salic law so that she could become
queen. Carlos Hugo is a direct descendant of
King Philip V of Spain through the male line.
He married Princess Irene, second daughter of
former Queen Juliana of the Netherlands, and
they have four children. Carlos Hugo and his
children have Farnese, Borgia, Visconti, Orsini
and Medici blood.

Medici

The relationship of Bourbon princes to
these papal families is readily explained. Philip
V, first Bourbon king of Spain, was the great-
great-grandson of King Henry IV of France
and his wife Maria de' Medici. Maria was the
great-great-granddaughter of Lorenzo de'
Medici, the Magnificent, and his wife Clarice

TABLE XXd: DESCENDANTS OF POPE ALEXANDER VI (RODRIGO BORGIA), LORENZO THE MAGNIFICENT AND POPE PAUL III (ALESSANDRO FARNESE) INTO THE ROYAL HOUSES OF EUROPE

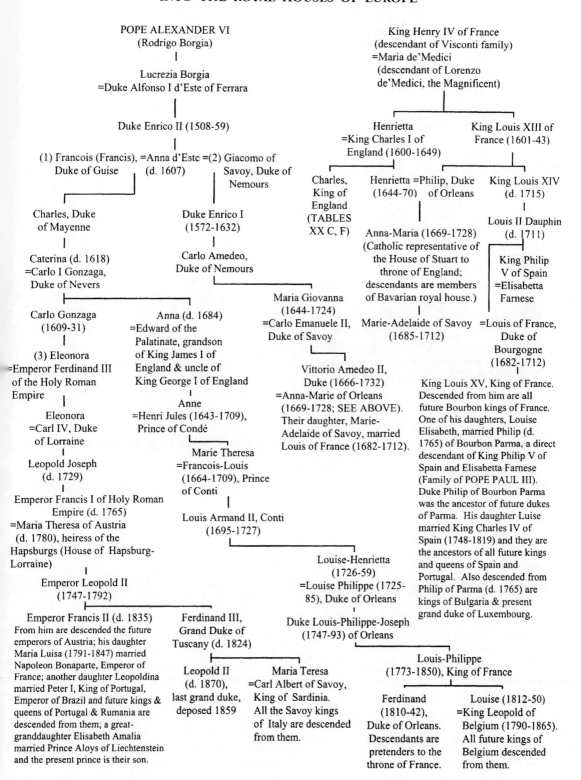

Orsini. King Henry IV of France was the great-great-great-grandson of Valentina Visconti (d. 1408) (see Table XXb). King Philip (Filippo) V's wife, Elisabetta Farnese, was descended from Pier Luigi Farnese and Girolama Orsini — whose ancestors included members of the Gaetani and Conti families — and from Ottavio Farnese and Margherita of Austria, natural daughter of the emperor Charles V of the Hapsburg Family.

Margherita of Austria was also married to the first duke of Florence, Alessandro de' Medici. The Medici grand dukes married the daughters of Austrian archdukes as well as members of the Gonzaga, d'Este, Farnese and della Rovere families. When Maria de' Medici, daughter of grand duke Francesco I (1541–87) espoused Henry IV, she became the ancestor of the remaining Bourbon-Orléans kings of France, the Bourbon kings of Spain and the kings of Belgium. The Medici epitomized the elevation of a papal and political dynasty into a royal one. The descendants of the Renaissance popes were primarily to be found in the royal families of the Catholic kingdoms since the Protestant Reformation, which took place at the same time, prevented the intermarriage between Catholic and Protestant royal houses.[20]

Lorenzo de' Medici (d. 1492) was the father of Pope Leo X, the uncle of Pope Clement VII and the great-grandfather of Pope Leo XI; while his descendants, the grand dukes of Tuscany, were to become extinct, he had many other descendants from the female lines. They included the Gonzaga, dukes of Mantova; the d'Este and Hapsburg-de'Este, dukes of Modena; and the last Farnese dukes of Parma (see Table XXc). A great-granddaughter of Cosimo I de' Medici married the prince of Savoy-Carignano from whom all the kings of Italy are descended as well as the royal family in Bulgaria (see Table XXe). All the Holy Roman emperors and the emperors of Austria, descended from Maria Theresa and her husband the emperor Franz I, as well as the present royal house of Wurttemberg and the prince of Liechtenstein, are direct descendants of both Cosimo, first grand duke of Tuscany and Lorenzo the Magnificent.

della Rovere

The rival of Pope Alexander VI and the Borgia children was Pope Julius II (Guiliano della Rovere). That pope's daughter Felice della Rovere married Giangiordano Orsini, and her descendants married into the Sforza (counts of S. Fiora), the Borghese family (princes Borghese, princes Aldobrandini and princes Torlonia) and the present princely house of Boncompagni-Ludovisi of Piombino. Julius' nephew Niccolò's daughter Elena married Stefano Colonna of Palestrina; they become the ancestors of the present-day Barberini-Colonna family and the Corsini family of Florence. The della Rovere dukes of Urbino, who were descended from another nephew of Pope Julius II, became extinct in 1623. Vittoria della Rovere, daughter and heiress of Duke Federico Ubaldo, last della Rovere duke of Urbino, married Ferdinando II de' Medici.

With Ferdinando and Vittoria's grandson Gian Gastone de' Medici (1671–1737), the Medici dukedom came to an end. Francesco Maria I della Rovere, Duke of Urbino, had a daughter Elisabetta who became the wife of Alberico Cibo, the duke of Massa, a direct descendant of Lorenzo de' Medici and Pope Innocent VIII; Elisabetta and Alberico's offspring, as noted, married first into the d'Este, later into the Hapsburg-d'Este and finally into the royal house of Bavaria.[21] [Refer to Table X.]

Farnese

As for the Farnese family, it was descended directly from Pope Paul III, and members of that illustrious ducal house married into the Orsini, Aldobrandini, Savoy and d'Este families. Pope Paul's mother belonged to the Caetani family of Pope Boniface VIII.

Ottavio Farnese, grandson of the pope, was the husband of the daughter of the emperor Charles V, and his brother Orazio Farnese married the daughter of Henry II, King of France. Duke Ranuccio Farnese I united into matrimony with Margherita; daughter of Gianfrancesco Aldobrandini, nephew of Pope Clement VIII.

TABLE XXe: BORGIA AND MEDICI DESCENDANTS AND THE HOUSES OF SAVOY AND SAVOY-CARIGNANO

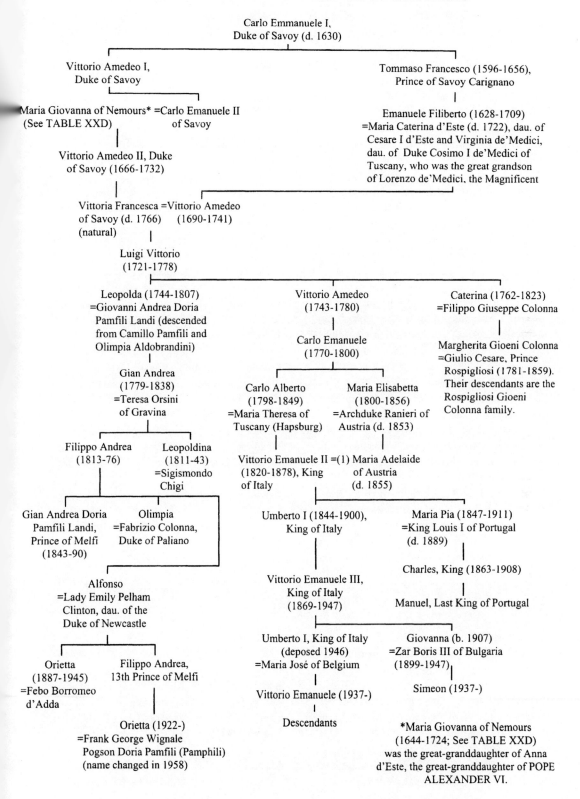

Carlo Emmanuele I,
Duke of Savoy (d. 1630)

Vittorio Amedeo I,
Duke of Savoy

Tommaso Francesco (1596-1656),
Prince of Savoy Carignano

Maria Giovanna of Nemours* =Carlo Emanuele II
(See TABLE XXD)   of Savoy

Emanuele Filiberto (1628-1709)
=Maria Caterina d'Este (d. 1722), dau. of
Cesare I d'Este and Virginia de'Medici,
dau. of Duke Cosimo I de'Medici of
Tuscany, who was the great grandson
of Lorenzo de'Medici, the Magnificent

Vittorio Amedeo II, Duke
of Savoy (1666-1732)

Vittoria Francesca =Vittorio Amedeo
of Savoy (d. 1766)   (1690-1741)
(natural)

Luigi Vittorio
(1721-1778)

Leopolda (1744-1807)
=Giovanni Andrea Doria
Pamfili Landi (descended
from Camillo Pamfili and
Olimpia Aldobrandini)

Vittorio Amedeo
(1743-1780)

Caterina (1762-1823)
=Filippo Giuseppe Colonna

Gian Andrea
(1779-1838)
=Teresa Orsini
of Gravina

Carlo Emanuele
(1770-1800)

Margherita Gioeni Colonna
=Giulio Cesare, Prince
Rospigliosi (1781-1859).
Their descendants are the
Rospigliosi Gioeni
Colonna family.

Filippo Andrea
(1813-76)

Leopoldina
(1811-43)
=Sigismondo
Chigi

Carlo Alberto
(1798-1849)
=Maria Theresa of
Tuscany (Hapsburg)

Maria Elisabetta
(1800-1856)
=Archduke Ranieri of
Austria (d. 1853)

Gian Andrea Doria
Pamfili Landi,
Prince of Melfi
(1843-90)

Olimpia
=Fabrizio Colonna,
Duke of Paliano

Vittorio Emanuele II =(1) Maria Adelaide
(1820-1878), King   of Austria
of Italy   (d. 1855)

Alfonso
=Lady Emily Pelham
Clinton, dau. of the
Duke of Newcastle

Umberto I (1844-1900),
King of Italy

Maria Pia (1847-1911)
=King Louis I of Portugal
(d. 1889)

Charles, King (1863-1908)

Vittorio Emanuele III,
King of Italy
(1869-1947)

Manuel, Last King of Portugal

Orietta
(1887-1945)
=Febo Borromeo
d'Adda

Filippo Andrea,
13th Prince of Melfi

Umberto I, King of Italy
(deposed 1946)
=Maria José of Belgium

Giovanna (b. 1907)
=Zar Boris III of Bulgaria
(1899-1947)

Vittorio Emanuele (1937-)

Simeon (1937-)

Orietta (1922-)
=Frank George Wignale
Pogson Doria Pamfili (Pamphili)
(name changed in 1958)

Descendants

*Maria Giovanna of Nemours
(1644-1724; See TABLE XXD)
was the great-granddaughter of Anna
d'Este, the great-granddaughter of POPE
ALEXANDER VI.

The Farnese females became the wives of members of the d'Este of Modena, Sforza, Borromeo, Pallavicini, della Rovere and Conti families. Violante Farnese, the natural daughter of Duke Ottavio, married Torquato Conti, Duke of Poli, and was thus an ancestor of Pope Innocent XIII (1721–24). Violante was the great-granddaughter of Pope Paul III; thus, in this case, one pope was the direct forebear of another (see Table XXf).

The marriage of Elisabetta Farnese, noted above, into the royal house of Bourbon-Spain catapulted that family into its most prestigious ties to the Catholic royal dynasties of Europe. King Philip V of Spain and his wife Elisabetta Farnese's descendants include the present king of Spain, the royal houses of Bourbon and Orléans in France, the present grand duke of Luxemborg and the king of Belgium. The coat of arms of the ducal family of Parma (Bourbon), of the royal family of the Two Sicilies (Bourbon) and of H.R.H Juan, Count of Barcelona, father of the present king of Spain, contain both the six fleur-de-lys of the Farnese family and the three fleur-de-lys of the de' Medici family.

Pope Paul III (Alessandro Farnese), through his daughter Costanza (wife of Bosio, Count of S. Fiora), became the ancestor of the Sforza (Sforza-Cesarini) family, members of which married into the Conti, della Rovere, Orsini, Colonna-Barberini and Boncompagni-Ludovisi families. The Sforza (Conti-Cesarini) family was the legitimate inheritors of the Conti family, and while there was no Sforza pope, that family allied itself with many of the Roman-Italian papal families of the seventeenth and eighteenth centuries. [Refer to tables 5a–5b in Appendix A.)

The Medici, Farnese, Visconti and Borgia — even though the main branches of these families are extinct — have been distinguished by their presence in many of the major royal houses in Europe. These descendants of the popes are found in all walks of life and can be located throughout the world. Gabriel (1752–88), the son of King Charles III of Spain — with the blood of the Visconti, Farnese and Medici families — had a son Pedro Carlos

whose wife, Maria Teresa, was a descendant of Pope Alexander VI (Rodrigo Borgia). Pedro Carlos and Maria Teresa's great-granddaughter Maria, Duchess of Durcel, married Antenor Patino, "the Tin King" of Bolivia, and their daughter Isabel (1936–54) became the wife of the British billionaire Sir James Goldsmith. Another Farnese-Medici-Visconti descendant is Miguel Braganza, brother of Duarte, pretender of the royal house of Portugal. Miguel, who renounced his rights to the Portugese throne, married into American society when Anita (1886–1923), the daughter of William Rhinelander Stewart, became his wife. Miguel's two sons, John and Miguel, became U.S. citizens, and John's son Michael lives on Long Island. Descended from Antonia Visconti (d. 1405) is Mariga (Marie-Gabrielle), granddaughter of the duke of Urach, a member of the royal house of Wurttemberg. She married the Hon. Desmond Guinness of the brewery family, and with Guinness money she has done much to preserve Georgian architecture in Ireland. Descended from Verde Visconti, whose present-day offspring constitute most of the royal houses of Europe, is Georg Timo (b. 1923), whose grandfather was King Friedrich Augustus III of Saxony. As his first wife, Georg Timo married Margrit, daughter of Carl Lucas, a master butcher.[22] It is obvious that the present-day descendants of the families of the popes contain members who engage in a multitude of various pursuits and who may be found most anywhere.

Descendants in England

British nobility holds not only Bourbon royal blood but also that of the Visconti, Medici and Orsini families. King Henry IV, founder of the Bourbon dynasty in France, married Maria de' Medici. King Henry was descended from Valentina Visconti, and his queen had as her ancestors Lorenzo de' Medici and his wife Clarice Orsini, whose mother was a Conti. A daughter of King Henry IV and Maria de' Medici, Henrietta Maria, married King Charles I, one of the four Stuart kings of

TABLE XXf: CONTI-FARNESE FAMILIES
(Families of Popes Innocent III and Innocent XIII)

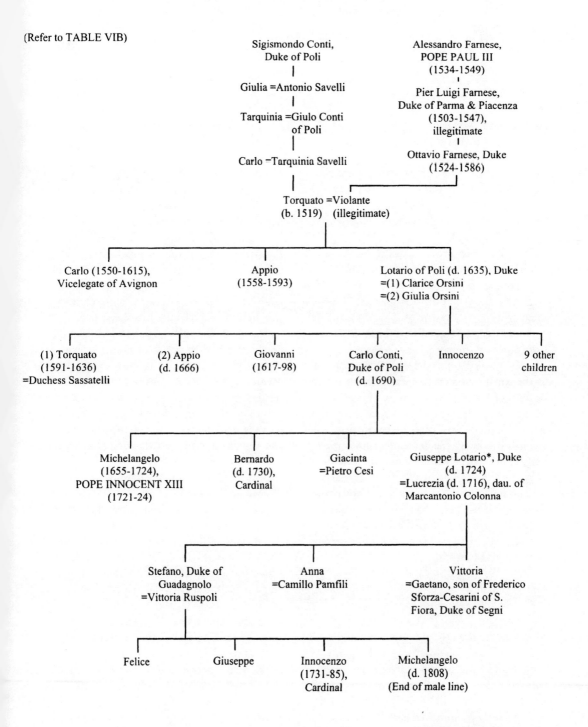

(Refer to TABLE VIB)

Sigismondo Conti,
Duke of Poli

Giulia =Antonio Savelli

Tarquinia =Giulo Conti
of Poli

Carlo −Tarquinia Savelli

Alessandro Farnese,
POPE PAUL III
(1534-1549)

Pier Luigi Farnese,
Duke of Parma & Piacenza
(1503-1547),
illegitimate

Ottavio Farnese, Duke
(1524-1586)

Torquato =Violante
(b. 1519)   (illegitimate)

Carlo (1550-1615),
Vicelegate of Avignon

Appio
(1558-1593)

Lotario of Poli (d. 1635), Duke
=(1) Clarice Orsini
=(2) Giulia Orsini

(1) Torquato
(1591-1636)
=Duchess Sassatelli

(2) Appio
(d. 1666)

Giovanni
(1617-98)

Carlo Conti,
Duke of Poli
(d. 1690)

Innocenzo

9 other
children

Michelangelo
(1655-1724),
POPE INNOCENT XIII
(1721-24)

Bernardo
(d. 1730),
Cardinal

Giacinta
=Pietro Cesi

Giuseppe Lotario*, Duke
(d. 1724)
=Lucrezia (d. 1716), dau. of
Marcantonio Colonna

Stefano, Duke of
Guadagnolo
=Vittoria Ruspoli

Anna
=Camillo Pamfili

Vittoria
=Gaetano, son of Frederico
Sforza-Cesarini of S.
Fiora, Duke of Segni

Felice

Giuseppe

Innocenzo
(1731-85),
Cardinal

Michelangelo
(d. 1808)
(End of male line)

*Sometimes spelled
Lottario

England, and they had two sons who became English kings, Charles II (1630–85) and James II (1633–1701).

Charles II had no children from his wife Catherine of Braganza, but he had numerous children, whom he ennobled, from his well-known mistresses, who included Lucy Walters (1630–58); Barbara Villers, Duchess of Cleveland (1641–1709); Louise de Kéroualle, Duchess of Portsmouth (1649–1734); Nell Gwyn and Catherine Peg. Charles II's illegitimate children became the dukes of Monmouth, Southampton, Grafton, Northumberland, Richmond and St. Albans and the earl of Plymouth. Charles II's brother James II had illegitimate children with Arabella Churchill.

The descendants of Charles II and James II, resulting from their illegitimate children, have married into England's most prominent, aristocratic families including the Spencers. Princess Diana (Spencer), ex-wife of Charles, Prince of Wales, was descended from both kings and from such Italian families as the Visconti, Medici, Orsini and Conti — the historical core of the papal dynasties (see Table XXg). If either or both of her sons, William and Henry, become king of England, they too, along with so many members of present-day British nobility, will be among the descendants of Italian papal dynasties. The progeny of those families will sit on the throne of Protestant England.

The blood of the families of the popes runs through the royal and noble houses of Europe especially in Italy, Spain, Germany, France and England; other descendants are scattered throughout the world.[23]

Carafa and Pignatelli

While the Renaissance popes, belonging to such families as the della Rovere, Borgia, Medici and Farnese, glaringly enriched and ennobled their relatives, others did so to a lesser degree, if at all. Some families attained their princely prominence before a member acquired the tiara.

The Carafa family was one of old Neapolitan nobility, and its eminence did not result from the fact that Pope Paul IV Giampietro Carafa, (1555–59) came from that family. The Carafa and the Pignatelli, with a similar lineage going back to the early Middle Ages, had often intermarried. Paul IV's distant cousin was Antonio Pignatelli, who became Pope Innocent XII (1691–1700) of the Baroque period. Other papal families married into the Carafa and Pignatelli families such as the Gaetani, Aldobrandini, Borgia, Colonna and Orsini. But these two families of southern Italy were deeply inbred, not only did Pignatelli and Carafa often intermarry but Pignatelli married Pignatelli and Carafa married Carafa, often with papal dispensations provided. Pope Paul IV of the Carafa family and Pope Innocent XII of the Pignatelli were not responsible for the princely status attained by the prosperous and existing branches of these two families. Their fortunes, lands and titles were gained despite the fact that pontiffs were family members.

But, in general, Renaissance and Baroque popes tended to enrich their families. Even the reform pope Pius IV (Giovanni Angelo de' Medici of Marignano) was generous to relatives — to his nephews and nieces, to members of the Borromeo family, which married into the della Rovere and Colonna families, and to the Altemps family, which married into the Orsini, Medici and Corsini families. (The Medici of Marignano may have been related to the Medici of Florence.) It is significant that the Borromeo family, a northern aristocratic family, was well-established before one of its members, Count Gilberto of Arona, married Pius IV's sister. The present Borromeo family, which for several centuries has married into many papal families, is descended from a brother of Count Gilberto, and its distinction as a noble family, like the Carafa and Pignatelli, antedates any papal connection.

On the other hand, while other Italian families were distinguished long before a member became a pope (e.g., the Medici and the Corsini), the eminence of the papacy and often the generosity of their papal relative placed the family into a new princely class. The Medici pope Clement VII created the dukedom of Florence for the Medici family, and Pope Clement XII

TABLE XXg: CHARLES II'S PROGENY; DUKES OF RICHMOND; ANCESTORS OF PRINCESS DIANA OF WALES

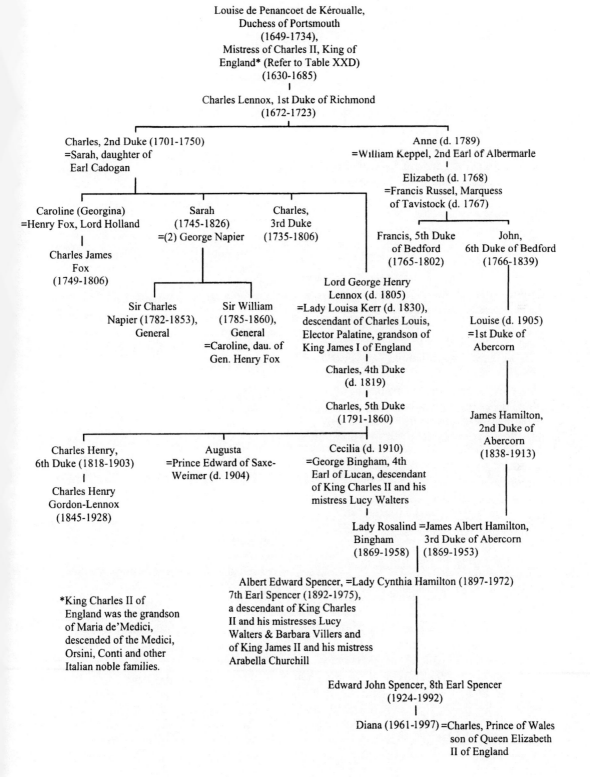

Louise de Penancoet de Kéroualle,
Duchess of Portsmouth
(1649-1734),
Mistress of Charles II, King of
England* (Refer to Table XXD)
(1630-1685)

Charles Lennox, 1st Duke of Richmond
(1672-1723)

Charles, 2nd Duke (1701-1750)
=Sarah, daughter of
Earl Cadogan

Anne (d. 1789)
=William Keppel, 2nd Earl of Albermarle

Elizabeth (d. 1768)
=Francis Russel, Marquess
of Tavistock (d. 1767)

Caroline (Georgina)
=Henry Fox, Lord Holland

Charles James
Fox
(1749-1806)

Sarah
(1745-1826)
=(2) George Napier

Charles,
3rd Duke
(1735-1806)

Francis, 5th Duke
of Bedford
(1765-1802)

John,
6th Duke of Bedford
(1766-1839)

Sir Charles
Napier (1782-1853),
General

Sir William
(1785-1860),
General
=Caroline, dau. of
Gen. Henry Fox

Lord George Henry
Lennox (d. 1805)
=Lady Louisa Kerr (d. 1830),
descendant of Charles Louis,
Elector Palatine, grandson of
King James I of England

Louise (d. 1905)
=1st Duke of
Abercorn

Charles, 4th Duke
(d. 1819)

Charles, 5th Duke
(1791-1860)

James Hamilton,
2nd Duke of
Abercorn
(1838-1913)

Charles Henry,
6th Duke (1818-1903)

Charles Henry
Gordon-Lennox
(1845-1928)

Augusta
=Prince Edward of Saxe-
Weimer (d. 1904)

Cecilia (d. 1910)
=George Bingham, 4th
Earl of Lucan, descendant
of King Charles II and his
mistress Lucy Walters

Lady Rosalind =James Albert Hamilton,
Bingham   3rd Duke of Abercorn
(1869-1958) | (1869-1953)

*King Charles II of
England was the grandson
of Maria de'Medici,
descended of the Medici,
Orsini, Conti and other
Italian noble families.

Albert Edward Spencer, =Lady Cynthia Hamilton (1897-1972)
7th Earl Spencer (1892-1975),
a descendant of King Charles
II and his mistresses Lucy
Walters & Barbara Villers and
of King James II and his mistress
Arabella Churchill

Edward John Spencer, 8th Earl Spencer
(1924-1992)

Diana (1961-1997) =Charles, Prince of Wales
son of Queen Elizabeth
II of England

(Lorenzo Corsini) made Corsini family members into the Roman princes of Sismano and the dukes of Casigliano. This practice of ennobling papal families was especially true of the popes during the Baroque period.

The Baroque Popes

Pope Gregory XIII (1572–85) of the Boncompagni family of Bologna saw to it that his son was created the duke of Sora. Members of the Boncompagni family married the heiresses of such papal families as the Ottoboni and the Ludovisi, from which the family inherited the principality of Piombino. Recognizing the princely role of the pope, the Holy Roman emperors began to make members of the pontiff's family into princes of the Holy Roman Empire (SRI). This was a tradition to last into the eighteenth century, dramatically elevating papal families into a new princely class. The families of papal princes tended to intermarry with other titled papal families, and intermarriages between members of these families are still taking place in the twentieth century. While the popes during the Renaissance and Baroque periods advanced their families by officially presenting them with territories, titles and payments, their descendants often married into the old papal families as the Colonna, Orsini, Sforza-Conti-Cesarini (heirs of the Conti) and Caetani. But since the seventeenth century, the families of the Baroque popes (i.e., the Boncompagni, Ludovisi, Chigi, Albani, Altieri, Borghese, Aldobrandini, Ottoboni, Barberini, Pamphili, Rospigliosi, Odescalchi and Corsini) have been more inclined to intermarry with each other (see tables XXI and XXII).

Later papal families that emerged during the Baroque period attained the same illustrious status of earlier dynasties. One such family was the Borghese; that family not only married into aristocratic and princely families in Italy, but into British, French, German and Spanish families as well. The Borghese serve as an example of the elevation of a papal family that has survived into the present period.

III: The Borghese — Case in Point

The Borghese, a princely family that descended from Giovan Battista, a brother of Pope Paul V (Camillo Borghese), demonstrates the interrelationship between its lineage and that of other papal families. The family exemplifies how a new papal dynasty — very much in the tradition of the Boncompagni and Chigi-Albani families — was attached by marriage to both the old Roman families as well as newer papal families of the Renaissance and the Baroque periods. Tables 6A–6C in Appendix A show that the present descendants of the Borghese family have such ancestors as Pope Paul III, Pope Julius II and Pope Gregory XIII. It also should be pointed out that the great-grandfather of Pope Paul V was Agostino Borghese, husband of Girolama, daughter of Danese Orsini. The Orsini were a key to the papacy, and it was highly desirable for any Italian family who wished to move and advance in Vatican circles to be a member of that family.

It is no wonder then that the heir of the Borghese family, Marcantonio, the son of Giovan Battista and nephew of Pope Paul V, married an Orsini, offspring of Orsini and Damasceni-Peretti parents and granddaughter of a Medici. The Damasceni-Peretti family was that of Pope Sixtus V (Felice Peretti). Camilla Orsini was a direct descendant of Pope Paul III (Alessandro Farnese) and Pope Julius II (Giuliano della Rovere). Pope Paul's mother was a Caetani and Julius II was a nephew of Pope Sixtus IV (Francesco della Rovere).

Related to Camilla and her descendants were:

the Medici popes — Leo X, Leo XI
and Clement VII;
the Orsini popes — Stephen II, Paul I,
Celestine III, Nicholas III and Benedict XIII;
the Pierleoni popes — Gregory VI, Gregory VII
and antipope Anacletus II.

Camillo, fourth Prince Borghese and the great-grandson of Camilla Orsini, married Agnese Colonna. She was a direct descendant of the

TABLE XXI: BARBERINI, PAMFILI, LUDOVISI, BONCOMPAGNI AND OTTOBONI PAPAL FAMILY RELATIONSHIPS

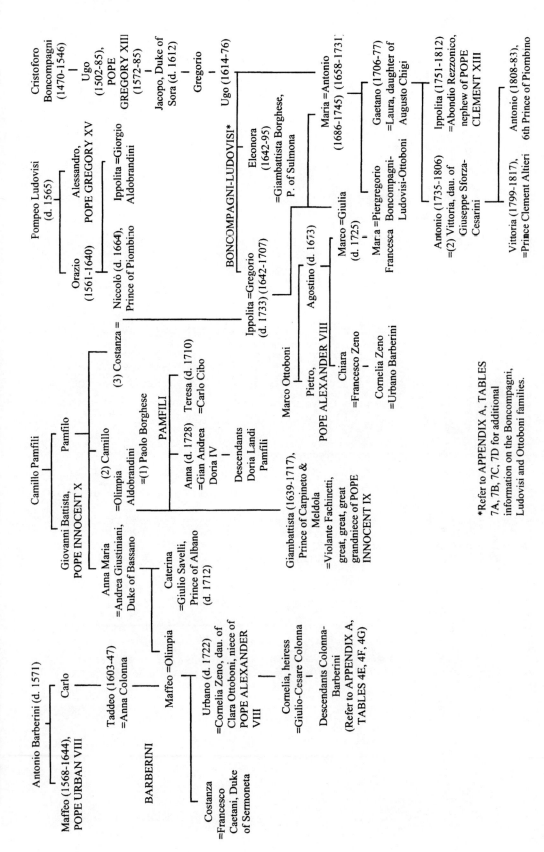

*Refer to APPENDIX A, TABLES 7A, 7B, 7C, 7D for additional information on the Boncompagni, Ludovisi and Ottoboni families.

TABLE XXII: ALBANI, CHIGI, BORGHESE AND ALDOBRANDINI PAPAL FAMILY RELATIONSHIPS

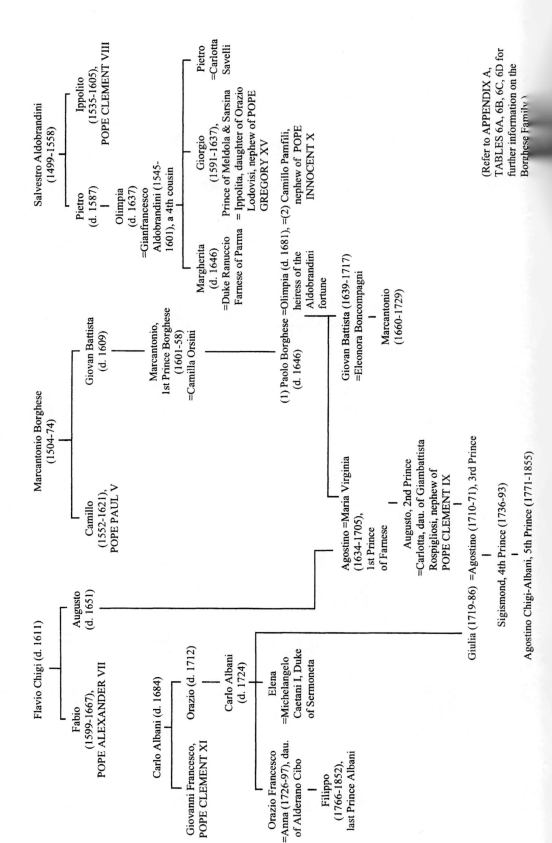

(Refer to APPENDIX A, TABLES 6A, 6B, 6C, 6D for further information on the Borghese Family.)

Pamfili family of Pope Innocent X, and was related to the Medici family of Marignano that produced Pope Pius IV, as well as to the Caetani, Orsini and della Rovere families. Both the Orsini and the Colonna families had the blood of the counts of Tusculum. The Orsini and Colonna also married into the Caetani, Conti and Savelli families. (Refer to tables 1a–1g and 4a–4g in Appendix A). At least seventeen popes came from these dynasties:

the Conti of Tusculum popes —
Hadrian I, Hadrian III, Sergius III,
John XI, Benedict VII, John XII, John XIX,
Benedict VIII and Benedict IX, as well as
antipopes Benedict X and Victor IV;
the Conti of Segni popes — Innocent III
Gregory IX, Alexander IV and Innocent XIII;
the Crescenzi pope — John XIII;
the Caetani popes — Gelasius II and
Boniface VIII;
the Savelli popes — Gregory II, Honorius III
and Honorius IV;
the Colonna pope — Martin V.

Future members of the Borghese clan would marry into the Aldobrandini and Boncompagni families.

Paolo the son of Marcantonio, first Prince Borghese, married Olimpia Aldobrandini, grandniece of popes Clement VIII and Gregory XV. Olimpia later married Camillo Pamfili, nephew of Pope Innocent X.[24] Olimpia and Paolo's son Giovan Battista, second Prince Borghese, was the husband of Eleonora Boncompagni, great-great-granddaughter of Pope Gregory XIII. That pope's son Giacomo (Jacopo) had married the niece of Pope Julius III (Giovanni del Monte). Accordingly the Borghese family is today closely or distantly related to these papal families. Moreover, since the beginning of the seventeenth century, Borghese princesses have united the Borghese family with numerous other papal dynasties: Virginia, daughter of Paolo, married Agostino Chigi, of the family of Pope Alexander VII; Maria, sister of Camillo, fourth Prince Borghese, married Prince Carafa; and Flaminia, sister of Camillo, fourth Prince, married Baldassarre Erba Odescalchi, of the family of Innocent XI.

The Borghese family divided into four main branches, assuming new names after distinguished ancestral families. Francesco, seventh Prince Borghese, had a son, Marcantonio, who succeeded him as eighth Prince Borghese; his second son, Camillo, took the name Prince Aldobrandini, and the third son, Scipione, became Duke Salviati. In this way the Borghese family acknowledged its descent from the family of Pope Clement VIII (Ippolito Aldobrandini, 1592–1605). Marcantonio's eldest son, Paolo (1844–1920), became the ninth Prince Borghese; another son, Giulio (1847–1926), married an heiress of the Torlonia family and took that name, forming a fourth branch with a distinct cognomen.

Similar to other papal dynasties, the Borghese continued to marry into those noble families related to popes — the daughter of the eighth prince Borghese became the wife of Rodolfo Boncompagni-Ludovisi, Prince of Piombino, of the family of Popes Gregory XIII and XV. Papal families were also inclined to marry within themselves in order to ensure that the family's wealth remained its own. The most notorious example was the marriage of Antonio Boncompagni to his niece Maria so that the princedom of Piombino would remain with the Boncompagni family. In the Borghese family, Francesco Borghese, ninth Prince, married his first cousin Francesca (1847–1926), the daughter of Duke Scipione (Borghese) Salviati. Maria, daughter of Camillo (Borghese), Prince Aldobrandini, married her first cousin Antonino, son of Scipione Salviati, Camillo's brother.[25]

During the nineteenth and twentieth centuries, the Borghese family — much like the other papal families such as the Boncompagni-Ludovisi, Chigi-Albani, Barberini-Colonna and Orsini — could not depend on receiving vast sums of money or estates from the papal treasury. Since the Vatican was no longer the source of financial success and since expenses were increasing, the Borghese made new efforts to attain money through matches with wealthy English, French, German and Hungarian heiresses. Camillo (1775–1832), sixth Prince Borghese, wedded the princess Pauline, sister of the Emperor Napoleon Bonaparte. Marcantonio,

eighth Prince, was married to Gwendaline
Talbot of the English earls of Shrewsbury; his
second wife was Teresa de la Rochefoucauld.
Camillo, Prince Aldobrandini, was first the
husband of Maria, Princess Arenberg, and then
the husband of Maria, Countess Hunyady de
Kéthely. The wife of Scipione, Duke Salviati,
was Jacqueline-Arabelle de Fitz-James. The
eighth prince's son Paolo (1844–1920) married
Ilona Appony.[26]

Marriage for fortunes became essential in
the nineteenth and twentieth centuries in order
for papal dynasties to retain the glories of
years past. Giulio Borghese (1847–1914), son of
Marcantonio, eighth Prince Borghese, married
Anna Maria Torlonia. She was the heiress
of Alessandro Torlonia (1800–1886), the son of
Giovanni, head of Banca Torionia and
entrepreneur, who established a fortune and
purchased the dukedoms of Poli and Guadagnolo. Alessandro increased the family wealth
and was recognized as the duke of Ceri,
marchese of Romavecchia and prince of
Civitella Cesi. Giulio Borghese changed his
surname to that of his wealthy father-in-law,
and his descendants are know as princes Torlonia. Giulio and Anna's grandson Alessandro
Torlonia married H.R.H Princess Maria Luisa
Beatrice, daughter of King Alfonso XIII of
Spain.[27] They reside in Palazzo Torlonia in
Rome. The present prince Borghese also lives
in Rome — appropriately, in the Palazzo
Borghese. It would appear that the Borgheses
have moved through the twentieth century
with their wealth intact and with an impressive
family history derived from those papal ancestors who reigned during the Middle Ages and
the Renaissance and Baroque periods.

CHAPTER SEVEN

Papal Dynasties and Nepotism

I: Early History

When Peter the Apostle came to preach in Rome, he laid the foundations of what was to become a church — the Roman Catholic Church. Jesus had told him that what he bound "on earth shall be bound in heaven," and with these words Peter was granted a special authority over the Christian community.

The early bishops of Rome, as successors to Peter, espoused the view that they were "primate of all the bishops." The bishop of Rome eventually established supremacy over the church, and assumed the title of Supreme Pontiff. There have been a total of 262 popes (see Appendix C), though this number is disputed since at various times there have been rival popes selected, called antipopes. The last antipope was Felix V, who abdicated in 1449.

During the first three centuries, the bishop of Rome was in fear of his life. He was often hounded and killed by orders of Roman emperors persecuting the new, Christian religion. In the fourth century, these persecutions ended. Constantine the Great helped to establish the Christian church as the religion of the state; consequently, the church prospered.

In the eighth century, the king of the Franks gave the papacy territory adjacent to Rome. This territory became the Papal States, and the pope thus acquired both spiritual and temporal power since he, or his agents, became the rulers of these states.

The first bishops of Rome were elected by the Christian community; soon, however, greater power was given to the Roman senate, controlled by the Roman aristocracy. Later, final choices for pope needed to be approved by the emperors or their delegates. It was not until 1179 that the Sacred College of Cardinals was established, becoming solely responsible for choosing the pope.

During that same period of time in the twelfth century, the church constructed its views on celibacy and clerical marriage. During much of its early history, many of the clergy — including bishops — married or kept concubines. It was not until Gregory VII (1073–85) that clerical celibacy was vigorously enforced; but concubinage for prelates remained fairly common during the Renaissance period.

Bishops of Rome were sometimes related to one another; several were elected from the same (usually aristocratic and Roman) family. The Orsini (Bobo-Orso or Bobone-Orsini) were such a family, attaining prominence during this early period. Family control over the papacy was to become more prevalent when the Conti family of Tusculum, guided by Senator Teofilatto and his wife Senatrix Teodora and later by their daughter Marozia and her son Alberico II, established the Alberichi papal dynasty.

Alberico took the titles of *princeps et senator Romanorum*, and he virtually ruled the Papal States, placing those prelates on the papal throne whom he could control and would limit themselves to "spiritual" matters. As some of Alberico's descendants became popes, others, such as Alberico III and Gregorio, acquired the titles of Prince of Tusculum and *Caput Factionum* (Factional Leader) and took command of Rome. The granting of titles was to flourish in the church and evolved over succeeding centuries. Friends and relatives of the pope would be made captain of the guard, captain general of the papal forces, governor of the Borgo, legate, apostolic protonotary, marshal of the church, vice-chancellor, high chamberlain, camerlengo (treasurer) and *gonfaloniere* (standard-bearer). With these titles came substantial stipends from the treasury of the church.

Teofilatto and Teodora had another daughter, called Teodora II. She was the mother of Teodora III, the wife of Giovanni Crescenzi. They were parents of another pope, John XIII. The Crescenzi family — the children, grandchildren and great-grandchildren of Teodora III and her husband — determined the course of the papacy for almost fifty years. Crescenzio II and Giovanni Crescenzi (d. 1012) were granted the title of Patrician, and they ruled Rome.

To protect their own interests and because of the arrogance of the Roman nobles, especially the families of the Alberichi and the Crescenzi who felt that they had a divine right to appoint popes, the Holy Roman emperors began placing prelates of their own choice on the papal throne. When the emperors controlled the papacy, they filled the position with German nobles who were often related to themselves, just as the Romans placed their own relatives on the throne.

The Romans were dissatisfied when the emperors interfered with the election of their bishop, and various Roman families emerged to challenge the authority of the emperors and to elect popes of their own choice. Two of these families were the Frangipane and the Pierleoni. The Pierleoni family, descended from the Jewish banker Baruch who converted to Christianity, accumulated both wealth and influence. Two popes, Gregory VI and Gregory VII (the famous Hildebrand who became the pope of reform) were members of the Pierleoni family, as was the antipope Anacletus II (1130–38) whose sister married a nephew of Peter Colonna of the House of Tusculum (Alberici), and was thereby related to Roman aristocracy.

The Frangipane, a rival family, managed the election of several of their own candidates, including Honorius II (1124–30) and Innocent II (1130–43); they also deposed Celestine (II) (1124). In 1187, after a period of conflict between the popes and the emperor Frederick I, Paolo Scolari was elected pope, as Clement III. This was the beginning of a new dynasty of popes — the Conti of Segni, descended from the Conti of Tusculum. Clement III (1187–91) was the uncle of the powerful Innocent III (Lotario Conti, 1198–1216), son of the count of Segni. Other popes of this same family included Gregory IX (1227–1241) and Alexander IV (1254–61), whose niece Emilia Conti was the mother of Pope Boniface VIII (1294–1303). It was during the reign of Boniface that the papacy came into conflict with the king of France, with the result that the papal court moved to Avignon, France, from which seven popes, instruments of the French king, ruled until the papacy returned to Rome in 1377.

In Avignon, the popes (e.g., Clement V, John XXII and Clement VI) generously gave titles, papal territory, cardinalates and gifts to family members. This was in the tradition of Boniface VIII, who had bought numerous fiefdoms for the Caetani family. The use of the papal treasury for family gain had commenced with Pope Nicholas III (Giovanni Gaetano Orsini, 1277–80). The Orsinis had given several popes to the Holy See: Stephen II, Paul I and Celestine III. Nicholas was extremely liberal to his four brothers, whose descendants became lords, dukes and princes. His great-grandfather Orso had married Gaetana, daughter of Crescenzii Caetani (Gaetani, Cajetan), descended of the papal families Crescenzi and Caetani. His mother was Perna Caetani, also of the family of Boniface VIII. Related to the Orsinis were their allies the Savellis who also gave two popes to the church: Honorius III (1216–27) and Honorius IV (1285–87).

A rival of the Orsinis and Savellis was the Colonna family, descended from Pietro "da Columna." He was the son of Gregory II of the House of Tusculum (Alberichi), descended from Duke Alberico II and his wife, Alda, who was a direct descendant of Charlemagne.

Pietro's brother Tolomeo served as consul in Rome and was a count of Tusculum. Tolomeo's son, who had the same name, also distinguished himself by being the consul of the Romans. He first married the daughter of the emperor Henry V and then the daughter of a Pierleoni.

These aristocratic Roman families — the Crescenzi, Pierleoni, Colona, Orsini, Gaetani, Conti and Savelli — frequently intermarried; and, even though they were sometimes rivals, marriage between these dynasties became essential for both power and wealth. These were families who wished to control the Holy See. They were not only related to each other, but they continued to marry into the subsequent papal families of the Renaissance and Baroque periods. While some families — in particularly the Conti and Orsini — may have dreamed of having popes elected only from their own families, similar to a hereditary monarchy, they were thwarted in this attempt. Since the same families could not always elect a member, it was deemed appropriate that the Supreme Pontiff should be Roman (this too became an impossibility) and thus somewhat related to the ancient papal nobility.

The old Roman families maintained papal dynasties with the assistance of their appointments to the College of Cardinals. From the early thirteenth century until the beginning of the nineteenth century, hundreds of cardinals came from these few families: the Conti, Caetani (which alone gave seventy-three cardinals to the church), Colonna, Orsini, Savelli, Piccolomini, della Rovere, Borgia, Medici, Barberini, Ottoboni, Corsini, Albani, Altieri-Paluzzi, Farnese, Fieschi, (Doria)-Pamfili and Aldobrandini. Cardinals were also taken from allied Italian families, including the d'Este, Sforza, Pallavicino, Gonzaga and Borromeo. Without question, during this same period of time, the cardinals and their family interests exerted a decisive influence on the selection of the Supreme Pontiff.

Genealogical charts of the Colonna, Orsini and Savelli families in the Middle Ages, as delineated by Litta, readily show how these families were intertwined. A genealogical table focusing on ten generations of the Orsini family from the twelfth to the fourteenth centuries graphically demonstrates this interrelationship. (Refer to the previous tables IIIA and IIIB.) Appendix B gives a brief description of these families, including their acquisition of titles and property, until either the present time or the family became extinct.

In later periods, in order to retain their power in the Papal States, these old papal families married into new ones, as shown by the Boncompagni, Borghese and Barberini. All of these Italian families realized that both their prosperity and future, lacking a direct papal relative, depended on a friendly, new pope. When a family or foreign extraction like the Borgias were elected, they were only interested in their own domination of the Holy See and the Papal States, and they quickly destroyed their Italian rivals — the Caetani, the Orsini and the della Rovere. The history of papal dynasties is a history of Italian families seeking to protect themselves in the States of the Church by allying with the families of the new popes. This was usually accomplished by a matrimonial union. The practice was to last for hundreds of years.

II: The Late Middle Ages and the Renaissance

During the late Middle Ages, several popes were selected from aristocratic and prosperous Roman families. Martin V (1417–31) was of the Colonna, a family which possessed territories, such as Palestrina, inherited from their forefather Pietro Colonna. The Colonna family was probably related to the counts of Tusculum. The Orsini family, to which Nicholas III (1277–80) belonged, had been a prominent and prosperous family since the 600s. Innocent III (1198–1216) was descended from the Conti, Dukes of Segni, and from the Scotti family: Honorius III (1216–27) and Honorius IV (1285–87) were of the aristocratic Savelli family. Boniface VIII (1294–1303) was of a noble family, the Caetani, related to the Orsini. These families were considered old Roman aristocracy. Those popes who were members of these families placed their relatives in positions of honor within the Vatican and granted fiefdoms and vast areas of land to them. This was the nepotism that was to be greatly refined and augmented by the Renaissance popes.

The popes had become secular princes "little by little," writes Giucciardini, "forgetting about the salvation of souls and divine precepts, and turning all their thoughts to worldly greatness." Their objectives were no longer religious but warlike:

> Their concern and endeavors began to be no longer the sanctity of life or the propagation of religion, no longer zeal and charity toward their neighbors, [rather] they began to accumulate treasures, to make new laws, to invent new tricks, new cunning devices in order to gather money from every side; for this purpose, to use their spiritual arms without respect for this end, to shamelessly sell sacred and profane things. The great wealth spreading amongst them and throughout their court was followed by pomp, luxury, dishonest customs, lust and abominable pleasures;... no thought of the perpetual majesty of the pontificate, but instead, an ambitious and pestiferous desire to exalt their children, nephews and kindred, not only to immoderate riches but to principalities, to kingdoms; no longer distrib-uting dignities and emoluments among deserving and virtuous men, but almost always either sell-ing them for the highest price or wasting them on persons opportunistically moved by ambition, avarice, or shameful love of pleasure.

Guicciardini laments the condition of the Renaissance papacy, noting that the popes are held "in the greatest respect by men," but they are "motivated by greed, incite wars, and use their title to attain their own ends for them-selves and for their families."[1] His mournful account of the condition of the papacy, written between 1537 and 1540, was to serve as an accurate portrayal of papal behavior for the next two hundred years.

From 1471 to 1585, there were fifteen popes:

Sixtus IV (Francesco della Rovere, 1471–84)
|
Innocent VIII (Gioranni Battista Cibo, 1484–92)
|
Alexander VI (Rodrigo Borgia, 1492–1503)
|

Pius III (Francesco Todeschini-Piccolomini, 1503)
|
Julius II (Giuliano della Rovere, 1503–1513)
|
Leo X (Giovanni de' Medici, 1513–21)
|
Hadrian VI (Adrian Florensz, 1522–23)
|
Clement VII (Giulio de' Medici, 1523–34)
|
Paul III (Alessandro Farnese, 1534–49)
|
Julius III (Giovanni Maria Ciocchi del Monte, 1534–55)
|
Marcellus II (Marcello Cervini, 1555)
|
Paul IV (Giampietro Carafa, 1555–59)
|
Pius IV (Giovanni Angelo de' Medici, 1559–65)
|
Pius V (Michele Ghislieri, 1565–72)
|
Gregory XIII (Ugo Boncompagni, 1572–85)

Of these fifteen popes, at least seven had chil-dren, and the popes during this period worked for the aggrandizement of both their children and their relatives. While Leo X had no actual children, one might consider his child to be the city of Florence; he spent a fortune to maintain an army and keep it under de' Medici control.

Sixtus IV made several of his nephews cardi-nals, including Cardinal Riario, who had com-plete control of the papal treasury, and Giu-liano della Rovere, later to be Pope Julius II. Another nephew, Leonardo, received the fiefs of Sora and Arpino, and Girolamo Riario was made the count of Bosco and given the fief of Imola. Pope Innocent XIII liberally bestowed wealth on his son Franceschetto from the church's treasury and presented him with the territories of Cervetri and Anguillara.

Like a master chess player, Pope Alexander VI used his children for his political ambi-tions — Lucrezia married into families that the pope selected and Caesar was given vast sums of papal money to pursue military actions to increase the Papal States, which became the personal domain of the Borgia family. The Borgia family profited enormously from both

Callistus III (1455–58) and Alexander VI. Using his influence—first as the nephew of Pope Callistus III, second as a cardinal and finally as pope—Alexander VI persuaded the Spanish king to make two of his sons dukes of Gandia. When he was allied with Naples, he had his son Goffredo marry a princess from that kingdom and receive the princedom of Squillace. He permitted his son Caesar to conquer Romanga and become its duke. When his daughter Lucrezia married Alfonso d'Este, he arranged a dowry of 100,000 ducati.[2] Lucrezia also received Sermoneta, which became the dukedom of her son. Many Borgia relatives were named cardinals, and the brother of Pope Alexander's lover Giulia Farnese was elevated to the purple.

Like the Roman Contis, the Borgias, too, were intent on establishing an hereditary papacy; both Calustus III and Alexander VI had numerous relatives named to the cardinalate and appointed to the Spanish clergy—as if to create a Spanish, rather than an Italian, papacy. Caesar Borgia with his military might was intent on insuring this Spanish domination, but his own illness and the shrewdness and simony of Giuliano della Rovere (Pope Julius II) thwarted the ambitions of the Borgias.

Julius II greatly expanded the fortunes of the della Rovere family. His nephew Francesco Maria was given the vicarate of Pesaro. The pope's daughter Felice was treated poorly and was only given 15,000 ducats upon her marriage to Giangiordano Orsini, who was made vice-chancellor of the palace.

While the Medici popes, Leo X and Clement VII, certainly assisted their Medici kin, they were also politically interested in the welfare of Florence under Medici control. Numerous relatives were made cardinals and given significant positions in the Vatican. Leo X's nephew Lorenzo obtained an army from the pope, and he conquered Urbino and became its duke. His sister Maddalena was given "the emoluments and exactions of the indulgences of many parts of Germany."[3] Clement VII indulged his son Alessandro, whom he made duke of Florence. Alessandro's illegitimate daughter Giulia married

a distant cousin Bernardetto, brother of pope Leo XI (d. 1605). Bernardetto and Giulia de' Medici's descendants were the dukes of Sarno and princes of Ottaiano. The fortunes of the Medici reached their apex when Pope Clement placed his cousin Caterina, great-granddaughter of Lorenzo the Magnificent and grandniece of Pope Leo X, on the throne of France by marrying her to King Henry II.

Clement's successor, Paul III, lavishly advanced his children, one of whom (Pier Luigi Farnese) became *gonfaloniere* of the church, commander-in-chief of the papal forces and duke of Castro. Finally, he was rewarded with the entire principality of Parma and Piacenza, which eventually became independent as a fief of the Papal States. The pope's daughter Costanza was presented with extensive territories upon her marriage to Bosio, Count of S. Flora. Three of the pope's grandchildren were made cardinals. Cardinal Alessandro Farnese became the pope's trusted advisor and vice-chancellor.

It is not known what happened to the three children of Pope Pius IV, but he made his nephews cardinals. He especially loved his Borromeo nephews—Cardinal Carlo Borromeo and Federico Borromeo who, unfortunately, died at a young age and left no children.

As the Renaissance period was coming to a close, new Roman families were to rise. The Boncompagni were to become prominent when Gregory XIII (1572–1585) became pope and made his son Giacomo (Jacopo) the duke of Sora. The succeeding popes and their families were to intermarry for a period of over 150 years. This was a period of transition for the Roman nobility.

III: The Late Renaissance and the Baroque Periods

And so the Renaissance period came to an end, and the Baroque now began to thrive. The old Roman papal families—the Colonna. Caetani, Orsini, Conti and Savelli—were beginning to lose most, if not all, of their political significance. The new families surpassed the old ones especially in terms of wealth. As the authority of the ancient families declined, they were forced to marry into the new papal dynasties — the Boncompagni, Peretti, Aldrobrandini, Borghese, Ludovisi, Barberini and Pamfili — which were eager to conclude matrimonial alliances with the ancient aristocracy.[4]

The goal of the popes in regard to their own families was to obtain "hereditary wealth and influence." Succeeding Supreme Pontiffs assisted their families to become established as members of the Roman elite, and the popes justified their distribution of moneys from the Holy See on the grounds that "the surplus proceeds of the spiritual office" was their own property and they "possessed the right of bestowing this superfluity on their kindred."[5] And these new aristocratic families began to absorb millions of scudi directly from the Apostolic Camera." "Paul V's nephews had received 260,000 scudi, those of Urban VIII 1,700,000, those of Innocent X, 1,400,000, those of Alexander VII, 900,000, those of Clement X 1,200,000, and those of Alexander VIII, 700,000 scudi, from the Apostolic Camera alone, to which must be added the revenues of the Dataria and the income derived from the various vacant offices."[6]

Nepotism became a game of family gain and opportunity, with each pope trying to do more for his kin than the previous Supreme Pontiff. Sixtus V (Felice Peretti, 1585–90) made his grandnephew a cardinal, granting him income of 100,000 scudi; his other grandnephew the pope made marchese of Mentana, giving him the principality of Venafro and the county of Celano. He also married his grandnieces into the Colonna and Orsini families, tying the new papal family with the old aristocracy. Clement VIII (Ippolito Aldobrandini, 1592–1605) helped his cardinal-nephew Pietro Aldobrandini to secure 60,000 scudi yearly from church property. Another nephew, by marriage, Gian Francesco Aldobrandini was appointed castellan of Castle Sant' Angelo, governor of the Borgo, captain of the guard and general of the church. "His [Gian Francesco's] income, so early as the year 1599, was 60,000 scudi, and he often received sums of money from the Pope." During

his pontificate Clement gave over 1,000,000 scudi in cash to relatives. Much of this money was wisely invested both by Cardinal Pietro and Gian Francesco. Again, in order to make permanent contact with older papal dynasties, marriages were arranged. The new papal families advanced themselves by having a member acquire a prestigious name, and in exchange the ancient noble families acquired substantial sums of money, usually in the form of dowries. When Gian Francesco Aldobrandini's daughter Margherita married Ranuccio I Farnese (1569–1622), the Aldobrandini family provided a dowry of 400,000 scudi. The Farnese family was one of distinction because of its position. Members were the dukes of Parma and Placenza, but they had need for the influx of money from the papal treasury, which had been denied them after the death of Pope Paul III (Alessandro Farnese).[7]

The older papal families often suffered from indebtedness and lack of income and were jealous of the abundance of wealth enjoyed by the new aristocracy. It should be noted that in 1664 Ranuccio II Farnese (1630–94) was in debt to the amount of 1,620,000 scudi and was unable to purchase Castro from the Holy See. These enormous debts began to proliferate throughout the old aristocracy.

As for the new papal nobility, Pope Paul V (Camillo Borghese, 1605–1621) placed great power into the hands of his cardinal-nephew Scipione, who in 1612 was receiving an income of 150,000 scudi annually from church benefices. Another nephew of the pope, Marcantonio Borghese, received the principality of Sulmona, palaces in Rome, as well as gifts of precious jewels and furniture. In 1620 the family was the recipient of 689,627 scudi in money and of other invested assets amounting to nearly a million. This great fortune was used to buy eighty estates in Campagna, often from Roman nobles of the ancient aristocracy who were heavily in debt and needed to sell their hereditary domains.[8]

The pope to follow Paul V was Gregory XV (Alessandro Ludovisi, 1621–23), and he pursued the same path of nepotism as his predecessor. His cardinal-nephew Ludovico Ludovisi had "unlimited authority" from his uncle, serving as vice-chancellor and high chamberlain, receiving more than 200,000 scudi a year. The pope's brother Don Orazio became general of the church, and the family was quick to acquire enormous wealth and property. They bought the duchy of Fiano from the Sforza family and the duchy of Zagarolo from the Colonna family. And by auspicious marriages Niccolò Ludovisi acquired Venosa and the principality of Piombino. The wealth of these papal families was "equal and even surpassed the possessions of kings themselves."[9]

The family of Pope Urban VIII (Maffeo Barberini, 1623–44) was obviously the most excessive of all the papal families. Their ambitions were "immoderate." The pope's brother Carlo Barberini was made governor of the church; it was he who wished to create an impressive family estate so that "the position of kinsmen to a pope should [not] appear in straitened circumstances after his death." The nephews of the pope played a leading role in the administration of Urban VIII. Antonio, a cardinal, became high chamberlain and easily had an income of 100,000 scudi a year. From benefices as vice-chancellor and legations, Cardinal Francesco also had an income in 1627 amounting to 100,000 scudi. Taddeo Barberini, the third nephew of the pope, was made general of the church, commander of Castle Sant' Angelo and governor of the Borgo, and he owned numerous estates. He became the prefect and "enjoyed a yearly income of 100,000 scudi. It has been estimated that the Barberini came into possession of 150,000,000 scudi in the twenty-one-year period when Pope Urban VIII reigned. The Barberini family had acquired Palestrina, Monterotondo and Valmontone, which the Colonna and Sforza families had been forced to sell; they possessed sumptuous palaces, magnificent works of art, gold, silver and precious stones. Meanwhile the pope — Urban VIII — instructed a commission to investigate the lawfulness of having kin obtain such enormous wealth. The commission felt that the pontiff had a right to bestow surplus revenues upon family members.[10] It was not until the evil of nepotism was abolished by Innocent XII in 1692 that the question was somewhat resolved. Many offices

and titles were removed, large incomes were forbidden, and the pope could not enrich relatives.[11]

During the seventeenth century before the papal bull to end nepotism, the practice continued with the Chigi, Rospigliosi, Altieri, Odescalchi and Ottoboni families; even during the eighteenth century, family enrichment moved ever onward with the Albanis and Corsinis. These families began to intermarry in order to sustain riches. Tables XXI, XXII and XXIII show the interrelations of the new papal dynasties, as well as the titles that these families received. (Refer also to Appendix B.)

Another problem occurred: male heirs for many families were scarce — especially in families with several clerical members — and their surnames were threatened with extinction. And so families began to hyphenate their names: the Chigi-Albani, Boncompagni-Ludovisi-Ottoboni and Barberini-Colonna; or the family name was revived by a younger son of another family as in the case of the Borghese member who assumed the name Aldobrandini to perpetuate that illustrious family's ancestry. Other ingenious methods were used so that these celebrated papal-dynastic names would survive.

IV: Papal Families Never Die

The names of Italian aristocratic families seemingly remain in the *Almanach de Gotha* forever. Even though some families have terminated and others have declined, the tendency is to have the husband of a surviving heiress assume the name of the noble family. Maria Barberini-Colonna di Sciarra (1872–1935), only child of Duke Enrico, had her husband, Luigi Sacchetti (1863–1936), take the name Colonna di Sciarra and become the prince of Palestrina; it is Maria and Luigi's descendants who retain the name and title. Maria's cousin Mirta (b. 1938), only child of Prince Urbano Barberini-Colonna di Sciarra, tenth Prince of Carbognano, married Don Alberto Riario Sforza (descended from the della Rovere family). Her husband was adopted by her aunt Stefanella Barberini-Colonna di Sciarra. This cognomen was added to that of Don Alberto's. Orietta (b. 1922) only child of

TABLE XXIII: CORSINI, ODESCALCHI, ROSPIGLIOSI AND ALTIERI PAPAL FAMILY RELATIONSHIPS

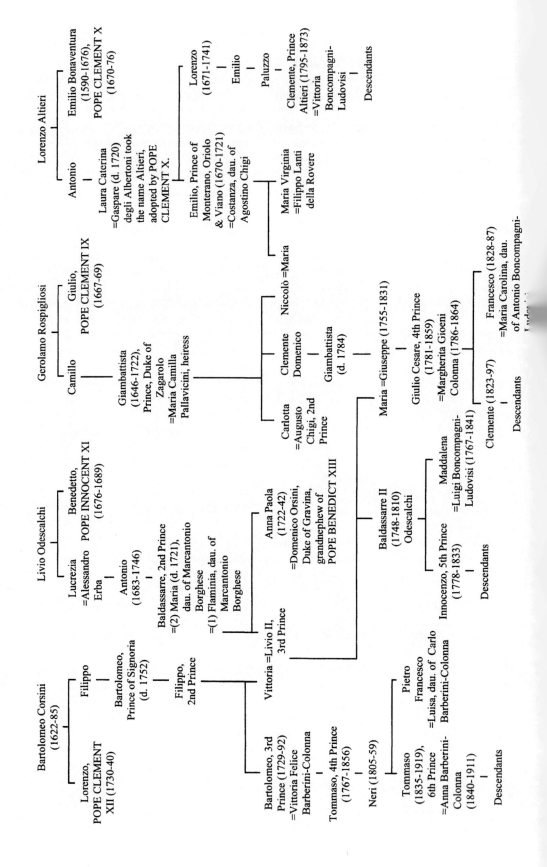

Filippo Andrea Doria-Pamfili-Landi, Prince of Melfi, had her husband, Frank George Wignale Pogson, add Doria-Pamfili to his name. The name change was made in London in 1958. Francesco Rospigliosi (1828–87), who had inherited the principality of Gallico from a Pallavicini(o) ancestor, took the name Rospigliosi-Pallavicini (now shortened to just Pallavicini). His son Giulio (1871–1941) adopted Guglielmo, the son of Armando of Pierre of Bernis, Marchese of Courtavel, in 1937. In 1940 a daughter Maria Camilla was born to Prince Guglielmo Pallavicini and Elvina de' Medici del Vascello. By adoption, the Pallavicini name was retained.

As time went on, the old Roman aristocracy came into particularly difficult times. While they wished to retain both pomp and status, they were simply running out of funds and owed enormous amounts. And so the Savelli was forced to sell Albano to the Pamfili family in 1650.[12] Nettuno was purchased for 400,000 scudi by the Apostolic Camera, and Virginio Orsini "sold the territory of Matrice to the brother of Cardinal Montalto for 130,000 scudi."[13] Not only were the old families losing their territories, many were ceasing to exist. The Savelli and Conti of Segni, as well as major branches of the Orsini family, became extinct. The need for the old nobility to marry into the new, rich families became essential, and thus the Colonna married into the Altieri and Barberini families and the Orsini into the Altieri, Odescalchi and Boncompagni-Ludovisi.

An additional problem emerged during the seventeenth century. The papal families began to have difficulty acquiring wealth superior to their predecessors "chiefly because the papal treasury had been gradually exhausted. The Chigi could no longer venture to aspire at surpassing their predecessors; the Rospigliosi did not even wish to do so...."[14] And so the munificent rewards of nepotism gradually diminished — but did not come to an end. Members of these families continued to acquire wealth by benefices they received as cardinals. Cardinal Luigi Caetani tried to help his family pay off their debts by using his resources from the cardinalate.[15] Other member of these prominent families served as governmental officials. Most

prominent were the members of the Caetani and Corsini families. When, during the economic hardships of the late nineteenth century, a powerful family like the Borghese was forced to sell its assets, many members of the old and new aristocracies were affected. But many of these families have survived to the present.

What these families retained, if not their vast material possessions, were titles. The old and new Roman papal families were conferred as Roman princes or princes of the Holy Roman Empire (Reichsfürst or S.R.I.—*Sacro Romano Impero*): Albani in 1719, Chigi in 1659, Doria-Pamfili-Landi in 1760, Odescalchi in 1714 and Rospigliosi in 1668. Besides being princes, they were created dukes, counts, lords and marchesi. Many of these families are conspicuous even today — the Orsini, Colonna and Caetani of the ancient aristocracy, and the Rospigliosi, Corsini, Boncompagni-Ludovisi, Borghese (Aldobrandini), Doria-Pamfili-Landi and Odescalchi of the newer aristocracy. The major branches of those families of the Renaissance — the della Rovere, Borgia, Medici, Farnese and Peretti — have disappeared, even though their blood runs through the present papal nobility and into the royal families of Europe.

V: The Modern Papacy and a Renewed Reverence for the Supreme Pontiff

The modern period for papal history begins with the decree *Romanum decet pontificem* of June 22, 1692, when Pope Innocent XII tried to stop the pernicious evil of nepotism. His acknowledgment of this practice and the decree's eventual acceptance in the church has altered the course of papal history. But it would take the Roman Catholic Church another 170 years to shift its focus from temporal concerns to spiritual ones and achieve the reverential position that the papacy enjoys in the contemporary period.

Throughout the past 250 years the papacy has been modified. The changes have been sweeping, but many of the old ways have persisted. In spite of the ban on nepotism, Pius VI

Giovanni (Angelo Braschi, 1775–99) continued that practice and overindulged his unworthy nephew Luigi Braschi-Onesti. During his administration, Pius had to contend with the aftereffects of the French Revolution and the remarkable military leadership of Napoleon, who in 1796 conquered the Papal States. For a brief period these lands were returned to pontifical authority, but two years later a Roman republic was proclaimed, and Pius was no longer head of the States of the Church. His successor, Pius VII (1800–23), was also dominated by the policies of Napoleon. Pius VII went to Paris, where he participated in the coronation of Napoleon as emperor in 1804. Five years later, Napoleon imprisoned the pontiff and was again in command of the Papal States. Only after Napoleon's defeat did Pius return to Rome and receive the Papal States back into the Holy See.

The Papal States were poorly administered and their citizens dissatisfied with papal rule. Pope Gregory XVI (1831–46) had to put down infrequent revolts. It was this Gregory who had the wife of his valet as his mistress. His successor, Pius IX (1846–78), moved into the papacy during a period of popular rebellion throughout Europe. In 1849 a Roman republic again came into existence, and the pope was forced to flee from Rome. While he was able to return the following year, the climate in Italy had changed. The Risorgimento (the movement for Italian independence) was vigorously developing and finally succeeded. In 1860 the Papal States were lost forever to the Supreme Pontiff, and ten years later Rome was occupied by the Italian state. For the remainder of his pontificate, Pius IX concentrated on spiritual and religious matters.

The loss of the Papal States can be considered a blessing for the popes. It was those states, which the popes perpetually wished to retain or to increase in size, that had been the cause of numerous battles and wars. It was for control of those states that political rivalries such as those between the Orsini and Colonna and their adherents had raged. It was around the year 900 when Teofilatto and his family began to govern Rome. He relied on the military might of dukes Alberico I and Alberico II. Misrule by the Roman nobles encouraged the emperors — Otto I, Otto II, Henry III and Frederick I — to appoint popes or antipopes of their persuasion to administer Rome and the papal territories in a more hospitable way.

Later, when nepotism reigned supreme, the popes extravagantly began to give parcels of the Papal States to various relatives, incurring jealousies and disagreements between other papal dynasties and the European powers. Pope Eugene IV (1431–47) spent most of his pontificate trying to regain the vast territories that his predecessor Martin V had given to his family, the Colonna. When the son of Pope Innocent VIII, Franceschetto Cibo, sold the land given to him by his papal father, Pope Alexander VI (Rodrigo Borgia, 1492–1503) protested, insisting that the sold land belonged to the church; Alexander VI proceeded to obtain them militarily. He confiscated the dukedom of Sermoneta from the Caetani family and gave it to his daughter Lucrezia and her son. When Alexander VI died, his successor, Pope Julius II (Giuliano della Rovere, 1503–13), promptly returned Sermoneta to the Caetani. Julius sanctioned the accession of his nephew Francesco Maria della Rovere to the dukedom of Urbino. Julius was followed on the papal throne by Leo X (Giovanni de' Medici, 1513–21), who sent an army to Urbino, deposed Francesco Maria della Rovere and in turn placed his own nephew Lorenzo de' Medici as the duke. Later, Urbino was returned to the della Rovere family.

The conflicts among Renaissance princes were appallingly harmful to the church as the Supreme Pontiffs themselves instigated and fought battles and sought wealth for their families at the church's expense. Needing endless amounts of money, the popes and their relatives inspired a repulsion for and dissatisfaction with the church. Their excesses thus served as the seed for the Protestant Reformation. The argument that the Reformation succeeded as a result of German princes' desires to gain political power at the expense of the papacy cannot be ignored, but the inabilities of the popes to concentrate on religious and spiritual matters certainly contributed to the development of Protestantism.

The new papal dynasties of the Baroque period also prospered on the acquisition of money and power, and the consequence was again dissension. The Barberini nephews acquired vast hoards of moneys and possessions during the reign of Urban VIII (Maffeo Barberini, 1523–44), who at times had a guilty conscience about nepotism. His successor Innocent X (Giambattista Pamfili, 1644–55) tried to recoup some of the church's possessions by bringing the Barberinis to trial. They managed to escape to France; later they were able to arrange a marriage between a Barberini and a Pamfili, thus ending the feud. The two Barberinis were allowed to return to Rome in triumph. As Innocent was dying, his sister-in-law Olimpia Pamfili swiftly trotted around the Vatican grabbing what wealth remained; she had already acquired immense sums during Innocent's pontificate. When the pope died, his successor, Alexander VII (Fabio Chigi, 1655–67), threatened to bring Olimpia up on charges of confiscating church property, and she quickly went into exile. It was now the turn of Alexander VII to grant estates, palaces and fortunes to members of his family.

And so, when the Papal States were removed in 1860 from the control of the popes, a new era commenced. The church became more concerned about ecclesiastical matters. Pius IX (1846–78) issued encyclicals, drew up concordats and summoned the First Vatican Council, renewing the spiritual life of the church. As the church marched into the twentieth century, it continued to concentrate on religious matters, but it also began — especially under Pope Pius XII (Eugenio Pacelli, 1939–58) — to acquire great wealth by investments in corporations. Financial advisors had helped the church to accumulate valuable assets, and now a new nepotism came into being. Pius XII's nephews became princes, served as his chief advisors (similar to the cardinal-nephews of the sixteenth and seventeenth centuries) and were placed in directorships of these multinational organizations. It remains to be seen whether future popes will use their position to aggrandize their families in the way that Pius XII did. Certainly, his successors have not moved in that direction.

It is significant that the present pope, John Paul II, is Polish. There is no question that traditional Italian society is family oriented. The Romans, placing the father at the very head, defined the closeness of the family. That tradition has permeated all strata of Italian society for centuries. Italian life centers on the family — a family that even in contemporary times retains its cohesiveness. It seemed only natural that the Italian popes should assist however possible the other members of their families. The treasury and lands of the church became the treasury and lands of the Roman popes to distribute to family members.

The avariciousness, however, of the families of the popes was unrelenting and inexcusable. The popes' concern for their families and friends was remarkably unscrupulous and unspiritual. The popes were all too human in their indulgence of their relatives, and the pontiffs' kinsfolk graspingly took whatever they could from the Holy See. The disposal of Vatican money had little to do with the church and its needs; rather, it evinced the maxim that "greed knows no bounds." The pace of this avidity was accelerated by the fact that the pontiff's tenure in office was limited. The family's access to papal riches would be curbed upon the pope's death.

There was often the further abuse of forcing kinswomen into so-called advantageous and strategic marriages for the advancement of the dynasty. Without any regard to their desires, young girls — not even in their teens — were sometimes thrown into marriage with members of other noble families. Young men could also be forced to marry heiresses. These politically arranged matches were often not only loveless, but joyless. Often the popes themselves served as the agents for engineering these matrimonial alliances. While it emulated the custom of European royal houses, this papal practice cannot be condoned because it was so often motivated by cupidity.

Often, too, it was the least deserving family members who received titles and positions of power. One conspicuous example was the elevation of Innocenzo del Monte, a depraved keeper of monkeys and a murderer, to the cardinalate by his benefactor Pope Julius III. Even popes like Alexander VII (Fabio Chigi), who at first refused to have his family come to Rome, soon relented and encouraged his kin to acquire offices and possessions from the Holy See. It then became incumbent upon Alexander's relatives to marry into other papal dynasties, a time-honored tradition.

"Tradition" is a potent word in the Vatican. For hundreds of years, for example, the Chigi family (Chigi-Albani)—unlike many other papal dynasties—has continued to serve the church as marshals of the church and guardians of the conclave. This role was executed even in the last election of a pope in 1978. The Chigi-Albani family still lives in the Palazzo Chigi in Rome. The Eternal City is where descendants of such distinguished papal dynasties as the Orsini, Colonna, Sforza-Cesarini, Boncompagni-Ludovisi, Borghese and Odescalchi continue to have their residences.

And, as we are well aware, it is in Rome where the papacy and papal families have thrived for over a thousand years; it is in Rome, after all, where it all began. For over a millennium, the papacy sustained the Roman nobility; the pontiffs and Italian aristocratic families were inextricably allied. These dynasties realized that they depended on the treasury and the power of the Holy See, and thus they vigorously supported and sustained the papacy in Rome.

Additional Genealogical Tables of Papal Families

TABLE 1a: ORSINI FAMILY

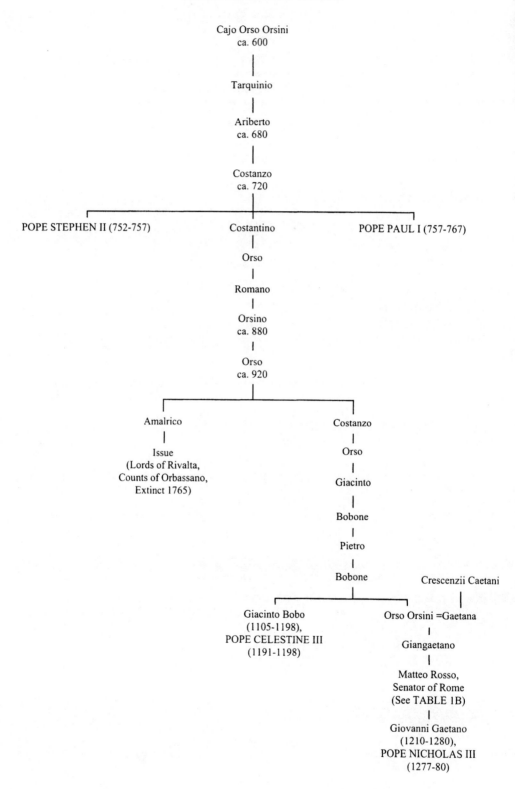

TABLE 1b: ORSINI FAMILY (continued from TABLE 1a)

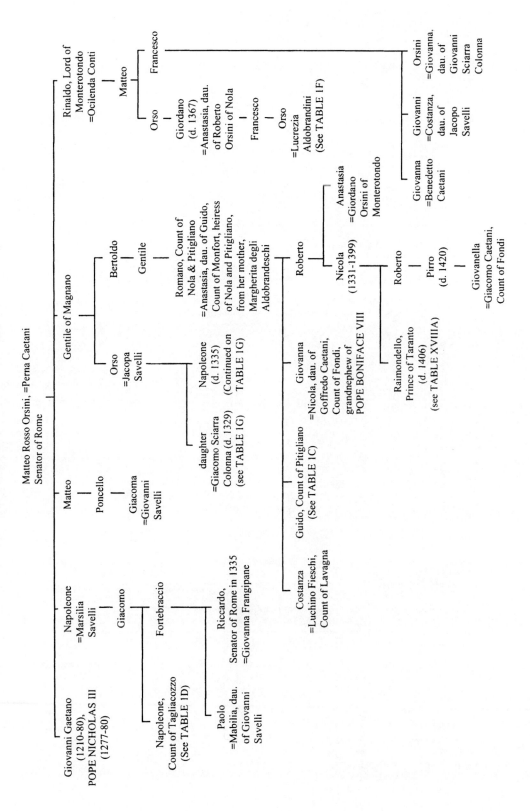

TABLE 1c: ORSINI COUNTS OF NOLA AND PITTIGLIANO
(continued from TABLE 1b)

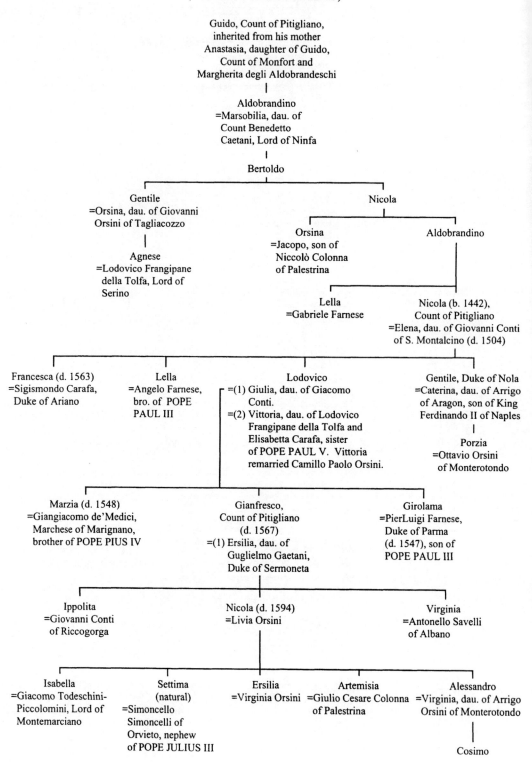

Guido, Count of Pitigliano,
inherited from his mother
Anastasia, daughter of Guido,
Count of Monfort and
Margherita degli Aldobrandeschi
|
Aldobrandino
=Marsobilia, dau. of
Count Benedetto
Caetani, Lord of Ninfa
|
Bertoldo

Gentile
=Orsina, dau. of Giovanni
Orsini of Tagliacozzo
|
Agnese
=Lodovico Frangipane
della Tolfa, Lord of
Serino

Nicola

Orsina
=Jacopo, son of
Niccolò Colonna
of Palestrina

Aldobrandino

Lella
=Gabriele Farnese

Nicola (b. 1442),
Count of Pitigliano
=Elena, dau. of Giovanni Conti
of S. Montalcino (d. 1504)

Francesca (d. 1563)
=Sigismondo Carafa,
Duke of Ariano

Lella
=Angelo Farnese,
bro. of POPE
PAUL III

Lodovico
=(1) Giulia, dau. of Giacomo
Conti.
=(2) Vittoria, dau. of Lodovico
Frangipane della Tolfa and
Elisabetta Carafa, sister
of POPE PAUL V. Vittoria
remarried Camillo Paolo Orsini.

Gentile, Duke of Nola
=Caterina, dau. of Arrigo
of Aragon, son of King
Ferdinando II of Naples
|
Porzia
=Ottavio Orsini
of Monterotondo

Marzia (d. 1548)
=Giangiacomo de'Medici,
Marchese of Marignano,
brother of POPE PIUS IV

Gianfresco,
Count of Pitigliano
(d. 1567)
=(1) Ersilia, dau. of
Guglielmo Gaetani,
Duke of Sermoneta

Girolama
=PierLuigi Farnese,
Duke of Parma
(d. 1547), son of
POPE PAUL III

Ippolita
=Giovanni Conti
of Riccogorga

Nicola (d. 1594)
=Livia Orsini

Virginia
=Antonello Savelli
of Albano

Isabella
=Giacomo Todeschini-
Piccolomini, Lord of
Montemarciano

Settima
(natural)
=Simoncello
Simoncelli of
Orvieto, nephew
of POPE JULIUS III

Ersilia
=Virginia Orsini

Artemisia
=Giulio Cesare Colonna
of Palestrina

Alessandro
=Virginia, dau. of Arrigo
Orsini of Monterotondo

Cosimo

TABLE 1d: ORSINI DUKES OF BRACCIANO, DUKES OF GRAVINA
(continued from TABLE 1b)

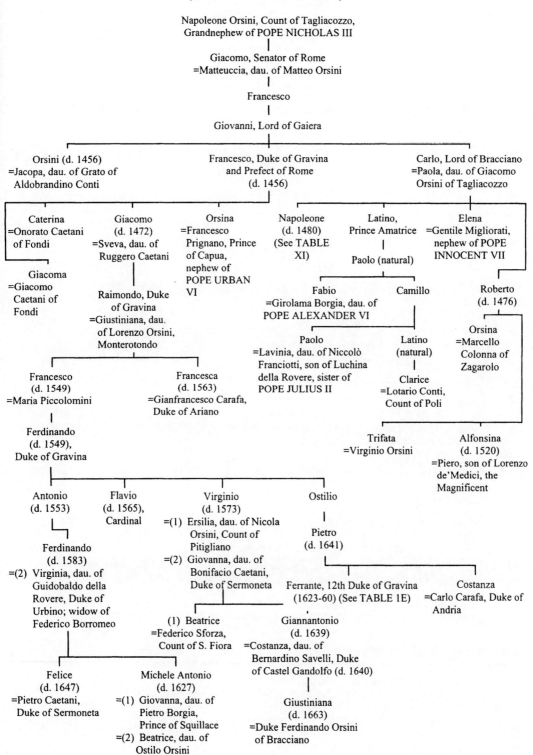

Napoleone Orsini, Count of Tagliacozzo,
Grandnephew of POPE NICHOLAS III

Giacomo, Senator of Rome
=Matteuccia, dau. of Matteo Orsini

Francesco

Giovanni, Lord of Gaiera

Orsini (d. 1456)
=Jacopa, dau. of Grato of
Aldobrandino Conti

Francesco, Duke of Gravina
and Prefect of Rome
(d. 1456)

Carlo, Lord of Bracciano
=Paola, dau. of Giacomo
Orsini of Tagliacozzo

Caterina
=Onorato Caetani
of Fondi

Giacomo
(d. 1472)
=Sveva, dau. of
Ruggero Caetani

Orsina
=Francesco
Prignano, Prince
of Capua,
nephew of
POPE URBAN
VI

Napoleone
(d. 1480)
(See TABLE
XI)

Latino,
Prince Amatrice

Paolo (natural)

Elena
=Gentile Migliorati,
nephew of POPE
INNOCENT VII

Giacoma
=Giacomo
Caetani of
Fondi

Raimondo, Duke
of Gravina
=Giustiniana, dau.
of Lorenzo Orsini,
Monterotondo

Fabio
=Girolama Borgia, dau. of
POPE ALEXANDER VI

Camillo

Roberto
(d. 1476)

Paolo
=Lavinia, dau. di Niccolò
Franciotti, son of Luchina
della Rovere, sister of
POPE JULIUS II

Latino
(natural)

Orsina
=Marcello
Colonna of
Zagarolo

Francesco
(d. 1549)
=Maria Piccolomini

Francesca
(d. 1563)
=Gianfrancesco Carafa,
Duke of Ariano

Clarice
=Lotario Conti,
Count of Poli

Ferdinando
(d. 1549),
Duke of Gravina

Trifata
=Virginio Orsini

Alfonsina
(d. 1520)
=Piero, son of Lorenzo
de'Medici, the
Magnificent

Antonio
(d. 1553)

Flavio
(d. 1565),
Cardinal

Virginio
(d. 1573)
=(1) Ersilia, dau. of Nicola
Orsini, Count of
Pitigliano
=(2) Giovanna, dau. of
Bonifacio Caetani,
Duke of Sermoneta

Ostilio

Pietro
(d. 1641)

Ferdinando
(d. 1583)
=(2) Virginia, dau. of
Guidobaldo della
Rovere, Duke of
Urbino; widow of
Federico Borromeo

Ferrante, 12th Duke of Gravina
(1623-60) (See TABLE 1E)

Costanza
=Carlo Carafa, Duke of
Andria

(1) Beatrice
=Federico Sforza,
Count of S. Fiora

Giannantonio
(d. 1639)
=Costanza, dau. of
Bernardino Savelli, Duke
of Castel Gandolfo (d. 1640)

Felice
(d. 1647)
=Pietro Caetani,
Duke of Sermoneta

Michele Antonio
(d. 1627)
=(1) Giovanna, dau. of
Pietro Borgia,
Prince of Squillace
=(2) Beatrice, dau. of
Ostilo Orsini

Giustiniana
(d. 1663)
=Duke Ferdinando Orsini
of Bracciano

TABLE 1e: ORSINI DUKES OF GRAVINA
(continued from TABLE 1d)

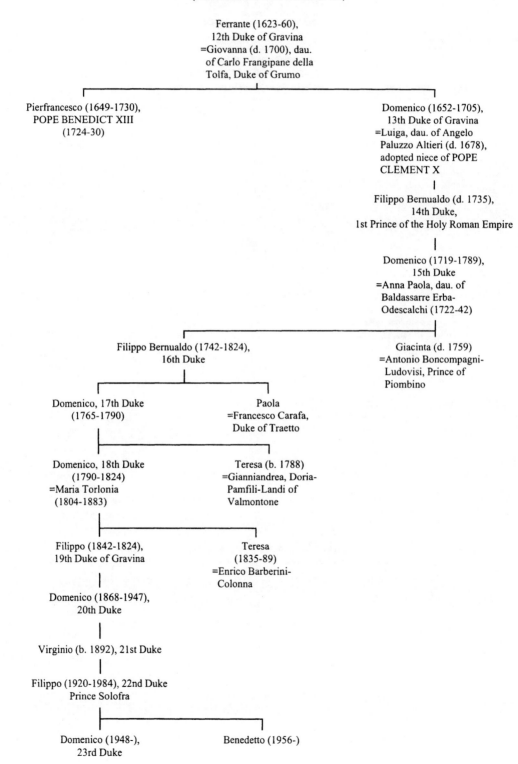

Ferrante (1623-60),
12th Duke of Gravina
=Giovanna (d. 1700), dau.
of Carlo Frangipane della
Tolfa, Duke of Grumo

Pierfrancesco (1649-1730),
POPE BENEDICT XIII
(1724-30)

Domenico (1652-1705),
13th Duke of Gravina
=Luiga, dau. of Angelo
Paluzzo Altieri (d. 1678),
adopted niece of POPE
CLEMENT X

Filippo Bernualdo (d. 1735),
14th Duke,
1st Prince of the Holy Roman Empire

Domenico (1719-1789),
15th Duke
=Anna Paola, dau. of
Baldassarre Erba-
Odescalchi (1722-42)

Filippo Bernualdo (1742-1824),
16th Duke

Giacinta (d. 1759)
=Antonio Boncompagni-
Ludovisi, Prince of
Piombino

Domenico, 17th Duke
(1765-1790)

Paola
=Francesco Carafa,
Duke of Traetto

Domenico, 18th Duke
(1790-1824)
=Maria Torlonia
(1804-1883)

Teresa (b. 1788)
=Gianniandrea, Doria-
Pamfili-Landi of
Valmontone

Filippo (1842-1824),
19th Duke of Gravina

Teresa
(1835-89)
=Enrico Barberini-
Colonna

Domenico (1868-1947),
20th Duke

Virginio (b. 1892), 21st Duke

Filippo (1920-1984), 22nd Duke
Prince Solofra

Domenico (1948-),
23rd Duke

Benedetto (1956-)

T.ABLE 1f: ORSINI LORDS OF MONTEROTONDO
(continued from TABLE 1b)

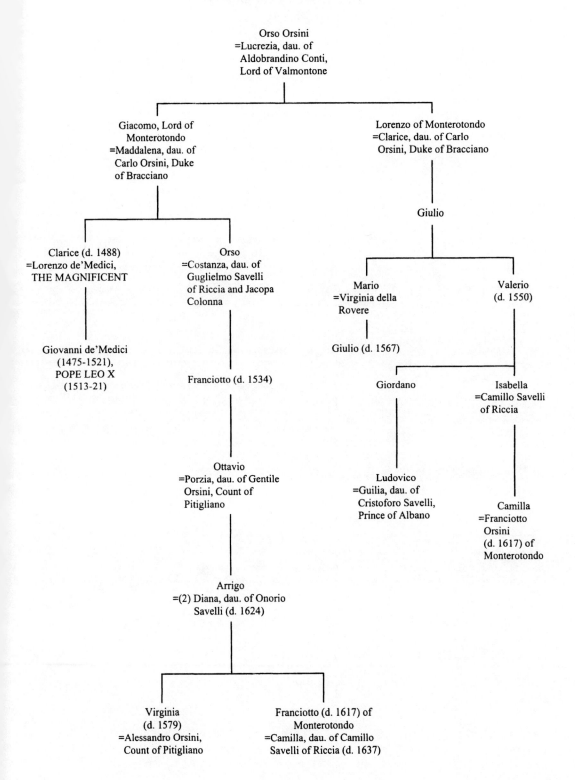

TABLE 1g: ORSINI BORGHESE COLONNA FAMILY
(continued from TABLE 1b)

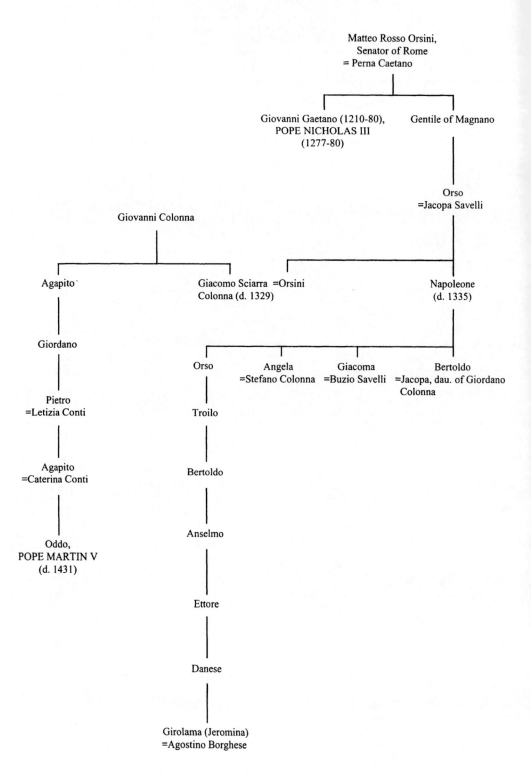

TABLE 2a: SAVELLI FAMILY

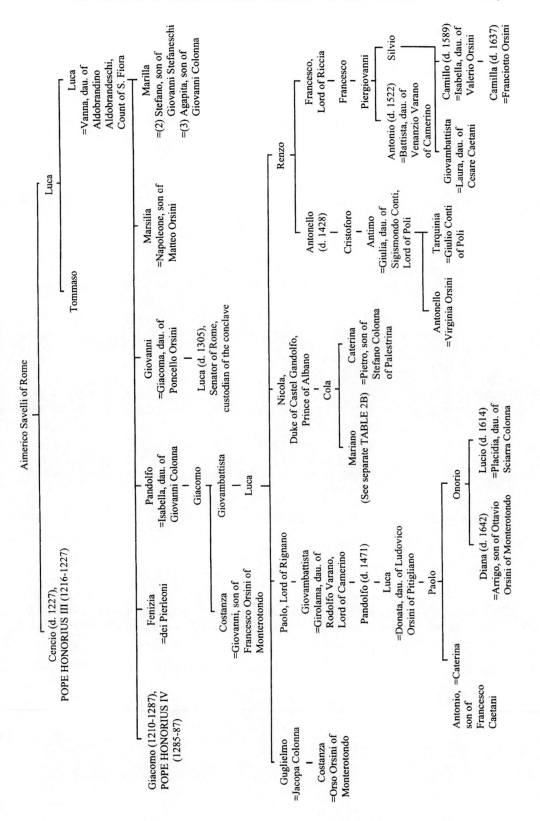

TABLE 2b: SAVELLI FAMILY
(continued from TABLE 2a)

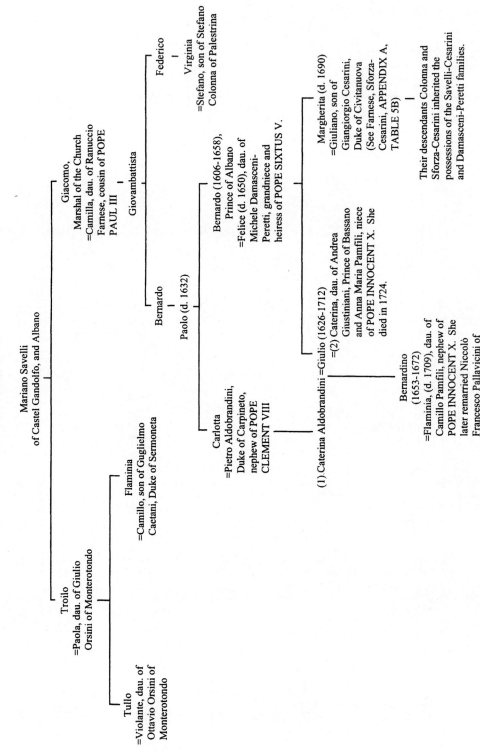

TABLE 3a: CAETANI FAMILY

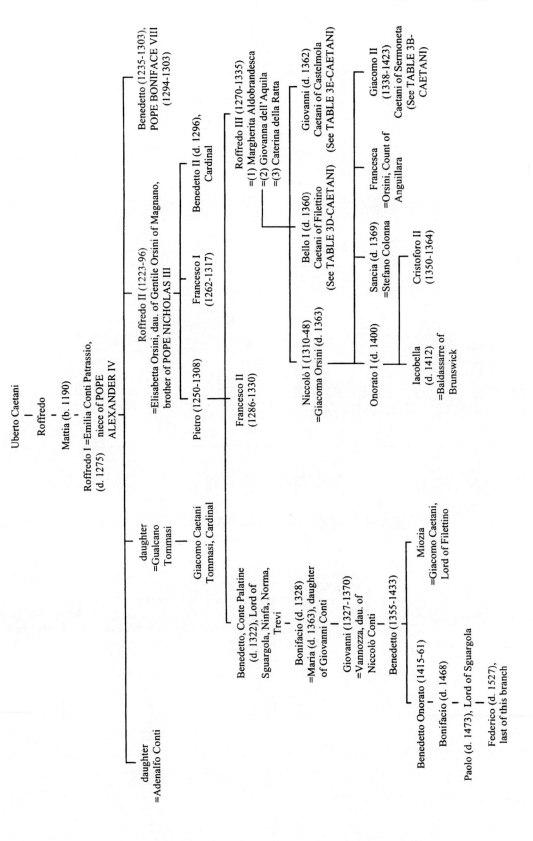

Uberto Caetani
|
Roffredo
|
Mattia (b. 1190)
|
Roffredo I =Emilia Conti Patrassio,
(d. 1275) niece of POPE
ALEXANDER IV

daughter
=Adenalfo Conti

daughter
=Gualcano
Tommasi

Roffredo II (1223-96)
=Elisabetta Orsini, dau. of Gentile Orsini of Magnano,
brother of POPE NICHOLAS III

Benedetto (1235-1303),
POPE BONIFACE VIII
(1294-1303)

Giacomo Caetani
Tommasi, Cardinal

Francesco I
(1262-1317)

Benedetto II (d. 1296),
Cardinal

Pietro (1250-1308)

Roffredo III (1270-1335)
=(1) Margherita Aldobrandesca
=(2) Giovanna dell'Aquila
=(3) Caterina della Ratta

Francesco II
(1286-1330)

Benedetto, Conte Palatine
(d. 1322), Lord of
Sguargola, Ninfa, Norma,
Trevi

Niccolò I (1310-48)
=Giacoma Orsini (d. 1363)

Bello I (d. 1360)
Caetani of Filettino
(See TABLE 3D-CAETANI)

Giovanni (d. 1362)
Caetani of Castelmola
(See TABLE 3E-CAETANI)

Bonifacio (d. 1328)
=Maria (d. 1363), daughter
of Giovanni Conti

Giovanni (1327-1370)
=Vannozza, dau. of
Niccolò Conti

Onorato I (d. 1400)

Sancia (d. 1369)
=Stefano Colonna

Francesca
=Orsini, Count of
Anguillara

Giacomo II
(1338-1423)
Caetani of Sermoneta
(See TABLE 3B-
CAETANI)

Iacobella
(d. 1412)
=Baldassarre of
Brunswick

Cristoforo II
(1350-1364)

Miozia
=Giacomo Caetani,
Lord of Filettino

Benedetto (1355-1433)

Benedetto Onorato (1415-61)

Bonifacio (d. 1468)

Paolo (d. 1473), Lord of Sguargola

Federico (d. 1527),
last of this branch

TABLE 3b: CAETANI FAMILY
(continued from TABLE 3a)

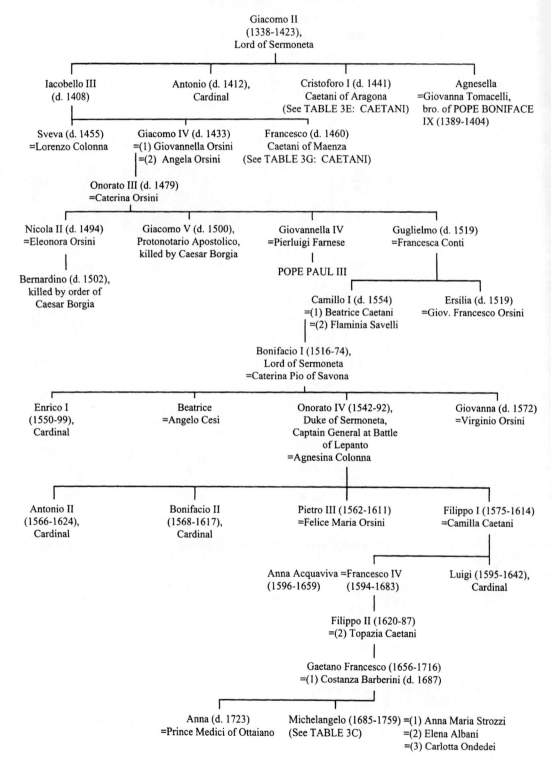

Giacomo II
(1338-1423),
Lord of Sermoneta

Iacobello III
(d. 1408)

Antonio (d. 1412),
Cardinal

Cristoforo I (d. 1441)
Caetani of Aragona
(See TABLE 3E: CAETANI)

Agnesella
=Giovanna Tomacelli,
bro. of POPE BONIFACE
IX (1389-1404)

Sveva (d. 1455)
=Lorenzo Colonna

Giacomo IV (d. 1433)
=(1) Giovannella Orsini
=(2) Angela Orsini

Francesco (d. 1460)
Caetani of Maenza
(See TABLE 3G: CAETANI)

Onorato III (d. 1479)
=Caterina Orsini

Nicola II (d. 1494)
=Eleonora Orsini

Giacomo V (d. 1500),
Protonotario Apostolico,
killed by Caesar Borgia

Giovannella IV
=Pierluigi Farnese

Guglielmo (d. 1519)
=Francesca Conti

Bernardino (d. 1502),
killed by order of
Caesar Borgia

POPE PAUL III

Camillo I (d. 1554)
=(1) Beatrice Caetani
=(2) Flaminia Savelli

Ersilia (d. 1519)
=Giov. Francesco Orsini

Bonifacio I (1516-74),
Lord of Sermoneta
=Caterina Pio of Savona

Enrico I
(1550-99),
Cardinal

Beatrice
=Angelo Cesi

Onorato IV (1542-92),
Duke of Sermoneta,
Captain General at Battle
of Lepanto
=Agnesina Colonna

Giovanna (d. 1572)
=Virginio Orsini

Antonio II
(1566-1624),
Cardinal

Bonifacio II
(1568-1617),
Cardinal

Pietro III (1562-1611)
=Felice Maria Orsini

Filippo I (1575-1614)
=Camilla Caetani

Anna Acquaviva =Francesco IV
(1596-1659)   (1594-1683)

Luigi (1595-1642),
Cardinal

Filippo II (1620-87)
=(2) Topazia Caetani

Gaetano Francesco (1656-1716)
=(1) Costanza Barberini (d. 1687)

Anna (d. 1723)
=Prince Medici of Ottaiano

Michelangelo (1685-1759) =(1) Anna Maria Strozzi
(See TABLE 3C)   =(2) Elena Albani
                                        =(3) Carlotta Ondedei

TABLE 3c: CAETANI-GIUSTINIANI FAMILY

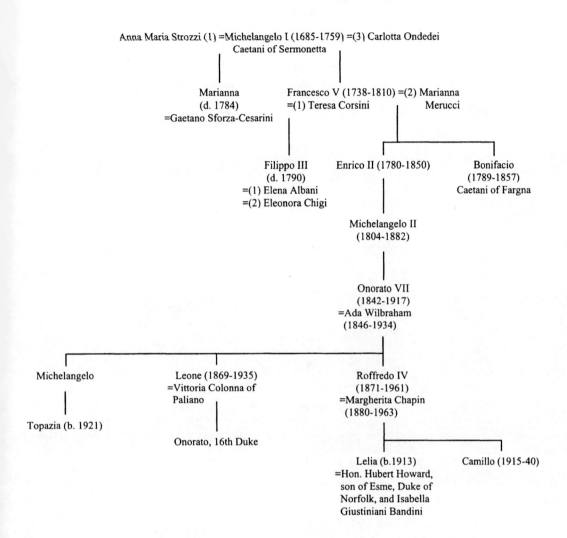

Anna Maria Strozzi (1) =Michelangelo I (1685-1759) =(3) Carlotta Ondedei
Caetani of Sermonetta

Marianna
(d. 1784)
=Gaetano Sforza-Cesarini

Francesco V (1738-1810) =(2) Marianna
=(1) Teresa Corsini   Merucci

Filippo III
(d. 1790)
=(1) Elena Albani
=(2) Eleonora Chigi

Enrico II (1780-1850)

Bonifacio
(1789-1857)
Caetani of Fargna

Michelangelo II
(1804-1882)

Onorato VII
(1842-1917)
=Ada Wilbraham
(1846-1934)

Michelangelo

Topazia (b. 1921)

Leone (1869-1935)
=Vittoria Colonna of
Paliano

Onorato, 16th Duke

Roffredo IV
(1871-1961)
=Margherita Chapin
(1880-1963)

Lelia (b.1913)
=Hon. Hubert Howard,
son of Esme, Duke of
Norfolk, and Isabella
Giustiniani Bandini

Camillo (1915-40)

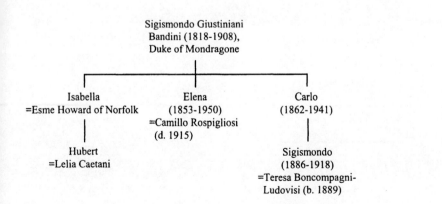

Sigismondo Giustiniani
Bandini (1818-1908),
Duke of Mondragone

Isabella
=Esme Howard of Norfolk

Hubert
=Lelia Caetani

Elena
(1853-1950)
=Camillo Rospigliosi
(d. 1915)

Carlo
(1862-1941)

Sigismondo
(1886-1918)
=Teresa Boncompagni-
Ludovisi (b. 1889)

TABLE 3d: CAETANI FAMILY
(continued from TABLE 3a)

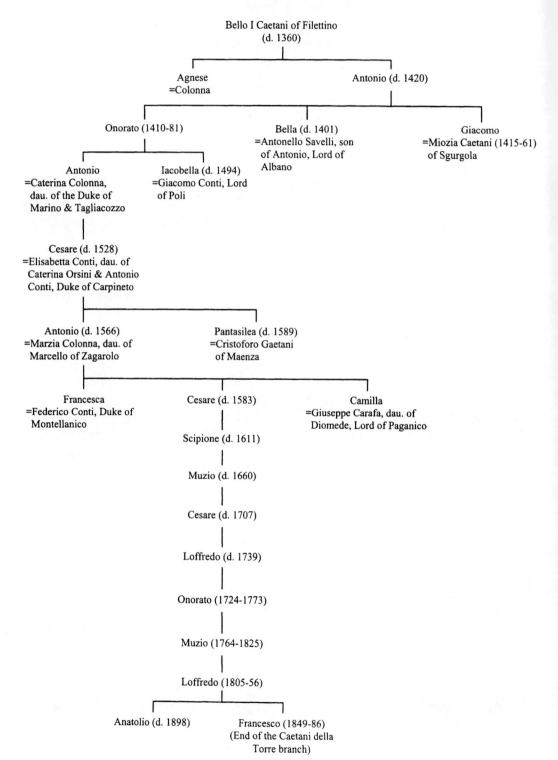

Bello I Caetani of Filettino
(d. 1360)

Agnese
=Colonna

Antonio (d. 1420)

Onorato (1410-81)

Bella (d. 1401)
=Antonello Savelli, son
of Antonio, Lord of
Albano

Giacomo
=Miozia Caetani (1415-61)
of Sgurgola

Antonio
=Caterina Colonna,
dau. of the Duke of
Marino & Tagliacozzo

Iacobella (d. 1494)
=Giacomo Conti, Lord
of Poli

Cesare (d. 1528)
=Elisabetta Conti, dau. of
Caterina Orsini & Antonio
Conti, Duke of Carpineto

Antonio (d. 1566)
=Marzia Colonna, dau. of
Marcello of Zagarolo

Pantasilea (d. 1589)
=Cristoforo Gaetani
of Maenza

Francesca
=Federico Conti, Duke of
Montellanico

Cesare (d. 1583)

Camilla
=Giuseppe Carafa, dau. of
Diomede, Lord of Paganico

Scipione (d. 1611)

Muzio (d. 1660)

Cesare (d. 1707)

Loffredo (d. 1739)

Onorato (1724-1773)

Muzio (1764-1825)

Loffredo (1805-56)

Anatolio (d. 1898)

Francesco (1849-86)
(End of the Caetani della
Torre branch)

TABLE 3e: CAETANI D'ARAGONA, COUNTS OF FONDI AND OF MORCONE, DUKES OF TRAETTO, DUKES OF LAURENZANA, PRINCES OF PIEDIMONTE
(continued from TABLE 3b)

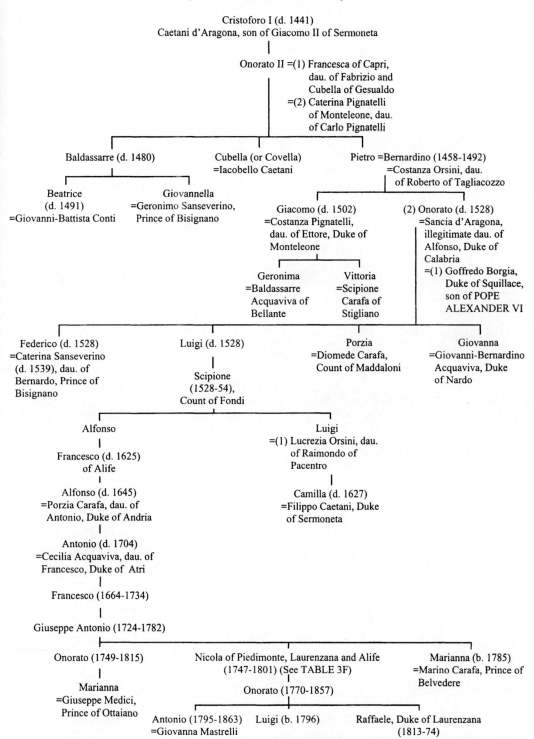

Cristoforo I (d. 1441)
Caetani d'Aragona, son of Giacomo II of Sermoneta

Onorato II =(1) Francesca of Capri,
dau. of Fabrizio and
Cubella of Gesualdo
=(2) Caterina Pignatelli
of Monteleone, dau.
of Carlo Pignatelli

Baldassarre (d. 1480)

Cubella (or Covella)
=Iacobello Caetani

Pietro =Bernardino (1458-1492)
=Costanza Orsini, dau.
of Roberto of Tagliacozzo

Beatrice
(d. 1491)
=Giovanni-Battista Conti

Giovannella
=Geronimo Sanseverino,
Prince of Bisignano

Giacomo (d. 1502)
=Costanza Pignatelli,
dau. of Ettore, Duke of
Monteleone

(2) Onorato (d. 1528)
=Sancia d'Aragona,
illegitimate dau. of
Alfonso, Duke of
Calabria
=(1) Goffredo Borgia,
Duke of Squillace,
son of POPE
ALEXANDER VI

Geronima
=Baldassarre
Acquaviva of
Bellante

Vittoria
=Scipione
Carafa of
Stigliano

Federico (d. 1528)
=Caterina Sanseverino
(d. 1539), dau. of
Bernardo, Prince of
Bisignano

Luigi (d. 1528)

Scipione
(1528-54),
Count of Fondi

Porzia
=Diomede Carafa,
Count of Maddaloni

Giovanna
=Giovanni-Bernardino
Acquaviva, Duke
of Nardo

Alfonso

Francesco (d. 1625)
of Alife

Alfonso (d. 1645)
=Porzia Carafa, dau. of
Antonio, Duke of Andria

Antonio (d. 1704)
=Cecilia Acquaviva, dau. of
Francesco, Duke of Atri

Francesco (1664-1734)

Giuseppe Antonio (1724-1782)

Luigi
=(1) Lucrezia Orsini, dau.
of Raimondo of
Pacentro

Camilla (d. 1627)
=Filippo Caetani, Duke
of Sermoneta

Onorato (1749-1815)

Marianna
=Giuseppe Medici,
Prince of Ottaiano

Nicola of Piedimonte, Laurenzana and Alife
(1747-1801) (See TABLE 3F)

Onorato (1770-1857)

Marianna (b. 1785)
=Marino Carafa, Prince of
Belvedere

Antonio (1795-1863)
=Giovanna Mastrelli

Luigi (b. 1796)

Raffaele, Duke of Laurenzana
(1813-74)

TABLE 3f: CAETANI FAMILY
(continued from TABLE 3d)

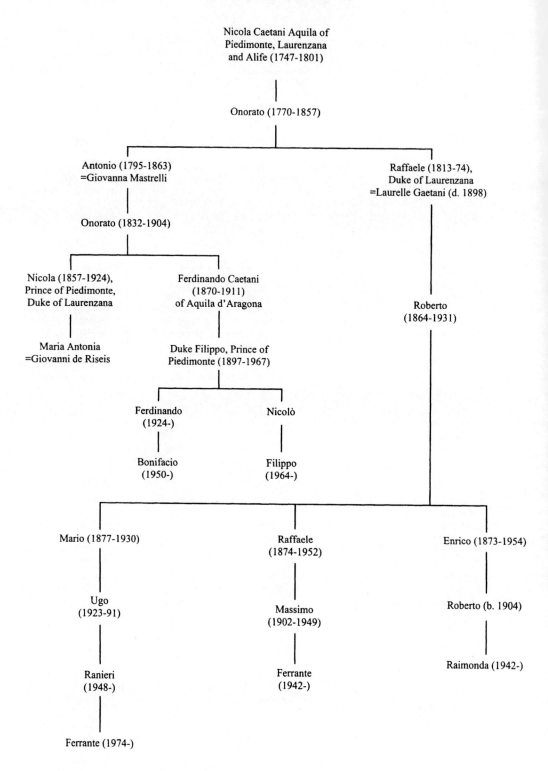

TABLE 3g: CAETANI OF MAENZA, NORMA AND ROCCAGORGA
(continued from TABLE 3b)

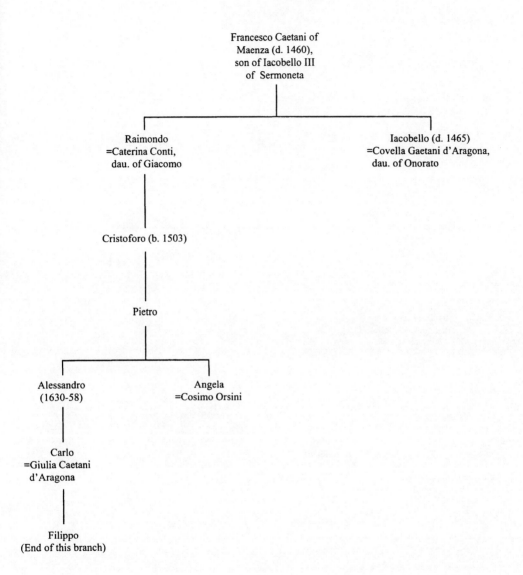

Francesco Caetani of
Maenza (d. 1460),
son of Iacobello III
of Sermoneta

Raimondo
=Caterina Conti,
dau. of Giacomo

Iacobello (d. 1465)
=Covella Gaetani d'Aragona,
dau. of Onorato

Cristoforo (b. 1503)

Pietro

Alessandro
(1630-58)

Angela
=Cosimo Orsini

Carlo
=Giulia Caetani
d'Aragona

Filippo
(End of this branch)

TABLE 4a: COLONNA FAMILY

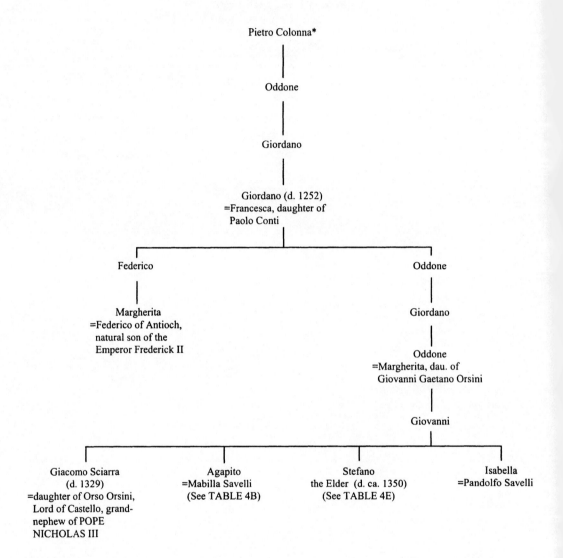

Pietro Colonna*

Oddone

Giordano

Giordano (d. 1252)
=Francesca, daughter of
Paolo Conti

Federico

Margherita
=Federico of Antioch,
natural son of the
Emperor Frederick II

Oddone

Giordano

Oddone
=Margherita, dau. of
Giovanni Gaetano Orsini

Giovanni

Giacomo Sciarra
(d. 1329)
=daughter of Orso Orsini,
Lord of Castello, grand-
nephew of POPE
NICHOLAS III

Agapito
=Mabilla Savelli
(See TABLE 4B)

Stefano
the Elder (d. ca. 1350)
(See TABLE 4E)

Isabella
=Pandolfo Savelli

*Pietro Colonna may have been the son of Gregorio II Conti of Tusculum (See TABLE I), or the son of Aemilia of
Palestrina and Duke Stefano (Refer to TABLE I and TABLE IV) or the brother of POPE BENEDICT IX (Teofilatto
Conti, d. 1056), or none of the above. It appears that he belonged to the House of Tusculum and acquired, probably
through inheritance, the lordships of Colonna, Palestrina, and Paliano.

TABLE 4b: COLONNA
(continued from TABLE 4a)

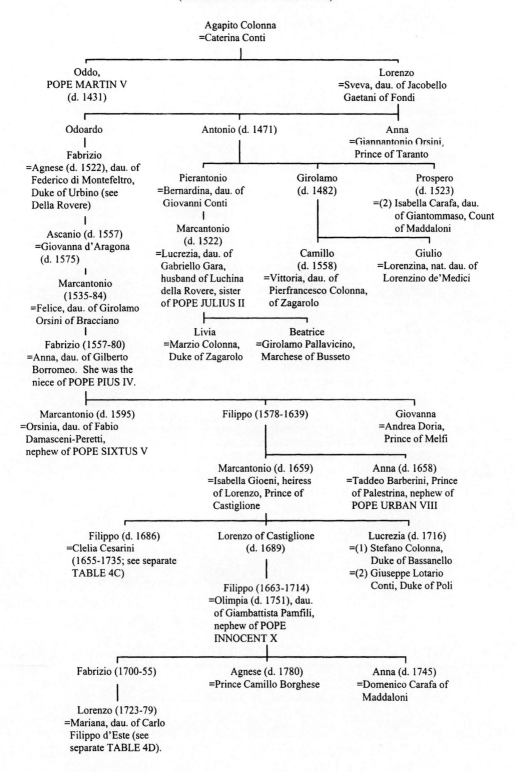

Agapito Colonna
=Caterina Conti

Oddo,
POPE MARTIN V
(d. 1431)

Lorenzo
=Sveva, dau. of Jacobello
Gaetani of Fondi

Odoardo
|
Fabrizio
=Agnese (d. 1522), dau. of
Federico di Montefeltro,
Duke of Urbino (see
Della Rovere)
|
Ascanio (d. 1557)
=Giovanna d'Aragona
(d. 1575)
|
Marcantonio
(1535-84)
=Felice, dau. of Girolamo
Orsini of Bracciano
|
Fabrizio (1557-80)
=Anna, dau. of Gilberto
Borromeo. She was the
niece of POPE PIUS IV.

Antonio (d. 1471)

Anna
=Giannantonio Orsini,
Prince of Taranto

Pierantonio
=Bernardina, dau. of
Giovanni Conti
|
Marcantonio
(d. 1522)
=Lucrezia, dau. of
Gabriello Gara,
husband of Luchina
della Rovere, sister
of POPE JULIUS II

Girolamo
(d. 1482)

Prospero
(d. 1523)
=(2) Isabella Carafa, dau.
of Giantommaso, Count
of Maddaloni

Camillo
(d. 1558)
=Vittoria, dau. of
Pierfrancesco Colonna,
of Zagarolo

Giulio
=Lorenzina, nat. dau. of
Lorenzino de'Medici

Livia
=Marzio Colonna,
Duke of Zagarolo

Beatrice
=Girolamo Pallavicino,
Marchese of Busseto

Marcantonio (d. 1595)
=Orsinia, dau. of Fabio
Damasceni-Peretti,
nephew of POPE SIXTUS V

Filippo (1578-1639)

Giovanna
=Andrea Doria,
Prince of Melfi

Marcantonio (d. 1659)
=Isabella Gioeni, heiress
of Lorenzo, Prince of
Castiglione

Anna (d. 1658)
=Taddeo Barberini, Prince
of Palestrina, nephew of
POPE URBAN VIII

Filippo (d. 1686)
=Clelia Cesarini
(1655-1735; see separate
TABLE 4C)

Lorenzo of Castiglione
(d. 1689)
|
Filippo (1663-1714)
=Olimpia (d. 1751), dau.
of Giambattista Pamfili,
nephew of POPE
INNOCENT X

Lucrezia (d. 1716)
=(1) Stefano Colonna,
Duke of Bassanello
=(2) Giuseppe Lotario
Conti, Duke of Poli

Fabrizio (1700-55)
|
Lorenzo (1723-79)
=Mariana, dau. of Carlo
Filippo d'Este (see
separate TABLE 4D).

Agnese (d. 1780)
=Prince Camillo Borghese

Anna (d. 1745)
=Domenico Carafa of
Maddaloni

TABLE 4c: COLONNA-STIGLIANO FAMILY
(continued from TABLE 4b)

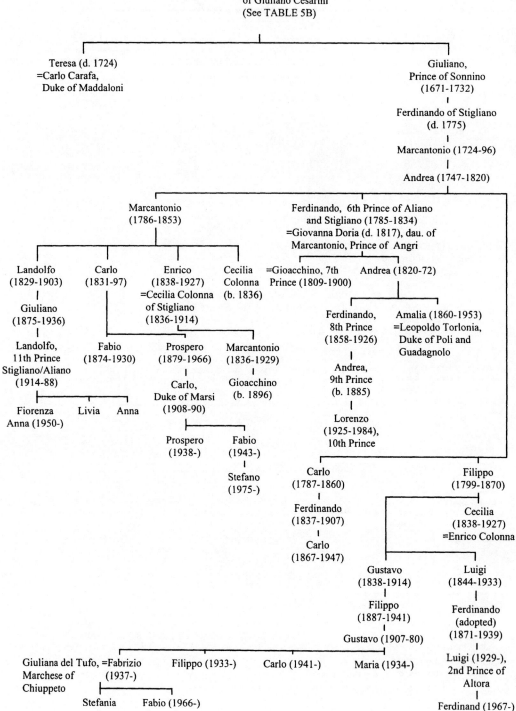

TABLE 4d: COLONNA-PALIANO FAMILY
(continued from TABLE 4b)

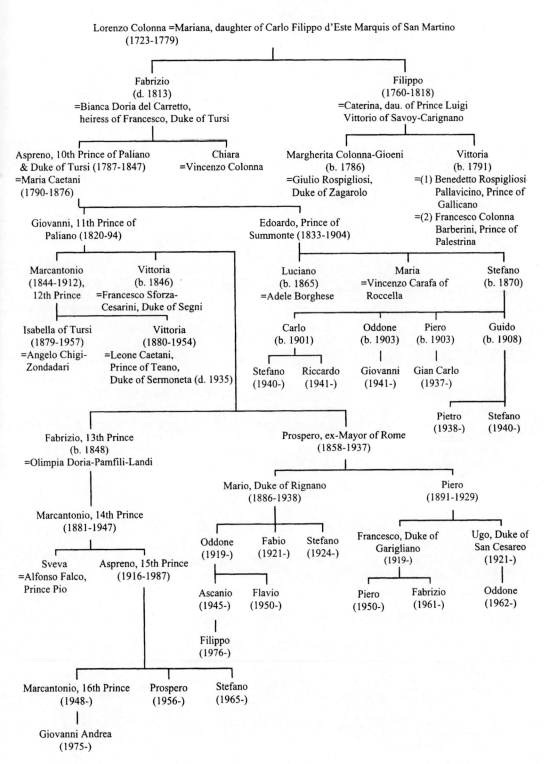

TABLE 4e: COLONNA FAMILY
(continued from TABLE 4a)

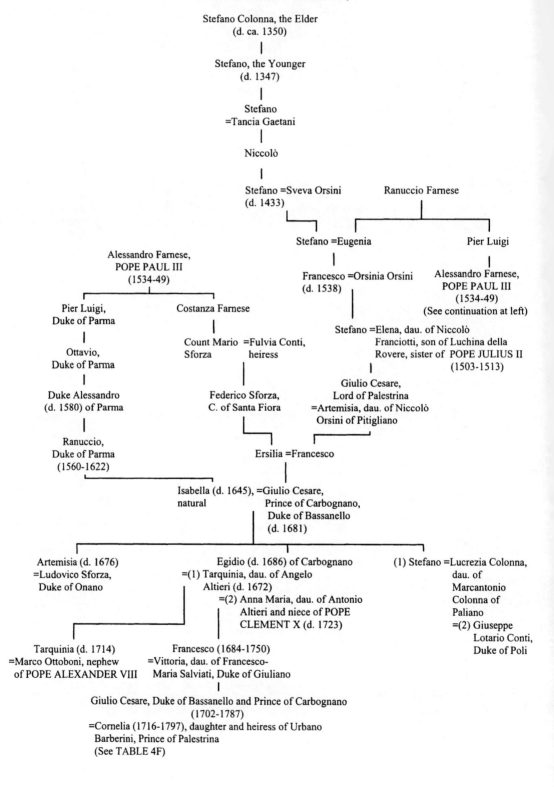

Stefano Colonna, the Elder
(d. ca. 1350)

Stefano, the Younger
(d. 1347)

Stefano
=Tancia Gaetani

Niccolò

Stefano =Sveva Orsini   Ranuccio Farnese
(d. 1433)

Stefano =Eugenia   Pier Luigi

Alessandro Farnese,
POPE PAUL III
(1534-49)

Francesco =Orsinia Orsini   Alessandro Farnese,
(d. 1538)   POPE PAUL III
(1534-49)
(See continuation at left)

Pier Luigi,   Costanza Farnese
Duke of Parma

Ottavio,   Count Mario =Fulvia Conti,   Stefano =Elena, dau. of Niccolò
Duke of Parma   Sforza   heiress   Franciotti, son of Luchina della
Rovere, sister of POPE JULIUS II
(1503-1513)

Duke Alessandro   Federico Sforza,   Giulio Cesare,
(d. 1580) of Parma   C. of Santa Fiora   Lord of Palestrina
=Artemisia, dau. of Niccolò
Orsini of Pitigliano

Ranuccio,   Ersilia =Francesco
Duke of Parma
(1560-1622)

Isabella (d. 1645), =Giulio Cesare,
natural   Prince of Carbognano,
Duke of Bassanello
(d. 1681)

Artemisia (d. 1676)   Egidio (d. 1686) of Carbognano   (1) Stefano =Lucrezia Colonna,
=Ludovico Sforza,   =(1) Tarquinia, dau. of Angelo   dau. of
Duke of Onano   Altieri (d. 1672)   Marcantonio
=(2) Anna Maria, dau. of Antonio   Colonna of
Altieri and niece of POPE   Paliano
CLEMENT X (d. 1723)   =(2) Giuseppe
Lotario Conti,
Tarquinia (d. 1714)   Francesco (1684-1750)   Duke of Poli
=Marco Ottoboni, nephew   =Vittoria, dau. of Francesco-
of POPE ALEXANDER VIII   Maria Salviati, Duke of Giuliano

Giulio Cesare, Duke of Bassanello and Prince of Carbognano
(1702-1787)
=Cornelia (1716-1797), daughter and heiress of Urbano
Barberini, Prince of Palestrina
(See TABLE 4F)

TABLE 4f: COLONNA-BARBERINI

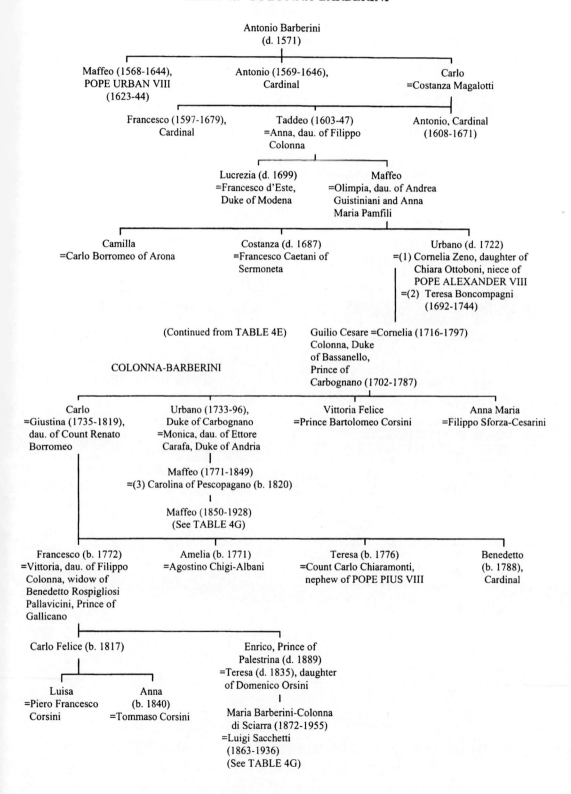

Antonio Barberini
(d. 1571)

Maffeo (1568-1644),
POPE URBAN VIII
(1623-44)

Antonio (1569-1646),
Cardinal

Carlo
=Costanza Magalotti

Francesco (1597-1679),
Cardinal

Taddeo (1603-47)
=Anna, dau. of Filippo
Colonna

Antonio, Cardinal
(1608-1671)

Lucrezia (d. 1699)
=Francesco d'Este,
Duke of Modena

Maffeo
=Olimpia, dau. of Andrea
Guistiniani and Anna
Maria Pamfili

Camilla
=Carlo Borromeo of Arona

Costanza (d. 1687)
=Francesco Caetani of
Sermoneta

Urbano (d. 1722)
=(1) Cornelia Zeno, daughter of
Chiara Ottoboni, niece of
POPE ALEXANDER VIII
=(2) Teresa Boncompagni
(1692-1744)

(Continued from TABLE 4E)

COLONNA-BARBERINI

Guilio Cesare =Cornelia (1716-1797)
Colonna, Duke
of Bassanello,
Prince of
Carbognano (1702-1787)

Carlo
=Giustina (1735-1819),
dau. of Count Renato
Borromeo

Urbano (1733-96),
Duke of Carbognano
=Monica, dau. of Ettore
Carafa, Duke of Andria

Vittoria Felice
=Prince Bartolomeo Corsini

Anna Maria
=Filippo Sforza-Cesarini

Maffeo (1771-1849)
=(3) Carolina of Pescopagano (b. 1820)

Maffeo (1850-1928)
(See TABLE 4G)

Francesco (b. 1772)
=Vittoria, dau. of Filippo
Colonna, widow of
Benedetto Rospigliosi
Pallavicini, Prince of
Gallicano

Amelia (b. 1771)
=Agostino Chigi-Albani

Teresa (b. 1776)
=Count Carlo Chiaramonti,
nephew of POPE PIUS VIII

Benedetto
(b. 1788),
Cardinal

Carlo Felice (b. 1817)

Enrico, Prince of
Palestrina (d. 1889)
=Teresa (d. 1835), daughter
of Domenico Orsini

Luisa
=Piero Francesco
Corsini

Anna
(b. 1840)
=Tommaso Corsini

Maria Barberini-Colonna
di Sciarra (1872-1955)
=Luigi Sacchetti
(1863-1936)
(See TABLE 4G)

TABLE 4g: BARBERINI-COLONNA DI SCIARRA FAMILY
(continued from TABLE 4f)

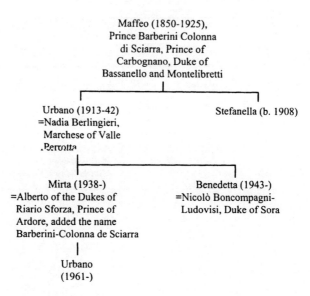

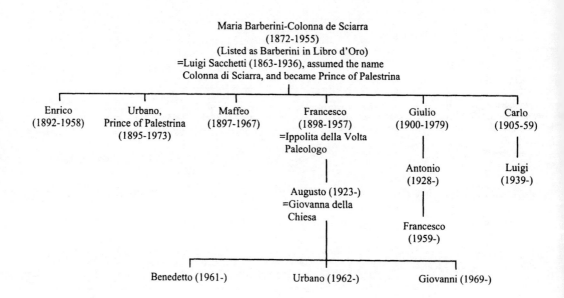

TABLE 5a: SFORZA OF SANTA FIORA

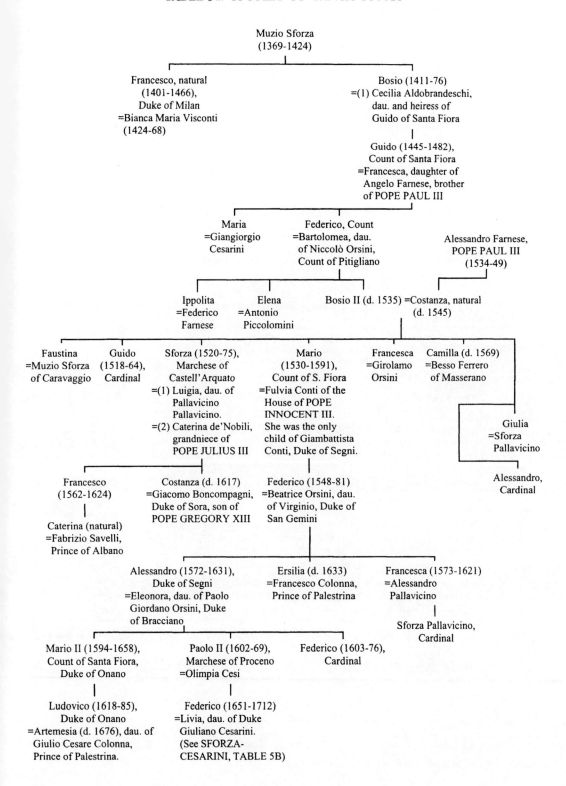

Muzio Sforza
(1369-1424)

Francesco, natural
(1401-1466),
Duke of Milan
=Bianca Maria Visconti
(1424-68)

Bosio (1411-76)
=(1) Cecilia Aldobrandeschi,
dau. and heiress of
Guido of Santa Fiora

Guido (1445-1482),
Count of Santa Fiora
=Francesca, daughter of
Angelo Farnese, brother
of POPE PAUL III

Maria
=Giangiorgio
Cesarini

Federico, Count
=Bartolomea, dau.
of Niccolò Orsini,
Count of Pitigliano

Alessandro Farnese,
POPE PAUL III
(1534-49)

Ippolita
=Federico
Farnese

Elena
=Antonio
Piccolomini

Bosio II (d. 1535) =Costanza, natural
(d. 1545)

Faustina
=Muzio Sforza
of Caravaggio

Guido
(1518-64),
Cardinal

Sforza (1520-75),
Marchese of
Castell'Arquato
=(1) Luigia, dau. of
Pallavicino
Pallavicino.
=(2) Caterina de'Nobili,
grandniece of
POPE JULIUS III

Mario
(1530-1591),
Count of S. Fiora
=Fulvia Conti of the
House of POPE
INNOCENT III.
She was the only
child of Giambattista
Conti, Duke of Segni.

Francesca
=Girolamo
Orsini

Camilla (d. 1569)
=Besso Ferrero
of Masserano

Giulia
=Sforza
Pallavicino

Francesco
(1562-1624)

Costanza (d. 1617)
=Giacomo Boncompagni,
Duke of Sora, son of
POPE GREGORY XIII

Federico (1548-81)
=Beatrice Orsini, dau.
of Virginio, Duke of
San Gemini

Alessandro,
Cardinal

Caterina (natural)
=Fabrizio Savelli,
Prince of Albano

Alessandro (1572-1631),
Duke of Segni
=Eleonora, dau. of Paolo
Giordano Orsini, Duke
of Bracciano

Ersilia (d. 1633)
=Francesco Colonna,
Prince of Palestrina

Francesca (1573-1621)
=Alessandro
Pallavicino

Sforza Pallavicino,
Cardinal

Mario II (1594-1658),
Count of Santa Fiora,
Duke of Onano

Paolo II (1602-69),
Marchese of Proceno
=Olimpia Cesi

Federico (1603-76),
Cardinal

Ludovico (1618-85),
Duke of Onano
=Artemesia (d. 1676), dau. of
Giulio Cesare Colonna,
Prince of Palestrina.

Federico (1651-1712)
=Livia, dau. of Duke
Giuliano Cesarini.
(See SFORZA-
CESARINI, TABLE 5B)

TABLE 5b: SFORZA-CESARINI FAMILY

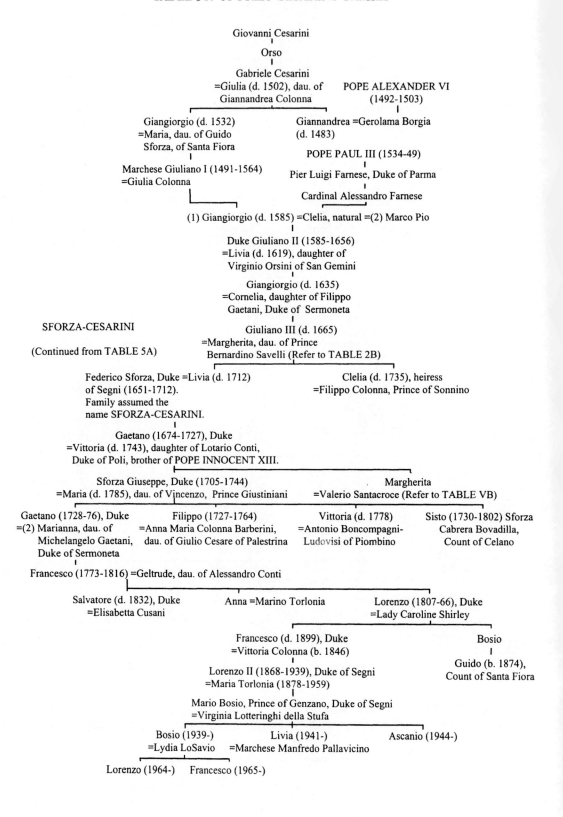

Giovanni Cesarini

Orso

Gabriele Cesarini
=Giulia (d. 1502), dau. of   POPE ALEXANDER VI
Giannandrea Colonna   (1492-1503)

Giangiorgio (d. 1532)   Giannandrea =Gerolama Borgia
=Maria, dau. of Guido   (d. 1483)
Sforza, of Santa Fiora
                               POPE PAUL III (1534-49)
Marchese Giuliano I (1491-1564)
=Giulia Colonna   Pier Luigi Farnese, Duke of Parma

                               Cardinal Alessandro Farnese

(1) Giangiorgio (d. 1585) =Clelia, natural =(2) Marco Pio

Duke Giuliano II (1585-1656)
=Livia (d. 1619), daughter of
Virginio Orsini of San Gemini

Giangiorgio (d. 1635)
=Cornelia, daughter of Filippo
Gaetani, Duke of Sermoneta

SFORZA-CESARINI   Giuliano III (d. 1665)
                               =Margherita, dau. of Prince
(Continued from TABLE 5A)   Bernardino Savelli (Refer to TABLE 2B)

Federico Sforza, Duke =Livia (d. 1712)   Clelia (d. 1735), heiress
of Segni (1651-1712).   =Filippo Colonna, Prince of Sonnino
Family assumed the
name SFORZA-CESARINI.

Gaetano (1674-1727), Duke
=Vittoria (d. 1743), daughter of Lotario Conti,
Duke of Poli, brother of POPE INNOCENT XIII.

Sforza Giuseppe, Duke (1705-1744)   Margherita
=Maria (d. 1785), dau. of Vincenzo, Prince Giustiniani   =Valerio Santacroce (Refer to TABLE VB)

Gaetano (1728-76), Duke   Filippo (1727-1764)   Vittoria (d. 1778)   Sisto (1730-1802) Sforza
=(2) Marianna, dau. of   =Anna Maria Colonna Barberini, =Antonio Boncompagni-   Cabrera Bovadilla,
Michelangelo Gaetani,   dau. of Giulio Cesare of Palestrina Ludovisi of Piombino   Count of Celano
Duke of Sermoneta

Francesco (1773-1816) =Geltrude, dau. of Alessandro Conti

Salvatore (d. 1832), Duke   Anna =Marino Torlonia   Lorenzo (1807-66), Duke
=Elisabetta Cusani   =Lady Caroline Shirley

Francesco (d. 1899), Duke   Bosio
=Vittoria Colonna (b. 1846)
                                             Guido (b. 1874),
Lorenzo II (1868-1939), Duke of Segni   Count of Santa Fiora
=Maria Torlonia (1878-1959)

Mario Bosio, Prince of Genzano, Duke of Segni
=Virginia Lotteringhi della Stufa

Bosio (1939-)   Livia (1941-)   Ascanio (1944-)
=Lydia LoSavio   =Marchese Manfredo Pallavicino

Lorenzo (1964-)   Francesco (1965-)

TABLE 6a: BORGHESE FAMILY

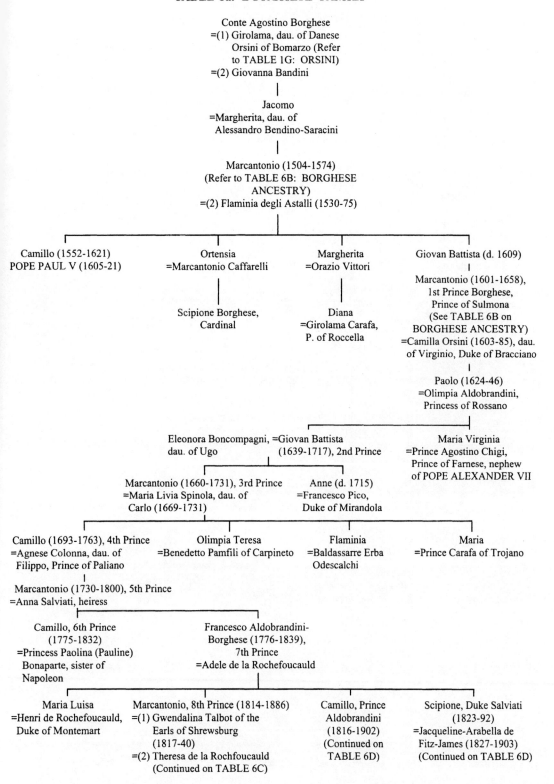

Conte Agostino Borghese
=(1) Girolama, dau. of Danese
Orsini of Bomarzo (Refer
to TABLE 1G: ORSINI)
=(2) Giovanna Bandini

Jacomo
=Margherita, dau. of
Alessandro Bendino-Saracini

Marcantonio (1504-1574)
(Refer to TABLE 6B: BORGHESE
ANCESTRY)
=(2) Flaminia degli Astalli (1530-75)

Camillo (1552-1621)
POPE PAUL V (1605-21)

Ortensia
=Marcantonio Caffarelli

Scipione Borghese,
Cardinal

Margherita
=Orazio Vittori

Diana
=Girolama Carafa,
P. of Roccella

Giovan Battista (d. 1609)

Marcantonio (1601-1658),
1st Prince Borghese,
Prince of Sulmona
(See TABLE 6B on
BORGHESE ANCESTRY)
=Camilla Orsini (1603-85), dau.
of Virginio, Duke of Bracciano

Paolo (1624-46)
=Olimpia Aldobrandini,
Princess of Rossano

Eleonora Boncompagni, =Giovan Battista
dau. of Ugo   (1639-1717), 2nd Prince

Maria Virginia
=Prince Agostino Chigi,
Prince of Farnese, nephew
of POPE ALEXANDER VII

Marcantonio (1660-1731), 3rd Prince
=Maria Livia Spinola, dau. of
Carlo (1669-1731)

Anne (d. 1715)
=Francesco Pico,
Duke of Mirandola

Camillo (1693-1763), 4th Prince
=Agnese Colonna, dau. of
Filippo, Prince of Paliano

Olimpia Teresa
=Benedetto Pamfili of Carpineto

Flaminia
=Baldassarre Erba
Odescalchi

Maria
=Prince Carafa of Trojano

Marcantonio (1730-1800), 5th Prince
=Anna Salviati, heiress

Camillo, 6th Prince
(1775-1832)
=Princess Paolina (Pauline)
Bonaparte, sister of
Napoleon

Francesco Aldobrandini-
Borghese (1776-1839),
7th Prince
=Adele de la Rochefoucauld

Maria Luisa
=Henri de Rochefoucauld,
Duke of Montemart

Marcantonio, 8th Prince (1814-1886)
=(1) Gwendalina Talbot of the
Earls of Shrewsbury
(1817-40)
=(2) Theresa de la Rochfoucauld
(Continued on TABLE 6C)

Camillo, Prince
Aldobrandini
(1816-1902)
(Continued on
TABLE 6D)

Scipione, Duke Salviati
(1823-92)
=Jacqueline-Arabella de
Fitz-James (1827-1903)
(Continued on TABLE 6D)

TABLE 6b: BORGHESE ANCESTRY (PARTIAL); PAPAL FAMILY INTERRELATIONSHIPS

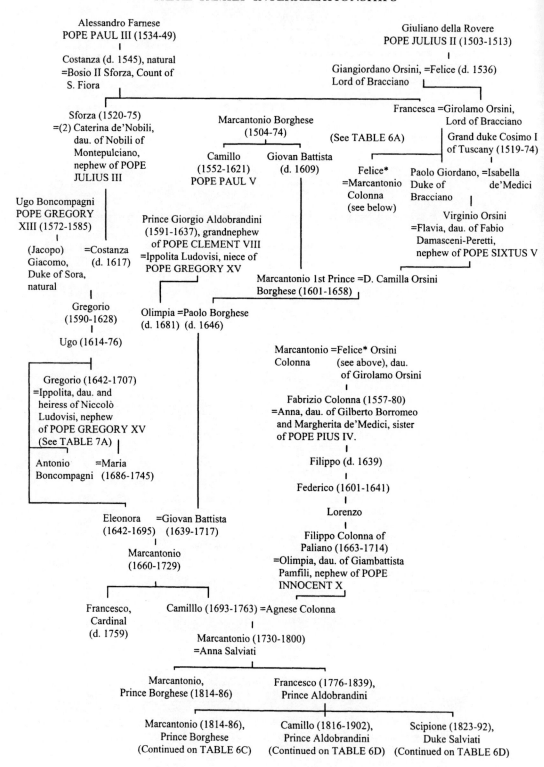

TABLE 6c: BORGHESE FAMILY
(continued from TABLES 6a and 6b)

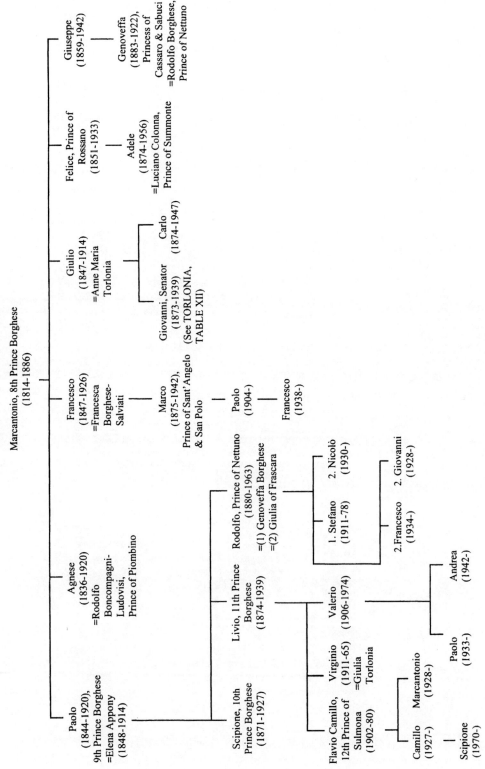

Marcantonio, 8th Prince Borghese
(1814-1886)

Paolo
(1844-1920),
9th Prince Borghese
=Elena Appony
(1848-1914)

Agnese
(1836-1920)
=Rodolfo
Boncompagni-
Ludovisi,
Prince of Piombino

Francesco
(1847-1926)
=Francesca
Borghese-
Salviati

Giulio
(1847-1914)
=Anne Maria
Torlonia

Felice, Prince of
Rossano
(1851-1933)

Giuseppe
(1859-1942)

Marco
(1875-1942),
Prince of Sant'Angelo
& San Polo

Giovanni, Senator
(1873-1939)
(See TORLONIA,
TABLE XII)

Carlo
(1874-1947)

Adele
(1874-1956)
=Luciano Colonna,
Prince of Summonte

Genoveffa
(1883-1922),
Princess of
Cassaro & Sabuci
=Rodolfo Borghese,
Prince of Nettuno

Paolo
(1904-)

Francesco
(1938-)

Scipione, 10th
Prince Borghese
(1871-1927)

Livio, 11th Prince
Borghese
(1874-1939)

Rodolfo, Prince of Nettuno
(1880-1963)
=(1) Genoveffa Borghese
=(2) Giulia of Frascara

1. Stefano
(1911-78)

2. Nicolò
(1930-)

2.Francesco
(1934-)

2. Giovanni
(1928-)

Flavio Camillo,
12th Prince of
Sulmona
(1902-80)

Virginio
(1911-65)
=Giulia
Torlonia

Valerio
(1906-1974)

Paolo
(1933-)

Andrea
(1942-)

Camillo
(1927-)

Marcantonio
(1928-)

Scipione
(1970-)

TABLE 6d: BORGHESE-SALVIATI AND BORGHESE-ALDOBRANDINI FAMILIES
(continued from TABLES 6a and 6b)

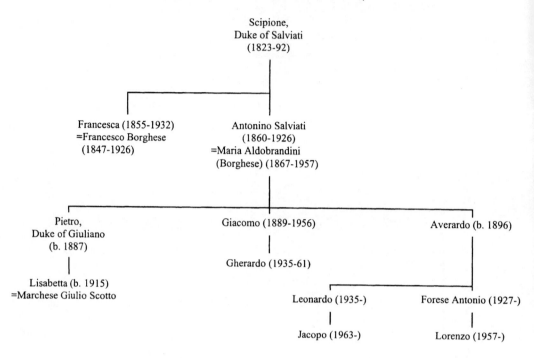

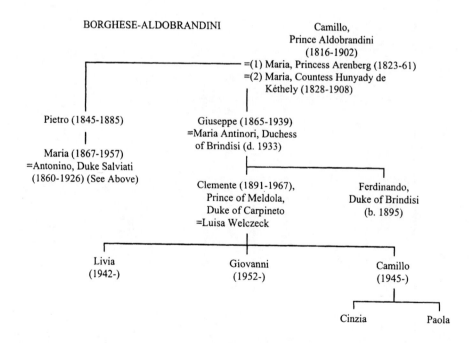

TABLE 7a: BONCOMPAGNI DI BOLOGNA AND BONCOMPAGNI-LUDOVISI FAMILIES

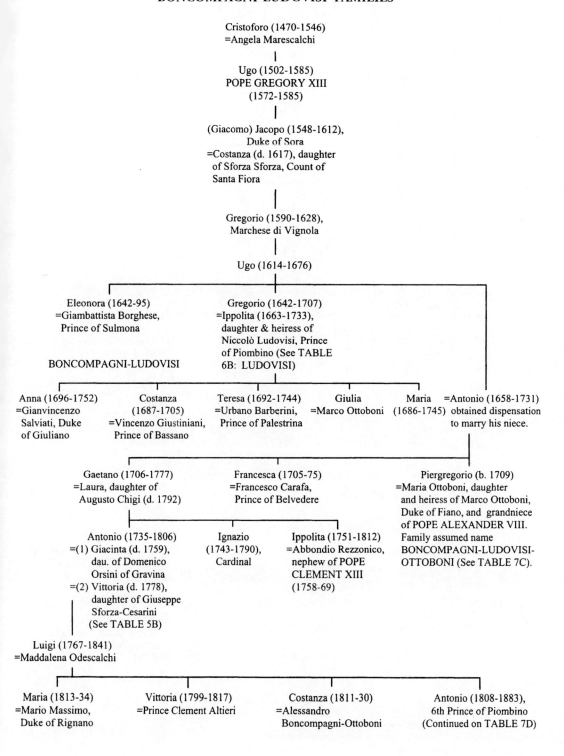

Cristoforo (1470-1546)
=Angela Marescalchi

Ugo (1502-1585)
POPE GREGORY XIII
(1572-1585)

(Giacomo) Jacopo (1548-1612),
Duke of Sora
=Costanza (d. 1617), daughter
of Sforza Sforza, Count of
Santa Fiora

Gregorio (1590-1628),
Marchese di Vignola

Ugo (1614-1676)

Eleonora (1642-95)
=Giambattista Borghese,
Prince of Sulmona

Gregorio (1642-1707)
=Ippolita (1663-1733),
daughter & heiress of
Niccolò Ludovisi, Prince
of Piombino (See TABLE
6B: LUDOVISI)

BONCOMPAGNI-LUDOVISI

Anna (1696-1752)
=Gianvincenzo
Salviati, Duke
of Giuliano

Costanza
(1687-1705)
=Vincenzo Giustiniani,
Prince of Bassano

Teresa (1692-1744)
=Urbano Barberini,
Prince of Palestrina

Giulia
=Marco Ottoboni

Maria
(1686-1745)

=Antonio (1658-1731)
obtained dispensation
to marry his niece.

Gaetano (1706-1777)
=Laura, daughter of
Augusto Chigi (d. 1792)

Francesca (1705-75)
=Francesco Carafa,
Prince of Belvedere

Piergregorio (b. 1709)
=Maria Ottoboni, daughter
and heiress of Marco Ottoboni,
Duke of Fiano, and grandniece
of POPE ALEXANDER VIII.
Family assumed name
BONCOMPAGNI-LUDOVISI-
OTTOBONI (See TABLE 7C).

Antonio (1735-1806)
=(1) Giacinta (d. 1759),
dau. of Domenico
Orsini of Gravina
=(2) Vittoria (d. 1778),
daughter of Giuseppe
Sforza-Cesarini
(See TABLE 5B)

Ignazio
(1743-1790),
Cardinal

Ippolita (1751-1812)
=Abbondio Rezzonico,
nephew of POPE
CLEMENT XIII
(1758-69)

Luigi (1767-1841)
=Maddalena Odescalchi

Maria (1813-34)
=Mario Massimo,
Duke of Rignano

Vittoria (1799-1817)
=Prince Clement Altieri

Costanza (1811-30)
=Alessandro
Boncompagni-Ottoboni

Antonio (1808-1883),
6th Prince of Piombino
(Continued on TABLE 7D)

TABLE 7b: LUDOVISI DI BOLOGNA
(antecedent for TABLE 7a)

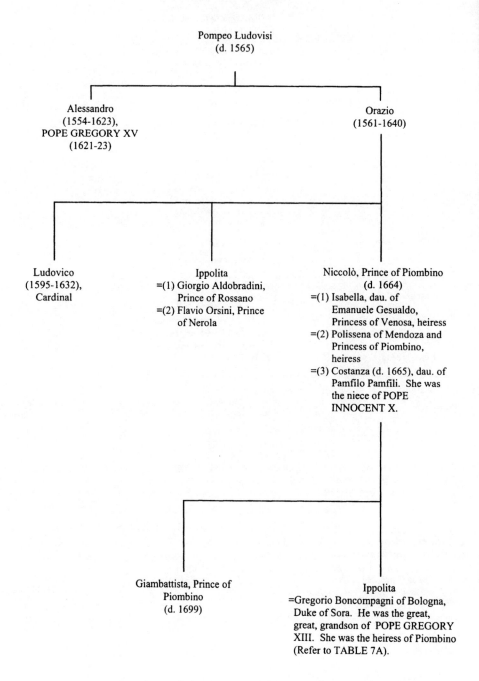

Pompeo Ludovisi
(d. 1565)

Alessandro
(1554-1623),
POPE GREGORY XV
(1621-23)

Orazio
(1561-1640)

Ludovico
(1595-1632),
Cardinal

Ippolita
=(1) Giorgio Aldobradini,
Prince of Rossano
=(2) Flavio Orsini, Prince
of Nerola

Niccolò, Prince of Piombino
(d. 1664)
=(1) Isabella, dau. of
Emanuele Gesualdo,
Princess of Venosa, heiress
=(2) Polissena of Mendoza and
Princess of Piombino,
heiress
=(3) Costanza (d. 1665), dau. of
Pamfilo Pamfili. She was
the niece of POPE
INNOCENT X.

Giambattista, Prince of
Piombino
(d. 1699)

Ippolita
=Gregorio Boncompagni of Bologna,
Duke of Sora. He was the great,
great, grandson of POPE GREGORY
XIII. She was the heiress of Piombino
(Refer to TABLE 7A).

TABLE 7c: BONCOMPAGNI-LUDOVISI-OTTOBONI FAMILY
(continued from TABLE 7a)

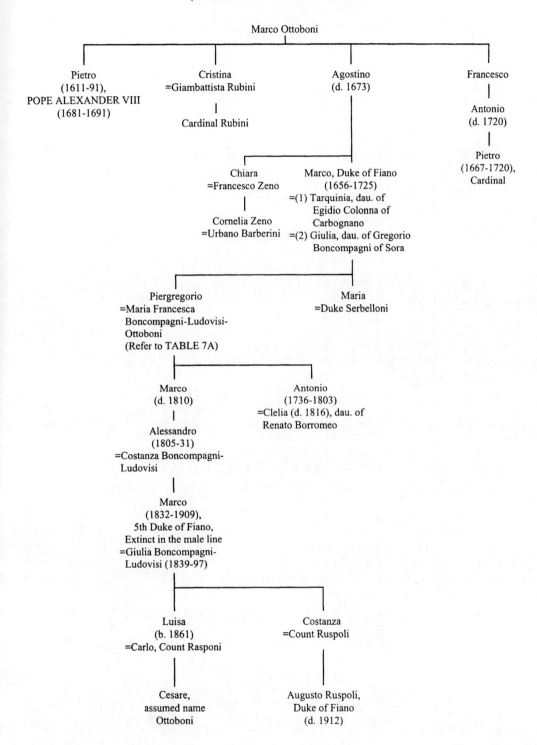

Marco Ottoboni

Pietro
(1611-91),
POPE ALEXANDER VIII
(1681-1691)

Cristina
=Giambattista Rubini

Cardinal Rubini

Agostino
(d. 1673)

Francesco

Antonio
(d. 1720)

Pietro
(1667-1720),
Cardinal

Chiara
=Francesco Zeno

Cornelia Zeno
=Urbano Barberini

Marco, Duke of Fiano
(1656-1725)
=(1) Tarquinia, dau. of
Egidio Colonna of
Carbognano
=(2) Giulia, dau. of Gregorio
Boncompagni of Sora

Piergregorio
=Maria Francesca
Boncompagni-Ludovisi-
Ottoboni
(Refer to TABLE 7A)

Maria
=Duke Serbelloni

Marco
(d. 1810)

Alessandro
(1805-31)
=Costanza Boncompagni-
Ludovisi

Antonio
(1736-1803)
=Clelia (d. 1816), dau. of
Renato Borromeo

Marco
(1832-1909),
5th Duke of Fiano,
Extinct in the male line
=Giulia Boncompagni-
Ludovisi (1839-97)

Luisa
(b. 1861)
=Carlo, Count Rasponi

Costanza
=Count Ruspoli

Cesare,
assumed name
Ottoboni

Augusto Ruspoli,
Duke of Fiano
(d. 1912)

TABLE 7d: BONCOMPAGNI-LUDOVISI FAMILY
(continued from TABLE 7a)

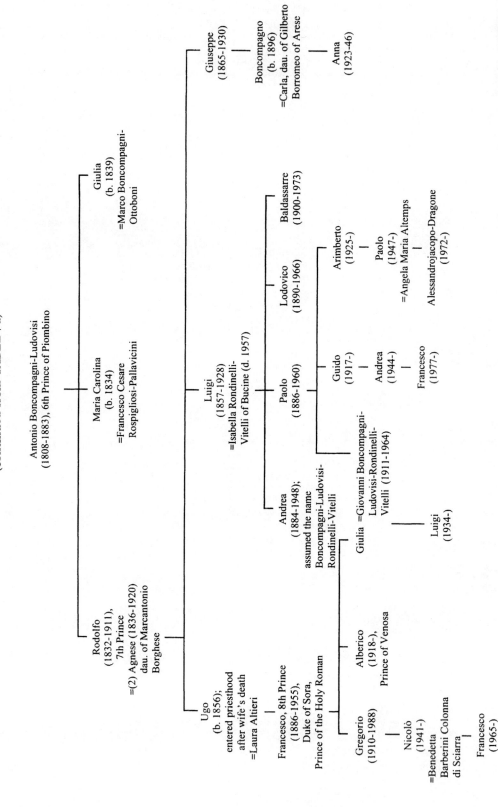

Reference Guide
to the Papal Dynasties

THE OLD PAPAL ARISTOCRACY

ALBERICHI (CONTI, HOUSE OF TUSCULUM)

The Contis of Tusculum were a family much involved in the history of the church during the Middle Ages. Supposedly Pope Hadrian I (772–95), Hadrian III (884–85) and Sergius III (904–911) were members of this family. Alberico I (d. 925), Margrave of Camerino and of Spoleto, may have belonged to the Conti. His wife Marozia, daughter of Senator Teofilatto and Senatrix Teodora I, is more likely to have been related to this family. Pope John XI (931–35) was the son of Marozia and either her husband or her lover, Pope Sergius III. One of Marozia and Alberico's sons, Prince Alberico II (905–954), after whom the Alberichi dynasty is named, was the father of Pope John XII (955–64). Alberico II established himself as the ruler of Rome and the surrounding lands of the church. He appointed popes at will, and the Conti family, the counts of Tusculum and Roman princes, wished to continue the policy set up by Prince Alberico II. At least four other popes and two antipopes — Benedict VII (974–83), Benedict VIII (1012–24), John XIX (1024–1032) and Benedict IX (1032–44, 1045, 1047–48) and antipopes Benedict X (1058–59) and Victor IV (1138) — were descended from Alberico II and his wife, Alta, whose ancestor was Charlemagne. The family attempted to create an hereditary papacy. In this they were unsuccessful, because of opposition from other Roman families and from the emperors, who selected their own candidates.

The Alberichi, the Conti family of Tusculum, claimed Tolomeo II and his wife Bertha, daughter of the emperor Louis I the Pious, son of Charlemagne, as ancestors. They also put forth the assertion that they were related to the royal houses of Europe. Both the Colonna family and the Contis (Comis), dukes of Segni — the family of Pope Innocent III (1198–1216) — maintained that they were descended from the Contis (Comis) of Tusculum. (Refer to tables I, IIIa, IIIb, IV, VIa, IIIb, IV, VIa and VIb. Tables I and IV present different versions of the genealogical background of the family. See also CONTI.)

CAETANI (GAETANI, CAJETAN)

Family of Popes Gelasius (1118–19) and Boniface VIII (1294–1303). Boniface's mother was Emilia Conti, niece of Pope Alexander IV of the Conti family. Using the church's treasury, Pope Boniface acquired numerous fiefs for members of his family; those territories include Anagni, Marino, Ninfa, Norma, Sermoneta, Alife, Piedimonte and Carpineto. Some areas, such as Fondi and Traetto, were acquired by marriage. The Caetani family was allied with the Orsini. The family retained some connections with the Holy See during the succeeding generations. Bonifacio Caetani became a cardinal in 1606, and Francesco Gaetano was a trusted advisor to Pope Innocent X (1644–55), serving as archbishop of Rhodes, nuncio to Spain and a negotiator of the Treaty of Westphalia (1648). The last Caetani cardinal was Luigi, who died in 1642. The last of the male members of the princely Caetani family to hold the titles Duke of Sermoneta, Prince of Teano, Duke of San Marco, Marchese of Cisterna and Lord of Bassiano, Norma, Ninfa and San Donato was Duke don Roffredo Caetani (1871–1961). At the present time, there are four branches of the princely Gaetani (Caetani) dell'Aquila d'Aragona. The current duke of the "primogeniture branch" is don Ferdinando Gaetani dell'Aquila d'Aragona, Prince of Piedimonte, Duke of Laurenzana and Count of Alife. He was born in 1924 and has a son Bonifacio who is the father of Giovanni, born in 1973, and two daughters. (Refer to tables 3a–g in Appendix A and tables IIIa, IIIb and XVII.)

COLONNA

The founder of the family is considered to be Pietro "de Columna," of the House of Tusculum and the Alberichi. He was probably descended from Duke Alberico II of Spoleto and his wife, Alda, a direct descendant of Charlemagne. Or he may have been the son of Duke Stefano and Aemelia, Countess of Palestrina of the Crescenzi family. Pietro acquired Palestrina around 1100. His son Oddone married the niece of Pope Honorius II (1124–30). Oddo Colonna, a descendant of Pietro and Oddone, became Pope Martin V in 1417 and reigned for fourteen years. In that time he added vast possessions to those already held by the Colonna family. He secured Ardea, Marsico, Nettuno, Astura, Soriano, Paliano, Rocca di Papa, Cave, Olevano, Capranica, Serrone and other territories. Pope Eugene IV (1431–47) undertook the task of having the vast territories appropriated by the Colonna returned to the Papal States.

During much of the Middle Ages they were the archenemies of the Orsini and Caetani families. The fiefs of the Colonna family were principally in the kingdom of Naples. In the 1600s, some members of the Colonna family went into debt and sold some of their territories such as Zagarolo and Palestrina — Zagarolo to the Ludovisi family and Palestrina to the Barberini. When Cornelia, heiress of the Barberini family, married Giulio Cesare Colonna (1702–1787) in 1728, Palestrina was returned to this branch of the "Barberini-Colonna" family, which had hyphenated the names. (See Barberini-Colonna.) The Colonna regained much of their fortune by marrying heiresses of the Barberini, Doria (Bianca Doria del Carretto, heiress of the duke of Tursi), Borromeo (Anna Borromeo, niece of Pope Pius IV), Cesarini (Clelia Cesarini, one of the heiresses of the count of Celano), Gioeni (Isabella Gioeni, Princess of Castiglione) and Franciotti della Rovere families (Elena, daughter of Niccolò Franciotti della Rovere and Laura Migliorati, brought the dukedoms of Carbognano and Bassanello to the Colonna family).

In 1710 the reigning lord of the Paliano branch of the Colonna family was made assistant prince to the pontifical throne, a title held at the present time. The male head of the family became duke of Paliano in 1520 and prince in 1569. The members of the Colonna family were active in church relations, as can be demonstrated by the number of cardinals who as late as the eighteenth century were members of that family. During the pontificate of Benedict XIV (1740–58), there were Cardinal Girolamo Colonna; Cardinal Marcantonio Colonna,

major-domo of the church; and Cardinal Prospero Colonna di Sciarra who became prefect of propaganda; at the end of the century under Pope Pius VI (1775–99), there were Cardinals Niccolò Colonna di Stigliano and Cardinal Carlo Antonio Colonna, influential members of the Curia. After the unification of Italy, Prospero Colonna became mayor of Rome and was appointed an Italian senator. In the twentieth century, there are several branches of this family, as represented by the Colonnas of Paliano at Palazzo Colonna in Rome. They are the prince and duke of Paliano, duke of Marino, prince of Sonnino and Avella, duke of Tursi and lord of Genazzano. (The present prince and duke of Paliano is Marcantonio Colonna, born in 1948, who has a son Giovanni Andrea, born in 1975, and a daughter.) Another branch is the Prince Colonna of Stigliano, Villa Colonna and Naples; this Colonna prince carries the titles Prince of Stigliano and Aliano, Prince of Galatro, Marchese of Castelnuovo, Baron of Alianello, S. Arcangelo, Roccanova, Melito and Giugliano. (The present duke is Don Prospero, born in 1938; he has a son Fabio Marzio, born 1943, who has two sons and a daughter.) The Prince Barberini-Colonna of Sciarra, Prince of Carbognano and Nerola, Duke of Bassanello and Montelbretti, Marchese of Corese and Count of Palazzuolo, represents another branch of the family. (The present head is Donna Mirta, born in 1938, wife of Alberto Riario Sforza, who adopted the surname of his wife, and their son is Urbano Riario Sforza-Barberini-Colonna de Sciarra, born in 1961.) (Refer to 4A–4E tables in Appendix A and tables I, IIIa, IIIb, XIII and XVII.)

CONTI.

The Conti dukes of Segni gave three popes to the Holy See: Innocent III (1198–1216), Gregory IX (1227–1241) and Alexander IV (1254–61). The Conti as a family descended from the Conti of Tusculum (refer to Alberichi) that had given so many popes to the Holy See. Riccardo, brother of Pope Innocent III, received the lordships of Poli and Guadagnolo in 1204, Valmontone in 1208, and in the same year the dukedom of Sora. And from Riccardo's sons

Paolo and Giovanni emerged the two branches of this family, the counts of Valmontone and Segni and the counts of Poli and Guadagnolo. Fulvia Conti, the only child of Giambattista, last duke of Segni of the Conti family, married Mario Sforza (d. 1591). Their son Federico Sforza (1548–81) became the duke of Segni, and he had numerous descendants. A son of the count of Poli, another branch of the Conti family, was Michelangelo, who in 1721 became Pope Innocent XIII. The last count of Poli, another Michelangelo, died in 1808, and this branch of the House of Conti became extinct. Salvatore Sforza-Cesarini sold Poli and Guadagnolo to Giovanni Torlonia in 1820 for 73,582 scudi and 80 baiocchi. (Refer to tables I, IIa, IIIb, IV, VIa, VIb, XVII and XX.g.)

CRESCENZI.

Descended from Senator Teofilatto and his wife Teodora I, through their daughter Theodora II, this family possibly gave only one pope to Rome, John XIII (965–72). The Crescenzi family for three generations were pope makers or pope destroyers. Members included Giovanni Crescenzi, husband of Teodora III; Crescenzio di Teodora; Crescenzio a Caballo Marmoreo, whose daughter Teodoranda married Benedetto, son of Count Benedetto of Campagna and Stefania of Palestrina (daughter of Giovanni Crescenzi and Teodora III); and Giovanni Nomentano and his son Giovanni. (Refer to table I.) The family deposed Benedict VI (973–74), put Boniface VII (974, 984–85) on the papal throne and enthroned John XV (985–96), John XVII (1003), John XVIII (1003–09) and Sergius IV (1009–12). A branch of the family settled in Sabina. In 1045 the Crescenzi family proposed Bishop John of Sabina as pope, and he reigned as Pope Silvester III for approximately twenty-one days. The Crescenzi family had little political importance in the history of the church after that period, but the surname occasionally surfaces. Pope Paul V (1605–21) named Pietro Paolo Crescenzi a cardinal in 1611.

FIESCHI.

An aristocratic feudal family of Genoa (Genova) that gave two popes to the See of Peter: Innocent IV (1243–54) and his nephew Hadrian V (1276). They belonged to the Fieschi branch of the family that were the counts of Lavagna. During the late Middle Ages, the family established close ties with the church: seventy-two members of the family became cardinals. Alberto Fieschi, nephew of Pope Innocent IV, was appointed captain general of the papal forces. The Fieschi family became the rival for political power of the Doria in the city of Genoa. Members of the family married into prominent Italian dynasties including the Visconti, della Rovere, Orsini, Savoia and Pallavicino families. The main branches became extinct, but one branch, the counts of Savignone, gave a cardinal, Lorenzo (1642–1726), to the church. He was archbishop of Genova and acted as the papal nuncio to France. (Refer to Table V.)

FRANGIPANE.

A Roman family (gens Anicia) that for a period of time became pope makers, placing Honorius II (1124–30) and Innocent II (1130–43) on the papal throne. During this period of time, Cardinal Aimerico Frangipane, the chancellor, was influential in formulating church policies. While the Frangipanes were headquartered in Rome, they did have lands outside of Rome (e.g., Cisterna, Terracina, Nettuno and Astura), which became the property of the Colonna family. The Colonnas, especially after the papacy of Martin V, became more powerful in the affairs of the church, while the Frangipanes lost much of their importance in church circles. However, Fabio Frangipane (d. 1587) was a cardinal, nuncio to Paris and bishop of Barletta and Nazareth. His nephew Ottavio Mirto Frangipane was appointed by Pope Paul V (1605–21) as archbishop of Taranto and papal nuncio to the Spanish Netherlands and Cologne. Mario Frangipane, Marchese of Nemi, who died in 1654, was the last male representative of the main arm of the family. Nemi was sold to Luigi Braschi-Onesti, nephew of Pope Pius VI. However, other branches such as the Frangipane of Friuli, lords of Tarcento, are still in existence. The family married into prominent families such as the Orsini. Beatrice

Frangipane (d. 1524) married Georg the Pious, Margrave of Ansbach (d. 1536), a member of the Hohenzollern family that later became kings of Prussia and kaisers of Germany. Giovanna, daughter of Carlo Frangipane della Tolfa, duke of Grumo, was the mother of Pierfrancesco Orsini (1649–1730), who was elected Pope Benedict XIII.

ORSINI (BOBO-ORSO OR BOBONE-ORSINI).

A Roman family that from the 600s became increasingly important in the history of the church. At least five popes belonged to this family: Stephen II (752–57), Paul (757–67), Celestine III (1191–98), Nicholas III (1277–90) and Benedict XIII (1724–30). The prosperity of the family can be attributed to church offices, benefices and possessions granted by papal relatives and obtained by lucrative marriages. In 1195 Senator Matteo Rosso Orsini became lord of Mugnano, Galeria, Licenza, Marino and Monterotondo. His son Pope Nicholas III (Giovanni Gaetano Orsini) was particularly generous with his relatives. Members became counts of Monterotondo, counts of Nola and Pitigliano, princes of Taranto, dukes of Gravina, dukes of Bracciano and Roman princes and princesses of the Holy Roman Empire. The Orsini received the title of Reichfurst, Prince of the Holy Roman Empire in 1629.

Allied with the Caetani when Pope Boniface VIII was in power, the Orsini captured Nepi from the Colonna, and it was given to them. Pope Eugene IV named Francesco Orsini as duke of Gravina in 1435. Giangiordano, Duke of Bracciano, married Felice della Rovere, the natural daughter of Pope Julius II, whom he served as captain on military expeditions. Later Virgino Orsini married Flavia Damasceni-Peretti, the niece of Pope Sixtus V. Both Felice della Rovere and Flavia Damasceni-Peretti brought considerable dowries to the Orsini family. The land and wealth of the family was threatened by Ceasar Borgia who captured the castle of Bracciano. He took as his prisoner Gentile Virginio Orsini, Lord of Bracciano, who was poisoned. Cardinal Giovan Battista Orsini and Paolo Orsini, Duke of Gravina, were

murdered. The Borgias readily confiscated property as Sermoneta from the Caetani and Bracciano from the Orsini. Fortunately, the papacy of Pope Alexander VI (Rodrigo Borgia) came to an abrupt end in 1503, and the Orsinis ingratiated themselves with Pope Julius II and regained their power. Pope Benedict XIII (Pietro Francesco Orsini, 1724–1730) conferred the title of Roman Prince on the family in May 1724.

There were numerous branches of this family, and members often intermarried with one another. Seemingly the most prolific and powerful of all the Roman aristocracy — hereditary prince assistant to the pontifical throne like the Colonnas — the family dwindled to one main branch. The dukes of Bracciano became extinct in 1698. Most of the other branches, including the princes of Taranto, counts of Nola and Pitigliano and lords of Monterotondo, died out in the male line by 1700. Today, the present Orsini standard-bearer, who lives in Palazzo Orsini in Rome, is prince of the empire and duke of Gravina. He is Don Domenico Napoleone Orsini, twenty-third Duke of Gravina, who was born in 1948 and has two daughters: Leonthia and Kayetana. (Refer to tables 1a–1g in Appendix A and tables IIIa, IIIb, XI and XVII.)

PIERLEONI.

This family was descended from the Jewish banker Baruch who converted to Christianity and took the name Benedetto Christiano. Members of the Pierleoni family married into the Colonna and Orsini families. Gregory VI (1045–46), Gregory VII (1073–85) and the antipope Anacletus II (1130–38) belonged to this family. They were very influential in the church affairs in Rome and frequent rivals of the Frangipane. In the papal election of 1124, the Pierleoni proposed deacon Teobaldo Boccapecci who became Pope Celestine (II). Meanwhile the Frangipane had Cardinal Lamberto of Ostia become pope (Honorius II), forcing Celestine to resign by force of arms. The Pierleonis' influence in church affairs now declined, but the family continued to maintain its residences in Rome. Various branches, those of Matelica and Citta' de Castello, are still in existence. From the latter Pierleoni branch was descended Florido, prelate, who died in 1829, friend of Pope Pius VII. He was named bishop of Acquapendente.

SAVELLI.

Honorius III (1216–27) and his grand-nephew Honorius IV (1285–87) were members of this Roman family. Gregory II (715–31) was also supposed to be a member of the Savelli. It was tied by marriage to the papal dynasties of the Conti, Colonna and Orsini. The Savelli family held a hereditary appointment as mar-shals of the church and custodians of the con-clave. Through Honorius IV, the family acquired the possessions of Albano, Castel Gandolfo, Palombara, Riccia, Cesano, Scrofano, Turrita, Castelleone and Monteverde in Sabina. It was a family allied to the interests of the Orsini. The last prince of Albano, Giulio Savelli of Rome, died in 1712, whereupon the office of marshal of the church was given to the Chigi family. The Savelli lands and possessions were inher-ited by the children of Margherita Savelli (sister of Giulio) and her husband Giuliano Cesarini of Civitanuova; the Savelli and Cesarini for-tunes eventually found their way into the Colonna and Sforza-Cesarini families. (Refer to tables 2a–2b in Appendix A and tables IIIa–IIIb.)

VISCONTI.

Tebaldo (Teobaldo, Tedaldo) Visconti was elected Pope Gregory X (1271–76). The Visconti family of Lombardy (Pavia-Milan) attained prominence when Ottone Visconti (1207–1295) was appointed archbishop of Milan (1262–95). Both Tebaldo and Ottone were descended of Guido (Guidone) Visconti who was the father of (1) Otto II (Ottone II) Visconti, the ancestor of the two prelates and the dukes of Milan; (2) Beatrice of Geneva, wife of Tommaso I of Savoy whose son Tommaso II married Beatrice Fieschi, sister of Pope Hadrian V (1276); and (3) Guglielmo, Count of Geneva, who was the forefather of Roberto of Geneva, the antipope Clement VII (1378–94).

The Visconti family claimed descent from Adalberto, King of Italy, who was a direct descendant of Charlemagne and was thus a cousin of the Conti family of Tusculum and the royal houses of Europe (the German emperors and the French and English kings asserted that Charlemagne was their ancestor). The nephew of Ottone, Archbishop of Milan, Matteo (d. 1322), was proclaimed lord of Milan, and his descendants were the dukes of Milan. Another descendant was Valentina Visconti, ancestor of the kings of France and Spain. Bernabò Visconti, grandson of Matteo, fathered over twenty children and was, as humorously as it sounds, the ancestor of Euro-pean royalty.

It seems Tebaldo, Pope Gregory X, had little to do with the success of this illustrious family; but the church, through the efforts of Ottone, Milanese archbishop, was responsible for its emergence as a leading Italian noble family. The principal ducal branch, dukes of Milan, is extinct.

The lord of Milan, Matteo (1250–1322) had a nephew Vercellino, cousin of Pope Gregory X, who was the forefather of the Visconti di Modrone family, very much in existence at the present time. This ducal family resides in Milan. One of its members, Anna Visconti of Modrone, was the mother of Pope Gregory XIV (1590–91) of the Sfondrati family. Cur-rently there are four main branches of the Vis-conti di Modrone family. The head of the pri-mogeniture branch is Duke Uberto Visconti di Modrone, Marchese of Vimodrone, born 1927, and he has a daughter Chiara. (See Sfondrati. Also refer to tables V, XXa and XXb, which focus on the Visconti. Table V and Table XXa present slightly different versions of the origins of the family.)

THE FAMILIES OF THE RENAISSANCE POPES

BORGIA.

Family of Pope Callistus III, Alfonso de Borja or Borgia of Valencia in Spain (1455–58) and his nephew Pope Alexander VI Rodrigo de Borja y Borja (1492–1503). Alexander's mother and father had the surname Borja, and it was his mother who was a sister of Callistus III. Rodrigo had numerous mistresses. From one of them was born Pedro Luis, who in 1485 was created duke of Gandia by the king of Aragon. Upon his death in 1488, his widow, Maria Enriquez, married Juan, son of Pope Alexander and Vannozza Catanei, who became the second duke of Gandia. King Alfonso II of Naples bestowed upon Juan the principality of Tricarico in 1494, and he as also named prince of Treano and duke of Benevento. These were his rewards from the papal wars against the Orsini. This family became extinct through the male line in 1748, but continues through the female line.

Financed by the pope, Caesar, another of Alexander VI's sons by Vannozza Catanei, conquered Romanga, Urbino and Camerino, becoming duke (1502). Another son Goffredo (Goeffre or Jofre) was made prince of Squillace and count of Cariati in 1484 after he married Sancia d'Aragona, daughter of King Alfonso II of Naples. After the death of Pietro, the fourth Prince of Squillace, the male line came to an end. Pietro's daughter Anna married a cousin, Francesco Borgia, son of the duke of Gandia. Their descendant Maria Antonia of Borgia died in 1728, and the principality of Squillace reverted to the crown.

Rodrigo (1499–1512), son of Lucrezia Borgia and Alfonso, Duke of Bisceglie, was named duke of Sermoneta in 1501 when Alexander was still pope. Lucrezia was the daughter of the pope and Vannozza Catanei. Alexander VI's son by Giulia Farnese (probably), Giovanni, the Infante Romano (being the son of a pope, he was known by this title, meaning princely heir of Rome), born in 1498, was created duke of Nepi and then duke of Camerino in 1501. The death of Pope Alexander VII and the military collapse of his son Caesar brought a quick end to these Borgia dukedoms. Alexander VI bestowed on Orsino Orsini Migliorati, the husband of his lover Giulia Farnese, the lordship of Carbognano, which was inherited by their daughter Laura, wife of Niccolò Franciotti della Rovere. (Refer to tables IX, XIX, XXd and XXe.)

CARAFA.

This is an aristocratic family that distinguished itself in the kingdom of Naples and goes back into the Middle Ages. In the fourteenth century one Bartolomeo Carafa was active in the political life of Naples as a chief judicial officer and diplomat and was able to accumulate vast riches. Various and numerous branches, descendants of Bartolomeo, of the Carafa family emerged. In 1594 Fabrizio I Carafa was made prince of Roccella and Girolamo (1564–1633) became the marchese of Montenero. He was also made prince of the Holy Roman Empire (1620). For services rendered to the Neapolitan state, various branches of the Carafa clan had been ennobled and rewarded with such fiefdoms as Policastro, Ruvo, S. Severina, Nocera, Mariglianella, Andria, Montenero, Maddaloni, Montorio and Stigliano. Family members of one branch often married those of another. The Carafa married into the Pignatelli, Orsini, Borgia, Colonna and Caetani families. Many members of this family were military leaders and prelates. Several members, such as Oliviero, archbishop of Naples in 1458, and Vincenzo, archbishop of Naples in 1504, were appointed princes of the church.

Giampietro Carafa, son of the count of Montorio, was elected to the papacy and took the name Paul IV (1555–59). His chief advisor was his unworthy and corrupt nephew Carlo Carafa (1518–61) whom he brought to the purple in 1555. A grandnephew Alfonso (d. 1565) also became a cardinal and was named archbishop of Naples. His father Antonio, nephew of the pope, was proclaimed marchese of Montebello by the pontiff in 1556. Paul IV was anxious to please his family; urged by Cardinal Carlo, his secretary of state, he even went to war against Spain. Carlo's brother Giovanni (d. 1561) was made duke of Paliano, taken from the Colonna family. After the death of the pope, Carlo and Giovanni were tried for treason (and in the case of Giovanni for murdering his wife). They were executed and their possessions were confiscated by the church. The Carafa family benefited little from having one of its members rise to become Supreme Pontiff.

It should be noted that, since there were so many different family lines, Pope Paul IV was often distantly related to other members of this huge family. He was a cousin of Antonio Pignatelli (Pope Innocent XII, 1691–1700), whose mother was Portia Carafa. Her father, grandfather and great-grandfather had all married women who belonged to the Carafa family. (Refer to Table XIV.)

Existing at the present time are two main branches: (1) the prince of Roccella, duke of Bruzzano and prince of the Holy Roman Empire (the current prince is Don Gregoria, born in 1945 and he has two daughters) and (2) the duke of Andria and Castel del Monte (headed by Duke Riccardo, born in 1937 and father of daughter Donna Paola, born in 1973). The heads of these families are located in Naples.

CIBO (CYBO).

Pope Innocent VIII (Giovanni Battista Cibo, 1484–92) had two children, Teodorina and Franceschetto. Teodorina married Gherardo Usodimare, and that branch of the family was known as Usodimare-Cibo. Franceschetto was made count of Anguillara. He was the husband of Maddalena de' Medici, daughter of Lorenzo the Magnificent. One of their sons, Lorenzo (1500–49), married Ricciarda Malaspina, heiress of the Marchese Antonio Alberico of Massa. The family assumed the name Cibo-Malaspina and ruled Massa and Carrara. The son of Lorenzo and Ricciarda, Alberico I (1529–1623), was made marchese in 1554 and prince of the Holy Roman Empire in 1568. His great-grandson Alberico II (d. 1690) became the duke of Massa in 1664. Alderano (1690–1731), Alberico II's grandson, was the last prince of the Cibo dynasty. His daughter and heiress, Maria Teresa Cibo, married Ercole Rinaldo

d'Este of Modena. Members of the Cibo-Malaspina family married into the della Rovere, Fieschi, Pamfill, Sfondrati and Albani families. (Refer to Table X.)

DELLA ROVERE.

Sixtus IV (Francesco della Rovere, 1471–84) provided amply for his brother Bartolomeo's son Leonardo who was made duke of Sora and Arce and prefect of Rome. The pope was also generous to his brother Raffaele's children: Giuliano was made a cardinal and became Pope Julius II and Giovanni was made lord of Senigallia and then duke of Sora after the death of his cousin Leonardo. Giovanni's son Francesco Maria I della Rovere inherited from his uncle Giudabaldo Montefeltro the dukedom of Urbino in 1508, which was sanctioned by the pope. Pesaro was given to him by his uncle Pope Julius II. When a descendant, Francesco Maria II, died in 1631 the dukedom reverted to the church. The last member of this family was Vittoria della Rovere who died in 1695. Another branch of the family were the descendants of Giulio della Rovere, son of Duke Francesco Maria I of Urbino, who elected to enter the clergy and became a cardinal. One of Cardinal Giulio's natural sons, Ippolito, Marchese of S. Lorenzo in Campo (d. 1620), was the father of Lucrezia who in 1609 married Marcantonio Lante. Their son Ippolito Lante della Rovere received in 1645 the title of duke of Bomarzo. This family, Lante Montefeltro della Rovere, remains in existence, members marrying into the Colonna, Altieri, Altemps, Odescalchi and Rospigliosi families. The present duke, Don Pietro Lante della Rovere, was born in 1928, and is the father of four children, including a son Marcantonio, born in 1957, who has two sons and a daughter.

A sister of Pope Sixtus IV, Bianca, married Paolo Riario of Savonna. Their children benefited from the generosity of the pope. One of their sons, Pietro Riario, became an extravagant and dissolute cardinal; the other, Girolamo Riario (d. 1488), received Imola from his uncle the pope in 1473. He married Caterina Sforza, illegitimate daughter of Duke Galeazzo Maria Sforza of Milan; in 1480 they became the lords of Forli. These territories were lost to the Riario-Sforza family when Caesar Borgia conquered them, and the family was reestablished in Bologna (Riario-Sforza of Bologna). One descendant, Alessandro (1585), became a cardinal; another, Giulio, was marchese of Oria; and another, Ferdinando, was made duke of the Empire and marchese of Castiglione. This branch of the family became extinct in 1676. The present-day Riario-Sforza family, marchese of Corleto, live in Naples and are descended from a brother of Paolo Riario. Duke Don Nicola Riario Sforza was born in 1934; his brother Don Alberto (b. 1937) married Mirta Barberini-Colonna di Sciarra and took the cognomen of his wife.

Another branch of della Rovere family was descended from Luchina, sister of Pope Julius II, whose first husband was Gian Francesco Franciotti. One of their sons, Niccolò Franciotti della Rovere, married Laura Migliorati, daughter of Orsino Orsini Migliorati and Giulia Farnese, the lover of Pope Alexander VI (see BORGIA). Niccolò and Laura's daughter Elena Franciotti della Rovere married Stefano Colonna, Lord of Palestrina. Her substantial dowry (from Borgia, Migliorati and della Rovere ancestors) included the lordships of Carbognano and Bassanello, which were subsequently inherited by this branch of the Colonna family. (Refer to tables VII, VIII and XI.)

FARNESE.

Alessandro Farnese of an illustrious family was elected pope, becoming Pope Paul III. He had at least three children. One of them, Costanza, was given sizable territories by her father. She married Bosio Sforza II, Lord of S. Fiora; it is this family for which information is provided in this section. But the pope paid special attention to his son Pier Luigi Farnese (1503–47). He was first made duke of Castro; then the pope created the dukedom of Parma and Piacenza in 1545 for him. One of Pier Luigi's sons, Ottavio, husband of Margherita of Austria (natural daughter of the emperor Charles V), succeeded him as duke. The pope made two of Pier Luigi's sons, Alessandro

(1520–89) and Ranuccio (1519–65), into cardinals. Alessandro became a cardinal at the age of fourteen and Ranuccio at twenty-six. Ottavio, a shrewd politician, was duke of Parma, Piacenza and Guastalla. His son Alessandro, the third duke, was the famous general who fought for King Philip II of Spain, his uncle. Members of the family married into the Italian ducal families of Gonzaga, d'Este and Medici. Ranuccio I (1569–1622), son of Duke Alessandro, married Margherita daughter of Gianfrancesco Aldobrandini, nephew of Pope Clement VIII. The last Farnese duke of Parma was Antonio I (1679–1731), and his niece Elisabetta (1692–1766), heiress of Parma and Piacenza, married King Philip V, the first Bourbon king of Spain. Their children became the kings of Spain, of the Two Sicilies and the Bourbon dukes of Parma. (Refer to tables X, XVII, XIX, XXb and XXg.)

MEDICI.

Lorenzo de' Medici, the Magnificent (1449–92), was the father of a pope, Leo X (1513–21) and uncle of a pope, Clement VII (1523–34), and great-grandfather of a pope, Leo XI (1605). The Medici family was vitally concerned about the power of the Medici in Florence; and the aggrandizement of the Medici family was paramount to popes Leo X and Clement VII. In 1516 Leo X conferred the dukedom of Urbino on his nephew Lorenzo, who died soon after in 1519. Pope Clement VII made his son Alessandro the duke of Florence in 1532. Upon Alessandro's death, the offices of the House of Medici were placed upon Cosimo I de'Medici, Duke of Florence, in 1537. He was made grand duke of Tuscany in 1569. Cosimo belonged to another branch of the Medici family, but through his mother he was a great-grandson of Lorenzo de' Medici, the Magnificent. The Medici dukedom lasted until the year 1737. It was a family that married into the prominent ones of the period — the Orsini, d'Este, della Rovere, Hapsburg, Bourbon, Farnese and Gonzaga. Future emperors of the Holy Roman Empire as well as the kings of France and Spain were descended from the Medicis.

Duke Alessandro de' Medici had an illegitimate daughter Giulia who married Bernadetto de' Medici, the brother of Pope Leo XI and great-grandson of Lorenzo the Magnificent. Bernadetto and Giulia's descendants became the dukes of Sarno and the princes of Ottai(j)ano, and members married into aristocratic Italian families such as the Caetani, Chigi and Pignatelli; this family remains in existence. The primogeniture branch is headed by Don Giovan Battista de' Medici, fourteenth Prince of Ottaiano and eleventh Duke of Sarno, born in 1939. He has three sons. This family resides in Naples. (Refer to tables X, XVII, XXc and XXd.)

MEDICI (OF MARIGNANO).

The family of Pope Pius IV (Giovanni Angelo de' Medici 1559–65) belonged to a family from Milan, known as Medici di Marignano. The family was probably related to the Medici of Florence. The pope's brother Gian Giacomo de' Medici de Marignano was a soldier and obtained in 1530 the marchesa of Marignano. He married Marzia Orsini and died in 1555, before his brother was elected pope. Agosto (d. 1586), brother of both the pope and Gian Giacomo di Marignano, inherited the title of marchese di Marignano. The family, descendants of Agosto, reside in Milan.

During the reign of Pope Pius IV, in 1560, his nephew Federico (son of Giberto Borromeo and Margherita de' Medici) married Virginia della Rovere. He was proclaimed duke of Camerino. In 1559 the king of Spain had given him the principality of Oria in Calabria. He died without children in 1560, leaving the principality of Oria to his brother Carlo Borromeo, who was the pope's principal advisor. In 1560 Carlo (Charles, later St. Carlo) was made a cardinal by his uncle. None of the male descendants of the pope's sister Margherita Borromeo had children. The Borromeo family of Arona, which exists today, is descended from Giberto's brother Giulio Cesare. A sister of St. Carlo's, Anna, married Fabrizio Colonna (1557–80), who was created cavalier of Toson d'Ora by King Philip II of Spain. He was twenty-three when he died. The descendants of Fabrizio and Anna Colonna were the princes and dukes of Paliano and the princes of Stigliano.

Pope Pius IV had one son of his sister Chiara, Jacob Hannibal, made count of the empire in 1560; another son, Marcus Sittich (Marco Sittico, 1533–95), was made a cardinal in 1561. They were of the House of Hohenems. The descendants of Jacob Hannibal I became the counts of Gallarate (sold to the Visconti in 1645) and the counts of Harrach. The last male count was Franz-Wilhelm-Maxmilian who died in 1759.

The illegitimate son of Cardinal Marco Sittico, Roberto, became the duke of Gallese and took the family name Altemps. Roberto married Cornelia Orsini. Descendants married into the Medici and Corsini families, and the Altemps family resided in Rome. The last duke, Don Alessandro Eugenio Maria Marco Amiceto Altemps, died in 1964, leaving two daughters Altea and Angela. (Refer to tables VIII, XIII and XIX.)

PICCOLOMINI.

This Sienese family gave two popes to the church: Pius II (Enea Silvio Piccolomini, 1458–64) and Pius III (Francesco Todeschini-Piccolomini, 1503). The two principal branches of the papal family were the Todeschini-Piccolomini (descended of Laudomia, sister of Pope Pius II) and the Piccolomini of Sticciano (descended from Caterina, another sister of that pope). The future pope Pius III's brother Antonio Todeschini-Piccolimini married the daughter of King Ferdinando I of Naples and was proclaimed duke of Amalfi in 1461. This was encouraged by Pius II to advance the position of the family, and Ferdinando I was a willing accomplice to gain favor with the pope. Pius II promoted the interests of the Piccolomini family. The Todeschini-Piccolimini descendants of Pope Pius III's brother Giacomo, Lord of Camporsevoli and Montemarciano, became the dukes of Montemarciano. Another brother, Andrea, was made the lord of Castiglione, which became extinct in 1717.

Later a descendant of Caterina, sister of Pius II, Ottavio Piccolomini (d. 1656) was declared duke of Amalfi in 1639 and prince of the Holy Roman Empire in 1650. This branch of the family (Piccolomini of Sticciano) became extinct in 1757 with the death of Ottavio Enea, great-grandnephew of Prince Ottavio. Alfonso (d. 1493), Duke of Amalfi, of the Todeschini-Piccolomini branch of the family, had a great-grandson Giovanni who became the prince of Valle: that branch became extinct in 1783 with the death of Prince Giuseppe. Other branches, but not the papal line, of the Piccolomini family are still in existence. (Refer to table XIX.)

SFORZA (OF S. FIORA).

They were the descendants of both the Conti family of Pope Innocent III (1198–1216), who were the counts of Segni and Valmontone, and the Farnese family of Pope Paul III (1534–49). While there were no popes who bore the name Sforza or who were descendants of Munzio Sforza, uncle of the first Sforza duke of Milan, this family is certainly a papal dynasty. They were the counts of Santa Fiora because Munzio's son Bosio I (1411–76) married Cecilia Aldobrandeschi, heiress of Santa Fiora. The Sforzas of Santa Fiora enriched themselves by their marriages to heiresses. Their great-grandson Bosio II (d. 1535) married Costanza,

the daughter of Pope Paul III, and received considerable land and wealth from her father. The pope proclaimed Bosio II the marchese of Proceno. Constanza and her offspring had the same ties to the pope as her brother Pier Luigi Farnese and his descendants, the dukes of Parma and Piacenza. The pope made his grandson Guido Ascanio Sforza into a cardinal.

In 1548 Mario Sforza, the son of Bosio II and Costanza Farnese, married Fulvia Conti, an heiress of the family of Pope Innocent III, and he obtained both the lordships of Segni and Valmontone which had been bequested to the Conti family by that pope. Alessandro Sforza-Conti, grandson of Mario Sforza (1530–91) and Fulvia Conti, was proclaimed the duke of Segni by the pope in 1585, and his son Mario II (1594–1658) was given the title Duke of Onano in 1612. Because of financial reverses, the family was forced to sell Valmontone in 1634 to the Barberinis, and they sold Segni in 1639 to that same family. The history of the Sforza family of Santa Fiora, which changed its name to Sforza-Cesarini, will be continued in the following section on the Baroque period. (Refer to table 5 in Appendix A.)

PAPAL ARISTOCRACY DURING THE BAROQUE PERIOD, 1572–1740

ALBANI.

Family of Pope Clement XI (1700–21). The family immigrated to Italy from Albania in the fifteenth century and settled in Urbino. In 1710 the family received the title of Reichsfürst, Prince of the Holy Roman Empire and, in 1721, Prince of Soriano. The last Prince Albani died in 1852, and the name was attached to that of the Chigi family. In 1735, Giulia Albani (1719–89), aunt of the last prince, had married Prince Agostino Chigi (1710–69). (Refer to table XXII.)

ALDOBRANDINI.

Family of Pope Clement VIII (1592–1605). The pope's niece Olimpia married her cousin Gianfrancesco Aldobrandini (1545–1601), and he was named count of Sarsina and Meldola. His granddaughter Olimpia first married Prince

Paolo Borghese, nephew of Pope Paul V, and then Camillo Pamfili, nephew of Pope Innocent X. Olimpia brought an enormous fortune to these families as well as the title Prince of Rossano, which was granted to the Borghese family. (Refer to Borghese.) In 1839 Camillo Borghese (1816–1902), son of Francesco, seventh Prince Borghese, assumed the name Aldobrandini, after that illustrious family, his ancestors. The family's home is Palazzo Aldobrandini in Rome. (Refer to table XXII and table 6d in Appendix A.)

ALTIERI (ALBERTONI).

Emilio Altieri became Pope Clement X (1670–76), and one of his first acts as pope was to adopt the Albertoni family since his only niece Laura had married the marchese of

Rasina, Gaspare Albertoni dei Paluzzi dei
Piermallei. Their descendants took the name
Altieri. The pope had his newly adopted
nephew-in-law receive such titles as Prince of
Oriolo and Viano and Duke of Monterano in
1672. Four cardinals came from this family, and
other members married into the Colonna,
Orsini, Borromeo, Chigi, Rospigliosi, della
Rovere and Boncompagni-Ludovisi families.
The last prince of this family is listed as
Lodovico (1878–1955). (Refer to table XXIII.)

BARBERINI.

The family of Pope Urban VIII (1623–44).
Urban VIII's three nephews, Antonio, Francesco and Taddeo, all acquired riches. The
family purchased Palestrina, Antiocoli Corrado,
Lugnano, Labico, Valmontone and Pimpinara.
Two of the pope's nephews, Antonio and
Francesco, were appointed cardinals. Francesco
governed various monasteries, castles and territories in the Papal States, living in the magnificent Palazzo alle Quattro Fontane in Rome.
Another nephew, Taddeo, whose descendants
inherited the Barberini fortune, was named
grandee of Spain. The heiress of the family,
Cornelia Barberini, great-granddaughter of
Taddeo, was only eleven years of age in 1728
when she married Giulio Cesare Collona, Duke
of Bassanello and Prince of Carbognano. The
family assumed the name Barbarini-Colonna.
(See below and refer to table 4f in Appendix A.)

BARBERINI-COLONNA.

The family of Pope Urban VIII (1623–44)
and Pope Martin V (1417–31). (Refer to
Colonna.) When Giulio Cesare Colonna, Duke
of Bassanello and Prince of Carbognano (1702–
87) married the heiress Cornelia, daughter
of Urbano Barberini, Prince of Palestrina, he
acquired Palestrina, upon the death of Cornelia's father, and took the name Barberini.
Their two sons formed two different branches
of this family: the Colonna di Sciarra, princes
of Carbognano and Nerola, which is living in
Naples, and the Barberini-Colonna, princes of
Palestrina and Monte Castel S. Pietro and lords
of Capranica and S. Vittorino. Maria Barberini-
Colonna, Princess of Palestrina and di Monte

Castel S. Pietro and Countess of Capranica and
S. Vittorino, married Luigi Sacchetti in 1891,
and he was authorized by royal decree to carry
the name Barberini and the title of Prince
of Palestrina. Members of the Barberini and
Barberini-Colonna families were united in
marriage with the Ottoboni, Colonna, Chigi,
Corsini and Doria-Pamfili families. The present prince of Palestrina is Prince don Augusto
Barberini, born in 1923, whose wife is Giovanna della Chiesa. They have three sons,
Benedetto, Urbano and Giovanni, and a daughter Francesca. (Refer to tables 4e and 4f in
Appendix A.)

BONCOMPAGNI-LUDOVISI.

Family of Pope Gregory XIII (1572–85).
The son of the pope Giacomo (Jacopo) received
the marquisate of Vignola and the dukedom of
Sora. He married Costanza Sforza, the grand-
daughter of Pope Paul III. His great-grandson
Gregorio (1642–1707) married Ippolita, the
daughter and heiress of Niccolò Ludovisi,
Prince of Piombino. The Ludovisi surname
was attached to the Boncompagni name, and
the descendants became the princes of Piom-
bino. Family members married into the
Chigi, Odescalchi, Altieri, Ottoboni, Orsini,
Rospigliosi and Borghese families. (Refer to
LUDOVISI.) The present prince of Piombino,
Prince don Nicolò Francesco, born in 1941,
lives in the Boncompagni-Ludovisi palace,
Villa Aurora. His marriage to Benedetta Maria
Barberini-Colonna di Sciarra was annulled
by the church in 1989. They had three sons:
Francesco Maria, Ignazio Maria and Bante
Maria. (Refer to tables 7a, 7b and 7d.)

BORGHESE.

Family of Pope Paul V (1605–1621). The
pope made his nephew Marcantonio the prince
of Sulmona, in 1610. In 1614 the family acquired
the title Prince of Rossano when Marcantonio's
son Paolo married the heiress Olimpia Aldobrandini. In 1809 the family secured the dukedom of Giuliano, inherited from Anna Salviati
who married the fifth prince Borghese. Their
grandson Scipione (1823–92) became the duke
Salviati.

Pope Gregory XVI (1831–46) gave the title Prince of Nettuno to the family, which in 1836 also acquired the dukedom of Bomarzo. The present prince Borghese is also prince of Sulmona, prince of Rossano, prince of Vivaro, prince of Montecompatri, duke of Palombara, duke of Castelchiodato, marchese of Mentana, marchese of Norma, etc. The family lives in Rome and there are several branches, including Aldobrandini, Salviati and Torlonia. Francesco, the seventh prince Borghese (1776–1839), divided the inheritance of the family with his three sons. Marcantonio (1814–86) became the eighth prince Borghese; the second son, Camillo (1816–1902), received the title Prince Aldobrandini and Aldobrandini possessions as a descendant of Olimpia Aldobrandini; and the third son, Scipione (1823–92), received the Salviati inheritance from his grandmother Anna Salviati. The head of the last branch is called Duke Salviati. When Giulio (1847–1914), son of the eighth prince Borghese, married the heiress Anna Maria Torlonia, he took the name Torlonia, by which their descendants are known. The Borghese family married into other papal dynasties, including the Boncompagni-Ludovisi, Orsini, Doria-Pamfili, Odescalchi, Colonna and Chigi. The present family are direct descendants of popes Paul III, Julius II and Gregory XIII. The present prince Borghese is Don Camillo, born in 1927, who has a daughter Flaminia and a son Don Scipione. (Refer to tables 6a–6d in Appendix A.)

CHIGI-ALBANI.

The family of Pope Alexander VII (1655–67). The pope ennobled his nephew Agostino Chigi, who was made Roman prince of Farnese (Province of Rome) in 1658. Other titles include Reichsfürst, prince of the Holy Roman Empire in 1659; prince of Campagnano in 1661; and duke of Ariccia and Formello. In 1712 the Chigi family was named as the hereditary marshal of the church and guard of the conclave. With the death of the last prince Albani, that name was affixed to that of Chigi because the third prince Chigi inherited that right by marrying Giulia Albani (1719–86). The Chigi family of Rome married into the Borghese,

Piccolomini, Rospigliosi, Boncompagni, Albani and Doria-Pamfili families.

The Chigis were originally from Siena, and became influential bankers in Rome. The family enjoyed a friendship with popes Julius II and Leo X. Julius X conferred the right for the family to affix della Rovere to its cognomen, and the family is listed in the *Libro d'oro* as Chigi-Albani-della Rovere. Prince Don Agostino Chigi-Albani-della Rovere, born in 1929, is the head of the family. (Refer to table XXII.)

CORSINI.

The family of Pope Clement XII (1730–40). This family became very active in the political life of Florence (Tuscany) where the family is presently located. It was ennobled and members became the marchese of Sismano, Casigliano and Civitella, Lajatico and Orciatico, Giovagallo and Tresana. In 1731 the pope made the head of the family, his nephew Bartolomeo (1683–1752), Roman prince of Sismano, duke of Casigliano and duke of Civitella. Bartolomeo also served as viceroy and captain-general in the kingdom of Sicily, and in 1739 he was named a grandee of Spain by King Philip V. His brother Neri Maria (1685–1770) was appointed a cardinal by his uncle, the pope. The descendants of Bartolomeo Corsini married into the Barberini-Colonna family. The present duke is Prince don Filippo Corsini, born in 1937, and he has four children, including one son Duccio. (Refer to table XXIII.)

DORIA-PAMFILI-LANDI (SOMETIMES SHORTENED TO DORIA-PAMFILI).

The family of Pope Innocent X (1644–55). Pope Innocent X made the Pamfili family patriarchs of Rome and princes of San Martino and Valmontone. His nephew Camillo married the heiress Olimpia Aldobrandini. The male line is extinct. Anna Pamfili, a daughter of Camillo, brought to her husband (Gian Andrea Doria IV, Prince of Melfi) the Pamfili inheritance, and Pamfili was added to the Doria name. The Doria had already added Landi to their surname. Members of the Landi family had been rules of Val di Taro, Bardi and Compiano. The heiress of the Landi had married into and enriched the Doria family. The Pamfili family had married into such papal families as the Barberini, Savelli, Conti and Facchinetti, while the Doria-Pamfili-Landi, now living in Rome, had been united with the Chigi, Orsini and Colonna as well as into the princely family of Savoy-Carignano, members of which became the kings of Italy. Prince Filippo (1886–1958) had an only daughter, Orietta, who married Frank George Wignall Pogson, who changed his surname in 1958 to Doria-Pamfili. Princess Orietta's children, Gesine (married to Massimiliano Floridi) and Jonathan Doria-Pamfili, operate the Doria-Pamfili Gallery (of art acquired by the family) in Rome. (*New York Times*, 22 December 1996, A14). The Doria-Pamfili family is descended from Pope Alexander VI (Borgia), whose illegitimate daughter Isabella (1467–1541) married Pietro Matuzzi. Their daughter Giulia married Ciriaco Mattei, whose daughter Oraziana was the wife of Pamfilio Pamfili. Their son Camillo Pamfili was the father of Giambattista Pamfili, who became Pope Innocent X, and Pamfilio Pamfili, the ancestor of the Doria-Pamfili dynasty as well as of other Roman aristocratic families that married into this clan. (Refer to tables XXe and XXI.)

LUDOVISI.

The family of Pope Gregory XV (1621–23). The pope's brother Orazio Ludovisi was created duke of Fiano and Zagarolo and general of the church. One of his sons Ludovico was "the Cardinal Boss" ("il Cardinal Padrone") under his uncle and acquired enormous wealth for the Ludovisi family. Another nephew of the pope, Niccolò, married as his first wife, Isabella Gesualdi, the heiress of the prince of Venosa, and as his second wife, Polissena di Mendoza, the heiress of the principality of Piombino. He acquired these territories. In 1634 Niccolò Ludovisi (d. 1664) was officially granted Piombino from the emperor. His third marriage was to the niece of Pope Innocent X, for whom he served as commander of the pontifical fleet. The Ludovisi also purchased the dukedom of Zagarolo from the Colonna family. These titles and estates were inherited by Gregorio Boncompagni,

who married Ippolita, the Ludovisi heiress of her brother Giambattista, Prince of Piombino. Ippolita was the daughter of Niccolò and the niece of another Ippolita who was the wife first of an Aldobrandini and then of an Orsini. The descendants of Gregorio Boncompagni and Ippolita Ludovisi assumed the name Boncompagni-Ludovisi. Although Piombino was eventually sold, the family retains the title, and family members are princes of the Holy Roman Empire. (Refer to table 7b in Appendix A.)

ODESCALCHI-ERBA.

The family of Pope Innocent XI (1676–1689). The pope's nephew Livio (1652–1713) received various titles, including Prince of the Holy Roman Empire (1689), Duke of Ceri and Duke of Syrmia in Hungary. In 1689, with the death of the last Colonna duke, he purchased the dukedom of Bracciano. These titles were inherited by his cousin Baldassarre, second prince, whose descendants (the Roman branch as opposed to the Hungarian branch of the family) live in the Odescalchi Palazzo in Piazza S.S. Apostoli in Rome. The present prince, Don Ladislao, born in 1920, father of three daughters, is also the prince of Bassano, duke of Bracciano, marchese of Roncofreddo and Montiano, count of Pisciarelli and lord of Palo. The family married into the Borghese, Orsini, Rospigliosi, and Boncompagni-Ludovisi families. (Refer to table XXIII.)

OTTOBONI.

The family of Pope Alexander VIII (1689–91). The pope's niece Chiara married Francesco Zeno, and their daughter Cornelia married Urbano Barberini, the last Barberini prince of Palestrina. His nephew Marco Ottoboni (1656–1725) married members of the Colonna and Boncompagni families. In 1690 Marco was made duke of Fiano. His daughter Maria-Francesca Ottoboni in 1731 became the wife of Pietro Gregorio Boncompagni-Ludovisi, and their descendants took the name Boncompagni-Ludovisi-Ottoboni, dukes of Fiano. This branch is extinct in the male line. The last Boncompagni-Ludovisi-Ottoboni duke of the family was Prince Marco (1832–1909), Senator of the Italian kingdom and Patrician of Venice, Rome, Genoa and Naples, who married his cousin Giulia Boncompagni-Ludovisi. His grandson Cesare, son of one of Prince Marco's daughters took the name Ottoboni. In 1977 Don Domenico Serlupi Crescenzi, an Ottoboni descendant from the female line, took the name Ottoboni. (Refer to table XXI and table 7c in Appendix A.)

PIGNATELLI.

Family of Pope Innocent XII (1691–1700). The family traces its descent from the princes of Benevento, prominent in the Middle Ages. One early ancestor, Lucio Pignatelli (ca. 1102), was the constable of Naples. In 1505 the family received the lordships of Cerchiara and Noya (or Noja). King Philip II of Spain bestowed the title Marchese of Cerchiara in 1556, and in 1600 King Philip III made one branch of the Pignatelli the princes of Noya. When Ettore Pignatelli, fourth prince of Noya, married the heiress Giovanna Tagliavia d'Aragona Cortes, the family were made princes of the Holy Roman Empire. There are numerous branches of this family, which have acquired such titles as princes of Noya, marchesi of Cerchiara, dukes of Monteleone and Terranova, princes of Monteroduni, dukes of Montecalvo and princes of Strongoli. Ferdinando Pignatelli (1689–1767), admiral for the kingdom of Naples and Grandee of Spain, was made into the prince of Strongoli, count of Melissa and duke of Tolve upon his marriage to the heiress Lucrezia Pignatelli (1704–1760), Princess of Strongoli, Countess of Melissa and Duchess of Tolve. Her family had been made princes of Strongoli in 1620, counts of Melissa in 1591 and dukes of Tolve in 1678. These titles had been acquired before one of their family had become pope and without the intervention of the papacy.

Pope Innocent XII (Antonio Pignatelli) was the son of Francesco, Prince of Minervino, and Porzia Carafa of Andria. Francesco's uncle Giulio was the marchese of Cerchiara. Pope Innocent XII was a distant cousin of Pope Paul IV (Giampietro Carafa), and his great-grandfather Luigi Carafa, Prince of Stigliano, married as his first wife Clarice Orsini, daughter of Duke Giangiordano Orsini of Bracciano and Felice della Rovere (daughter of Pope Julius II). Among the main existing divisions and branches of the Pignatelli family are the Pignatelli della Leonesse, princes of Monteroduni; the Pignatelli, dukes of Montecalvo, princes of the Holy Roman Empire (S.R.I.), dukes of Terranova (Tagliavia-Aragona-Pignatelli-Cortes, the S.R.I. princes of Strongoli; now Ferrara-Pignatelli); and the Pignatelli di Cerchiara, princes of the S.R.I. (Refer to table XIV.)

ROSPIGLIOSI.

Family of Pope Clement IX (1667–1669). In 1668 the pope's nephew Giambattista Rospigliosi (1646–1722) became prince of the Holy Roman Empire (Reichsfürst) and soon after (1668) acquired the dukedom of Zagarolo from the Ludovisi family. He married Marie-Camille Pallavicini, who inherited the principality of Gallicano. One branch, Rospigliosi-Gioeni (Colonna), live in the Palazzo Rospigliosi in Rome. The family acquired the principality of Castiglione when Giulio Rospigliosi, great-great-grandson of Giambattista married Margherita Gioeni (Colonna) in 1803. Their oldest son Clemente (1825–1899) was the ancestor of the Rospigliosi-Gioeni (or simply Rospigliosi) branch of the family whose titles include Prince of the Holy Roman Empire, Prince of Castiglione, Duke of Zagarolo, Marchese of Giuliana, etc. The present prince Don Filippo, born in 1942, has a daughter, Donna Benedetta; his brother Don Francesco has a son Alessandro, born in 1978.

Francesco Cesare (1828–87), the second son of Giulio and Margherita, took the name Rospigliosi-Pallavicini (now just Pallavicini). He and his descendants were known as the prince Pallavicini, prince of Gallicano and marchese of Colonna. The family lived in the Palazzo Rospigliosi-Pallavicini in Rome. Francesco (1828–87) married Carolina Boncompagni-Ludovisi (1834–1910), and their son Giulio in 1937 adopted the son of Armando of Pierre of Bernis, Marchese of Courtavel. This adopted son took the name Guglielmo Pallavicini and had a daughter Maria Camilla, born in 1940. Members of the Rospigliosi married into the Odescalchi, Altieri, Colonna, Boncompagni-Ludovisi and Chigi families. (Refer to table XXIII.)

SFONDRATI.

Family of Pope Gregory XIV (1590–91). Pope Gregory XIV (Niccolò Sfondrati) was the son of Francesco Sfondrati and Anna Visconti di Modrone. This branch of the Visconti family was related to that of Pope Gregory X (1271–76), who was Tebaldo Visconti, and to the dukes of Milan. After Anna Visconti died, Francesco Sfondrati (1493–1550) entered the clergy, serving as archbishop of Amalfi and bishop of Cremona, from where the family originated. In 1544 he was appointed a cardinal. His son Pope Gregory XIV was pope for less than a year. He appointed his nephew Paolo Emilio (1561–1618) a cardinal on December 19, 1590, fourteen days after becoming pope. Gregory's brother Paolo (d. 1587), husband of Sigismonda, daughter of the Marchese Sigismondo d'Este, Lord of S. Martino, was the baron of Valsassina. He was created count of the Riviera and of the Holy Roman Empire. His eldest son Ercole (1559–1637) was made duke of Montemarciano and commander of the pontifical forces by his uncle the pope. His wife Lucrezia was the daughter of Alberico Cibo, Prince of Massa, of the family of Pope Innocent VIII (1484–92). Their grandson Celestino Sfondrati (1644–1696) was also a cardinal, and their great-great-grandson Carol died without issue in 1788, leaving the rights to use the Sfondrati name to his friend Alessandro Serbelloni. His property was inherited by his niece Ricciarda d'Este, daughter of Teresa Sfondrati and Carlo Filiberto d'Este of S. Martino. Ricciarda was the wife of Alberico di Barbiano, Prince of Belgioioso (1725–1813), and their descendants continue to flourish. While the pope benefited his family, Gregory XIV's reign was too short to heap upon them the titles and sums that had been given to other families, and the Sfondrati dynasty never achieved the importance of other papal families during the Baroque period. (Refer to table X.)

SFORZA-CESARINI.

This family were descended from Pope Paul III (1534–49) through his daughter Costanza Farnese and were the inheritors of the Conti family of Pope Innocent III (1198–1216). The Sforza family had been forced to sell much of its territory in the first half of the seventeenth century. With the marriage of Federico, grandson of Duke Alessandro Sforza (1572–1613), the family was able to repurchase the dukedom of Segni in 1695. Federico Sforza (1651–1712) was the husband of Livia, heiress of Duke Giuliano III Cesarini, Count of Celano, of an immensely wealthy family, whose wife Margherita (d. 1690) was the heiress of the Savelli and Damasceni-Peretti families. The Sforzas added Cesarini to their name.

Federico and Livia's son Gaetano was the husband of Vittoria, daughter of Lottario Conti of Poli, brother of Pope Innocent XIII (1721–24), and the Sforza-Cesarini became the heirs of this branch of the Conti family after Michelangelo Conti, the last duke, died in 1808. Duke Salvatore Sforza-Cesarini sold Poli and Guadagnolo, the lands of this branch of the Conti family, to banker Giovanni Torlonia. Marino Torlonia, husband of Anna, sister of Duke Salvatore, tried to prevent Anna's younger brother Lorenzo (1807–66) from obtaining the Sforza-Cesarini inheritance. Marino was unsuccessful, and Lorenzo succeeded as the duke of Segni and head of the Sforza-Cesarini family.

The Sforza-Cesarini family has intermarried with the Boncompagni-Ludovisi, the Colonna-Barberini, the Colonna and Caetani families. Their titles include Prince of Genzano, Duke of Segni, Duke of Civitalavinia as well as Count of S. Flora, the original title of this branch of the Sforza family. The Sforza-Cesarini currently reside in Rome. Duke don Bosio was born in 1939 and has two sons: Lorenzo and Francesco. (Refer to Table 5b in Appendix A.)

MARRIAGES BETWEEN THE PAPAL FAMILIES DURING THE NINETEENTH AND TWENTIETH CENTURIES

For much of the Middle Ages and throughout the Renaissance and Baroque periods, many of the Supreme Pontiffs were instrumental in providing for their families, helping them to obtain huge sums of money, prestigious titles as well as territories. To keep intact this precious heritage, these families tended to marry each other, so that they are often related many times over. In the nineteenth and twentieth centuries, the papal dynasties of the past continued to form marital alliances. This is only a partial listing of some of the marriages formed between these families, but it serves to show how these papal dynasties perpetuated themselves:

ALDOBRANDINI

Maria Aldobrandini married Antonino-Stefano-Camillo, Duke (Borghese) Salviati, on September 12, 1885.

Anna Aldobrandini, daughter of Prince Aldobrandini of Sarsina, married Ludovico Chigi-Albani, eighth prince on June 5, 1893.

ALTEMPS (SEE MEDICI OF MARIGNANO)

Angela Maria of Altemps married on June 24, 1971, Paolo Boncompagni-Ludovisi-Rondinelli-Vitelli.

ALTIERI (ALBERTONI)

Laura Altieri married Ugo Boncompagni-Ludovisi on July 6, 1884.

BARBERINI-COLONNA

Enrico Barberini-Colonna di Sciarra, Prince of Palestrina, married Teresa Orsini on October 2, 1853.

Anna Barberini-Colonna di Sciarra of Palestrina married Tommaso, sixth Prince Corsini, on October 3, 1858.

Luisa Barberini-Colonna di Sciarra of Palestrina married Pietro-Francesco Corsini, Marchese of Lajatico, on October 3, 1863.

Augusto Barberini, Prince of Palestrina, married Giovanna del marchese della Chiesa, on October 4, 1960.

Donna Mi(y)rta Barberini-Colonna di Sciarra, Princess of Carbognano, married Alberto Riario Sforza, Prince of Ardore, on June 30, 1960.

Benedetta Barberini-Colonna di Sciarra married Nicolò Boncompagni-Ludovisi, Duke of Sora, on July 8, 1964.

BONCOMPAGNI-LUDOVISI (INCLUDING BONCOMPAGNI-LUDOVISI-RONDINELLI-VITELLI)

Rodolfo Boncompagni-Ludovisi of Piombino married Agnese Borghese on May 31, 1854.

Carolina Boncompagni-Ludovisi married Francesco Cesare Rospogliosi-Pallavicini on October 4, 1854.

Giulia Boncompagni-Ludovisi married Prince Marco Boncompagni-Ludovisi-Ottoboni on September 21, 1857.

Prince Ugo Boncompagni-Ludovisi married Laura, daughter of Prince Altieri, on July 6, 1884.

Princess Giulia Boncompagni-Ludovisi married Prince Giovanni Boncompagni-Ludovisi-Rondinelli-Vitelli on June 11, 1932.

Prince Nicolò Boncompagni-Ludovisi, Duke of Sora, married Benedetta Barberini-Colonna di Sciarra of Carbognano on July 8, 1964.

Prince Paolo Boncompagni-Ludovisi-Rondinelli-Vitelli married Angela Maria of Altemps on June 24, 1971.

BONCOMPAGNI-LUDOVISI-OTTOBONI (FAMILY OF ALEXANDER VIII)

Prince Marco Boncompagni-Ludovisi-Ottoboni, fifth Duke of Fiano, married Giulia Boncompagni-Ludovisi on September 21, 1857.

BORGHESE (INCLUDING SALVIATI)

Agnese Borghese married Rodolfo Boncompagni-Ludovisi of Piombino on May 31, 1854.

Francesca (Borghese) Salviati married Francesco Borghese, Duke of Bomarzo, on June 5, 1873.

Maria (Borghese) Aldobrandini married Antonino (Borghese) Salviati on September 12, 1885.

Adele Borghese married Luciano Colonna, Prince of Summonte, on September 12, 1895.

Maria, daughter of Prince Giullo (Borghese) Torlonia and Anna Torlonia, married Duke Lorenzo Sforza-Cesarini (1868–1939) on June 2, 1897.

Rudolfo Borghese, Prince of Nettuno, married Genoveffa Borghese on July 16, 1905.

CAETANI

Leone, fifteenth Duke of Sermoneta, married Vittoria Colonna of Paliano in June 1901.

Emilio G(C)aetani dell Aquila d'Aragona married Giuila Pignatelli on September 28, 1939.

CARAFA

Prince Vicenzo Carafa of Roccella married Marina (Maria) Colonna of Paliano on August 15, 1904.

CHIGI-ALBANI

Sigismondo, sixth Reichsfurst, married Leopoldina Doria-Pamfili on June 2, 1829.

Ludovico Chigi-Albani, eighth Prince, married Anna Aldobrandini (Borghese), daughter of the Prince of Sarsina, on June 5, 1893.

Chigi-Zondadari (family of Pope Alexander VII)

Angelo Chigi-Zondadari married Isabella Colonna of Paliano and Tursi on January 8, 1900.

COLONNA

Maria Luisa Colonna married Diego Pignatelli on September 3, 1834.

Enrico Colonna married Cecilia Colonna-Stigliano on May 18, 1862.

Vittoria Colonna of Paliano married Francesco Sforza-Cesarini, Duke of Segni, on November 30, 1867.

Gioacchino Colonna, seventh Prince of Stigliano and Aliano, married Cecilia Colonna of Stigliano on March 26, 1873.

Prince Luciano Colonna of Summonte married Adele Borghese on November 26, 1874.

Fabrizio, Prince Colonna, of Paliano married Olimpia Doria-Pamfili-Landi, Princess of Torriglia, on May 20, 1878.

Isabella Colonna of Paliano and Tursi married Angelo Chigi-Zondadari, Marchese of S. Quirico, on January 8, 1900.

Vittoria Colonna married Leone Caetani, Duke of Sermoneta, on June 20, 1901.

CORSINI

Tommaso, sixth Prince Corsini, married Anna Barberini-Colonna di Sciarra of Palestrina on October 3, 1858.

Pietro-Francesco Corsini, Marchese of Lajatico, married Luisa Barberini-Colonna di Sciarra of Palestrina on October 3, 1863.

DELLA CHIESA (FAMILY OF POPE BENEDICT XV)

Giovanna del marchese della Chiesa married Augusto Barberini (Colonna) on October 4, 1960.

DORIA-PAMFILI-LANDI (OR DORIA-PAMFILI)

Leopoldina Doria-Pamfili married Sigismondo Chigi-Albani, sixth Reichsfurst on June 2, 1829.

Olimpia Doria-Pamfili married Prince Fabrizio Colonna of Paliano on May 20, 1878.

DELLA ROVERE (LANTE MONTEFELTRO DELLA ROVERE)

Duke Antonio Lante Montefeltro della Rovere (1904–1954) married Elena Rospigliosi on November 25, 1926.

Amelia Lante Montefeltro della Rovere married Prince Alessandro Odescalchi on January 25, 1954.

ODESCALCHI

Prince Alessandro Odescalchi married Amelia Lante Montefeltro della Rovere on January 25, 1954.

ORSINI

Teresa Orsini married Enrico Barberini-Colonna di Sciarra, Prince of Palestrina, on October 2, 1853.

PIGNATELLI

Diego Pignatelli married Marie Luisa Colonna of Stigliano on September 3, 1834.

Princess Emilia Pignatelli of Strongoli married Ferdinando Ferrara Pignatelli on April 3, 1903.

Prince Valerio Pignatelli of Cerchara married Maria Gioria Argona-Pignatelli-Cortes of Terranova in January 1924.

Princess Ludovica Pignatelli married Sosthénes Argona-Pignatelli-Cortes on July 26, 1928.

Giulia Pignatelli married Emilio Gaetani dell'Aguila d'Argona on September 28, 1939.

RIARIO-SFORZA (THE DELLA ROVERE FAMILY OF POPES SIXTUS IV AND JULIUS II)

Alberto Riario Sforza married Myrta Barberini-Colonna di Sciarra, Princess of Carbognano, on June 30, 1960.

ROSPIGLIOSI (ROSPIGLIOSI-PALLAVICINI, NOW PALLAVICINI)

Prince Francesco-Cesare Rospigliosi-Pallavicini, Prince of Gallico, married the princess Carolina Boncompagni-Ludovisi on October 4, 1854.

Elena Rospigliosi married Duke Antonio Lante Montefeltro della Rovere on November 25, 1926.

Prince Giulio Rospigliosi of Castiglione married Giulia of the dukes of Visconti di Modrone on November 25, 1940.

SFORZA-CESARINI

Duke Francesco Sforsa-Cesarini of Segni married Vittoria Colonna of Paliano on November 30, 1867.

Duke Lorenzo Sforza-Cesarini, Prince of Genzano (1868–1939), married Maria (Borghese) Torlonia on June 1, 1897.

VISCONTI (DI MODRONE)

Giulia of the dukes of Visconti di Modrone married Prince Giulio Rospigliosi of Castiglione on November 25, 1940.

APPENDIX C

Chronological List
of the Popes and Antipopes*

Note: For the first four centuries, the title Bishop of Rome was used. Information here is given in the following order: papal name, birthplace, original name and year(s) of reign. The years for the early popes are uncertain. For most of the first ten centuries, the popes took their own given names. The first pope to assume a new name was John II (533–35), whose actual name was that of the pagan god Mercury. He changed it to John for logical reasons.

1. St. Peter the Apostle, Bethsaida in Galilee, Symeon or Simon Bar-Jona (ca. 40–67).

2. St. Linus, Volterra in Tuscany (ca. 67–76).

3. St. Anacletus, Rome (ca. 76–88).

4. St. Clement I, Rome (ca. 88–97).

5. St. Evaristus-Bethlehem in Judea (ca. 97–105).

6. St. Alexander I, Rome (ca 105–115).

7. St. Sixtus I, Rome (ca. 115–125).

8. St. Telesphorus-Terranuova in Calabria (ca. 125–36).

9. St. Hyginus, Athens in Greece (ca. 136–40).

10. St. Pius I, Acquileia (ca. 140–55).

11. St. Anicetus-Homs in Syria (ca. 155–66).

12. St. Soter-Fondi in Campania (ca. 166–75).

13. St. Eleutherius, Nicopolis in Epirus (ca. 175–89).

14. St. Victor, Africa (189–99).

15. St. Zephyrinus, Rome (199–217).

16. St. Callistus (or Calixtus) I, Rome (217–222).

(1.) Antipope St. Hippolytus, Rome (217–235)

17. St. Urban I, Rome (222–30).

18. St. Pontian, Rome (230–35).

19. St. Anterus, Greece (235–36).

20. St. Fabian, Rome (236–50).

21. St. Cornelius, Rome (251–53).

(2.) Antipope Novatian, Rome (251–58).

22. St. Lucius I, Rome (253–54).

23. St. Stephan I, Rome (254–57).

24. St. Sixtus II, Greece (257–58).

25. St. Dionysius, probably Greece (259–68).

26. St. Felix I, Rome (269–74).

27. St. Eutychian, Luni in Etruria (Tuscany) (275–83).

28. St. Caius (or Gaius), Dalmatia (283–96).

29. St. Marcellinus, Rome (296–304).

30. St. Marcellus I, Rome (308–09).

31. St. Eusebus, Greece (309–10).

32. St. Miltiades (or Melchiades), Africa (311–14).

33. St. Silvester I, Rome (314–35).

34. St. Mark, Rome (336).

35. St. Julius I, Rome (337–52).

36. Liberius, Rome (352–66).

(3.) Antipope St. Felix II, Rome (355–65).

37. St. Damasus, Spain (or Rome) (366–84).

(4.) Antipope Ursinus, probably Rome (366–67).

*Listings of popes can also be found in Foy, Almanac (123–27); Rendina, I papi (825–30); Enciclopedia Italiana, "Papato," Vol. XXVI (240–51); and Dizionario Enciclopedico Italiano, "papa," Vol. IX (7–8).

38. St. Siricius, Rome (384–99).
39. St. Anastasius I, Rome (399–401).
40. St. Innocent I, Albano (401–417).
41. St. Zosimus, Greece (417–18).
42. St. Boniface I, Rome (418–22).
    (5.) Antipope Eulalius, probably Greece (418–19)
43. St. Celestine I, Campagna (422–32).
44. St. Sixtus III, Rome (432–40).
45. St. Leo I, Volterra in Tuscany (440–61).
46. St. Hilarus, Sardinia (461–68).
47. St. Simplicius, Tivoli (468–83).
48. St. Felix III, Rome (483–92).
49. St. Gelasius, Rome (of African descent) (492–96).
50. Anastasius II, Rome (496–98).
51. St. Symmachus I, Sardinia (498–514).
    (6.) Antipope Lawrence, probably Rome (498 and 501–05).
52. St. Hormisdas, Frosinone (514–23).
53. St. John I, Tuscany (523–26).
54. St. Felix IV, Sannio (526–30).
55. Boniface II, Rome (of German descent) (530–32).
    (7.) Antipope Dioscorus, Alessanaria (530).
56. John II, Rome, Mercury (533–35).
57. St. Agapi(e)tus I, Rome (535–36).
58. St. Silverius, Campania (536–37).
59. Vigilius, Rome (537–55).
60. Pelagius, Rome (556–61).
61. John III, Rome, Catelinus (561–74).
62. Benedict I, Rome, probably Bonosio (575–79).
63. Pelagius II, Rome (579–90).
64. St. Gregory I, Rome (590–604).
65. Sabinian, Blera, Viterbo (604–606).
66. Boniface III, Rome (607).
67. St. Boniface IV, della Marsica in l'Aquila (608–615).
68. St. Deusdedit (also Adeodatus I), Rome (615–18).
69. Boniface V, Naples (619–25).
70. Honorius I, Campania (625–38).
71. Severinus, Rome (640).
72. John IV, Dalmatia (640–42).
73. Theodore I, Greece (642–49).
74. Martin I, Todi in Umbria (649–54).
75. St. Eugene, Rome (654–57).
76. St. Vitalian, Segni (near Rome) (657–72).
77. Adeodatus II, Rome (672–76).
78. Donus, Rome (676–78).
79. St. Agatho, Palermo in Sicily (678–81).
80. St. Leo II, Sicily (682–83).

81. St. Benedict II, Rome (684–85).
82. John V, Antioch in Syria (685–86).
83. Conon, origin unknown but raised in Sicily (686–87).
84. St. Sergius I, Palermo (of Syrian descent) (687–701).
    (8.) Antipope Theodore, Rome (687).
    (9.) Antipope Paschal, possibly Rome (687).
85. John VI, Greece (701–705).
86. John VII, Greece (705–707).
87. Sisinnius, Syria (708).
88. Constantine, Syria (708–715).
89. St. Gregory II, Rome (715–31).
90. St. Gregory III, Syria (731–41).
91. St. Zacharias, S. Severina in Calabria (of Greek descent) (741–52).
92. Stephen II, Rome, of the Bobo-Orso or Orsini family (752–757).
93. St. Paul I, Rome, of the Bobo-Orso or Orsini family (757–67).
94. Stephen III, Sicily (768–72).
    (10.) Antipope Constantine, Nepi (767–69).
    (11.) Antipope Philip, origin unknown (768).
95. Hadrian I, Rome, probably of the Conti family (772–95).
96. St. Leo III, Rome (795–816).
97. Stephen IV, Rome (816–817).
98. St. Paschal I, Rome (817–24).
99. Eugene II, Rome (824–27).
100. Valentine, Rome (827).
101. Gregory IV, Rome (827–44).
102. Sergius II, Rome (844–47).
    (12.) Antipope John, probably Rome (844).
103. St. Leo IV, Rome (847–55).
104. Benedict III, Rome (855–58).
    (13.) Antipope Anastasius Bibliothecarius, probably Rome (855).
105. St. Nicholas I, Rome (858–67).
106. Hadrian II, Rome (867–72).
107. John VIII, Rome (872–882).
108. Marinus, Gallese in Tuscany (882–84).
109. St. Hadrian III, Rome (884–85).
110. Stephen V, Rome (885–91).
111. Formosus, Rome (891–96).
112. Boniface VI, Rome (896).
113. Stephen VI, Rome (896–97).
114. Romanus, Gallese in Tuscany (897).
115. Theodore II, Rome (897).
116. John IX, Tivoli (898–900).

117. Benedict IV, Rome (900–903).

118. Leo V, Ardea (903).

(14.) Antipope Christopher, Rome (903–904).

119. Sergius III, Rome of the Conti family of Tusculum (904–911).

120. Anastasius III, Rome (911–13).

121. Lando, Sabina (913–14).

122. John X, Tossignano, Imola in Romagna (914–28).

123. Leo VI, Rome (928).

124. Stephen VII, Rome (928–31).

125. John XI, Rome of the Alberichi/Conti family (931–35).

126. Leo VII, Rome (936–39).

127. Stephen VIII, Rome (939–42).

128. Marinus II, Rome (942–46).

129. Agapi(e)tus II, Rome (946–55).

130. John XIII, Rome, Ottaviano dei Conti di Tusculum (955–64).

131. Leo VIII, Rome (963–65).

132. Benedict V, Rome (964–66).

133. John XIII, Rome (965–72).

134. Benedict VI, Rome (973–74).

(15.) Antipope Boniface VII, Rome, Franco (974 and 984–85).

135. Benedict VII, Rome (974–83).

136. John XIV, Pavia, Pietro Canepanova (983–84).

137. John XV, Rome (985–96).

138. Gregory V, Germany, Bruno (son of the duke of Carinthia in Saxony) (996–99).

(16.) Antipope John XVI, Rossano in Calabria (of Greek descent), Giovanni Filigato (Philagathos) (997–98).

139. Silvester II, Belliac in Auvergne in France, Gerbert (999–1003).

140. John XVII, Rome, Giovanni (John) Sicco (1003).

141. John XVIII, Rome, Giovanni Fasano (Fasanus) (1004–1009).

142. Sergius IV, Rome, Pietro (1009–1012).

143. Benedict VIII, Rome, Teofilatto (Theophylact) of the Conti of Tusculum (1012–24).

(17.) Antipope Gregory VI, Rome (1012).

144. John XIX, Rome, Romano (Romanus) of the Conti of Tusculum (1024–32).

145 (*also* 147 and 150).* Benedict IX, Rome, Teofilatto (Theophylact) of the Conti of Tusculum (1032–44; 1045 and 1047–48).

146. Silvester III, Rome, Giovanni (John) of Sabina (1045).

148. Gregory VI, Rome, Giovanni Graziano (John Gratian) (1045–46).

149. Clement II, Germany, Suitgero (Suidger) of Morsleben and Hornburg in Saxony (1046–47).

151. Damasus II, Germany, Poppone (Poppo) of Bavaria (1048).

152. St. Leo IX, Germany, Bruno of the counts of Egisheim (1049–54).

153. Victor II, Germany, Gebhard of Dollnstein-Hirschberg (1055–57).

154. Stephen IX, Lorraine, Frederick of the dukes of Lorraine (1057–58).

155. Nicholas II, Chevron in Savoy, Gerard (1058–61).

(18.) Antipope Benedict X, Rome, Giovanni (John) Mincius (1058–59).

156. Alexander II, Baggio (near Milan), Anselmo (Anselm) (1061–73).

(19.) Antipope Honorius II, Verona, Pietro Cadalo (Cadalus) (1061–72).

157. Saint Gregory VII, Soana in Tuscany, Ildebrando (Hildebrand) (1073–85).

(20.) Antipope Clement III, Parma-Guilberto (Guibert) (1080; 1084–1100).

158. Victor III, Benevento, Desiderio (Desiderius) (1086–87).

159. Urban II, Châtillon-sur-Marne in France, Eudes (Odo) de Lagery (1088–99).

160. Paschal II, Blera (Viterbo) in Romagna, Raniero (Rainerius) (1099–1118).

(21.) Antipope Theoderic, origin unknown (1100–1102).

(22.) Antipope Albert, origin unknown (1102).

(23.) Antipope Silvester IV, Rome, Maginulfo (Maginulf) (1105–1111).

161. Gelasius II, Gaeta, Giovanni (John) Caetani (1118–19).

(24.) Antipope Gregory VIII, Limoges in France, Maurice Bourdin (Burdinus) (1118–21).

162. Callistus II, Burgundy in France, Guy (Guido) of the counts of Burgundy (1119–24).

163. Honorius II, Fiagnano in Imola, Lamberto (1124–30).

(25.) Antipope Celestine (II), Rome, Tebaldo Boccadipecora (Teobaldo Boccapecci) (1124). Canonically elected but considered an antipope.

164. Innocent II, Rome, Gregorio Papareschi (1130–43).

*There have been 262 popes. Benedict IX, having served three times, accounts for numbers 143, 147 and 150.

(26.) Antipope Anacletus II, Rome, Pietro Pierleoni (1130–38).

(27.) Antipope Victor IV, Ceccano in Frosinone, Gregorio Conti (1138).

165. Celestine II, Città di Castello in Umbria, Guido (1143–44).

166. Lucius II, Bologna, Gerardo Caccianemici (1144–45).

167. Eugene III, Pisa, Bernardo Pignatelli (or Paganelli di Montemagno) (1145–53).

168. Anastasius IV, Rome, Corrado (1153–54).

169. Hadrian IV, Langley in England, Nicholas Breakspear (1154–59).

170. Alexander III, Siena, Rolando (Orlando/Roland) Bandinelli (1159–81).

(28.) Antipope Victor IV, Tivoli, Ottaviano Monticelli (1159–64).

(29.) Antipope Paschal III, Crema, Guido (1164–68).

(30.) Antipope Callistus III, Strumi in Arezzo, Giovanni (1168–78).

(31.) Antipope Innocent III, Sezze in Latina, Lando (1179–80).

171. Lucius III, Lucca, Ubaldo Allucingoli (1181–85).

172. Urban III, Milan, Uberto Crivelli (1185–87).

173. Gregory VIII, Benevento, Alberto de Morra (1187).

174. Clement III, Rome, Paolo Scolari (1187–91).

175. Celestine III, Rome, Giacinto Bobone-Orsini (1191–98).

176. Innocent III, Gavignano (near Rome), Lotario of the Conti of Segni (1198–1216).

177. Honorius III, Rome, Cencio Savelli (1216–27).

178. Gregory IX, Anagni, Ugolino of the Conti of Segni (1227–41).

179. Celestine IV, Milan, Goffredo da Castiglione (1241).

180. Innocent IV, Genoa (Genova), Sinibaldo Fieschi (1243–54).

181. Alexander IV, Jenne (Anagni), Rinaldo of the Conti of Segni (1254–61).

182. Urban IV, Troyes in France, Jacques Pantaléon (1261–64).

183. Clement IV, Saint-Gilles-sur-Rhone in France, Guy Foulques (1265–68).

184. Gregory X, Piacenza, Tebaldo Visconti (1271–76).

185. Innocent V, Val d'Isère in Savoy, Pierre de Tarentaise (1276).

186. Hadrian V, Genoa, Ottobono Fieschi (1276).

187. John XXI, Lisbon, Pietro Juliani (1276–77).

188. Nicholas III, Rome, Giovanni Gaetano Orsini (1277–80).

189. Martin IV, Brie (Seine-et-Marne) in France, Simon de Brion (Brie) (1281–85).

190. Honorius IV, Rome, Giacomo Savelli (1285–87).

191. Nicholas IV, Lisciano (Ascoll Piceno), Girolamo Masci (1288–92).

192. St. Celestine V, Isernia in Molise, Pietro Angeleri (Pietro del Morrone) (1294).

193. Boniface VIII, Anagni, Benedetto Caetani (1294–1303).

194. Benedict XI, Treviso, Niccolò Boccasini (1303–1304).

195. Clement V, Villandraut (Gironde) in France, Bertrand de Got (1305–14).

196. John XXII, Cahors in France, Jacques Arnaud d'Euse (Deuse) (1316–34).

(32.) Antipope Nicholas V, Corvaro (Rieti) in Abruzzi, Pietro Rainalducci (1328–30).

197. Benedict XII, Savardin (Foix) in France, Jacques Fournier (1334–42).

198. Clement VI, Maumont in France, Pierre Roger de Beaufort (1342–52).

199. Innocent VI, Mont-Beyssac in France, Etienne Aubert (1352–62).

200. Urban V, Grisac (Alvernia) France, Guillaume de Grimoard (1362–70).

201. Gregory XI, Rosier-d'Egleton in France, Pierre Roger de Beaufort (1370–78).

202. Urban VI, Naples, Bartolomeo Prignano (1378–89).

(33.) Antipope Clement VII, Geneva, Robert of the counts of Geneva (1378–94).

203. Boniface IX, Naples, Pietro Tomacelli (1389–1404).

204. Innocent VII, Sulmona in Abruzzi, Cosimo Gentile de'Migliorati (1404–1406).

205. Gregory XII, Venice, Angelo Correr (1406–1415).

(34.) Antipope Benedict XIII, Illueca (Aragon) in Spain, Pedro de Luna (1394–1417).

(35.) Antipope Alexander V, Crete, Pietro Philarghi (1409–1410).

(36.) Antipope John XXIII, Naples, Baldassarre Cossa (1410–15).

206. Martin V, Genazzano in Rome, Oddo(ne) Colonna (1417–31).

(37.) Antipope Clement VIII, Teruel in Spain, Gil Sanchez Muñoz (1423–29).

(38.)*Antipope Benedict XIV, France, Bernhard Garnier (1425–30).

207. Eugene IV, Venice, Gabriele Condulmer (Condulmaro) (1431–47).

(39.) Antipope Felix V, Chambéry in Savoy, Amedeo (Amadeus) VIII Duke of Savoy (1439–49).

208. Nicholas V, Sarzana, Tommaso Parentucelli (1447–55).

209. Callistus III, Jativa in Valencia, Alonso (Alfonso) de Borja (Borgia) (1455–58).

210. Pius II, Corsignano in Siena-Enea Silvio Piccolomini (1458–64).

211. Paul II, Venice, Pietro Barbo (1464–71).

212. Sixtus IV, Celle Ligure (Savona), Francesco della Rovere (1471–84).

213. Innocent VIII, Genoa, Giovanni Battista Cibo (1484–92).

214. Alexander VI, Jativa in Valencia, Rodrigo de Borja (Borgia) (1492–1503).

215. Pius III, Siena, Francesco Todeschini-Piccolomini (1503).

216. Julius II, Albisola in Savona, Giuliano della Rovere (1503–1513).

217. Leo X, Florence, Giovanni de' Medici (1513–21).

218. Hadrian VI, Utrecht, Adrian Florensz (1522–23).

219. Clement VII, Florence, Giulio de' Medici (1523–34).

220. Paul III, Canino in Viterbo, Alessandro Farnese (1534–49).

221. Julius III, Rome, Giovanni Maria Ciocchi del Monte (1550–55).

222. Marcellus II, Montepulciano in Siena, Marcello Cervini (1555).

223. Paul IV, S. Angelo della Scala (Avellino), Giampietro Carafa (1555–59).

224. Pius IV, Milan, Giovanni Angelo de' Medici (1559–65).

225. St. Pius V, Bosco Marengo in Alessandria, Michele Ghislieri (1566–72).

226. Gregory XIII, Bologna, Ugo Boncompagni (1572–85).

227. Sixtus V, Grottammare (Ascoli Piceno), Felice Peretti (1585–90).

228. Urban VII, Rome, Giambattista Castagna (1590).

229. Gregory XIV, Somma Lombardo (Cremona), Niccolò Sfondrati (1590–91).

230. Innocent IX, Bologna, Giovanni Antonio Fachinetti (1591).

231. Clement VIII, Fano, Ippolito Aldobrandini (1592–1605).

232. Leo XI, Florence, Alessandro Ottaviano de' Medici (1605).

233. Paul V, Rome, Camillo Borghese (1605–1621).

234. Gregory XV, Bologna, Alessandro Ludovisi (1621–23).

235. Urban VIII, Florence, Maffeo Barberini (1623–44).

236. Innocent X, Rome, Giambattista Pamfili (1644–55).

237. Alexander VII, Siena, Fabio Chigi (1655–67).

238. Clement IX, Pistoia, Giulio Rospigliosi (1667–69).

239. Clement X, Rome, Emilio Altieri (1670–76).

240. Innocent XI, Como, Benedetto Odescalchi (1676–89).

241. Alexander VIII, Venice, Pietro Ottoboni (1689–91).

242. Innocent XII, Spinazzola (Puglia), Antonio Pignatelli (1691–1700).

243. Clement XI, Urbino, Giovanni Francesco Albani (1700–21).

244. Innocent XIII, Poli (Palestrina), Michelangelo of the Conti of Poli (1721–24).

245. Benedict XIII, Gravina (Bari), Pietro Francesco Orsini (son of the duke of Gravina) (1724–30).

246. Clement XII, Florence, Lorenzo Corsini (1730–40).

247. Benedict XIV, Bologna, Prospero Lorenzo Lambertini (1740–58).

248. Clement XIII, Venice, Carlo della Torre Rezzonico (1758–69).

249. Clement XIV, S. Arcangelo (Rimini),

*The 1995 Catholic Almanac (ed. Foy) states that most of the popes before St. Sylvester I (314–35) were married. This same source names thirty-seven antipopes. Rendina also lists that number. The source is the "Annuario Pontificio." The Encyclopædia Britannica (1958) gives the names of thirty-seven antipopes, but they are not the same as those in the Catholic Almanac. Kelly in Oxford Dictionary of Popes describes thirty-nine antipopes, and the Encyclopædia Britannica: Micropaedia (15th edition) presents a "tentative list" of thirty-nine antipopes. Because of the ambivalence regarding the election of schismatic popes or antipopes, the number (as well as the names and dates) varies with different sources.

Giovanni Vincenzo Antonio Ganganelli (1769–74).

250. Pius VI, Cesena (Emilia), Giovanni Angelo Braschi (1775–99).

251. Pius VII, Cesena (Emilia), Barnaba Gregorio Chiaramonti (1800–23).

252. Leo XII, Genga (Ancona), Annibale Sermattei della Genga (1823–29).

253. Pius VIII, Cingoli (Macerata), Francesco Saverio Castiglione (1829–30).

254. Gregory XVI, Belluno in Venetia, Bartolomeo Alberto (Mauro) Cappellari (1831–46).

255. Pius IX, Senigallia in Ancona, Giovanni Maria Mastai-Ferretti (1846–78).

256. Leo XIII, Carpineto in Anagni, Gioacchino Pecci (1878–1903).

257. St. Pius X, Riese in Treviso, Giuseppe Sarto (1903–1914).

258. Benedict XV, Genoa, Giacomo della Chiesa (1914–22).

259. Pius XI, Desio in Milan, Achille Ratti (1922–39).

260. Pius XII, Rome, Eugenio Pacelli (1939–58).

261. John XXIII, Brusicco di Sotto II Monte in Bergamo, Angelo Giuseppe Roncalli (1958–63).

262. Paul VI, Concesio in Brescia, Giovanni Battista Montini (1963–78).

263. John Paul I, Forno di Canale d'Agordo in Belluno, Albino Luciani (1978).

264. John Paul II, Wadowice in Poland, Karol Wojtyla (1978–).

Notes

One: In the Beginning — The First 1,200 Years*

1. Saba, *Storia della chiesa* I, pp. 337–40, 363–67 and 467–68.
2. Ibid., pp. 168–69.
3. Mann, *The Lives of the Popes* I, pp. 356 and 358.
4. Ibid., p. 357.
5. Saba, I, pp. 206–209.
6. Mann, I, pp. 16 and 177.
7. Saba, II, pp. 153–161.
8. The Anici (gens Anicia) was a family clan going back to ancient Rome and related to other noble Roman families such as the Annii and Petronii. The consul Lucio Anicio Gallo was of this family. Aristocratic Roman families, including the Pierleoni, Frangipane, Conti, Colonna and C(G)aetani claimed descent from the Anici. Popes Felice III (483–92) and Pope Gregory I (590–604) belonged to this family.
9. Mann, IV, pp. 79–82.
10. Rendina, *I papi*, p. 312.
11. Mann, IV, pp. 137–41.
12. Rendina, p. 314.
13. Mann, IV, pp. 151–52.
14. Raffaello Morghen, "Teodora da Roma," in *Enciclopedia Italiana* XXXIII, p. 509, from P. Fedele's *Ricerche per la storia di Roma e del papato al sec. X in Archivo della R. Società Romana de storia patria,* XXXIII (1910) and XXXIV (1911), and Liutprand's *Anatapodosis,* Chapter XIV.
15. Rendina, p. 320.
16. Mann, VI, pp. 137–41.
17. Ibid., pp. 137–238.
18. Saba, pp. 188–94.
19. Mann, IV, p. 163.
20. Ibid., p. 194

*Agostino Saba's Storia della chiesa *and Mann's* The Lives of the Popes *are scholarly accounts which have served as the basis for this expository study of the early history of the popes. Mann has a tendency to defend the papacy, including offensive or unsavory actions of the church and popes. His study was written to present this early history of the papacy to supplement the study of Pastor who deals with the popes from the end of the Middle Ages. Rendina's *I papi, Storia e segreti *often focuses on the scandalous, bizarre and sensational in the history of the popes, but his account is corroborated by other histories. In 1986 Oxford University Press published its dictionary of popes by J. N. D. Kelly. Using primary and period sources, Kelly brings a fresh approach to this subject, often refuting information previously reported or questioning the accuracy of other purported facts. He also lists and describes the antipopes so often ignored in other studies. Some of his facts, though, are in conflict with other works on the popes and are questionable.*

*Several sources — Prinz, Stroll, MacDonald and Piscotta — deal with the controversial Pierlioni family, its Jewish origins and its ascendancy to the papacy under Gregory VII. Robinson's *The Papacy, 1073–1198 *looks at this same pope, the period which follows his pontificate and the influence on the powerful Roman families on the papacy.*

Other studies on genealogical information in this chapter, including material used for the genealogical tables, have been gathered from sources such as Dugast Rouillé, Ratti, Litta, Pompeo Colonna, Stovis, Mann, Caetani, Longhi, Amayden and Kircheri. The author has interpreted these studies and has drawn his own conclusions and prepared his own tables, based upon his research.

*Since this chapter deals with the earliest history of the church, it has been observed that much of the genealogical data of families and individuals who lived during those times vary and are inconsistent. Sometimes there is speculation about a particular family — as with the origins of the Colonna. Litta conjectures that Pietro Colonna was the son of a member of the Conti family or the son of Aemelia of Palestrina and Duke Stefano. These differences are shown in tables I and IV. Kircheri, in *Historia Eustachio-Mariana Foglio 77 *(the basis for table IV) is of the opinion that Alberico I (d. 925), Margrave of Camerini and husband of Marozia, belonged to the Conti family. It is far more likely that Teofilatto and Teodora, the parents of Marozia, were members or related to the Conti family. Teodora was possibly a member of the Stefaneschi family. They were certainly closely connected to Roman nobility. It also seems that Alberico I was originally from France. These and other contradictions are found in genealogical studies that center on the period.*

21. Ibid., p. 191.
22. Rendina, p. 322.
23. Mann, IV, p. 212.
24. Rendina, p. 328.
25. Ibid., pp. 329 and 331–332.
26. Giorgio Falco, "Crescenzi," in *Enciclopedia Italiana* XI, p. 840, from G. Bossi's I Crescenzi. *della Pontificia contributo alla storia di Roma e dintorni dal 900 ad 1012, in dissertazioni Academia Romana di Archeologia*, s.2ª, XII (1915), pp. 47ff.
27. Mann, IV, p. 311.
28. Rendina, p. 341.
29. Mann, IV, p. 317.
30. Ibid., p. 340.
31. Rendina, p. 345.
32. G. Falco, "Crescenzi," in *Enciclopedia Italiana* XI, p. 840; Saba, I, pp. 212–15.
33. Saba, II, pp. 213–28; Kelly, *The Oxford Dictionary of Popes*, pp. 136–40; Rendina, pp. 350–60.
34. Saba, II, pp. 230–32.
35. Mann, V, pp. 160–239.
36. Rendina, p. 365.
37. Gregorovius as quoted in Prinz, *Popes from the Ghetto*, pp. 113–14, footnote 36.
38. Dr. Dugast Rouillé in his study *Les Maisons Souveraines de l'Autriche* (p. 56) is unsure if Leo was the son of Hugh IV whose father Hugh II was the brother of Adelaide, or the son of Hugh, whose father Hugh of Egisheim was the brother of Eberhard IV. The latter (Eberhard IV) was the father of Hugh II and Adelaide. Eberhard IV was also the brother of Gontram, founder of the Hapsburg dynasty. The Engisheims were closely related to many royal houses, including those of Lorraine, Hohenzollern and Hohenstaufen.
39. There are different versions of the genealogy of the Teofilatto family, which includes the Crescenzi. Tables are provided by Mann, IV, facing p. 40; and by Stokvis, *Manuel d'Histoire*, Band III, Chapter XII. Table 39.
40. Prinz. pp. 114–15 and 120–28.
41. Ibid., pp. 128 and 239–41. Prinz states that even the *Cambridge Medieval History* accepts Gregory VII's relationship to the Pierleoni family, as does A. J. MacDonald in his work *Hildebrand: A Life of Gregory VII*.

42. Longhi, "Gil Stefaneschi" Table II.
43. Amayden, *La storia delle famiglie romane*, pp. 148–49, 332 and 403–404.
44. Litta, "Orsini di Roma," *Famialie celebri italiane*, Tome 9, names Giangaetano as the son of Orso and Gaetano Orsini and as the father of Matteo Rosso, while other sources such as Gelasio Caetani, *Caietanorum genealogia*, Table XXXVII, says that the father of Matteo Rosso was Teobaldo son of Matteo, son of Orso and Gaetana Orsini, adding another generation.
45. Saba, II, pp. 264–302; Mann, VII, pp. 116ff; see also MacDonald, *Hildebrand*.
46. Prinz, pp. 189–96.
47. Robinson, *The Papacy 1073–1198*, p. 10.
48. Mann, VIII, p. 122.
49. Ibid., pp. 122ff; Saba, II, pp. 309–11.
50. Saba, II, p. 325.
51. Litta, "Normanni Re di Sicilia," Tome 16.
52. Mann, IV, refer to tables facing page 40.
53. Rendina, p. 426.
54. Robinson, pp. 56 and 509.
55. Mann, XIII, p. 10. But Mann does not list the thirteen Conti popes. The following chapter will focus on that papal family. However, Ratti, *Della famiglia Sforza*, Part II, p. 243, lists seven Conti popes: Sergius III, John XI, John XII, Benedict VII, Benedict VIII, Benedict IX and John XIX; and two antipopes: Benedict X and Victor IX. Four other popes of the Conti family were Innocent III, Gregory IX, Alexander IV and Innocent XIII.
56. Athanasil Kircheri, *Historia Eustachio-Mariana*, Foglio 77. This study includes the genealogical tables prepared by Francesco Zazzera.
57. Cascioli, *Memorie storiche di Poli*, p. 236.

Two: The Papal Families at the Close of the Middle Ages*

1. Albert Hauck, "Innocent III Desired to Rule the World," in Powell, *Innocent III*, p. 2.
2. Rendina, *I papi*, p. 448.
3. Giovanni Battista Picotti, "Conti," in *Enciclopedia Italiana* XI, p. 232; Mann, *The Lives of the Popes* XI, pp. 10ff.

*The papacy at Avignon, with the extravagances of the French popes and their families is duly described in Wood's Clement VI, in Mollat's The Popes at Avignon and in the comprehensive study of Guillemain, La Cour Pontificale d'Avignon, which includes the genealogical tables of the French papal families. Wood deals with the reign of Pope Gregory XI in France and his return to Rome and is less involved with the excesses of the Avignon court.
   When Giovanni Gentile in the 1920s and 1930s put together the Enciclopedia Italiana, he brought together the scholars of his country to write the entries. Among them were Picotti, professor at the University of Pisa who specialized in medieval history, and Falco, professor at the University of Torino who was an expert in the history of the church. These entries were often superior to articles and books published on these topics.
   Several genealogical studies were used as references for this chapter and its tables, and they include Lorenz's Genealogisches Handbuch, de'Crescenzi Romano's Anfiteatro Romano (the section on the Visconti family) and Ratti's L'autenticità degil alberi genealogici (the section on the Conti family). Burke's Royal Families of the World presents all the names, dates of birth and marriages of European royal and princely families for the last four centuries. The parents and children for several generations are listed, and the names and titles of the children of the male members of the family are continued into the contemporary period.
(Continued on page 239.)

4. Mann, XI, pp. 10–12.

5. Mann, XIII, p. 170, states that Pope Gregory IX was the grandnephew of Pope Innocent III, but other sources indicate that the relationship was more distant. Refer to Table V.

6. Marc Dykmans, "D'Innocent III à Boniface VIII." In particular, refer to Tables I, facing p. 90; II, facing p. 96, and III, facing page 98.

7. Litta, "Sforza," *Famiglie celebri italiane*, Tome 7. Refer to Mario Sforza, Count of Santa Flora. See also Ratti, *L'autenticità degli alberi genealogici*.

8. Mann, XIV, p. 108.

9. Ibid., p. 21.

10. Lorenz, *Genealogisches Handbuchl*, Table 14.

11. Litta, "Visconti," Tome 7. Refer to Bernabò Visconti.

12. de'Crescenzi Romano, *Anfiteatro Romano*, pp. 311–39.

13. Ibid.

14. Burke's, *Royal Families of the World*, p. 172.

15. This section on the Orsini family is based on Litta, "Orsini di Roma," Tome 9. Refer, in particular, to Matteo Rosso Orsini, his son Giovanni Gaetano Orsini (Pope Nicholas III) as well as to other individual members of the family described in this chapter.

The Historian Gregorovius claimed that the Orsini family was descended from the Roman emperors (*Libro d'Oro*, Vol. XV, p. 33). Caio Orso Flavio, who may have belonged to this family, lived during the time of the emperor Constantius I (d. 306). The Orsinis belonged to the Roman aristocracy. It is believed that in the early history of the church at least three popes were members of this family: Pope Stephen II (752–57), his brother Pope Paul I (757–67) and Pope Eugene II (824–27).

The first historically recorded Orsini pope was Celestine III, Giacinto Bobo, (1191–98), who was a member of the Boboni (later called Orsini) family. The power of the Orsini was greatly enhanced by the nepotistic Pope Nicholas III (1277–80), son of Senator Matteo Orsini and Perna Caetani. The Orsini family benefited greatly from the church and was a consistent and powerful ally to the Roman Church for centuries.

The family history has been recorded in Francesco Sansovino's *Origini e fatti delle famiglie illustri d'Italia*. According to Prince Benedetto Orsini, "a copy of a book written by Sansovino concerning the Orsini family, of which only three copies in the world are still in existence," remains in possession of the Orsini family. Archival material from the Orsini family was sold to the University of California, Los Angeles. The J. Paul Getty Museum published *The Orsini Inventories*, edited by Gisela Rubsamen, in 1980. Other Orsini manuscripts became the possession of the city of Rome in 1905. They are held in the Archivio Storico Capitlino and the Archivio di Stato in Rome. It should be recognized, however, that available material about the Orsini family before 1000 A.D. is often not historical, but rather is based on myth, legend and conjecture.

16. Litta, "Orsini di Roma." Tome 9. Refer to Matteo Rosso Orsini. Matteo Rosso Orsini was married to Perna Gaetani and their son was Giovanni Gaetano (Pope Nicholas III, 1277–80), whose great-grandmother Gaetana Gaetani was the wife of Orso Orsini. This Gaetani family, which had close ties with the Orsini, is spelled with a "G," whereas the family of Benedetto Caetani (Pope Boniface VIII, 1294–1303), including the descendants of his brother is spelled with a "C" throughout this study. The two families were probably distantly related: even today, some members of the family spell Caetani with a "C" and others with a "G."

17. Mann, XVI, p. 355.

18. Litta, "Savelli di Roma," Tome 15. Refer to Giacomo Savelli (Pope Honorius IV) and his brothers and sisters.

19. Analecta Bollandiana, Tome IX. *Vita et miracula Sancti Petri Caelestini Auctore coaevo*, pp. 147–200.

20. *Memorie delle famiglie nobili*, "Gaetani," pp. 30–31.

21. Ibid; *Almanach de Gotha*, 1914 "Gaetani," pp. 302–303.

22. Giorgio Falco, "Bonificio VIII," in *Enciclopedia Italiana* VII, p. 410.

23. Ibid.

24. Saba, *Storia della chiesa* II, pp. 480–83.

25. Rendina, p. 514.

26. Giorgio Falco, "Bonifacio VIII," in *Enciclopedia Italiana* VII, p. 410.

(continued.)

Litta's tomes of noble Italian families were a lifelong study. Not only were thousands of sources used, but Litta wrote either a short or extremely lengthy biography of thousands of individual members of such families as the Orsini, Savelli, Colonna, Corraro, Barbo, Condulmero, Migliorati and Piccolomini. He did not do a study of the Conti family. He wrote penetrating accounts of the popes who were members of these families. The tomes are unpaginated; and while table numbers are given as well as the names of specific branches of these families, the names of the various family members may be difficult to find especially when there are numerous family members to account for, as in his study of the Orsini family. While Litta may have made errors, his scholarship has rarely been equated. His studies usually do not deal with these families during the early Middle Ages, as the sources are fewer and less reliable for genealogical purposes.

Litta is the major source for most of the tables in the book, including the tables in Appendix A. They have been modified considerably since Litta's study is such an extensive one. The genealogical table for the C(G)aetani Family (Appendix A, tables 3a–3g) is based upon Caetani's Caietanqum genealogia *and Spreti's* Enciclopedia, Storico-Nobiliare Italian, *pp. 305–309.*

27. Saba, II, pp. 463–495; see also T. S. R. Boase, *Bonaface VIII* (London: Constable, 1933).

28. Saba, III, pp. 4–7.

29. Mollat, *The Popes at Avignon*, p. 8.

30. Ibid., p. 10.

31. Ibid., p. 11.

32. Ibid., p. 24.

33. Ibid., p. 25.

34. Ibid.

35. Ibid., p. 29.

36. Thibault, *Pope Gregory VI*, pp. 2–4.

37. Ibid., p. 2.

38. Mollat, p. 300.

39. Thibault, p. 15.

40. Wood, *Clement VI*, p. 7.

41. Mollat, pp. 310–18; Wood, p. 52.

42. Mollat, p. 39.

43. Thibault, p. 3.

44. Mollat, p. 4.

45. Ibid., p. 52.

46. Guillemain, *La Cour Pontificale d'Avignon*. Refer to the first chapter, "Les Papes et leurs Parents," pp. 89–179.

47. Thibault, p. 33.

48. Ibid., p. 1.

49. Mollat. p. 308.

50. Ibid., p. 306.

51. Wood, p. 105.

52. Rendina, pp. 540–42.

53. Litta, "Colonna," Tome 2.

54. Giorgio Falco, "Cola di Rienzo," in *Enciclopedia Italiana* X, p. 711, from F. Gregorovius, *Storia della città di Roma nel Medioevo*; Litta, "Orsini di Roma," Tome 9.

55. Litta, "Orsini di Roma," Tome 9.

56. Ibid: Litta, "Colonna," Tome 2, refer to Stefano and Sciarra Colonna; Georgio Falco, "Cola di Rienzo," in *Enciclopedia Italiana* X, pp. 711–13.

57. Kelly, *The Oxford Dictionary of Popes*, p. 227.

58. Litta, "Orsini di Roma," Tome 9. Refer to Orsina, daughter of Francesco Orsini, Gravina.

59. Litta, "Migliorati di Sulmona," Tome 16. Refer to Cosimo Gentile de' Migliorati (Pope Innocent VII) and his nephew Ludovico.

60. Litta, "Orsini di Roma," Tome 9. Refer to Raimondello Orsini, Prince Taranto.

61. Saba, III, pp. 77–84.

62. Litta, "Corraro di Venezia," Tome 2.

63. Ibid. Refer to Angelo Corraro (Pope Gregory XII).

64. Ibid.

65. Litta, "Condulmero di Venezia," Tome 13. Refer to Gabriele Condulmer (Pope Eugene IV).

66. Litta, "Barbo di Venezia," Tome 14. Refer to Polissena Condulmer Barbo.

67. Ibid. Refer to Pietro Barbo (Pope Paul II).

68. Litta, "Colonna," Tome 2. The history of the Colonna family is described under Pietro da Colonna, founder of the family.

69. Ibid.

70. Ibid. Refer to Oddo Colonna (Pope Martin V).

71. Ibid.

72. Ibid. Refer to entry on Lorenzo Onofrio Colonna, the pope's brother, as well as to the entries on his children.

73. Ibid.

74. Litta, "Condulmero di Venezia," Tome 13. Refer to Gabriele Condulmer (Pope Eugene IV).

75. Pastor, *The History of the Popes*, II, p. 62.

76. Ibid., p. 149.

77. Litta, "Piccolomini," Tome 4. Refer to Pius II, Pius III, Laudomia and Caterina Piccolomini and their descendants.

78. Lorenz, Table 33.

79. Litta. "Piccolomini," Tome 4.

Three: The Renaissance Popes and Their Families, 1471–1565

I: The della Rovere and Cibo Families*

1. There are no precise dates as to when the Renaissance began and ended. This study on popes during the Renaissance begins with Sixtus IV (1471–84). It could be argued that an earlier pope, Nicholas V (1447–55), who restored the Vatican library and rebuilt churches and bridges in Rome could be recognized as a Renaissance pope. Certainly some of

---

*During the nineteenth century, Leopold von Ranke and Ludwig Pastor wrote their scholarly studies on the papacy. Both were interested in using documents previously ignored. At the end of each volume, Ranke lists verbatim documents of particular interest to this chapter. Pastor obtained such a wide variety of sources that his study of forty volumes contains a graphic, almost day-by-day account of the popes from the end of the Middle Ages to the nineteenth century. They are classic works and have often been referred to for a more complete understanding of a pontificate.

They add to the biographical information supplied by Litta in his tomes on various pontificate families including the della Rovere (Tome 12) and the Orsini (Tome 9). What is remarkable about Litta's study are his biographic entries. The studies of Sixtus IV and Julius II are minor masterpieces, filled with details of their papacy. Later, Litta gives pertinent accounts of the della Rovere dukes of Urbino so that this family history reaches beyond the pages and adds to our understanding of a family and its strategic role during the Renaissance.

It should also be noted that the erudite and experienced political leader and historian Francesco Guicciardini enlivens his The History of Italy so that it makes the period come alive. Working for many of the popes, in diplomatic missions, Giucciardini knew of what he wrote, and he placed it all down on paper. His work is a frequently used and reliable source for this historic

(continued on page 241)

the Roman pontiffs during the next one hundred years espoused learning and arts in the mode of the period, but others did not. This chapter deals with the popes from Sixtus IV to Pius IV (1559–65).

2. Pastor, *The History of the Popes* IV, p. 200. Refer also to Litta, "Della Rovere di Savonna," *Famiglie celebri italiane*, Tome 12. Refer to Francesco della Rovere (Sixtus IV).

3. Pastor, pp. 203, 231 and 245.

4. Ibid., p. 237.

5. dei Marchesi Della Rovere, *Memorie Istoriche alla noblissima ed antichissima famiglia Della Rovere*, pp. 15 and 31.

6. Litta, "Della Rovere di Savonna," Tome 12. Refer to Francesco della Rovere (Sixtus IV) and his nephews.

7. Pastor, IV, pp. 238–39.

8. Cloulas, *The Borgias*, p. 172.

9. This story is noted in a footnote in Giucciardini, *The History of Italy*, p. 152, and is cited in Guicciardini, *Storia d'Italia*, Torrentino edition (Firenze, 1561) p. 166. Caterina Sforza-Riario (1463–1509 was married three times. Her first husband was Girolamo Riario, nephew of Pope Sixtus IV, then Iacopo Feo, and finally Giovani de' Medici. Feo, known for his arrogance and cruelty, was murdered before her eyes in 1495, and she sought a terrible revenge. Anyone whom she considered to be conspirators, as well as their wives and children, were liquidated. Caterina Sforza's cruelty was very much in keeping with that practiced by her ancestors, the Sforzas and Viscontis of Milan. And her descendants, Duke Cosimo I de' Medici and Maria de' Medici, Queen of France, evinced similar ruthless tendencies.

10. Pastor, IV, pp. 250, 311, 316ff, and 356ff.

11. Ibid., VI, p. 450.

12. Guicciardini, as reported in Pastor, VI, p. 217.

13. Pastor, VI, p. 218.

14. Litta, "Della Rovere di Savonna," Tome 12. Refer to Giuliano della Rovere (Pope Julius II) and his sister Luchina and her children.

15. Litta, "Colonna di Roma," Tome 2.

16. According to Corvo's *History of the Borgias*, pp. 162 and 295, which tries to rehabilitate the Borgia family, Cardinal Giuliano della Rovere (later Pope Julius II) was the actual father of Caesar Borgia. He claims that la Vannozza was the mistress of both Cardinal della Rovere and Cardinal Borgia.

17. Litta, "Orsini di Roma," Tome 9. Refer to Giangiordano Orsini, Lord of Bracciano, and his wife Felice della Rovere.

18. Litta, "Della Rovere di Savonna," Tome 12. Refer to Felice della Rovere, wife of Giangiordano Orsini.

19. Guicciardini, *The History of Italy*, p. 272.

20. Litta, "Orsini di Roma," Tome 9. Refer to Felice della Rovere.

21. Refer to the Orsini (Part Three), Farnese, Damasceni-Peretti and Borghese dynasties in this study.

22. Refer to *Almanach de Gotha* and Libro d'Oro.

23. Pastor, V, pp. 238 and 352–53.

24. Sabatini, *The Life of Caesar Borgia*, pp. 59–60: Corvo, pp. 88–89.

25. Corvo, p. 80.

26. Vito Antonio Vitale, "Cybo," in *Enciclopedia Italiana* XII, p. 202.

27. Rendina, *I papi*, p. 597.

28. Burchard, *Diarium*.

29. Pastor, V. pp. 240 and 270; Rendina, *I papi*, p. 596.

30. Corvo, p. 80.

31. Pastor, V., pp. 282, 354 and 405.

32. Corvo, pp. 107–108.

33. Litta, "Varano di Camerino," Tome 13.

34. Vito Antonio Vitale, "Cybo," in *Enciclopedia Italiana* XII, p. 202.

35. Litta, "d'Este," Tome 5. Refer to Ercole d'Este and his wife Maria Teresa Cibo.

36. Lorenz, *Genealogisches Handbuch*, tables 33 and 34.

II: The House of Borgia[†]

37. Pastor, II, p. 461.

38. Guicciardini, *The History of Italy*, p. 166.

39. Baronius, *Annales eccesiastici*, p. 31.

40. Pastor, V., p. 383.

41. Pastor, VI, p. 107.

42. Corvo, pp. 19, 193, 314 and 317.

43. Pastor, V., pp. 363–65.

44. Sabatini, pp. 43–49; Corvo, p. 162. Vannozza Catanei had four children: Caesar (1475–1507), Juan (Giovanni in Italian, 1476–1497), Lucrezia (1480–1519), and Goffredo (also known as Jofre,

(continued.)

period. His study begins with the peace brought about by Lorenzo de' Medici, the Magnificent, and Pope Innocent VIII. Their deaths in 1492 fan the flames for the turbulence that follows. Guicciardini captures the upheaval and turmoil of the pontificates of the Borgia, della Rovera and de' Medici popes.

Additional genealogical material is found in Lorenz's Genealogisches Handbuch, *Table 32. It is used to supplement Litta. Since Litta does not study the "Cibo" family, other sources were here used, including Rendina, Vitale and Pastor.*

[†]Unfortunately, Litta's genealogical studies do not include the Borgia family, whose origins were Spanish, but whose members often married into prominent Italian families. For this reason a variety of other sources were used, including Burchard's At the Court of the Borgia, *Cloulas'* The Borgias, *Gregorovius's works and Mallett's* The Borgias, The Rise and Fall of a Renaissance Dynasty. (Continued on page 242.)

(1481–1516). It is believed that Rodrigo Borgia (who was a cardinal from 1456 to 1492 and then Pope Alexander VI from 1492 to 1503) was the father of these four children.

45. Corvo, pp. 152–53.
46. Pastor, V., pp. 497–99.
47. Corvo, p. 127.
48. Pastor, VI, p. 104.
49. Bellonci, *The Life and Times of Lucrezia Borgia*, pp. 155–57 and 316–19.
50. Sabatini, pp. 44, 48 and 169.
51. Erlanger. *Lucrezia Borgia*, p. 119.
52. Vrignault, *Généalogie de la Maison de Bourbon*, p. 12.
53. Guicciardini, *The History of Italy*, p. 152.
54. Litta, "Manfredi," Refer to Astorre Manfredi III.
55. Sabatini, pp. 277–83.
56. Guicciardini, *The History of Italy*, p. 161.
57. Sabatini, pp. 373 and 389.
58. Pastor, VI, p. 58.
59. Guicciardini, *The History of Italy*, pp. 154 and 165–66.
60. Ranke, *The History of the Popes*, III, p. 181.
61. Guicciardini, *The History of Italy*, p. 166.
62. Pastor, VI, pp. 200–204.
63. Ibid., p. 208.
64. Corvo, p. 309.
65. Pastor, V., p. 401; Rendina, 602; Litta, "d'Este," Tome 5, refer to Alfonso d'Este, Duke of Ferrara and his wife Lucrezia Borgia.
66. Pastor, V, p. 420; Rendina, p. 602.
67. Pastor, VI, p. 58.
68. Bellonci, pp. 116–17 and 133–40.
69. Pastor, VI, pp. 76 and 104.

70. Guicciardini, *The History of Italy*, p. 163.
71. Bellonci, pp. 181–83.
72. Pastor, VI, p. 110.
73. Corvo, pp. 309–310.
74. Litta, "d'Este," Tome 5. Refer to Ippolito d'Este and the other children of Duke Alfonso I and Lucrezia Borgia. The last male member of the Pico family died in 1747.
75. Ibid. Refer to children of Ercole II, Duke of Ferrara.
76. Ranke, III, p. 13; Pastor, XXIV, p. 394. Lucrezia d'Este even willed part of her estate to Cardinal Pietro Aldobrandini.
77. Sedgwick, *The House of Guise*, pp. 45, 161 and 303. The seventh and last duke of Guise was Francois (d. 1675). He was succeeded by a sister of the fifth duke, Maria of Lorraine, who sold her rights to the dukedom to Augustus, Duke of Maine. When she died in 1688, the numerous possessions of the Guise family were inherited by Anna Enrichetta, daughter of Catherine of Lorraine (wife of Duke Carlo Gonzaga), daughter of Charles, Duke of Mayenne, son of Francois I, second Duke of Guise, and Anna d'Este. Anna Enrichetta was the wife of Henry-Jules, Prince of Conde.
78. Pastor, VI, pp. 104 and 218.
79. Corvo, pp. 359–72, 375–76, 402 and 404.
80. R. Gervaso, *I Borgia*, (Milano, 1976), quoted in Rendina, p. 606.
81. Litta, "Farnesi," Tome 12. Refer to Rosa (la Vannozza) Farnese, daughter of Ranuccio and sister of Pier Luigi, father of Pope Paul III.
82. Pastor, V, p. 363.
83. Litta, "Farnesi," Tome 12.
84. Corvo, pp. 162 and 295.

(continued.)

Pope Alexander VI's son Goffredo became the prince of Squillace in southern Italy, and this Italian branch of the family lasted for several generations. The last prince of Squillace had an only daughter, Giovanna, who married Michele Antonio Orsini (d. 1627) of the dukes of Gravina, a cousin of Pope Benedict XIII. The Orsini genealogy is, of course, delineated in Tome 9 of Litta. Lucrezia Borgia, daughter of Pope Alexander VI, had many descendants from her marriage to Alfonso I d'Este, Duke of Ferrara, and they are described in Tome 5 (d'Este) of Litta. Other descendants of Lucrezia are noted in Sedgwick's The House of Guise. *A nineteenth century work on her life, such as Gregorovius'* Lucretia Borgia, *and later books on her life, such as Bellonci's* The Life and Times of Lucrezia Borgia *and Erlanger's* Lucrezia Borgia, *are remarkably dissimilar. Gregorovius depicts Lucrezia as an evil adventuress, whereas Erlanger's book shows her to be saintly, filled with piety and a victim of political intrigue and circumstances.*

The legitimate descendants of Caesar Borgia, the Bourbon-Bissets, are all detailed in Vrignault's Généalogie de la Maison de Bourbon, *and an account of Caesar's life is recorded in Sabatini's* The Life of Caesar Borgia. *The Spanish dukes of Gandia, descendants of Pope Alexander's son Juan, are given lengthy biographies in Corvo's* A History of the Borgias. *This work, which blames Pope Julius II "the Terrible" for many of the misdeeds attributed to the Borgias, is ludicrous because, while numerous facts are given, it deliberately glosses over the heinous deeds of the pope and his son Caesar. However, it should not be ignored that one of Alexander VI's major achievements—especially in terms of its consequences on history—was his decision to proclaim the Line of Demarcation (1493), dividing the New World between Spain and Portugal.*

Most works on Pope Alexander VI and his children give some details regarding his mistresses, the beautiful la Vannozza Catanci and Giulia Farnese, and both women are given a biographic entry in Litta's Tome 12, "The Farnesi." As indicated in the text, Vannozza probably was not a member of the Farnese family, but she is listed by Litta in the Farnese genealogy. Giulia is said by Litta to have married a member of the Orsini family, but she was the wife of Orsini Migliorati.

Guicciardini's The History of Italy *presents a vivid picture of the court of Alexander VI, and Pastor's* The History of the Popes *duly recalls the transgressions of the Borgias in Volumes V and VI. Litta in Tome 16 gives a good account of the Migliorati di Sulmona family, showing its close relationship to the Borgias. And while Litta does not center any study on the Borgias, there is certainly enough information about that family in numerous other sources to make up for the lack of material in Litta.*

85. Sabatini, pp. 43–54.
86. Pastor, V, p. 363.
87. Litta, "Farnesi," Tome 12; Bellonci, pp. 65–66.
88. Litta, "Farnesi," Tome 12.
89. Guicciardini, *The History of Italy*, p. 124.
90. Pastor, V, p. 363.
91. Bellonci, p. 314.
92. Pastor, VI, p. 80.
93. Litta, "Farnesi," Tome 12.
94. Ibid. Refer to Giulia Farnese, daughter of Pier Luigi Farnese and sister of Pope Paul III.
95. Litta, "Migliorati di Sulmona," Tome 16. Refer to Adriana, wife of Lodovico Migliorati, grandnephew of Pope Innocent VII.
96. Litta, "Farnesi," Tome 12. Refer to Giulia Farnese.
97. Gregorovius, *Lucretia Borgia*, p. 89.
98. Litta, "Migliorati di Sulmona," Tome 16. Refer to Giulia Farnese, wife of Orsino Migliorati.
99. Ibid.
100. Ibid.
101. Mallet, p. 103.

III: The Medici and Farnese Families*

102. Guicciardini, *History of Florence*, p. 5.
103. Alberi, *Documenti sull' assedio di Firenze*, p. 51.
104. Guicciardini, *History of Florence*, p. 76.
105. Ibid., p. 70.
106. Pastor, V, p. 359. While Giovanni de' Medici (Leo VI) acquired the reputation as a model cardinal, as pope, he was extravagant, pleasure-loving and a reputed homosexual.
107. Ibid., VII, p. 90 and 147.
108. Guicciardini, *History of Florence*, p. 302.
109. Pastor, VIII, p. 104 and 109–110.
110. Ibid., p. 348; Pastor, VII, pp. 291ff.
111. Guicciardini, *The History of Italy*, p. 321.
112. Ibid., pp. 296 and 324–28.
113. Pastor, IX, p. 4.
114. Ibid., pp. 233ff.
115. Ibid., pp. 422ff; Litta, "Medici," Tome 4. Refer to Giulio de' Medici (Pope Clemente VII).
116. Guicciardini, *History of Florence*, p. 409. Pope Clement VII pretended that Alessandro was

the illegitimate son of Lorenzo de' Medici, Duke of Urbino.
117. Pastor, X, pp. 161ff.
118. Ibid., p. 331.
119. Litta, "Medici," Tome 4. Refer to Alessandro, Duke of Florence.
120. Ibid.
121. Ibid. Refer to Lorenzo de' Medici and to Grand-duke Cosimo I.
122. Ibid. Refer to Ottaviano de' Medici and his sons Bernadetto and Alessandro (Pope Leo XI).
123. Ibid. Refer to Giambuono de' Medici.
124. Pastor, XI, pp. 17 and 35.
125. Rendina, p. 629; Litta, "Farnesi," Tome 12. Refer to Giulia Farnese.
126. Rendina, p. 635; Litta, "Farnesi," Tome 12, refer to Alessandro Farnese (Pope Paul III); Pastor, XII, pp. 631–35.
127. Pastor, XI, pp. 14 and 16.
128. Litta, "Farnesi," Tome 12. Refer to Ranuccio Farnese, grandfather of Pope Paul (Paolo) III, and his children.
129. Ibid. Refer to Alessandro Farnese (Pope Paul III) and his children.
130. Pastor, XI, pp. 19–20.
131. Litta, "Farnesi," Tome 12. Refer to Pier Luigi Farnese, son of Pope Paul (Paolo) III.
132. Ibid. Refer to Pope Paul III, his son Pier Luigi and his grandson Cardinal Alessandro.
133. Litta, "Sforza," Tome 7. Refer to Cardinal Guido Ascanio Sforza.
134. Litta, "Farnesi," Tome 12. Refer to Pier Luigi, son of the pope.
135. Ibid.
136. Ibid.
137. Pastor, XII, p. 370.
138. Pastor, XII, pp. 371–72; Litta, "Farnesi," Tome 12. Refer to Pope Paul III and his son Pier Luigi Farnese.
139. Ibid.
140. Pastor, XII, p. 452.
141. Litta, "Farnesi," Tome 12. Refer to Alessandro Farnese (Pope Paul III).
142. Pastor, XIII, pp. 92 and 101–155.
143. Litta, "Farnesi," Tome 12. Refer to Ottavio Farnese, son of Pier Luigi and grandson of Pope Paul III.
144. Pastor, XIII, pp. 132–33.

*An intimate of popes Leo X and Clement VII, Guicciardini presents accounts of their papacies that are revealing and gripping. Litta in Tome 4 focuses on the Medici family, and he has a great deal to say about the Medici dukes of Florence—including its first duke, Alessandro—emphasizing the decline of that dynasty from Cosimo I to Giovanni Gaston (d. 1737).

Litta does an outstanding biographical sketch of Pope Paul (Paolo) III in Tome 12, "I Farnesi," and it holds the reader's interest because of its poignancy. The Medicis treated Florence as their only child, and Paul III doted on his son Pier Luigi. Litta again writes excellent biographies on the dukes of Parma and Placenza as well as on Cardinal Alessandro Farnese.

In Tome 7 Litta examines the numerous branches of the Sforza family, which include the dukes of Milan and the counts of S. Flora. The latter branch married into illustrious papal families, such as the Conti and Farnese, and increased its social position and wealth with its subsequent union with the Cesarini family, described in Tome 1. The Sforza dynasty is also studied by Ratti in his Della famiglia Sforza, which stresses its relationship with the Conti family.

145. Litta, "Farnesi," Tome 12. Refer to Costanza Farnese and her father, Pope Paul (Paolo) III.

146. Litta, "Sforza," Tome 7. Refer to Bosio and Costanza Sforza and their children (Sforza di Santa Flora).

147. Ibid.

148. Ibid. Refer to children of Francesco Sforza (1520–75).

149. Pastor, XXX, p. 71.

150. Litta, "Pallavicino," Tome 8.

151. Litta, "Orsini di Roma," Tome 9. Refer to Eleanora Orsini of Bracciano.

152. Litta, "Cesarini," Tome 1. Refer to Livia and Clelia Cesarini.

153. Litta, "Sforza," Tome 7, and "Boncompagni di Bologna," Tome 2.

154. Pastor, XXX, pp. 372–73.

155. Corvo, p. 393.

156. Ratti, *L'autenticità degli alberi genealogici.*

157. Litta, "Cesarini," Tome 1, and "Sforza," Tome 7. Refer to Federico Sforza (1651–1712), his wife Livia Cesarini and their descendants.

IV: The Renaissance Comes to a Close*

158. Pastor, XIII, p. 66.

159. Ibid., p. 67.

160. Rendina, p. 637.

161. Litta, "del Monte di Sansavino," Tome 4, refer to Fabiano, nephew of Pope Julius (Giulio) III; see also Tettoni and Saladini, *Teatro Araldico*, VI.

162. Rendina, p. 638.

163. Pastor, XIII, pp. 70–73; Rendina, p. 638. Pastor's translator refers to Innocenzo del Monte as "the keeper of the ape," (p. 70) but it appears more likely that he was a keeper of monkeys. Because of this association, the Romans called him "Monkey" or "Ape,"—but in either case the monkeys or apes could only have been insulted by this appellation and comparison, as Innocenzo demonstrated the most peculiar, if not the most insufferable, behavior imaginable.

164. Pastor, XIII, pp. 99ff and 155; Litta, "del Monte di Sansavino," Tome 4. Refer to Giovanni Maria Ciocchi del Monte who became Pope Julius (Giulio) III for a history of his pontificate and to other members of his family for a detailed explanation of the role of his relatives.

165. Rendina (quoting Ranke), p. 639.

166. Litta, "Carafa," Tome 17. Refer to Giampietro Carafa (Pope Paul IV) and his nephews Carlo and Giovanni Carafa.

167. Kelly, *The Oxford Dictionary of the Popes*, p. 266.

168. Litta, "Medici," Tome 4. Refer to Giambuono de' Medici.

169. Litta, "Orsini di Roma," Tome 9. Refer to Ludovico Orsini, Count of Pitigliano.

170. Pastor, XV, p. 74.

171. Ibid., pp. 98 and 378.

172. Ibid., pp. 99, 101–102, 108–109 and 113–14.

173. Ibid., pp. 102–104; see also Rendina, p. 651.

174. Pastor, XV, p. 113, footnote 2.

175. Litta, "Carafa," Tome 17. Refer to Carlo Carafa.

176. Pastor, XV, p. 138. The court process, the verdict and effects on the Carafa brothers are dramatically explicated in Pastor, XV, pp. 135–177.

177. Litta, "Carafa," Tome 17. Refer to Giovanni and Carlo Carafa, nephews of Pope Paul IV.

178. Ibid. Refer to Alfonso and Agnese Carafa, grandnephew and niece of Pope Paul IV.

179. Pastor, XV, 175–176.

180. Ibid., p. 177.

181. Spreti, *Enciclopedia Storico-Nobiliare Italiana*, II, pp. 144–46; and Calvi, *Famiglie notabili milanese*, 2, "Borromeo," Tables VIII, IX, X, XI, XII, XIII and XIV. The present-day Borromeo family, nobility of Arona and Isola Bella, are descended from Giulio Cesare Borromeo (1515–72), brother of Gilberto Borromeo (d. 1558) who married Margherita de' Medici. She was the sister of Pope Pius IV (Giovanni Angelo de' Medici) and mother of St. Carlo Borromeo. Thus, the descendants of Giulio Cesare, who married into many of the papal dynasties, were cousins of St. Carlo Borromeo and not directly related to Pope Pius IV. This branch of the Borromeo family later married into many aristocratic and papal families, such as the della Rovere, Farnese, Barberini, Colonna, Boncompagni-Ludovisi, Rospigliosi, Albani, Altieri and Odescalchi. Eight cardinals came from the Borromeo family. Giulio Cesare (1517–72), ancestor of the present Borromeo family, and his brother Gilberto (d. 1558), the brother-in-law of Pius IV, were the sons of Federico Borromeo, Count of Arona, and his wife Veronica Visconti.

*Litta gives a biographical and genealogical account in Tome 4 of the "del Monte di Sansavino" family which has been supplemented by the studies of Tettoni and Saladini in Teatro Araldico, Pastor The History of the Popes (XIII), and Rendina I papi.

Litta (with collaborators) devotes almost the entire Tome 17 to the Carafa family—the family of Pope Paul IV; Volume XIV of Pastor is a magnificent description of the Carafa papacy. In the papacy of Pius IV, which follows in the succeeding volume, Pastor explains this "reform" pope's generosity to his relatives, especially to the Borromeo family. The aristocratic Borromeos, their lineage and history, are developed in Spreti's Enciclopedia Storico-Nobiliare Italiana (II) and in "Borromeo" in Calvi's Famiglie notabili milanesi (2). And while Litta does not place this family in his Famiglie celebri italiane, Calvi tries to emulate Litta by giving some biographic description of each member of the Borromeo family.

Although Litta indicates that Pius IV belonged to the Medici family of Florence, he does not show the specific ancestry and does not present a biographic sketch of that pope, so other sources as Pastor, Kelly and Rendina were used.

The Borromeo frequently intermarried with branches of the Visconti family. Giulio Cesare's son Renato (d. 1608) married Ersilia, daughter of Duke Ottavio Farnese of Parma-Piacenza, grandson of Pope Paul III. Renato and Ersilia's grandson Renato II (1613–85) was the husband of Giulia, heiress and daughter of Bartolomeo Arese, a name added to that of the Borromeo. Their eldest son Carlo and his descendants took the name Borromeo-Arese by which that branch of the family is known today. This Borromeo family is intricately entwined with the dynastic families of the Roman pontiffs.

182. Pastor, XV, p. 148, note 1. Pius V read the trial proceedings and revised them. Later, the original documents of these hearings were burned. Pastor explains Pope Pius V's account of his decision regarding the Carafas in Volume XVI. Suffice it to say that Pastor (XV, p. 154) states: "The choice of prejudiced judges effected the rest, and thus it may well have happened that crimes were attributed to the accused of which they were innocent."

Four: The Papal Dynasties of the Baroque Period, 1572–1740

I: From Boncompagni to Ludovisi*

1. Pastor, *The History of the Popes*, XIX, p. 23.
2. Ibid., p. 36.
3. Litta, "Boncompagni di Bologna," *Famiglie celebri italiane*, Tome 2. Refer to Ugo Boncompagni (Pope Gregory [Gregorio] XIII) and his son Giacomo.
4. Ibid.
5. Ibid.
6. Ibid.
7. Ibid.
8. Ibid.
9. Ibid. Refer to Giulia Boncompagni. Tasso wrote the song "Why Life Is Short" (*"Perchè la vita é breve"*) for her.
10. Litta, "Sforza," Tome 7. Refer to Franceso Sforza, Marchese di Varzi, Santa Fiora branch.
11. Pastor, XX, p. 539.
12. Ibid., p. 533.
13. Pastor, XI, p. 23.
14. Pastor, XXI, p. 67.
15. Rendina. *I papi*, pp. 660–62.
16. Pastor, XXI, pp. 72ff.
17. Pastor, XXII, pp. 233–303.
18. Ibid., p. 304.
19. Pastor, XXI, p. 67.
20. Ibid., p. 69.
21. Litta, "Savelli," Tome 15. Refer to Bernardo Savelli, his wife Maria Felice and their children Giulio and Margherita.
22. Ibid., see also Litta, "Cesarini," Tome 1.
23. Pastor, XXI, pp. 70–71.
24. Litta, "Colonna," Tome 2. Refer to Marcantonio Colonna and his wife Orsina Damasceni-Peretti.
25. Litta, "Sforza," Tome 7. Refer to Muzio Sforza of Caravaggio.
26. Litta, "Orsini di Roma," Tome 9. Refer to Giangiordano Orsini of Bracciano, his wife Felice della Rovere and descendants.
27. Ibid.
28. Litta, "Sforza," Tome 7. Refer to Alessandro Sforza, Duke of Segni, and his descendants, including the Sforza-Cesarini; Ratti, *Della famiglia Sforza*, Part 1, Tables on the Conti di Santa Fiora and Duchi Sforza.
29. Ibid.
30. Calvi, *Famiglia notabili milanesi* 2, Tables on the Sfondrati.
31. Ibid.
32. Litta, "Visconti," Tome 7. Refer to Bernabò Visconti and his son Sagromoro.

*Litta's studies concentrated on the old aristocracy—families like the Colonna (Tome 2), the Orsini (Tome 9), the Visconti (Tome 7), the Sforza (Tome 7) and the Savelli (Tome 15)—showing the relationships between these and newer emerging nobility; he also included the new noble families that were enhanced by the popes. These families include the Boncompagni of Bologna (Tome 2), the Ludovisi (Tome 14) and the Aldobrandini (Tome 2). He writes a noteworthy biography of Pope Gregory XIII's son Giacomo. Surprisingly, the Borghese family was not listed in Litta's works. Instead Spreti's Enciclopedia Storico-Nobiliare Italiana was here used as a reference. Spreti offered genealogical information and sometimes short biographical accounts of specific members of the family. A genealogical table with brief descriptions of members of the Sfondrati family is found in Volume 2 of Calvi, Famiglia notabili milanesi.

    Surviving members of Italian aristocratic families as the Borghese-Aldobrandini and the Boncompagni-Ludovisi are listed with titles and honors in the twentieth century publications of Libro d'Oro della Nobiltà Italiana and the Almanach de Gotha. The former is issued every four years; Volume XX, for example, is for the years 1986–89. The latter came out every year until 1944. To bring genealogical material into the contemporary period, these sources were among the primary ones consulted. On occasion, Chaffonjon's Le Petit Gotha and C. A. Starke's Genealogisches Handbuch des Adels, Band 3, served as references.

    In this chapter other references and studies, such as those by Rendina and Pastor, as well as a biography of Pauline Bonaparte by Dixon, captured the history of these papal families from the early Baroque into the modern and contemporary periods. Litta's Tome 2, which included the Aldobrandini, Boncompagni di Bologna and Colonna families, was published in 1838, so the need to update the history of these families is apparent. In fact, Litta's studies of the important Italian families were all published in the nineteenth century, most of them before 1852, the year of his death. As noted in the list of selected sources, other scholars continued Litta's work.

33. Pastor, XXIV, p. 377.
34. Litta, "Aldobrandini," Tome 2. Refer to Ippolito Aldobrandini (Pope Clement VIII) and his nephews.
35. Pastor, XXIII, p. 47.
36. Ibid., p. 50.
37. Ibid., p. 53–54.
38. Ibid., pp. 55–56.
39. Litta, "Savelli," Tome 15. Refer to Bernardo Savelli, his wife Felice, their son Giulio and his wife Caterina and their son Bernardino.
40. Litta, "Aldobrandini," Tome 2. Refer to Giorgio Aldobrandini and his daughter Olimpia.
41. Chaffanjon, Le Petit Gotha, p. 289.
42. Almanach de Gotha, 1914, "Borghese," pp. 289–90.
43. Pastor, XXIII, pp. 57–8.
44. Bentivoglio Memorie, as quoted in Pastor, p. 56.
45. Pastor, XXV, pp. 293–99.
46. Ibid., p. 61.
47. Ibid., pp. 61–2.
48. Pastor, XXVI, pp. 375–460.
49. Pastor, XXV, p. 65.
50. Ibid., p. 67.
51. Ibid., p. 68.
52. Spreti, Enciclopedia Storico-Nobiliare Italiana, II, pp. 131–33; Anderson, Royal Genealogies, p. 683.
53. Dixon, Pauline, pp. 89–90, 107–108, 154, 166 and 201–204.
54. Spreti, Enciclopedia Storico-Nobiliare Italiana, II, pp. 131–33.
55. Ibid., Almanach de Gotha, 1914, pp. 284–90.
56. Ibid.
57. Spreti, Enciclopedia Storico-Nobillare Italiana, II, pp. 131–33; "Borghese," in Libro d'Oro I–XXI. Prince Scipione Borghese (1871–1927) demonstrated the international importance of the automobile. In 1907 he traveled from Peking to Paris. The auto trip

took sixty days. He went a distance of 16,000 kilometers, of which only 4,000 were on real roads.
58. Pastor, XXV, pp. 71–72; also see Cascioli, Memorie storiche di Poli pp. 236ff.
59. "Torlonia" in Libro d'Oro I–XXI; Almanach de Gotha, 1880, p. 332.
60. Rendina, p. 680.
61. Pastor, XXVII, p. 54.
62. Litta, "Ludovisi di Bologna," Tome 14. Refer to Alessandro Ludovisi (Pope Gregory XV), his brother Orazio and Orazio's children: Lodovico, Ippolita and Niccolò.
63. Pastor, XXVII, p. 61.
64. Litta, "Ludovisi di Bologna," Tome 14.
65. Litta, "Orsini di Roma," Tome 9. Refer to Flavio Orsini of Bracciano and his wife Ippolita.
66. Litta. "Boncompagni di Bologna," Tome 2. Refer to Gregorio Boncompagni, his wife Ippolita and Antonio Boncompani, Gregorio's brother.
67. "Boncompagni Ludovisi" in Libro d'Oro, I–XXI; Almamach de Gotha, 1914, pp. 282–84.

II: From Barberini to Corsini*

68. Pastor, XXIX, pp. 43ff.
69. Pastor, XXVIII, p. 48.
70. Ibid., p. 43.
71. Ibid., pp. 44–45 and 49.
72. Ibid., pp. 39–42.
73. Ibid., pp. 42 and 47.
74. Pastor, XXIX, pp. 499ff.
75. Rendina, p. 685.
76. Pastor, XXVIII, pp. 46 and 48.
77. Ibid., p. 45.
78. Litta, "Colonna," Tome 2. Refer to Filippo Colonna of Paliano and his daughter Anna.
79. Pastor, XXIX, pp. 383–400.
80. Pastor, XXX, p. 56.
81. Ibid., pp. 62–64; Rendina, p. 688.

*In this section papal families such as the Barberini, Pamfili, Chigi, Rospigliosi, Altieri, Odescalchi, Ottoboni, Pignatelli, Albani and Corsini are not among those which were included by Pompeo Litta in his monumental work. Litta's account of the Orsini family in Tome 9 gives information about Pope Benedict XIII (Pietro Francesco Orsini). Previously noted sources, such as those by Pastor, Redina and Ranke, provided much of the core material for the chapter and substantial genealogical material was located in the Libro d'Oro della Nobilità Italiana, Almanach de Gotha, Lorenz's Genealogisches Handbuch, Spreti's Enciclopedia Storico-Nobiliare Italiana and Tettoni and Saladini's Teatro Araldico.
     Volumes XXVIII and XXIX in Pastor's The History of the Popes startles the imagination with its passages on the avidity of the Barberini family. The machinations of Donna Olimpia Maidalchini, sister-in-law of Pope Innocent X, are dramatically presented in his Volume XXX, in Ranke's Volume III, and in Rendina on pages 687–93. It was Donna Olimpia who let the pope's dead body sit for three days in a corner without proper burial.
     Biographical and genealogical material on the Chigi family is well-illustrated in Frittelli's Albero Genealogico della famiglia Chigi; the Odescalchi are delineated in Edmond de Syrmia's At the Head of Nations. The Pignatelli family, with genealogical tables, are described in volume 8 of Tettoni and Saladini's Teatro Araldico. The Pignatelli and Carafa family are jointly investigated because of striking similarities between these two noble Neapolitan families. The Carafa family is in Tome 17 of the Litta series, published in 1902 and edited by Luciano Basadonna. The Istituto della Enciclopedia Italiana's Dizionario biografico degli Italiani is an excellent source for the biographies of such family members as the Corsini who contributed so much to the political life of Tuscany and Italy. This dictionary, part of which is published and part of which has been placed on microfiche, contains substantial material on the life of individuals who have made historical or cultural contributions in Italy and as well gives an impressive bibliography at the end of each entry.

82. Litta, "d'Este," Tome 5. Refer to Francesco I, de'Este, Duke of Modena, his wife Lucrezia and their descendants.

83. Lorenz, *Genealogisches Handbuch*, N.G. 2.

84. Litta, "Colonna," Tome 2. Refer to Giulio Cesare Colonna, his wife Cornelia and descendants.

85. Ibid.

86. *Almanach de Gotha*, 1914, pp. 318–23; "Colonna" in *Libro d'Oro* I–XXI.

87. Pastor, XXX, pp. 57–64, 94 and 371.

88. Litta, "Farnesi," Tome 12. Refer to Ranuccio Farnese II, Duke of Parma.

89. Ranke, *The History of the Popes*, III, pp. 392–94.

90. Pastor, XXX, pp. 38–40.

91. Rendina, pp. 691–92.

92. Ranke, III, pp. 35 and 396.

93. Pastor, XXX, p. 38.

94. Ranke, III, p. 392.

95. Rendina, p. 693.

96. Pastor, XXX, p. 46.

97. Ranke, III, p. 36.

98. An account of the ducati obtained by Donna Olimpia is recorded in Cavalier Giustiniani's 1652 report in Ranke, III, p. 396.

99. Rendina, p. 693.

100. Pastor, XXX, pp. 389–400.

101. Rendina, p. 690.

102. Spreti, *Enciclopedia Storico-Nobiliare Italiana*, II, p. 632.

103. Ibid; *Almanach de Gotha*, 1829 and 1836; Tettoni and Saladini, *Teatro Araldico*, 4, "Doria"; Stokvis, *Manuel d'Histoire*, Band III, Chapter XII, Table 70.

104. Lorenz, Table 32.

105. Litta, "d'Este," Tome 5. Refer to Ercole III d'Este and his wife Maria Theresa.

106. Litta, "Savelli," Tome 15. Refer to Giulio and his son Bernardino Savelli.

107. Ibid.

108. Pastor, XXIV, p. 419.

109. Ranke, III, p. 47.

110. Litta, "Colonna," Tome 2, Stigliano branch.

111. Ibid., Paliano branch.

112. "Colonna" in *Libro d'Oro*, XV, pp. 426–32.

113. *Almanach de Gotha*, 1914, p. 319.

114. Litta, "Colonna," Tome 2. Stigliano branch.

115. Almanach de Gotha, 1914, pp. 320–22.

116. "Colonna" in *Libro d'Oro*, XV, pp. 429–31.

117. Pastor, XXXI, p. 16.

118. Ibid., p. 59.

119. Pastor, VIII, pp. 117–18.

120. Pastor, XXXI, pp. 19–28.

121. Frittelli, *Albero Genealogico della Famiglia Chigi*, pp. 137–41.

122. Ibid., pp. 142–50.

123. Almanach de Gotha, 1914, pp. 305–306; *Libro d'Oro* I–XXI; *Elenco Ufficiale della Nobilità Italiana*, p. 232; Frittelli, p. 145.

124. Ibid., "Albani" in *Almanach de Gotha*, 1846.

125. "Chigi Albani della Rovere" in *Libro d'oro* I–XXI.

126. Frittelli, p. XXV.

127. Istituto della Enciclopedia Italiana, *Dizionario biografica degli Italiani* 24, "Agostino Chigi" (1464–1520), p. 735.

128. Girelli, *Le Terre del Chigi ad Ariccia*, p. 8.

129. Ibid., p. 10; (Istituto della Enciclopedia Dizionario biografica degli Italiani, Italiana), 24, "Agostino Chigi" (1771–1855), p. 758.

130. Pastor, XXXI, p. 430.

131. Litta, "Pallavicino," Tome 8, Gallicano branch.

132. "Rospigliosi" in *Almanach de Gotha*, 1914, pp. 453–54; "Rospigliosi" in *Libro d'Oro*, XV, pp. 1313–14.

133. "Rospigliosi" and "Pallavicini" in *Almanach de Gotha*, 1944.

134. Pastor, XXXI, pp. 444–46.

135. Litta, "Colonna," Tome 2. Refer to descendants of Egidio and Tarquinia Colonna, Carbognano branch.

136. Pastor, XXXI, p. 401.

137. "Altieri" in *Almanach de Gotha*, 1914, pp. 258–259; Spreti, *Enciclopedia Storico-Nobiliare Italiana*, I, p. 365; "Altieri" in *Libro d'Oro*, XV, pp. 32–33; McNaughton, *The Book of Kings* II, pp. 541–42.

138. Syrmia, *At the Head of Nations*, pp. 70 and 78.

139. "Odescalchi" in *Almanach de Gotha*, 1914, pp. 404–405.

140. Litta, "Boncompagni di Bologna," Tome 2; Spreti, *Enciclopedia Storico-Nobiliare Italiana* pp. 883–84.

141. "Odescalchi" in *Libro d'Oro*, I–XXI.

142. Pastor, XXXII, p. 539.

143. Ibid., p. 536–38.

144. Litta, "Boncompagni di Bologna," Tome 2.

145. "Boncompagni Ludovisi" in *Almanach de Gotha*, 1915, pp. 282–84; see also "Boncompagni-Ludovisi-Ottoboni" in Spreti, *Enciclopedia Storico-Nobiliare Italiana*, II.

146. "Boncompagni Ludovisi" in *Libro d'Oro*, XV, pp. 199–201; *Almanach de Gotha*, 1943.

147. Litta, "Carafa," Tome 17. Refer to Luigi Carafa of Stigliano, his daughter Maria and her husband Fabrizio Carafa.

148. Tettoni and Saladini, 8, "Pignatelli," pp. 1172–78, and "Tagliavia-Aragona-Cortez."

149. *Archivio biografico italiana*, pp. 237–38.

150. Litta, "Carafa," Tome 17; Litta, "Caracciolo di Napoli," Tome 19.

151. Spreti, *Enciclopedia Storico-Nobiliare Italiana*, II, pp. 312–13.

152. Litta, "Carafa," Tome 17.

153. Ibid. Refer to Giovan Battista Carafa (Roccella branch) and his wife Lucrezia Borgia d'Aragona. Refer also to Antonio Carafa, son of Luigi and

Isabella Gonzaga Carafa (Stigliano-Bracciano branch), and his wife Elena Aldobrandini.

154. Pastor, XXXIV, pp. 128 and 343–45.

155. Litta, "Orsini di Roma," Tome 9. Refer to Gravina branch of the family.

156. "Orsini" in *Almanach de Gotha*, 1915, p. 404 and 1944; "Orsini" in *Libro d'Oro* I–XXI.

157. "Orsini" in *Almanach de Gotha*, 1915, p. 404 and 1944; "Orsini" in *Libro d'Oro* I–XXI. *Libro d'Oro*, XXI, pp. 234–35, states that Domenico Napoleone Orsini, born in 1948, is the twenty-third duke of Gravina and is the present head of the family. In the 1990s he and his family were living in Paris, France.

158. Spreti, *Enciclopedia Storico-Nobiliare Italiana*, II, p. 552.

159. Pastor, XXXIV, p. 359.

160. Spreti, *Enciclopedia Storico-Nobiliare Italiana*, II, pp. 552–55; see also Litta, "Colonna," Tome 2.

161. Ibid.

162. "Corsini" in *Almanach de Gotha*, 1915, pp. 323–24; "Corsini" in *Libro d'Oro* I–XXI.

163. Spreti, *Enciclopedia Storico-Nobiliare Italiana*, II, pp. 552–55. Refer to the *Dizionario biografico degli Italiani* by the Istituto della Enciclopedia Italiana for information on members of the Corsini family.

Five: The Papacy After 1740— The Modern Period*

1. Paster, *The History of the Popes* XXXVI, p. 41, and XXXVII, p. 361.

2. Paster, Vol. XXVIII, pp. 527–37.

3. Rendina, *I papi*, p. 743.

4. Pastor, XXXIX, pp. 35–36.

5. Ibid., pp. 36–37.

6. Rendina. pp. 763–64.

7. Ibid., p. 786.

8. Wynn, *Keepers of the Keys*, p. 152.

9. Murphy, *La Popessa*, p. 250.

10. Peter Nichols, *Politics of the Vatican*, as quoted in Vaillancourt. *Papal Power*, p. 249.

11. Vaillancourt, pp. 68 and 250.

12. Corraco Pallenberg, as reported in Murphy, p. 158.

13. Murphy, pp. 175–179, 203–209, 285 and 289.

14. Wynn, pp. 26–27.

15. Vaillancourt, p. 68.

16. Murphy, pp. 285–286.

Six: Papal Dynasties and Noble Houses†

I: The Italian Houses and the Papacy— A Retrospective

1. Mann, *The Lives of the Popes*, 1, pp. 19 and 177; Kelly, *The Oxford Dictionary of Popes*, p. 65. Rendina, in *I papi* (p. 142), has Agapitus I and Felix IV (526–30) in the same family. This is an error; the Roman Agapitus I belonged to the same family as Felix III (483–92).

2. Mann, p. 235. Mann refers to him as Stephen V. The popes with the name Stephen often have a dual numbering because Stephen II (752) was elected pope but never consecrated. Kelly, p. 109.

3. Rendina, p. 832.

*While Pastor and Rendina are the primary sources for this chapter, the contemporary period also utilizes such works as Wynn's Keepers of the Keys: John XXIII, Paul VI and John Paul II, Murphy's La Popessa, and Vaillancourt's Papal Power. All of these books give a critical analysis of the more recent events in papal history. This work does not deal with the present Pope John Paul II (who is not Italian) and his administration even though a good deal has been written about him. A quick understanding of recent pontiffs can be obtained by a reading of Kelly's scholarly study, The Oxford Dictionary of Popes.

The major source for genealogical information dealing with the families of the popes from northern Italy was Famiglie Nobili in Lombardia, IV. The della Chiesa family is listed in Libro d'Oro della Nobiltà Italiana, XV (1965–68), p. 393, as well as in other volumes of this book, issued every four years. The princely Pacelli family is listed in that same volume. In 1941, Victor Emmanuel III conferred the title of Marchese to the descendants of Francesco Pacelli, brother of Pope Pius XII.

†Chapter Six uses many of the sources already mentioned and described elsewhere in the book, especially in chapters One and Two. Sources such as Ratti, Lorenz, Kircheri and de' Crescenzi Romano contain genealogical tables and information about the families of the popes. This chapter, particularly in the first section, places the study in retrospect and at the same time looks at the relationships among the papal dynasties. The second section places its emphasis on some of the descendants, many of whom are members of European royal families that exist at the present time. Further members of the families of the popes are in noble as well as in untitled families throughout the world. However, it should be recognized that it would be impossible to note all the descendants of these prominent Italian, papal families. Their blood lines cross national boundaries, and all of their offspring are too numerable to count or ascertain.

Genealogical sources such as Litta and Spreti, along with Lorenz's Genealogisches Handbuch, de' Crescenzi's Anfiteatro Romano, Vrignault's Généalogie de la Maison de Bourbon, Tettoni and Saladini's Teatro Araldico and Burke's Royal Families of the World, are among the primary ones for this chapter. Burke's study lists all descendants of specific royal and titled families, including some papal families, from the seventeenth century to the present time. Contemporary family histories are found in the Almanach de Gotha and the Libro d'Oro della Nobiltà Italiana. They have served the author throughout most of this study. Litta's study is the most comprehensive of all since it not only includes genealogical tables but also significant biographical information. (Continued on page 249.)

4. Ratti, *Della Famiglia Conti di Segni*, p. 217; Zazzera in his history of the Conti says that they were descended from the House of Augusta Ottavia as reported in *La storia delle famiglie romane* by Teodoro Amayden (p. 332).

5. Prospero Colonna, *I Colonna dalle origini all 'inizio del secoio XIX*, p. 1.

6. Antipopes were popes who were elected or who established themselves as popes contrary to another who was elected in accordance to church law. This definition does not preclude the fact that many antipopes were of the opinion that they had been legitimately elected. Certainly the antipope reigned in opposition in another pope causing a schism in the church. It was this result which made an antipope a power to be reckoned with (as antipopes were often supported by kings, emperors, states or by influential families or clergy members) and which caused considerable dissension and conflict within the church.

7. Lorenz, *Genealogisches Handbuch*, tables 10, 10c, 13 and 35.

8. Kircheri, *Historia Eustachio-Mariana*, Foglio 77.

9. de' Crescenzi Romano, *Anfiteatro Romano*, p. 314.

10. When the family of King Ferdinando I of the House of Aragon(a) (1431–94) was forced out of Naples at the end of the 1490s, its influence, of course, decreased, and the papal families of the period no longer expressed interest in marrying into this royal but powerless Neapolitan family.

11. While the dukes of Gandia were descendants of Juan Borgia, there were many others as well. One of Juan's daughters married into the Moscoso family and their son Pablo de Moscoso settled in Peru. Paolo de Moscoso's great-great-granddaughter Mercedes de Moscoso married Joseph Joachim de Tristán, and their son Mariano had a daughter Flora de Tristán y Moscoso. Flora was a radical feminist and author of *The Emancipation of Women*. She married André Chazal. Their daughter Aline Chazal was the wife of Clovis Gauguin, and their son was the French painter Paul Gauguin (1848–1903), who had many descendants. Gauguin was a direct descendant of Pope Alexander VI. Refer to David Sweetman, *Paul Gauguin, A Life* (N.Y.: Simon & Schuster, 1995) pp. 5–28.

II: The Italian Houses and European Nobility

12. Litta, *Famiglia celebri Italiane*, tomes 4, 7 and 12 on the Visconti, Medici, della Rovere and Farnese families. Corvo in *A History of the Borgias* gives a fairly good account of the genealogy of the Borgia family.

13. de' Crescenzi Romano, Parte Prima, pp. 311–39.

14. Refer to Burke's, *Royal Families of the World*, I.

15. de' Crescenzi Romano, Parte Prima, pp. 311–39.

16. Lorenz, *Genealogisches Handbuch*, tables 32, NG 2: Tettoni and Saladini, *Teatro Araldico* 4, unpaginated.

17. Refer to Sedgwick, *The House of Guise*.

18. Vrignault, *Généalogie de la Maison de Bourbon*, pp. 13–27.

19. Ibid.

20. Lorenz, tables 32, 34, 35, 44, NG 34.

21. Ibid., tables 32, 34, NG 21, NG 2.

22. Refer to Burke's, *Royal Families of the World*, I.

23. Ibid; *Almanach de Gotha*, all volumes: *Libro d'Oro* I–XXI; Burke's, *Genealogical and Heralic History of the Peerage, Baronetage, and Knightage*; Debrett's, *Peerage, Baronetage, Knightage and Companionage*; Doyle, *The Official Baronage of England*.

24. The papal treasure, acquired during the pontificate of Innocent X (1644–55), who was a member of the Pamfili family, was confiscated by his sister-in-law Olimpia. Her descendants married into the Borghese, Ludovisi, Barberini, Savelli, Cibo, Facchinetti, Colonna and Conti families. Her son Camillo Pamfili was the second husband of the heiress Olimpia Aldobrandini (d. 1681) whose first husband was Paolo Borghese, grandnephew of Pope Paul V. Her children from these two members of papal families married into numerous other families of past and succeeding popes. One of Olimpia and Camillo's daughters, Anna, married Gian Andrea Doria IV. She brought with her some of the Pamfili inheritance, and the family took the name Doria-Pamfili-Landi. Members of this family married into the Orsini, Chigi, Colonna and Carafa families. Olimpia and Camillo Pamfili had a son Giambattista

(Continued.)

The descendants of King Charles II of England are numerous. James Doyle in The Official Baronage of England *lists the names of the sons of that king with biographical data. Burke's* Genealogical and Heraldic History *has been published since 1826, and Debrett's works on British nobility go back even farther. Both present a detailed genealogical record of each aristocratic British family so that they can be traced. The* Almanach de Gotha *records German, French, Italian, English, etc., royal and noble families. The dukes of Richmond and Gordon, descendants of King Charles II, for example, are duly noted in the third part of the* Almanach.

In the chapter's third section, the author has scrutinized the Borghese as a pertinent example of a family which epitomizes the innumerable and intricate relationships between these papal families — although the Colonna, Orsini and Boncompagni-Ludovisi would serve much the same purpose. The genealogical tables of these families are located in Appendix A.

whose daughter Olimpia was the wife of Filippo
Colonna. It was their daughter Agnese Colonna who
married Prince Camillo Borghese.

25. Spreti, *Enciclopedia Storico-Nobiliare Italiana*
II, pp. 131–33. Refer also to *Almanach de Gotha*,
1836 and 1914–44; and *Libro d'Oro* I–XXI.

26. Spreti, *Enciclopedia Storico-Nobiliare Italiana*
II, pp. 131–33. Refer also to *Almanach de Gotha*,
1836 and 1914–44; and *Libro d'Oro* I–XXI.

27. *Almanach de Gotha*, 1880 and 1914–44. *Libro
d'Oro* I–XXI. Refer to both "Borghese" and "Torlonia".

Seven: Papal Families and Nepotism*

1. Guicciardini, *The History of Italy*, p. 149.
2. Ibid., p. 163.
3. Ibid., p. 321.
4. Pastor, *The History of the Popes* XXIV, p. 418.
5. Ranke, *The History of the Popes* III, pp. 12 and
18.

6. Pastor, XXXII, p. 637.
7. Ranke, III, p. 13.
8. Ibid., p. 14.
9. Ibid., p. 15. Ranke states that Zagarolo was
bought from the Farnese family, but that seems to be
an error. Zagarolo had long belonged to the Colonna
family before that family was forced to sell the dukedom to the Lodovisis. In 1668 Zagarolo was sold
by the Ludovisi family to Giambattista Rospigliosi
(1646–1722), whose wife was the heiress Maria
Camilla Pallavicini. In Zagarolo is the Villa Rospigliosi. Giambattista, nephew of Pope Clement IX,
was created a prince of the Holy Roman Empire in
1658. Zagarolo exemplifies the acquired territory that
went from one papal family into the hands of
another.

10. Ibid., pp. 16–18.
11. Pastor, XXXII, pp. 637–38.
12. Pastor, XXX, p. 372.
13. Pastor, XXIV, p. 419.
14. Ranke, III, p. 45
15. Pastor, XXIX, p. 377.

*This chapter on "Papal Families and Nepotism" is one that emphasizes The History of the Popes by Ranke and by Pastor as its
primary sources because they constitute the definitive works on the subject. Both Ranke and Pastor were instrumental in opening
the Vatican Library so that sources, previously unknown, could be used by scholars. They saw the need to broaden the perspective
on a subject long closed to scrutinization and investigation. Guicciardini's History of Italy, which had not been translated into
English until recently, was a revelation for those who wished to know firsthand about the Renaissance pontiffs. His observations
on these popes is based upon his experiences and graphically demonstrates their insidious and pernicious manipulations to enhance
family members.
    Pastor and Ranke preferred firsthand documents rather than secondary sources, and their studies were indeed eye-openers for
the world. However, Pastor's forty-volume work is often ignored because of its length, and frequently the language in the translated version of the Ranke study sounds archaic. But it is what they had to say that stimulates the mind and opens new avenues
in the papal cloister.

Selected Sources

Alberi, E. *Documenti sull' assedio di Firenze, 1529–1530*. Firenze: Molini, 1840.

Almanach de Gotha, Annuaire généalogique, diplomatique et statistique. [Selected annuals]. Gotha: Justus Perthes, 1819, 1830, 1836, 1846, 1848, 1880, 1890, 1914, 1915, 1917, 1933, 1939, 1943 and 1944.

Almanacco nobiliare italiano. Under the direction of dott. prof. Conte Temistocle Bertucci, Araldista Istoriografo Accademico d' Arcadia. Milano: Ed. Dora, 1961. [A supplement, *Supplemento a carattere storico ed internationale dell'Almanacco nobiliare italiano*, also edited by Bertucci, was published by the Istoriografo Accademico d'Arcadia, in Roma, s.e., 1965.]

Ameyden, Teodoro. *La storia delle famiglie romane*. Bologna: Forni Ed., 1967.

Analecta Bollandiana. *Vita et miracula Sancti Petri Caelestini Auctore coaevo*. Tome IX. Brussels, 1890.

Anderson, James. *Royal Genealogies or the Genealogical Tables of Emperors, Kings, and Princes from Adam to There Time*. London: James Bellenham, 1736.

Annuario della nobiltà italiana. Pisa: Giornale Araldico, 1891.

Annuario della nobiltà italiana. Anno XVII. Bari: Direzione del Giornale Araldico e dell'Annuario della nobiltà italiana, 1895.

Archivio biografico italiano [Italian Biographical Archive]. Microfiche edition. Ed. Tommaso Nappo [(1987–1990): 1046 microfiches; Series II (1991–1994): 850 microfiches].

Baronius, Caesar. Continued by Raynaldus, *Annales ecclesiastici*, 1460.

Bellonci, Maria. *The Life and Times of Lucrezia Borgia*. Trans. Bernard and Barbara Wall. New York: Harcourt, Brace, 1953.

Boase, T. S. R. *Boniface VIII*. London: Constable & Co., 1933.

Boschetti, Anton Ferrante. *I Cataloghi dell'opera di Pompeo Litta "Famiglie celebri italiane."* Modena: Società Tipografica Modenese, 1930.

Brun, Guillaume. *Uzeste et Clemente V*. Bordeaux: [Soc. archéologique de Bordeaux] Cadoret, 1894.

Burchard, John. *Diarium, 1483–1506*. Vols. I–III. Ed. L. Thuasne. Paris: E. Leroux, 1883–1885.

Burchard, John. *At the Court of the Borgia*. Ed. Geoffrey Parker. London: The Folio Society, 1963.

Burke's Peerage. *Genealogical and Heraldic History of the Peerage, Baronetage and Knightage*. 104th edition. Ed. Peter Townsend. London: Burke's Peerage Limited, 1967.

Burke's Peerage. *Royal Families of the World*. Vol. I: Europe and Latin America. Ed. Hugh Montgomery-Massingberd. London: Burke's Peerage Ltd., 1977.

Burke's Peerage. "The Roche Ancestry of the Princess of Wales." London: Burke's Peerage Ltd., 1991.

Burke's Peerage. "The Spencer Ancestry of the Princess of Wales." London: Burke's Peerage Ltd., 1991.

Caetani, Gelasio. *Caietanorum genealogia*. Perugia: Unione Tipografica Cooperativa, 1920.

Calvi, Felice. *Famiglie notabili milanesi*. Milano: Antonio Vallardi Editore, 1881.

Cascioli, Giuseppe, Canonico. *Memorie storiche di Poli*. Roma: Editrice della "Vera Roma," 1896.

Chaffanjon, Arnaud. *Le Petit Gotha Illustré*, 1968.

Chenaye-Desbois et Badier. *Dictionnaire de la Noblesse de la Chenaye-Desbois et Badier*. Paris: Schlesinger, 1864.

Cloulas, Ivan. *The Borgias*. Trans. Gilda Roberts. New York: Franklin Watts, 1989.

Colonna, Prospero. *I Colonna dalle origini all'inizio del secolo XIX*. Roma: Istituto Nazionale Medico Farmacologico "Serono," 1927.

Corvo, Frederick Baron. *A History of the Borgias*. New York: Carlton House, 1901.

de'Crescenzi Romano, Gio. Pietro. *Anfiteatro Romano*. Milano: Gio. Battista e Giulio Cesare Fratelli Malatesta, Stampatori (Parte Prima), 1714.

Debrett's Peerage. *Peerage, Baronetage, Knightage, and Companionage*. Ed. C. F. J. Hankinson. 160th edition. London: Odhams Press, 1962.

Debrett's Peerage. *Peerage and Baronetage.* Ed. Patrick Montague-Smith. London: Debrett's Peerage Ltd., 1980.

Dionigi, D. Marco. *Genealogia di Casa Conti.* Parma: Vietti, 1653.

Dizionario Enciclopedico Italiano. Under the direction of Aldo Ferrabino. Roma: Istituto dell'Enciclopedia Italiana, 1970.

Dixon, Pierson. *Pauline, Napoleon's Favourite Sister.* New York: David McKay, 1964.

Doyle, James E. *The Official Baronage of England.* 3 volumes. London: Longmans, Green and Co., 1886.

Dugast Rouillé, Michel. *Les Maisons Souveraines de l'Autriche.* Paris: Printed by the author, 1967.

Dykmans, Marc. "D'Innocent III à Boniface VIII: Histore des Contes et des Annibaldi." *Institut historique belge de Rome, Bulletin* 45 (1975).

Elenco Ufficiale della Nobiltà Italiana. Roma: Presidenza del Consiglio dei Ministri, 1937.

Enciclopedia Italiana. Under the direction of Giovanni Gentile. Roma: Istituto della Enciclopedia Italiana, 1929–36.

Erlanger, Rachel. *Lucrezia Borgia.* New York: Hawthorne Books, Inc., 1978.

Famiglie Nobili in Lombardia. (Tavole Genealogiche.) 4 volumes. Milano: Arti Grafiche E. Milli, 1964.

Foy, Felician A., ed. *1995 Catholic Almanac.* Huntington, Ind.: Our Sunday Visitor, 1994.

Frittelli, Ugo. *Albero Genealogico della Famiglia Chigi.* Siena: Stab. Arti Grafiche Lazzeri, 1922.

Galletti, D. Pierluigi. *Del Vestarario della Santa Romana Chiesa.* Roma: Giovanni Generoso Salomoni, 1758.

Genealogisches Handbuch Des Adels. Bands II–IV. Glucksburg/Ostsee: Verlag von C. A. Starke, 1953, 1955, 1956.

Girelli, Angelo Maria. *Le Terre dei Chigi ad Ariccia Sec. XIX.* Milano: Casa Ed. Dott. A. Giuffrè, 1983.

Giulini, Alessandro. *Nozze Borromeo nel Quattrocento.* Milano: Tipografia Editrice L. F. Cogliati, 1910.

Giulini, Alessandro. *Lo stemma dei Borromeo.* Milano: Stabilimento Pontificio d'Arti Grafiche Sacre A. Bertarelli, 1910.

Giustiniani, Antonio. *Dispacci.* 1st and 2nd vols. Firenze: Successori Le Monnier, 1876.

Gregorovius, Ferdinand. *History of the City of Rome in the Middle Ages.* Trans. Mrs. Gustavus W. Hamilton. 8 volumes. London: G. Bell, 1903–1912.

Gregorovius, Ferdinand. *Lucretia Borgia: According to Original Documents and Correspondence of Her Day.* Trans. John Leslie Grant. London, 1903.

Gregorovius, Ferdinand. *Lucrèce Borgia.* Traduction de l'Allemand par Paul Regnaud, Tome second. Paris: Sandoz et Fischbacher, Editeurs, 1876.

Guicciardini, Francesco. *History of Florence.* Trans. Mario Domandi. New York: Harper & Row, 1970.

Guicciardini, Francesco. *The History of Italy.* Trans. Sidney Alexander. New York: The Macmillan Co., 1969.

Guillemain, Bernard. *La Cour Pontificale d'Avignon (1309–1376): Etude d'une Société.* Paris: Editions E. De Boccard, 1962.

Infessura, Stefano. *Diario della città di Roma di Stefano Infessura.* Nuova edizione a cura di Oreste Tommasini. Roma: Forzani, 1890.

Istituto della Enciclopedia Italiana. *Dizionario biografico degli Italiani.* Roma: Società Grafica Romana, 1970–83.

Isenburg, Wilhelm Karl Prinz von. *Stammtafeln zur Geschichte der Europaeischen Staaten.* Marburg: Verlag von J. A. Stargardt, 1965.

Kelly, J. N. D. *The Oxford Dictionary of Popes.* Oxford: Oxford Univ. Press, 1986.

Kircheri, Athanasii, (Kircherius, Athanasius). *Historia Eustachio-Mariana.* Roma: Varese: 1665. (Storia e genealogia dei Conti Tusculani)

Lea, Henry Charles. *History of Sacerdotal Celibacy in the Christian Church.* London: Watts, 1932.

Il Libro della Nobiltà Lombarda. Milano: Distribuzione Storica Lombarda, 1976–78.

Il Libro d'Oro del Campidogilo. Vol. 1. Roma: Tip. della "Vera Roma" di Enrico Filiziani, 1893.

Libro d'Oro della Nobiltà Italiana. 21 volumes, Vol. 1 (1910)–Vol XXI (1990–93). Roma: Collegio Araldico.

Lindeman, O. *Vorstenschemering: De Families, De Onderlinge Verhoudingen, De Huwelijken, De Paleizen En Hoven En De Val Der Europese Dynastieen Met Wat Daaran Voorafging En Wat Overbleef.* Zaltbommel: Europese Bibliotheek, 1974.

Litta, Pompeo. *Famiglie celebri italiane.* 19 volumes. Milano: Paolo Emilio Giusti, 1819–1881. [The first volume is entitled *Famiglie celebri d'Italia*, Milano, 1819. Litta died on August 17, 1852. Other authors continued with the second part from 1852 to 1883. They were Cav. Federico Odorici, Conte Luigi Passerini, Cav. Federico Stefani, Cav. Francesco Di Mauro di Polvica and Professor Costantino Coda.]

Litta, Pompeo. Ed. Luciano Basadonna, 2nd series. Napoli: Stab. tipo. litogr. Richter & Co., 1902–1923. [This work was continued by Luigi Passerini, Federico Odorici and Federico Stefani.]

Liudprand of Cremona. *Works.* Trans. F. A. Wright. London, 1930.

Longhi, Giuseppe Marchetti. "I Papareschi e I Romani." *Le grandi famiglie romane.* Roma: Istituto di Studi Romani, 1947.

Longhi, Giuseppe Marchetti. "Gli Stefaneschi." *Le grandi famiglie romane.* Roma: Istituto di Studi Romani, 1954.

Lorenz, Ottokar. *Genealogisches Handbuch der Europäischen Staatengeschichte.* Stuttgart & Berlin: J. G. Cotta'sche Buchhandlung Nachfolger, 1908.

MacDonald, A. J. *Hildebrand: A Life of Gregory VII.* London: Methuen, 1932.

Mallet, Michael. *The Borgias.* New York: Barnes & Noble, 1969.

Mann, Horace K. *The Lives of the Popes.* 18 volumes. London: Kegan, Paul, Trench, Trubner, 1925.

Mannucci, Conte Silvio. *Nobiliario e blasonario del Regno d'Italia.* Roma: Collegio Araldico.

McNaughton, Arnold M. *The Book of Kings: A Royal Genealogy.* 3 volumes. New York: Quadrangle, The N.Y. Times Book Co., 1973.

Memorie delle famiglie nobili. Napoli: De Angelis e figlio, 1875.

Mollat, G. *The Popes at Avignon, 1305–1378.* London: Thomas Nelson & Sons, 1963.

Murphy, Paul I. *La Popessa.* New York: Warner Books, Inc., 1983.

Nobiltà italiana. Roma: Collegio Araldico, 1910.

Paschini, Pio. *Le grandi famiglie romane, "I Chigi."* Roma: Reale Istituto di Studi Romani, 1946.

Paschini, Pio. *Le grandi famiglie romane, "I Colonna."* Roma: Istituto di Studi Romani, 1954.

Pastor, Ludwig. *The History of the Popes, from the Close of the Middle Ages.* Ed. Frederick Ignatius Antrobus. 6th edition. 40 volumes. Liechtenstein: Nendeln, 1909.

Picotti, G. B. *Della supposta parentèla ebraica di Gregorio VI e Gregorio VII.* n.p.: Archivio Storico Italiano, 1942.

Powell, James, M. *Innocent III, Vicar of Christ or Lord of the World.* Boston: D. C. Heath, 1963.

Prinz, Joachim. *Popes from the Ghetto.* New York: Horizon Press, 1966.

Ranke, Leopold von. *The History of the Popes.* Trans. E. Fowler. 3 volumes. Revised edition. New York: The Colonial Press, 1901.

Ratti, Nicola. *Della famiglia Sforza.* Roma: Presso il Salomoni, 1795. [It is in four parts and includes "Della famiglia Conti di Segni" in Part 2.]

Ratti, Nicola. *L'autenticità degli alberi genealogici, Primogenitura Conti.* Roma: Puccinelli, 1821.

Ravegnani Morosini, Mario. *Signorie e principati.* Rimini: Maggioli Ed., 1984.

Rendina, Claudio. *I papi, Storia e segreti.* Roma: Newton Compton Editori, 1983.

Robinson, I. S. *The Papacy, 1073–1198.* Cambridge: Cambridge Univ. Press, 1990.

della Rovere, Paolo dei Marchesi. *Memorie Istoriche alla nobilissima e antichissima famiglia Della Rovere.* Torino: Tipografia Italiana di F. Martinengo, 1858.

Ruvigny, Marquis de. *The Titled Nobility of Europe.* London: Harrison & Sons, 1914.

Saba, Agostino. *Storia della chiesa.* 4 volumes. Torino: Unione Tipografica Editrice Torinese, 1954.

Sabatini, Rafael. *The Life of Caesar Borgia.* New York: Brentano's, n.d.

Sansovino, Francesco. *Della Origine et de' Fatti delle famiglie illustri d'Italia.* Venice: Altobello Salicatu, 1582. [Libro Primo]

Sanudo, Marino. *I Diarii.* vol.s 1–7. Venezia: F. Stefani, 1879.

Sedgwick, Henry Dwight. *The House of Guise.* New York: Bobbs-Merrill, 1938.

Sternfeld, Richard. *Der Kardinal Johann Gaetan Orsini (Papst Nikolaus III), 1244–1277.* Berlin: E. Ebering, 1905.

Spreti, Vittorio. *Enciclopedia Storico-Nobiliare Italiana.* Milano: Enciclopedia Storico-Nobiliare Italiana, Arnaldo Forni Editore, 1928–36.

Spreti, Vittorio. *Enciclopedia Storico-Nobiliare Italiana.* Appendice Part I. Milano: Soc. An. Stirpe, 1935.

Stokvis, A. M. H. J. *Manuel d'Histoire de Généalogie et de Chronologie de Tous Les Etats du Globe, Depuis les Temps les Plus Reculés Jusqu'a nos Jours.* 4 volumes. B. M. Israel (H. V. Boekhandel & Antiquariat), 1966.

Stroll, Mary. *The Jewish Pope.* Leiden: E. J. Brill, 1987.

Syrmia, Edmond de. *At the Head of Nations: The Rise of the Papal and Princely House of Odescalchi.* Pleasant Valley, N.Y.: Cyclopedia Publishing Company, 1978.

Tettoni, L., and F. Saladini. *Teatro Araldico ovvero raccolta generale delle armi ed insegne gentilizie delle più illustri e nobili casate che esisterono un tempo e tuttora fioriscono in tutta l'Italia.* 8 volumes. Milano: Tipi di Claudio Wilmant. 1848 [Unpaginated.]

Thibault, Paul R. *Pope Gregory VI.* Landham: Univ. Press of the America, 1986.

Vaillancourt, Jean-Guy, *Papal Power.* Berkeley: Univ. of California Press, 1980.

Varaldo, Ottavio. *Compendio della Casa della Rovere di Bernardino Baldi.* Savona: D. Bertolotto, 1888.

Villiers, Hugo. *Debrett's Book of the Royal Family.* New York: Viking Press, 1981.

Vrignault, Henri. *Généalogie de la Maison de Bourbon.* Paris: Chez Henri Lefebvre, 1957.

Wood, Diana. *Clement VI.* Cambridge: Cambridge Univ. Press, 1989.

Wynn, Wilton, *Keepers of the Keys: John XXIII, Paul VI and John Paul II.* New York: Random House, 1988.

Index